TURKS IN EUROPE

TURKS IN EUROPE

From Guest Worker to Transnational Citizen

Nermin Abadan-Unat

Translated by Caterine Campion

Berghahn Books
New York • Oxford

First published in 2011 by

Berghahn Books

www.berghahnbooks.com

Library of Congress Cataloging-in-Publication Data

Abadan-Unat, Nermin, 1921–
[Migration ohne Ende. English]
Turks in Europe : from guest worker to transnational citizen / Nermin Abadan-Unat ; translated by Caterine Campion. — English-language ed.
p. cm.
Includes bibliographical references and index.
ISBN 978-1-84545-425-8 (hardback : alk. paper)
1. Foreign workers, Turkish—Europe. 2. Turkey—Emigration and immigration. 3. Europe—Ethnic relations. I. Title.
HD8378.5.T8A18513 2011
305.89'4304—dc22

2010048899

British Library Cataloguing in Publication Data

A catalogue record for this book is available from the British Library.

Printed in the United States on acid-free paper.

ISBN: 978-1-84545-425-8 Hardback

To Mustafa Kemal Abadan, Susan Abadan, and Taner Abadan with love

Contents

Figures

Tables

Appendix Tables

Foreword to the English Edition

This is an important book for more than one reason. The first reason is the personality of the author. Anyone who has studied international migration to Western Europe should be familiar with Nermin Abadan-Unat, who has been a central figure in charting Turkish labor migration to Germany, the Netherlands, France, and other European countries since the early 1960s. In addition, she has made major contributions to the broader social sciences. She is especially known for her research on the position of women—in Turkey, in international migration, and in processes of social development. But she has also worked on mass communication, electoral studies, and education. Her many books and scientific articles span the social sciences, and this has given her the ability to make linkages and to unravel complex processes of development, modernization, and globalization. Nermin Abadan-Unat is justly respected for the crucial role she has played in the emergence of a strong tradition of social-scientific research in Turkey.

The publication of this book coincides with the year of Abadan-Unat's ninetieth birthday. She remains an active and original researcher, and is a professor of political science and international relations at Boğaziçi University, one of Turkey's leading academic establishments. However, she is also known internationally as a sociologist and feminist researcher. She studied law at Istanbul University, was awarded a Fulbright scholarship to do graduate work at the University of Minnesota from 1952 to 1953, and then taught political science from 1953 to 1989 at Ankara University. She was also a member of the Turkish Senate from 1978 to 1980. Nermin Abadan-Unat is truly a public intellectual who has helped enrich Turkey's political culture.

Abadan-Unat's engagement in public affairs is no coincidence. Born in Vienna in 1921, she grew up bilingual in German and Turkish. Her 2004 autobiography—unfortunately available only in German—tells how she came to Istanbul as a student and was able to benefit from the reforms made by Mustafa Kemal Atatürk, the nationalist leader and first president of the Turkish Republic from 1923 to 1938. Atatürk was determined to make Turkey into a modern, secular democracy. Under the Turkish Civil Code, introduced in 1926 (and modelled on the Swiss Civil Code), women gained equal status with men—uniquely among Islamic countries. Atatürk saw the education of women as crucial for Turkey's development. This opened the door for women—like the young Nermin—to study at university and enter public life. No wonder then that this book is dedicated to her son, who also carries the name of Atatürk, as well as to family members. Abadan-Unat was—and remains—a passionate Kemalist, devoted to principles of secularity, emancipation, and equality. Her views on multiculturalism and religious symbols—as found later in this book—reflect that background.

The second reason why this book is so important is that it contains a unique longitudinal perspective on one of the most significant international migration experiences of the twentieth century. When Turkey—a nation without a tradition of emigration—adopted a policy of "export of excessive manpower" in the early 1960s, Abadan-Unat was asked to examine the experiences of the migrant workers and to explore the possible benefits of labor export for the development of then-economically backward Turkey. The main instrument of overseas deployment was a bilateral labor recruitment agreement with the German Federal Republic. Millions of Turkish workers were to take on the lower-skilled jobs in the land of the Economic Miracle. Abadan-Unat, with her fluent German and her understanding of both Turkish and German societies, was a natural choice to chronicle and analyze the movement—and in doing so she became the acknowledged "mother of Turkish migration research."

Abadan-Unat followed the fate of Turkish migrants, revealing their often disillusioning experience of work abroad, the inadequacy of protective measures by both the Turkish and German states, the exploitation and frequent racism encountered in Western Europe, and the consequences for the areas of origin. This book brings together and summarizes the many empirical studies, reports, articles, and books resulting from the work of Abadan-Unat and the generations of Turkish researchers whom she inspired and led. Her work has always been critical. Turkish planners saw labor export as a tool of development through acquisition of skills and industrial experience, and through productive investment of worker remittances, but Abadan-Unat exposed the misconceptions behind this hope. In many cases, skilled Turkish migrants were employed in dead-end jobs and were actually deskilled. When (and if) they returned, there were few opportunities to use industrial skills, and remittances were mainly used for consumption or small service businesses. Many migrants from rural Anatolia returned to big cities and spent their savings on real estate.

The third reason why this book is important is that it presents some important lessons for both researchers and policy-makers. Uniquely, Abadan-Unat's research spans fifty years: she shows how migrant workers became settlers when Western Europe stopped labor import in the 1970s; she investigates the educational dilemmas of the second generation in the 1980s; and she brings together the latest research on globalization and and transnationalism from the 1990s and the early twenty-first century. Her analysis shows the deficiencies of narrow, short-term understandings and the failures of misguided policies. The "Euro-Turks," as they are called in the German edition of this book, have not assimilated into German, Dutch, Swiss, or French society—nor have they wanted to. They have created new identities which are both Turkish and European. This can be uncomfortable for some—as the resurgence in racism in countries like Switzerland (e.g., the ban on minarets through the referendum of November 2009) and the Netherlands (e.g., the strong electoral performance of the anti-immigration Freedom Party in June 2010) reveals. But the Turkish migration experience—as documented in this book—shows how human mobility can bring about lasting change and interconnectedness that will continue to transform nations and communities in the future.

Stephen Castles
Sydney/Oxford, 2010

Acknowledgments

This work may be called a summary of my experiences, research, books, and articles on Turkish migration since 1963. During these forty-five years my aim has been threefold: To explain the journeys made by choice, necessity, or invitation of thousands of Turkish men and women to foreign lands in those years; to cast light on the difficulties they faced; and elaborate on how their lives were affected by the legal, political, social, and economic measures taken by the countries which accepted them. This book also constitutes a summary of the findings of much research undertaken both inside Turkey and in Europe into the lives of individuals directly and indirectly affected by the migration phenomenon. In brief, it is a synthesis of my life's work as an academic.

Throughout my career I have been afforded invaluable help and support from countless colleagues and institutions. The first such institution was the State Planning Department in Turkey, which, in the early 1960s, first broached the suggestion that a field study of Turkish workers in West Germany be done, which would engender new and better public policies. Here, once more I would like to thank Ziya Müezzinoğlu and the late Enver Ergun from the State Planning Organization and the late Professor Dr. Cahit Talas of Ankara University, all of whom gave me the opportunity to lead a team of five to travel to West Germany and realize the 1963 research. Dr. Gerhard von Walther, Ambassador of West Germany at that time, and his staff were very helpful in this undertaking.

The research was conducted during November 1963, during which time we visited 29 cities in West Germany and spoke with 494 Turkish employees in 56 companies. Those who accompanied me in this task and whom I wish to thank sincerely once again for their dedicated work were: Cafer Canlı, Erdoğan Güçbilmez, Alparslan Işıklı, Nihat Oğuz, and Şengül Şenel. The research, titled *Turkish Workers in West Germany and Their Problems,* was published in 1964 by the State Planning Department.

My second major study was conducted in Turkey in the Boğazlıyan district of Yozgat province. This was a combined Dutch-Turkish study with Turkey being represented by the Settlement and Urbanization Institute at Ankara University, and the Dutch team coming from the Institute for Social Science Research in Developing Countries affiliated to the International Foundation of Dutch Universities. Management of the project, which was titled *Migration and Development—Research into the effects of international labor migration on the Boğazlıyan district,* was in the hands of Dr. Ruşen Keleş, a professor from

Ankara University; and Herman van Renselaar, who represented Dutch universities. The project's scientific team was headed up by myself, with Herman van Renselaar, Rinnus Penninx, and Leo van Velzen joining us from Holland, and Leyla Yenisey from Turkey. During the fieldwork phase we were also accompanied by Dr. Birsen Gökçe from Hacettepe University, Dr. Doğu Ergil from Ankara University, and State Planning Organization representative Gül Ergil. I owe a debt of gratitude to each of these individuals. The study was published in Turkish as *Göç ve Gelişme* and also in English as *Migration and Development* in 1975. The late Dr. Ünsal Oksay undertook the Turkish translation and the English was completed by Dr. Donald Bloch. The late Dr. Mübeccel Kıray and Dr. Hamit Fişek from Middle East Technical University in Ankara played a consultative role.

Over the years and on various occasions there are many other colleagues to whom I owe my thanks: R. H. Böhning, for his contribution to the analyses conducted for ILO in Geneva; Professor Reginald Appleyard of the University of Western Australia, with whom I undertook the general reporting on the "Future of Migration" OECD conference in 1986; Dr. Serim Timur, ex-director of UNESCO's Population and Migration Unit, and organizer of the 1980 UNESCO "Conference on Women, Development and Population" in Paris, who gave a place to my presentation there in her book *Women on the Move;* Professors Laurence Michalak and Joseph Salacuse, who assisted in the publishing of the paper I presented at the 1986 "Social Legislation and Migration in the Middle East" conference in Rabat, Morocco; the late Dr. George Sabbath, who kindly invited me to spend a semester at UCLA participating in a series of seminars on "Migration and Returnees" in 1988; the president of the Sociology Institute at Zurich University, the late H.J. Hoffmann-Nowotny; Dr. D. J. Puchala, director of the European Research Centre at the University of South Carolina, and Dr. Emek Uçarer, for including in their publications my presentation at the Centre on "Ethnic enterprises, ethnic communities and ethnic politics"; and Dr. Lydio F. Tomasi, who afforded me the opportunity to be a contributor and adjudicator for the *International Migration Review* published by the U.S. Center of Migration. All of my meetings and relationships with these individuals enriched my knowledge of migration, and allowed me to meet those who were pioneers in research in this field.

My student Dr. Neşe Kemiksiz made an invaluable contribution to the completion of a commentated bibliography on works on Turkish migration in Turkish and foreign languages covering the period of 1960–1984. Dr. Faruk Şen, then director of the *Zentrum für Türkeisstudien* (Centre for Turkish Studies), played a major role in supporting the publishing of this work in 1986. I would also like to mention Dr. Ekkehard Eickhoff, former German ambassador to Turkey, who contributed immensely to the organization of a series of conferences by the Turkish-German Association held in Bonn and Hamburg.

From 1978 to 1996, I was the Turkish representative on the European Council Commission for Equality between Women and Men (CEDG), and I would like to express my gratitude to the general secretary of the Steering Committee for Equality between Women and Men (CDEG), Ms. Olöf Olafsdottir, who afforded me the opportunity to present my views as a member of the "Migrant Women" and "Racism and Tolerance" sub-committees.

Thanks too to Dr. Phillip L. Martin at Davis University in California for all the academic work we have done together over the years on Turkish emigration and the evaluation of policies related to it.

I consider myself fortunate to have had the opportunity to discuss and develop my ideas and perspectives on topics such as migration, globalization, transnationalism, development, and identity in debates and conversations with internationally well-known scholars in the field such as Saskia Sassen, Aristide Zolberg, M. Teitelbaum, Mark J. Miller, Deniz Kandiyoti, Riva Kastoryano, and Stephen Castles.

Dr. Kemal Kirişci, former head of the European Research Center at Bosphorus University, asked me to participate in the various "Migration and Asylum" seminars and workshops he organized, and helped me to establish new contacts. Dr. Necla Pur and İnci Beşpınar were largely responsible for the organization of an Istanbul conference on return migration on 28–30 March 2001. For similar dedication to organization, I thank Dr. Sema Erder and Dr. Günay Göksu Özdoğan for their contribution to the Swedish Turkish conference in May 2002.

Dr. Ahmet İçduygu, Director of the Migration Research Program at Koç University in Istanbul invited me on different occasions to contribute during his most enriching international encounters. As a representative of the SOPEMI organization of the OECD, he has on many occasions helped me by providing statistics and new data. It was a privilege to collaborate with Dr. Ayhan Kaya, director of the European Studies Center from Bilgi University, in presenting abroad and at home the finding of his research on Euro-Turks.

I consider Fahri Aral, director of Bilgi University Press, as an invaluable co-author of my last book in Turkish for his tireless support in its drafting and selection of photographs and other pictorial elements. For their work on the book's graphics and design I must thank Hüsnü Abbas and Mehmet Ulusel.

The German edition, *Migration ohne Ende—Vom Gastarbeiter zum Eurotürken,* was published in 2005 by Parabolis, Berlin. My thanks go to the Goethe Institute, which sponsored the translation. Ms. Çiçek Bacık and Ms. Beatrix Caner have kindly undertaken the task of shouldering the translation into German.

The English version, which represents an up-to-date interpretation of the available source materials, has required tireless efforts on behalf of many persons: I wish to acknowledge the dedication of my translator, Ms. Caterine

Champion; the encouragement of the director of Berghahn Books, Dr. Marion Berghahn; the generous help Mr. David J. Erstrin displayed during the re-editing of the English text; and the kindness, patience, and invaluable help Ms. Ann Przyzycki has displayed during the long e-mailing over the final text. Finalizing of the manuscript has been possible through the meticulous attention and care of Ms. Caitlin Mahon. My former student Derya Özkul not only helped me to overcome my shortcomings in the mastering of computerized writing, but was also a major helper in completing the book. My deep and sincere gratitude goes to all of them.

Throughout my fifty-one-year career, members of my family have always constituted my greatest support and encouragement. When I first began to undertake the study of migration, the criticisms and comments of my late first husband, Dr. Yavuz Abadan, were priceless in showing me the way, and I can never thank my son Mustafa Kemal Abadan enough for his cheerful and supportive presence from a very young age at many a migration conferences. His wonderful help and support continue to this day. In the completion of this book in Turkish, later in German, and finally in English, my late husband of thirty-seven years, Dr. İlhan Unat, was unstinting and steadfast in his support.

In tackling the English version, I have been many times encouraged and stimulated by the comments and suggestions from Susan Brady Abadan, a wonderful daughter-in-law and marvelous mother of my grandson, Taner. My gratitude to them is endless.

Finally, the heroes of this work are the countless thousands of migrants old and new, unknown to me, who, with their "national "or "transnational" identities, are introduced to the reader. I salute each and every one of them!

Nermin Abadan-Unat
Boğaziçi University Istanbul
December 21, 2010

A Short Summary on the Major Theories of International Migration

In the original Turkish edition of this book, the opening chapter examines the various theories that attempt to explain and elaborate on international migration. In doing this, the writer intended to make available to Turkish students material that they may not be able to access firsthand. Since all these resources are readily available in English, it has been considered sufficient to make a brief note in this introduction of these theories and cite the names of those who put them forward. Today there exists no single comprehensive theory of migration, and individuals working on this subject employ portions of each and every theory in their analyses.

The first academic and scientific attempt at an analysis of migration dates back to the nineteenth century when in 1885, and again in 1889, cartographer and geographer Georg Ravenstein presented a paper on "migration laws" to the Royal Statistical Society in London. Ravenstein espoused the theory that economic factors were the root cause of all migration, in as much as individuals moved from one place to another to better their financial circumstances.

The twentieth century witnessed the development of various models to explain migration, among which the primary are: the Macro Theory of Neoclassical Economics, developed by Lewis (1954), Ranis and Fei (1961), Harris and Todero (1970), and Todaro (1976); the Micro Theory of Neoclassical Economics, developed on a parallel with the Macro Theory, by Sjaastad (1962), Todaro (1969), and Borjas (1989); New Economics of Migration Theory, which grew out of what were criticisms of the older Macro and Micro theories, and was mainly propounded by Stark and Levhari (1982), Stark (1984), Katz and Stark (1986), and Stark (1991); and Segmented Labor Theory, of which the main protagonist is Piore. World Systems Theory was first put forward by Wallerstein in 1974 and has since been expanded upon by Sassen (1988, 1991), Castells (1989), and Moravska (1990). Network Theory, developed by Taylor (1986), Massey and Garcia Espana (1987), and Massey (1990), focuses on the relationship networks between migrants—old and new—and non-migrants, which fosters migration and constitutes social capital. Cumulative Causation Theory is mainly the work of Böhning (1972), Massey, Goldring, and Durand (1994), and Massey (1999). Migration Systems Theory is the product of work by Zlotnik.

Each of these theories may open the way to very different practices in migration policies and, depending on which is adopted, social scientists may suggest various alternatives to policy-makers, from alterations in the wage system and employment conditions in the country of acceptance, to strengthening the economy or creating a social insurance system in the sending country. Yet a more basic approach would be to adopt the stance that international movements of people arise simply out of the structure of the market economy.

Introduction

This book was first published in Turkish in 2002, then in German in 2005. The English edition presents the Turkish migration story in a new light with relevant revisions.

This book has several goals. I intend to explain how migration was used as an instrument of "social engineering" in Turkish politics, as a vehicle to realize the State Planning Organization's goals, and later as an unanticipated process generating economic and political structural changes in the sending and receiving countries. Planned migration was first presented as a goal in Turkey's First Five-Year Development Plan.[1] One of the most relevant aspects of Turkish migration is that although in the majority of cases immigration was and is an individual and/or familial decision, often encouraged by the existing external migrant network, large-scale Turkish migration started as government policy and eventually developed into a transnational phenomena.

In the First Five-Year Development Plan, the following paragraph appeared in the section dealing with "manpower, employment education and research":

> Another aspect of employment policy is the export of surplus labor to those countries of Western Europe which suffer from a dearth of labor. However, Turkey, while having surplus unskilled labor, is lacking in sufficient numbers of skilled labor. Therefore, it is essential that measures be taken to ensure that Turkey's deficiency in skilled labor not be exacerbated by Turkey's labor export policy.[2]

This proposal, lacking any humanitarian dimension, makes one wonder how many Turks actually wanted to establish a new life in a new country. One piece of research that provides an answer to this question was a joint study of seven Middle Eastern countries, completed in the spring of 1950 by the Massachusetts Institute of Technology and Columbia University. The published version, *The Passing of Traditional Society* by Daniel Lerner, became a classic in sociology literature. Of the "traditional" subjects of the study, 49 percent of Turks, when asked which country they would live in if they had to leave Turkey, answered that they would prefer death to leaving.[3] Now, almost sixty years

---

[1] The Plan was not considered to be mandatory, only indicative. However, its forecasts were widely used from 1965 to 1980 as a guideline for public policies.

[2] State Planning Organization, *Turkish Five-Year Development Plan* (Ankara: 1962), 456.

[3] Daniel Lerner, *The Passing of Traditional Society: Modernizing the Middle East* (Glencoe: Free Press, 1958), 148.

later, 4.5 million Turkish citizens are living in all corners of the globe. Of these, more than 4 million are in Europe, with 80 percent of these in Germany, having either been sent there or having chosen to go. There are more than 170,000 Turks in Berlin alone. Turkey, therefore, is one of only a few countries that has experienced such intense levels of human mobility, as huge numbers of its citizens, first through official encouragement, and later as a result of preference, family pressure, or encouragement by the experiences of friends and fellow citizens, left Turkey to start new lives and create new communities abroad. This reaffirms the opinion of Saskia Sassen that by incorporating international migration, the state and the city are also contributing to the expansion of different forms of globalization.[4]

Following the military coup of 1960, the interim government of Turkey decided to solve economic problems such as unemployment and shortage of foreign currency by introducing a "demographic" solution, briefly defined as the "export of excessive manpower." This is why I was asked by the State Planning Organization in 1963 to study the issue of exporting surplus labor and the potential of remitting savings from abroad. It also explains why I was commissioned to carry out a field survey in West Germany in November 1963.[5] This survey was one of the first empirical studies on migration conducted in Europe. It should not be overlooked that West Germany's (and other European countries') intense interest in importing foreign labor in those years was closely linked to the creation of the Berlin Wall and reduced the number of East German citizens coming to the West.

After completing the survey in 1963, my interest in the subject led me to explore the behavior of laid-off Turkish workers during the recession of 1966–1967 in the car industry of the Ruhr region. This was followed by a large-scale study in 1974–1975 (in cooperation with Ankara University School of Political Science and Netherlands Universities Foundation for International Cooperation [NUFFIC]) of family members of migrants who had been left in Turkey and the impact of migration.

In 1987, Reginald Appleyard and I acted as the *rapporteurs* of "The Future of Migration" conference organized by OECD. Over the years I repeatedly studied the impact of migration on Turkish migrant workers and their family on behalf of UNESCO and ILO. Thus, in this book I intend:

- to indicate the shortcomings of planning as related to migration
- to show that policy-makers can rarely obtain substantial results from blueprint recommendations, whereas unintended consequences of those policies may create new problems, e.g., an unwillingness to in-

[4] Saskia Sassen, *A Sociology of Globalization* (New York: W.W. Norton, 2007), 129.
[5] In the survey I questioned 494 Turkish male workers in 29 localities and in 56 companies.

tegrate, the formation of self-created "islands of isolation," ethnic conflicts, and religious fanaticism

- to discuss the emergence of new aspects of international migration as it affects Turks, e.g., the readiness to change citizenship and participate in the public sphere as an active citizen, positions taken concerning ethnic/religious schisms, and evaluating the merit or flaws of multicultural policies
- to discuss gender-related controversies related to segregation and human rights
- to explore the tendency of xenophobia, both in general and particularly concerning Turkish migrants
- to reveal the multifaceted reactions migration and asylum-seeking processes may yield in light of the political demands of the respective diasporas and the widening sphere of transnational social spheres and transnational links

Why Did Turks Migrate So Late?

An additional particularity of Turkish migration is that with few exceptions there was no rooted tradition for this behavior. In the past, migration was seen as a precondition for enlarging a country's territories, changing its borders, and accruing authority—it is inherent in all colonial conquests. It means resettling a group of people away from the established frontiers of a given state. This readiness to leave the homeland by going overseas or to far off lands had not been cultivated by the Turks. Historically, the enlargement of their state/empire occurred by pushing the frontiers. Settlement in newly conquered lands occurred only later and sparsely. Looking for a new job, or a new life in an unknown country was not a part of the common person's aspiration. Although there had been sporadic migratory waves to France and the United States in the early years of the twentieth century, the real surge occurred after the 1950s. It coincides with the rebuilding of postwar Europe.

Why was Germany their first goal? Here traditional ties, such as imperial Germany's zone of influence, Prussian training in the military schools of the Ottomans, and Turkey's alliance with Germany during World War I played a role. When West Germany began its reconstruction of its industry, geopolitics played a determining role.

As in other countries, it is clear that in Turkey emigration was a major element of the process of capitalism. Capitalism used migrant workers as a "security buffer" in times of economic crisis. For many years, policies based on the assumption of easily repatriating migrant workers once the need for them had been fulfilled was taken for granted. State planners in Turkey, meanwhile, were in search of short-term solutions to their problems. Indeed, interstate labor agreements between Turkey and Germany, and later with other European countries, were based on the principle of "rotation," according to which workers sent abroad would return after a year of training, ready and equipped with knowledge and expertise that would then be available in the economic development of Turkey. However, even in the early years of these experiments it became clear that this transfer of technical expertise and knowledge would not be possible in such a short period of time abroad. Indeed, it became clear in Turkey that, just as with other labor-exporting countries, migration primarily served to benefit migrant-accepting states and their financial capital. Through labor migration, developed industrial countries were able to increase their productivity and provide opportunities for upward mobility for their native labor forces. In other words, the process of labor migration only widened the gap between core and periphery countries while helping to give birth to a new global proletariat.

Having had the opportunity to follow the various phases of this primarily European migratory movement, I was able to document the changes that occurred during each phase. For half a century, I became a kind of historian, while retaining my primary interest in social and political issues.

The title of my original Turkish book was *Migration without End: From Guestworker to Transnational Citizen.* This title points to a phenomenon that came about as a direct result of globalization, a phenomenon that has led thousands to uproot themselves in the hope of reshaping their futures in new lands with new jobs and to endorse an identity that rests upon more than one aspect of loyalty. This is why I dealt so extensively with the subject of globalization.

Globalization and Migration

The notion that the time they were spending "in exile" was akin to military service was widespread among the first generation of Turkish migrants, and the dream of permanently returning to the homeland remains alive for them to this day. The second and third generations, however, envision their futures differently. They have five basic choices about how to live their lives. The first is to use their time in the country of settlement to gain experience and knowledge, after which they can move back to a homeland they have only known through time spent there on annual family holidays. The second is to establish a small enterprise in the country of settlement in order to secure an independent living without necessarily putting down roots there. A third choice is occupying a niche in the economy on a local level, which may not even entail learning a foreign language. A fourth option is to obtain the education and/or expertise that will open the way to upward social mobility. The final choice is adopting the citizenship of the country of settlement and thus engaging in full integration into its larger society and benefiting from all the rights that obtain to this status. Each of these five possibilities requires the individual to adopt a different identity. It also reveals that there are several possibilities when choosing integration or non-integration. It is also clear that these apparently simple (yet extremely complex) choices contain obstacles that cannot be overcome by the individual, his or her family, or a community of friends acting alone.

Many of the problems to be resolved lie in globalization, the notion that has become the "meta-narrative" of the twenty-first century. When considering migration within globalization, we are faced with a series of questions: What drives the emergence of globalization? Which powers are most influential in the globalization process? Which social groups benefit most from globalization? In dealing with these questions, it becomes clear that, above all, globalization means a "shift in horizons." When social realities take on an international character it leads to developments more important than those concerning local and nation-state relations. Not only must we look at the changing nature of the nation-state in relation to transnational organizations (e.g., the European Union, NATO, the International Monetary Fund, and the United Nations), but we must also take into account the transnational social spaces that are being created by worldwide networks with the aid of the Internet. The differing statuses offered to these transnational communities, many of which are made up of migrants and their families, in the form of work permits or dual citizenship, form the basis of new loyalties. This multifaceted process cannot be understood from the perspective of one criterion.

The Issue of Identity

Some of the most significant outcomes of globalization are new identities and fragmented personalities. In order to understand this immense change, we must look back and review the transformations that began to occur in the political, economic, and social arenas in the 1980s and that were greatly stimulated by the final collapse of socialism in 1989 in East Germany. The breathtaking development in communications technologies, the availability of low-cost travel, and the increasing allure of unknown people and places are all factors in inciting people to further mobility. Today, with the aid of the process we know as global outsourcing, businesses are able to provide for their needs and services from all corners of the globe, some basing their decisions on cost, some on the education levels of the potential workforce, and others on levels of "social peace" in the society they choose. As a result, a new international division of labor has emerged that has led to harsher levels of international competition in production costs, capital, and labor. These changes, in addition to having a deep and lasting impact on the social structure of societies, have also opened the way to all forms of migration, both legal and illegal, including asylum-seeking and human trafficking.

They have also led to heated debate on such issues as the functions of the nation-state, its position in opposition to supranational institutions, and the shifting in national borders, all of which are closely connected to the issue of the rights of individuals on the move.

The issues being debated revolve around the circumstances in which migrants become part of migration—as a result of actual danger to their lives or for purely economic reasons. As a result, is becomes impossible to examine the migration issue solely from an economic perspective.

In choosing an identity, it is clear that ethnic belonging and religion play a primary role for Turks and Kurds, Alevites and Sunnis. The religious principles of Islam and the application of its commandments in everyday life mean that it is open to fundamentalist theological commentary. As a result, the worldwide network of mosques and Islamic centers has been effective in the spread of a "third world ideology," and those most attracted to the debate on these issues are unemployed young men, the retired, and those who, through illness or incapacity, are unable to work.

Migration and State Policies

Even if we accept the fact that following World War II, the responsibilities of the nation-state changed and activity in the private sector expanded, it is still impossible to imagine the internationalization of the production process without the influence of state-based political strategies. The privatization and/or abolishment of monopolies by governments and parliaments as part of their economic policies marked the start of this process. The most striking example of this can be seen in West German policies of the 1950s and 1960s created to secure a labor force. Likewise, the Turkish state may also be said to have engaged in a form of social engineering when it began to apply the policy of surplus labor export as part of its First Five-Year Development Plan. Both states laid the economic and legal foundations of international migration during those years. The dominant image of the time was that people should be conceived as *Homo Economicus,* and both migrant-exporting countries and migrant-accepting countries that adopted this view saw the export of surplus labor as simply another form of "goods exchange."

However, with the spread of globalization and the dawning realization among nation-states of their growing inability to direct their individual economies, the debate shifted to new ground. Ulrich Beck claims that in this "century of similarities," the authenticity of nations and cultures will fade away and active citizens will interact with each other within a global network. With the opening up of new horizons, human rights will be judged according to international criteria, even in the face of resistance from individual states. Jürgen Habermas refers to a "post-nationalist" period in his work on political theory. Habermas analyzed the notion of "cosmopolitan global society" and, with the help of an institutionalized normative ethic that "takes the other into account," attempted to arrive at a peaceful solution. As can be seen, all these ideas ignore economic processes and have the goal of creating a better world society. Those viewing globalization with a critical eye declare that it represents a "project" rather than a "logical" process. Business and governments tried to overcome the crisis faced by post-war capitalism by encouraging cross-border trade, attracting investment opportunities in their own territories, reviewing social policies in the labor market, and limiting social welfare.

Oppositions to Globalization

The dream of neo-liberalism is ever better welfare of nations and happiness for individuals by what it calls the "trickle-down" approach. Those criticizing this notion claim that in such a social sharing project the rich Northern countries will always dominate the underdeveloped South. With the coming of globalization it was not long before it was realized that it brought with it a process of social exclusion that meant insecure living conditions and crisis for millions of people. This is the reason for the violent protests against globalization that began in the late 1990s, particularly those directed against the World Trade Organization in cities including Geneva, Seattle, and Porto Allegre. The Attac organization has been particularly active in these protests and with its slogan, "a better world is possible," makes use of its electronic network to promote the concept of "anti-globalization." Within the framework of these broad debates space is also given over to more specific developments, among which are the future of the welfare state, the role of nongovernmental organizations (NGOs), the positions of men and women in the labor market, and the effects of migration and global inequalities on individuals. Topics that continue to resurface as part of these debates are multiculturalism, minority rights, tolerance and diversity, and the expansion and establishment of fundamental democratic rights and freedoms. Another concept gaining greater importance is "transnationalism."

Transnationalism

This term was first used by Nigel Young in 1983 in relation to social movements based on Gandhi's ideas and the notion of communitarian solidarity.

Even though the concept is thematically used in the case of ethnic communities, local/urban groups (e.g., the black community), and feminist movements, it has not become widely accepted in the mainstream thinking of the new Left. However, it gained new strength through the activities of NGOs. Despite its principle that the United Nations may not interfere in the domestic affairs of its member states, with the help of transnational networks, issues concerning the lack of fundamental human rights and freedoms, continuous surveillance and torture, ethnic cleansing, and other overt violations of rights are being placed on the international agenda. In this context, the institutionalized and spontaneously established diasporas play an important role in relation to the problems of Turkish Kurds and Alevites. Islamist fundamentalists also benefit from these transnational networks in communicating and coordinating their activities.

The issue of identity constitutes an important part of any analysis of Turkish migration. Turkish society today remains in partly patriarchal, authoritarian, and vertical in structure. In such a situation the individual, and particularly the female, may only develop their personality with great difficulty. In contrast, in urban, industrialized Turkey, and in those regions that have come under the influence of tourism, we see a Turkish society more in line with Western societies, one that is liberal, modern, and dynamic. Be it in Turkey or abroad, youth in such segments of society interact and identify with other groups based on their preferences, level of education, and individual interests. Thus, we see the emergence of various groups creating networks based, for instance, on a love of a particular music, identity with city neighborhoods (e.g., Kreuzberg, Wedding, or Kadiköy), or the establishment of sports clubs in European ghettos and acting in solidarity with other fans in the homeland. The striking characteristic that all such identities share is their dynamism: these newly acquired identities developed on a horizontal plane constantly shift and alter, influenced by any change in political or economic circumstances. In a world that is becoming ever smaller, we now come across more than ever before the issue of identity within culture, and it is becoming a vitally important aspect of any mutual understanding.

Global/Local—Glocalism

The term "glocalism" was invented to highlight the vital importance of the cultural element between "local" and "global." For migrants in diaspora this means the necessity of having a dual identity. There are second and third generation children of migrants who must, on the one hand, transform their deep feelings of loyalty to the homeland (passed on to them by the first generation) into the creation of a "imagined paradise," and, on the other hand, work to have their voices heard in relation to their rights, demands, and criticisms of mainstream society in the country of settlement. As a result of this process, there emerges a state of mind best defined as "dual diasporic consciousness."

In lyrics of many popular songs it becomes clear how a local identity may cross borders to become a transnational news item. It is clear that, aided by the Internet, what Thomas Faist calls "transnational social spaces" are coming into existence, spaces that embrace not just Europe but the entire globe from the United States to Australia, India, and Russia. Slogans, computer generated animation, cartoons, and logos are all being fired into cyberspace by extreme nationalist groups, independence fighters, militant evangelists, and Islamist fundamentalists. These new transnational social spaces recognize no borders or limits.

The Structure of the Book

Covering a process of about half a century I was obliged to select meaningful time-bound sections. Chapter 1 delineates the rapid changes that took place between 1961—the year of the signature of bilateral labor exchange agreement between Turkey and Germany—and 1974, the year recruitment ended throughout Europe. It deals with the benefits obtained through the welfare state, the exclusionary situation of foreign laborers, and the essential role played by remittances in helping to close the hiatus of foreign currency in Turkey.

Chapter 2 covers migration to the Middle East and Russia—a different kind of migration, not handled by formal state administrative organizations but by entrepreneurs and middlemen. It has a temporary and dominant male character, and is sometimes labeled as "circular migration," i.e., migrants/expats who go home for a while and then take up a new job in a new country.

Chapter 3 focuses on the results of two empirical studies. The first is devoted to the problems of Turkish migrants in a divided Germany at the beginning of the "big exodus" in 1963. They were predominantly urban, with a primary school education, and inexperienced with an industrial world that focused on speedy production. These novices who did not know much about collective bargaining or trade union membership were unable to communicate with the co-workers of the host society, worried about not eating pork, and were anxious human beings whose sole aim was to save money in order to provide a better future for the children at home, or to realize some dream (e.g., buying a car, a tractor, a field, a house). The second study is focused on the life of the family members left behind in the district center of Boğazlıyan, province of Yozgat, in 1975. The lifestyle and change in gender roles among the women, decision-making, and investment patterns were closely monitored. The questions of whether migration contributes to regional development and the impact of remittances are discussed.

Chapter 4 deals exclusively with migrant women, the options they confronted, the social control that imposes conservative and religious values, the role of wearing a headscarf, and adopting an Islamic identity.

Turkey is the only country in the Islamic world to have constitutionally adopted the principle of secularism, and the principle of equality between the genders is also set out in its constitution. Following the abolition of *Shari'a* law, the first civil code of the new Turkish Republic was adopted almost in full from Swiss civil law in 1926. The 1930s were a period of great reforms during which all doors were opened to women in education and political participation. In appearance, Turkish women began to adopt a Western style of dress. Indeed, one of the most important elements of Mustafa Kemal Atatürk's legacy to Turkish women is undoubtedly his providing them with a place in the professional and political life of Turkey.

The process of emigration, however, brought new and different movements in its wake. In the European countries of settlement, the male-dominated Islamic communities consider freedom of conscience as a primary constitutionally guaranteed right. In particular, militant fundamentalist Islamic groups that settled in Europe systematically promoted the principle of gender distinction and women in many Turkish communities found themselves pressured into adopting traditional dress and behavior patterns. The great importance attached to religious belief began to make itself felt both in Turkey and abroad. Although the majority of young women in Turkey's urban areas work to achieve equal social status with men, the number of women who prefer to wear the veil is increasing among those migrating from rural areas to urban centers and those going overseas. Women in this group perceive the wearing of the traditional headscarf or veil as the essential symbol of freedom of conscience. In a group with a close-knit internal structure—and this is particularly characteristic of communities that resulted from chain migration—it is more difficult for young girls and women to resist the pressure to adopt traditional dress. Indeed, in countless cases, integration into mainstream society is closely linked to the will of the female. For a great number of women, setting out on the path individual independence means they may have to leave their families entirely—not an easy decision. Arranged marriages and marriage migration also play an important role in hindering integration.

Chapter 5 deals with the manifold problems of educating the second and third generations. The federal character of Germany, Austria, and Belgium sometimes makes it impossible to understand the different school systems. The teaching of the mother tongue, the Turkish government's insistence in urging the children of migrants to take voluntary lessons in Turkish history and geography, and the demands of parents to send their children to *Qur'an* courses creates an almost unbearable pressure for young children. The elitist character of Europe prevents a large part of the younger generation to attend university, and the unfriendly attitudes of business owners narrow the chances that professional school graduates obtain a job.

Chapter 6 focuses on the impact of Islamic organizations, the role Turkish clerics play in Europe, and the impact of fundamentalist sects using the democratic right of association to increase the rift between the migrants and mainstream society.

Chapter 7 analyzes the emergence of ethnic communities, the role of chain migration, the creation of migrant "niche economies," and the importance of migrants' political participation in states that grant them the right to vote in local elections.

Chapter 8 discusses the different systems of incorporating migrants by extending them the status of citizen; the trend of naturalization; and the model of dual citizenship.

Chapter 9 focuses on the issue of refugees. The military interventions in Turkey in 1972 and 1980 played an important role increasing the number of asylum-seekers, particularly among Turkish leftist militants and children of Kurdish origin. The collapse of the Berlin Wall, Germany's reunification, and the sudden swelling of new citizens in both Germany and other European countries created a favorable climate for ultra-nationalism and its logical consequence, xenophobia.

Chapter 10 presents the findings of two surveys about the values and opinions toward the EU among Turks abroad in 2005 and the number of "Euroskeptics" among Turks at home in 2003.

Finally, chapter 11 examines the relationship between globalization and the nation-state, and the existing contradictions, and plausible solutions to problems of globalization.

Those who conduct research on the topic of "migration without end" in the near future will probably have to deal with the topic of governance regarding migration, providing national security while granting free movement of labor, the step-by-step dissolution of existing ghettoes, the rewriting of history books from a global perspective, the creation of new models to intensify local participation, and the growing importance of NGOs. There is little doubt that the process of integration in Europe cannot be carried out by any single European welfare state. As we have seen in recent years, when dealing with their individual budget deficits and demographic shifts, EU member states have not displayed a willingness to work together in their migration and asylum policies. In this respect, national preferences and security analyses will be the determining factors.

As a researcher on migration I hope that the world of tomorrow will be more generous, open, and with good will toward those who desire to participate in the building of a global egalitarian world order. As Castles and Miller remark, the globalization of migration provides grounds for optimism, because it gives us some hope of increased unity in dealing with the pressing problems that beset our small planet.[6]

[6] Stephen Castles and Mark J. Miller, *The Age of Migration,* 3rd ed. (New York: Palgrave MacMillan, 2003), 290.

CHAPTER 1

Phases of Turkish Emigration

Figure 1.1. Waiting for Departure

Why stay behind? For a thousand green marks a month,
Let's go and spread out from eagle Anatolia, to the face of the earth.
Those foreign gentlemen are about to wake from their golden sleep,
Come on let's sweep their streets,
Huge brooms, towering garbage,
Feeling no shame in the face of the crimson sun.
Hands filthy, hearts filthy.
My forefathers were too mighty for today and tomorrow;
I fell, I flounder, a servant for foreigners now.

—Fazıl Hüsnü Dağlarca, *Our Street-Sweepers in Germany*
Translated by Talat Sait Halman

Towards the end of the twentieth century, events of historical importance wrought significant change in the social geography of people's lives. This was a time marked by revolutions in communication and information technology, which brought with them rapid changes to human life. World economies became more and more interrelated and dependent on each other, leading to the growth of new and different relationship networks among economy, state, and society. With the breakup of the former Soviet Union, international communism lost its global attractiveness. The ever-present risk of nuclear war seemed to recede, and radical shifts took place in the world of global geopolitics. Capitalism was restructured, and capital was granted superior status to the labor represented by the working class. Through existing political power and institutions, states began to intervene in market affairs and, by choosing the road to privatization, began moving away from the notion of the welfare state. At the same time, limits were put on the migratory movements that had offered individuals and groups new employment opportunities. Skilled labor (brain power) began to take priority over unskilled labor (muscle power) as countries accepting immigrants began to execute policies of selectivity. In this environment, many immigrating individuals who would not otherwise have been fit for selection gave the political conditions in their home country as justification for their migration, often with reference to discrimination and violence employed by the state. Thus, alongside groups migrating for economic reasons, these years witnessed a huge increase in the numbers of individuals looking for a safe haven from political violence and ethnic conflict.

In order to better understand the nature of the migratory movements that have radically transformed the social structure of Turkey in the past forty years, we must first briefly look at the changes migration has brought about on a world scale from a historical perspective.

Characteristics of Global Migration

European Imperialism and Migration

The first huge wave of migratory movements may be said to have occurred between the early seventeenth century and the end of World War I. During these three hundred years it was Europe that determined the direction of migration: England, Spain, Portugal, Holland, and France all looked overseas to secure lands and create colonies for their growing populations, and all in turn sent shiploads of immigrants to the Americas. The French settled Québec in Canada and then looked to South Africa. Between 1846 and 1932 England exported almost 18 million people to North America, Australia, New Zealand, South Africa, and the Caribbean. About 10 million Italians and 5 million Germans also chose this time to leave their homeland and seek their fortunes on other continents. Between 1821 and 1924, approximately 55 million Europeans went in search of new places to live, and 34 million of them chose the United States as their destination.[1] There can be little doubt that these migrations left a deep mark on political institutions and issues of national identity.

Involuntary Migration from the Third World

What we may call the second great wave of migration also occurred during this time but was of a very different nature. In the seventeenth and eighteenth centuries many European traders carried human cargo in the form of captured Africans, who were transported to work as slaves in South America, particularly Brazil, and the Caribbean. England began to operate the practice of transporting indentured labor collected from South Asia to work in its colonies in East Africa, Guyana, Jamaica, Surinam, and Trinidad, and used huge numbers of Chinese workers in a similar manner in Indonesia, Thailand, Malaya, and Indochina. Importation of African slaves was banned in the British colonies in 1807, to be followed by the United States in 1808. In 1863 U.S. President Abraham Lincoln freed the slaves in the Confederate States, and in 1865 slavery was prohibited throughout the United States. In Latin America it remained in practice up to 1876, particularly in the Spanish colonies of Cuba and Puerto Rico. In much of the Islamic world it persisted as a legal institution well into the twentieth century. Today child and adult slavery and forced labor are illegal in most countries as well as being against international law.

These great migrations of the time changed the face of the world. In the words of Louis Hartz, by "creating fragments of Europe"[2] in Canada, the United States, Australia, and New Zealand, European emigrants opened the way for the creation of new nation states. The creation of these new states brought massive change to the political systems of the "New World." The native populations of these colonies were reduced to the status of minority groups, and in places where this could not be achieved, the Europeans succeeded in maintaining political hegemony and exercising their political power through systems of discrimination, such as the *apartheid* system in South Africa. These changes might be looked upon as new forms of conquest or imperialism. One has also to keep in mind that the totality of what is called "New World" does not represent Europe.

The Aftermath of World War I

During World War I and the years that followed, the world of empires began to unravel and disintegrate, and the third wave of international migration co-

[1] Myron Weiner, *The Global Migration Crisis: Challenge to States and to Human Rights* (New York: HarperCollins, 1995), 21.

[2] Louis Hartz, ed., *The Founding of New Societies: Studies in the history of the United States, Latin America, South Africa, Canada, and Australia* (New York: Harcourt, Brace & World, 1964).

incides with this time. The deaths of the Ottoman and Hapsburg Empires led to new states being born in central, eastern, and southern Europe. With these new states, which identified themselves with nationalist politics, wished to create homogenous populations, the result was a huge increase in the number of refugees migrating across borders. In the 1920s, entire populations of Greeks and Jews from Russia and eastern European countries often emigrated to escape persecution, e.g., pogroms. People of Polish, Hungarian, Bulgarian, Serbian, and Turkish origin found themselves being sent on their way to find new places to call home as the subjects of population exchange agreements between these states. Added to this list must be the millions of White Russians who fled their homeland at the time of the revolution, and those Jews who managed to escape from Nazi Germany in the 1930s prior to the worst of the Nazi excesses.

The End of Colonialism and Independence Movements

The fourth wave of migration took place after World War II, when the last remnants of the empires finally collapsed, making way for the creation of dozens of independent states in Asia, Africa, and the Middle East. For the most part, these states were governed by authoritarian political regimes ruling weak, ethnically diverse societies, a situation that almost invariably allowed for the growth of violence and led once more to many millions of people becoming refugees. The partitioning of India and Pakistan in 1947 alone saw more than 14 million Hindus and Muslims move between the two countries seeking refuge and new lives in other lands, and similar patterns of movement were to be seen time and again between and among the new states of the time: Arabs fleeing from Israel, Jews from North Africa, Chinese from Indonesia, and South Asian peoples from East Africa, Burma (now Myanmar), and Ceylon (now Sri Lanka).

This international flow of refugees continued almost without interruption throughout the late twentieth century.[3] Just as the creation of colonies by the European powers eventually led to the birth of new states, the end of these old empires in the aftermath of World War II led to yet more states. The declaration of the Chinese People's Republic by the Chinese Communist Party in 1948 drove the political and military leaders of the old China to set up an independent state on the island of Taiwan. A new country, Pakistan, became home to 6 million Muslims who fled India when it became independent. In 1971, following another division, Muslims in what was then known as East Pakistan created the new state of Bangladesh. The independence movements that led to the emergence of these states allowed those in power to drive out

[3] By 1993, international refugee numbers were estimated at 18.9 million, in addition to domestic refugees (i.e., those forced to move in order to find safer and more secure living conditions within their own country), who numbered approximately 25 million. Weiner, *Global Migration Crisis*, 24.

groups whom they had had to tolerate while part of a greater empire. Algeria dispatched the French in 1962; Angola drove out the Portuguese in 1975; and Zimbabwe forced out the English in 1980. The fall of the Soviet Union in 1991 left 65 million Soviet citizens to find new homes for themselves, and today we see the same exclusion processes continuing in such states as Kazakhstan, Ukraine, Uzbekistan, Armenia, and Azerbaijan.

Economy, Productivity, and the Export of Labor

The fifth and final international migration movement coincided with the fourth, but was rooted in economics. In the 1950s and 1960s, Western Europe, the United States, and the oil-rich countries of the Middle East, in an effort to increase their economic productivity, began to import labor: laborers came to Western Europe from Turkey, Yugoslavia, and North Africa; the United States received workers from Mexico and the Caribbean; workers from Iraq went to Saudi Arabia and the United Arab Emirates; and workers from Palestine, Yemen, and South Asia traveled to Egypt. Each receiving country intended that the workers who entered its borders would remain only for a specified time, but from the beginning, the *Gastarbeiter* (guest worker) who went to Europe—and the *bracero* who went to the United States—showed every inclination to remain, the results of which were changes to the ethnic and religious makeup of the societies they entered.

These waves of international migration shared one characteristic: they grew out of and were shaped by the social and national needs of the sending and receiving countries, and resulted in many societies becoming either more homogenous or more heterogeneous. Moreover, migrations sometimes resulted in the formation of new states; at other times, states were responsible for new groups of immigrants.

Franklin D. Scott observes that the days of uncontrolled international migration based simply on the decision made by an individual have passed. Today's migration movements are governed by the "economic fluctuations and national wishes"[4] of the accepting countries, and it is from this perspective that we will now examine post–World War II Turkish migration.

Characteristics of Turkish Migration

The New "South Europe"

Rather than consider emigration from Turkey as a single event, we will examine it in the context of (1) labor migration from Mediterranean countries;

[4] Franklin D. Scott, *World Migration in Modern Times* (New York: Prentice Hall, 1968), 2–3.

(2) income differentials among countries; and (3) commentaries on "south Europe."

Since the end of World War II, it is possible to speak of certain groups of countries as constituting a new geography of "south Europe":

- The "classic" countries of south Europe: Portugal, Spain, southern Italy, and Greece.
- Turkey and Yugoslavia (and the Balkan states that succeeded it): with the dissolution of the Ottoman Empire, the former engaged in military struggle to define its own borders; the latter arose as a result of the disintegration of two empires.
- The ex-colonial states of Algeria, Morocco, Tunisia, Syria, and Lebanon, all under French rule at one time; Cyprus, Israel, Iraq, Jordan, and Egypt, which were ruled by the English; and Libya, which was once an Italian colony.[5]

It was these "periphery countries" that satisfied Europe's increasing need for labor in the 1950s, and they became the backbone of the European economy and transformed European capitalism. First concerned with centralizing its capital, European capitalism later internationalized itself and moved into the countries on its outer periphery in search of higher profits.

Underdevelopment and Migration

The European Common Market was created in 1956 with the signing of the Treaty of Rome. Following the creation of the EC, member states began to formulate a zone of migration that was somewhat similar to that created by the United States and Canada in the early years of the twentieth century. In Europe, it was claimed that this development would ultimately benefit labor-exporting countries. On the one hand, it would create employment opportunities that would help ease social tensions in these countries caused by high unemployment and rapid urbanization; on the other hand, it would guarantee a flow of hard currency into economies that needed it to bridge their balance of payments gap. Eventually, this perspective came to be seen for what it really was: a distinctly rose-colored view of the world and, as Johan Galtung[6] pointed out, an asymmetric interaction among the countries involved in a specific type of division of labor: Thus, although "core nations" were constantly engaged in

[5] Marios Nikolinakos, *Politische Ökonomie der "Gastarbeiter"* (Hamburg, Germany: Rowohlt, 1975), 142–143.

[6] Johan Galtung, "A Structural Theory of Imperialism," *Journal of Peace Research* 8 (1971): 81–117.

the effort to better educate and improve their native labor force, the "periphery countries" made do with being both the suppliers of raw materials and the markets for the "core nations," and they began exporting human resources for which they could not supply employment. This situation led to the creation of a new dependence that served only to prolong unemployment, poverty, and underdevelopment in periphery countries.[7] The flow of capital to periphery countries (in the form of workers' savings) resulted only in a dependent industrialization and prevented the cycle of underdevelopment from being broken. Today, through the much-discussed globalization process we can see that this imbalance, far from being corrected, is instead being exacerbated.

Thus, it is from the above-discussed perspective that I will examine the different phases of Turkish migration and the problems that have ensued. The reader should keep the following point in mind: apart from the general structure of the migration itself, each country that exports labor should take its own specific historical and societal factors into account and adopt political programs in light of these factors. In the case of Turkey, I believe these must include Turkish society's lack of a historical tendency to migrate for the purposes of settlement in a new place; the fact that the labor exported from Turkey was for the most part of rural origin and unskilled, with no strong roots in democracy and little experience of the labor union tradition; and the dominance of a Christian identity and culture in accepting countries and those cultures' discriminatory attitudes and lack of desire to accommodate and/or respond to the needs of Muslim social groups.

Phases of Turkish Emigration

This chapter deals with the problems during the five Turkish migrations to Europe, particularly to Germany, from 1950 to 2000. This period is characterized by the declaration of all German governments that "Germany is not a country of immigration." This position was shared by other European countries with large Turkish migrant concentrations such as Austria, the Netherlands, and Belgium. This policy changed consistently after the beginning of the new millennium, and problems deriving from this change will be treated in separate chapters.

1950s to 2000

As a player on the emigration stage, Turkey is a new arrival. Its citizens only gained the fundamental right to enter and leave the country freely when it was written into the 1960 constitution as a "basic right." Available statistics

[7] Stephen Castles and Godula Kosack, *Immigrant Workers and Class Structures in Western Europe* (London: Oxford University Press, 1973), 67.

can demonstrate how rapidly emigration progressed after 1960. In 1961 there were 6,700 Turks in Germany, accounting for 1 percent of the total foreign population. By 1987, Turks constituted 34.3 percent of foreigners there and numbered 1,453,700 (see table 1.1).

We may speak of five stages of Turkish emigration to Europe beginning in the latter half of the 1950s:

- 1950s: Individual enterprise and private agents
- 1960s: State-controlled "Surplus Labor Export," based on official agreements between states

TABLE 1.1.
Growth and percentage of total population of Turkish and other foreign populations in Germany

Year	*Total Foreign Pop.*	*No. of Turks*	*% of Total Population*	*Foreigners (% of total pop.)*
1961	686,200	6,700	1.2	1.0
1970	2,976,497	469,200	15.8	4.9
1973	3,966,200	605,000	15.2	6.4
1977	3,948,300	508,000	12.9	6.4
1987	4,240,500	1,453,700	34.3	6.9
1989	4,845,900	1,612,600	33.3	7.7
1990	5,342,500	1,675,900	32.0	8.4
1991	5,882,300	1,779,600	30.3	7.3
1992	6,495,800	1,854,900	28.6	8.0
1993	6,878,100	1,918,400	27.9	8.5
1994	6,990,510	1,965,577	28.1	8.6
1995	7,173,866	2,014,311	28.1	8.7
1996	7,314,046	2,049,060	28.0	8.9
1997	7,365,833	2,107,426	28.6	9.0
1998	7,319,600	2,110,223	28.8	9.0
1999	7,343,600	2,053,600	27.9	8.9
2000	7,296,800	1,998,500	27.3	8.8
2001	7,318,600	1,947,900	26.6	8.7
2002	7,335,592	1,912,169	26.2	8.9
2003	7,334,765	1,877,661	25.6	8.7
2004	6,717,115	1,877,661	27.9	8.1
2005	6,755,811	1,764,041	26.1	8.2
2006	6,751,000	1,738,000	25.7	8.2

Data from 1961–1990 the " old Laender "
Data from 1991 on for the " old " and " new "Laender
Source: Statistisches Jahrbuch für die Bundesrepublik Deutschland, 2007

- 1970s: economic crisis caused an absolute halt in acceptance of foreign labor, granting of legal status to illegal immigrants, unification of families, and child subsidies
- 1980s: problems in education of children, ghetto life, growth in associations, rise in asylum demands, visa requirement, laws promoting return to homeland
- 1990s: "foreigners laws," the process of foreigners gaining identity, growing xenophobia, spread of ethnic businesses, a growth in the number of ethnic and religious associations, increasing demands for political rights

The 1950s

In what has been called an "economic miracle," what was then called "West Germany" undertook an intensive employment process following World War II. During the initial stages all the extra labor West Germany required for this was provided by Germans from the east fleeing communism, and it was only later that West Germany began to look towards Europe's newly industrializing countries as a labor source. Initially, Italy, a fellow member of the Common Market, began to provide labor from its southern region. In turn, Spain, Greece, and Turkey became the wells from which West Germany drew skilled and unskilled labor.

Individual Enterprise

One characteristic distinguished the Turkish labor going to Germany at this time from labor going there from other countries: from the beginning, workers from the other Mediterranean countries entered the German labor market as a result of formal agreements between the states, whereas in the 1950s Turkish workers were, for the most part, invited by individuals to work in West Germany with a view to improving their job skills. These individuals—often businessmen active in Istanbul and married to German women, or Turkish entrepreneurs already settled in West Germany—played a crucial role in the early years of Turkish migration to Germany.

In 1956 the German Ministry of Foreign Affairs received a proposal that a specified number of young artisans from Turkey be invited to Germany for the purpose of training, with the idea that, if successful, the plan could be employed later in German investment projects. The proposal came from the World Economy Institute (attached to Kiel University).[8] It was also said that such an opportunity for study would ultimately benefit Turkey by serving to strengthen its economy and foreign trade.

[8] The proposal was the brainchild of Dr. Fritz J. Bade, who was at that time chair of the Institute. Dr. Bade had returned to the Institute following World War II, during which he had been forced to reside in Turkey.

In Turkey the Association of Technical Vocational School Alumni responded positively to this proposal, and the first group of ten trainees arrived in Kiel on 1 April 1957. From there they were sent to various institutions throughout Schleswig-Holstein by the German Employment Ministry.[9] All the trainees' traveling expenses, fees for a six-week language course in Kiel, and living expenses during the course were met by the West German Foreign Affairs Ministry. It was decided that another 200 trainees would follow later, and during a state visit to Turkey, Theodor Heuss, then president of the German Federal Republic, declared in a speech in Ankara that as a gift to the people of Turkey, preparations were being made for 150 Technical Vocational School graduates to undergo further training in West Germany.[10]

Private Agents

Also at this time the Hamburg-based Zentralverband des Deutschen Handwerks (Center for German Artisans) suggested additional exchanges to the Confederation of Turkish Businessmen and Artisans and, with the slogan of "middle class supports middle class," proposed that further cooperation would accelerate Turkey's industrial development. Within this framework of cooperation, there were even more exchanges of artisans working in various fields. In 1959, under the auspices of the Hamburg Chamber of Commerce, and headed by Dr. Selahattin Sözeri, the Institute for Research in Turkish-German Economic Affairs was established. The institute concentrated its efforts on securing skilled labor (e.g., welders and electricians) for shipyards in Hamburg and Bremen, and charged a fee for each worker it provided. Each worker was nominally recruited from Turkey, and travel expenses were paid by the German employer. However, at that time official responsibility for all placements of workers, both foreign and German, lay with the state-run Federal Institution for Employment and Social Insurance, and thus the Institute operating out of Hamburg was able to remain active for a period of only a year and a half.

In Turkey, early in 1960, an inter-ministry commission was established to deal with the Turkish-West German artisan exchange programs, but it had barely begun its activities when there was a military coup in May. This ushered in the new Constitution in 1961 that, as mentioned above, granted Turkish citizens the right to travel freely in and out of the country. With this, emigration from Turkey took on a new character.

---

[9] Statistisches Bundesamt, *Statistisches Jahrbuch* (Bonn, Germany: Metzler & Poeschel, 1995), 76, table 3.21.

[10] Those on the first list were: Nihat Cigalli, Hikmet Dağdelen, Mustafa Özbilgiç, Abbas Dorbek, Şerafettin Demirer, Hadi Ongun, Basri Yalınay, Galip Çankaya, Metin Büyükçizegin, Hilmi Akyıl, and Rıfat Tuncer. Nermin Abadan-Unat, *Batı Almanya'daki Türk İşçileri ve Sorunları* (Ankara, Turkey: Devlet Planlama Teşkilatı, Başbakanlık, 1964), 35.

The 1960s

State-Controlled "Surplus Labor Export" Based on Official Agreements Between States

With travel restrictions removed, Turkish citizens began to avail themselves of new opportunities. These were years of high unemployment, and many Turks looked to going abroad as a means of economic improvement. In 1960 it was estimated that 2,700 Turkish workers were employed abroad, and just one year later this figure had risen by almost 300 percent to 6,700. To facilitate the needs of these workers, private companies, known as translation and employment bureaus, were set up. At this time, as in the 1950s, the workers who were going abroad had been nominally recruited, with future employers guaranteeing them financially and meeting their travel expenses.

Meanwhile, in West Germany, unions, fearing unfair competition as a result of an influx of cheap labor, were warning the authorities of the dangers posed to the economy. In response, a German Liaison Office was set up in Istanbul, and began (unofficial) talks with the Turkish Employment Ministry and the state Employment Bureau. The outcome of these talks was a labor agreement signed on 1 September 1961. This was followed in later years by similar agreements with Austria, Belgium, and Holland (1964), France (1965), and Sweden (1967). Under these agreements, applications by Turks for vacancies in these countries were entered on a waiting list with the Turkish Employment Bureau and evaluated anonymously. Recruitment in its old nominal form continued to exist, however, until 1973.

TABLE 1.2.
Bilateral Labor and Social Security Agreements between Turkey and European states

Countries	*Labor Agreements*	*Social Security Agreements*
West Germany	30 Sept. 1961*	30 April 1964
Austria	15 May 1964	12 October 1966
Belgium	15 July 1964	4 July 1966
Holland	19 August 1964	5 April 1966
Switzerland	—	1 May 1969
France	8 April 1965	20 Jan. 1972
Sweden	10 March 1967	2 Sept. 1977
Denmark	—	13 Nov. 1970

(*) extended on 30 Sept. 1964

Source: Ahmet Y. Gökdere, 1978. *Yabancı Ülkelere İşgücü Akımı ve Türk Ekonomisi Üzerine Etkileri*, Türkiye İş Bankası Kültür Yayınları, s.275.

Gastarbeiter *(Guest Worker) Replaces Individual Immigrant*

During this second phase, emigration from Turkey underwent an important structural change. The first phase, undertaken by individuals or small groups acting independently, was of relatively small numbers. This changed in 1962, when the Berlin Wall was erected and Turkey's First Five-Year Development Plan came into being. Among the many targets of the plan were population control and the export of surplus labor. The latter meant bringing emigration under state control and the end of the days of the individual immigrant. The planners were operating on the hypothesis that sending an unskilled work force abroad would secure the return of the necessary skills with which to undertake Turkey's industrialization process. Meanwhile, the ever-increasing demand from West German employers for labor—preferably skilled—was set to bring about extraordinary changes in both West Germany's foreign population and emigration out of Turkey. A comparison of 1960 and 1963 is sufficient: 2,700 workers moved from Turkey to Germany in 1960 and 27,500 in 1963.[11]

Labor export in this second phase was bound up with policies of the governments involved, with state bureaucracies on both sides ultimately responsible for the dispatch and settlement of the workers. It was at this time that the concept of *Gastarbeiter* was born. Agreements were based on a principle of rotation: a worker was expected to return home after one's year employment abroad. Of course, history has shown that this principle rarely—if ever—operated in reality. The agreements stipulated that the health check and travel expenses of the worker were underwritten by the future employer, and contained detailed information concerning the treatment of those who wished to return prior to the end of the contract and those who were obliged to return.

Workers were not permitted to take their families with them, and were housed in group living quarters or dormitories known as *Heim*. Despite being separated from loved ones, the primary aim of all workers was to extend their work contracts and save enough to set up a business when they eventually returned home. Given that employers wanted to retain workers who had become accustomed to the work, the rotation principle mentioned above never became practice. The Confederation of German Unions, which had from the start supported the rotation model, failed almost completely to interest itself in the Turkish workers, out of concern no doubt for its own native work force. The German government, attempting to provide information for and regulate the leisure time interests of its *Gastarbeiters*, put responsibility for this in the hands of the Organization for Social Assistance of Workers, an offshoot of the German Social Democrat Party. One outcome of this was the establishment of *Türk-Danış*, a consultant/advisory organization that aimed to strengthen

[11] Bundesanstalt für Arbeitsvermittlung, *Erfahrungsbericht* 1961, 3; Bundesanstalt für Arbeitsvermittlung, *Erfahrungsbericht* 1964, 5.

cooperation among Turkish workers and encourage the formation of associations. German television and radio, recognizing the workers' need for news and information, began daily broadcasting of short programs in Turkish, and in attempts to prevent the workers' savings from draining away into the black market, a specified rate of exchange was agreed upon, which guaranteed the flow of these savings to Turkey.[12]

The economic crisis in Germany in 1966–1967, during which the motor industry was severely affected and over 70,000 Turkish workers lost their jobs, led to the first critical appraisal of the issue of foreign labor.[13] Intense debate began on the question of what, exactly, is a foreign worker—part of a reserve labor army or an element that occurs naturally in an industrialized society? The majority of the Turks whose jobs had disappeared tried to find jobs in Holland, Belgium, and Denmark; those who failed to find work were taken in by fellow Turks.[14] Few, if any, returned home, and when the crisis eased in the spring of 1967 almost all were reemployed. The experience, however, had taught them that union membership at least guaranteed payment of social insurance in the event of layoffs and Turkish works began to unionize in huge numbers. The unions responded by creating special units for Turkish workers.

The 1970s

These were the years in which European countries imported Turkish labor, and Turkey came to the realization that this was no longer a temporary phenomenon; the exported labor intended to stay. This led to the beginning of intergovernmental negotiations on the granting of social rights to foreign workers, the result of which was a series of social security agreements. Within the framework of these agreements, foreign workers gained access to state health care; social insurance in the event of accidents, disability, or death; unemployment and pension rights; and state assistance in childbirth and care.

Economic Crisis and the Halt in Flow of Foreign Labor

In 1973, events in world economics radically changed state policies regarding foreign labor. The 1973–1974 petrol embargo led to a worldwide economic recession as oil quadrupled in price, and growing unemployment throughout

---

[12] Nermin Abadan-Unat, *Turkish Workers in Europe 1960–1975 A Socio-Economic Reappraisal.* (Leiden: Brill, 1976), 15.

[13] In order to prevent black market activities, between 1964 and1970, workers received a special rate of 430.68 Turkish lira (TL) for 100 German marks (DM). Nermin Abadan-Unat, Ruşen Keleş, Rinus Pennix, *Herman van Renselaar, Leo Van Velzen,* and Leyla Yenisey, eds., *Migration and Development: A Study of the Impact of International Labor Migration on the District of Boğazlıyan* (Ankara University–NUFFIC, 1975), 48.

[14] Nermin Abadan-Unat, "La Récession de 1966/67 en Allemagne Fédérale et ses repercussions sur les ouvriers Turcs," *Turkish Yearbook of International Relations,* no. 11 (1971): 59.

TABLE 1.3.
In 1968–1980 numbers and distribution of Turkish workers throughout Europe

Country	*1968/69*	*1970/71*	*1973/74*	*Worker 1980*	*Adult 1980*	*Child 1980*	*Total*
Germany	171,016	373,000	605,000	590,623	287,377	584,400	1,462,400
France	4,000	10,000	29,600	38,000	20,695	34,077	92,772
Holland	13,243	16,512	46,018	47,326	38,137	36,249	121,712
Belgium	4,217	8,500	10,000	23,000	13,305	30,258	66,563
England	—	1,387	2,170	3,000	1,000	2,000	6,000
Denmark	—	2,377	7,000	9,321	250	6,264	15,841
Other EEC countries	—	—	—	395	30	75	500
Total (EEC)	**192,476**	**411,776**	**711,302**	**711,671**	**360,794**	**693,323**	**1,765,323**
Austria	5,259	12,316	29,764	30,130	17,331	17,539	65,000
Switzerland	5,227	6,502	23,158	20,119	2,143	13,604	35,857
Norway	—	200	449	1,370	163	719	2,252
Non-EEC countries	12,157	21,805	58,432	58,619	24,661	40,043	119,314
Total (Europe)	**204,633**	**435,581**	**769,734**	**770,290**	**385,455**	**733,366**	**1,885,102**

Source: N. Abadan-Unat, "Turkey: Late Entrant into Europe's Work Force," in D. Kubat (ed.), *The Politics of Migration Policies,* 2nd ed. (pp. 308–309) (New York: Center for Migration Studies, 1993).

Europe forced governments to halt all imports of foreign labor. At the same time, foreign workers already in Europe found that they were being blocked from employment opportunities, and governments began to actively encourage foreign labor to return home.

The dire economic circumstances polarized groups on the issue of migration policies. The Union of German Employers and local authorities, concerned about overloading hospitals, schools, and other public services, began to call for a return to the original rotation principle of migration, whereas the Confederation of German Unions made a plea for "integration," condemning the discriminatory character of the 1965 Foreigners Law promulgated to combat fears of illegal migration and unfair competition from cheap labor.[15]

This debate brought about significant changes in state migration policies. In 1973, 103,753 workers traveled to West Germany, but by 1975 only 640

[15] Nermin Abadan, "Le non-retour a l'industrie, trait dominant de la chaine migratoire Turque," *Sociologie du travail,* no. 3 (1972): 278–293. See also Nermin Abadan-Unat, "Federal Almanya'nın 1966/7'de geçirdiği ekonomik buhran açısından yabancı işgücü ve Türk işçilerin durumu," *A.U.S.B.F. Dergisi* 26, no. 4:159–180; and Klaus J. Bade, ed., *Deutsche im Ausland. Fremde in Deutschland. Migration in Geschichte und Gegenwart.* (Munich: C. H. Beck, 1993), 393–402.

individuals were granted work permits.[16] Despite this dramatic decline, the number of Turkish immigrant workers continued to increase as families were reunited: the total number of Turkish immigrant workers throughout the European Community, estimated at 711,302 in 1974, rose in 1977 to 1,765,788 with the arrival of spouses and children.[17]

The sudden rise in the number of illegal workers may be linked to the radical strategies adopted by governments to end legal migration. As far back as 1970–1971, the waiting list of potential immigrants with the State Employment Bureau in Turkey exceeded 1 million, many of whom, when faced with a six- or seven-year wait, decided to try other routes.[18] For example, many immigrants traveled to Europe on a tourist visa in the hope of finding an employer willing to turn a blind eye to employment laws. Another alternative was traveling by train through eastern Europe to East Berlin, and from there by subway to the west. However, this entryway was firmly locked before long.

The intense passion for migration among Turks at this time was documented in research undertaken by Dutch and Turkish academics in Yozgat province, Turkey, in 1975. One finding to emerge from this research showed that of a group of five hundred workers, 42.4 percent had gone abroad on tourist visas and later obtained work permits.[19]

TABLE 1.4.
Channels used when initially going abroad

Method	*Number leaving*	*%*	*Number returning*	*%*	*Total number*	*%*
State Employment Bureau	138	37.0	58	46.0	196	39.2
Nominal Recruitment	45	12.1	10	7.9	55	11.0
Tourist	158	42.4	54	42.5	212	42.4
Other	32	8.5	5	3.9	37	6.4
Total	373	100.0	127	100.0	500	100.0

Source: N. Abadan-Unat, R. Keleş et al, *Migration and Development,* s.193, Table 5.2.2.1.

[16] "Zur Reform der Auslaenderpolitik," *Theorie und Praxis der Sozialen Arbeit,* special edition (April 1973); Walter Arendt, "Aktionsprogramm fur Auslaenderbeschaefttigunng," *Bulletin, Presse und Informationsamt, Bonn* 70 (1973): 689.

[17] Ray C. Rist, *Guestworkers in Germany: The Prospect for Pluralism* (New York: Praeger, 1978), 113.

[18] Nermin Abadan-Unat, "Turkey: Late Entrant into Europe's Work Force," in *The Politics of Migration: Settlement and Integration,* 2nd ed., Daniel Kubat, ed. (New York: Center for Migration Studies, 1993b), 308–309.

[19] The total number of those on the waiting list to go abroad was 1,066,085 on 31 April 1971. IIBK, *Yurt Dışındaki Türk İşcileri ve Dönüs Eğilimleri,* Araştırma, no. 59 and no. 85 (İş ve İşçi Bulma Kurumu, Ankara, 1971).

Amnesty for Illegal Workers

Amnesty for illegal workers was introduced at various times in countries that found themselves with large numbers of illegal workers: Belgium in 1966 and 1974; the West German states of Hessen and Nordrhein-Westfalen in 1972; France in 1973; and the Netherlands in 1975. The amnesty programs were aimed both at protecting native workers from unfair competition (i.e., cheap labor), but also at curbing the exploitation of "tourist" workers and granting them equality under the law. To take advantage of the amnesty, illegal workers had first to return to their homeland, after which the country of acceptance guaranteed to mail them residence and work permits, which would enable them to reenter legally.

Thus, we can see that this third phase was a time of growing awareness in European countries and Turkey of the issue of foreign labor and the scope and gravity of the problems associated with it. This consciousness was also reflected in the print media in many publications and discussions on the subject of foreign labor and its influence on the social life of all societies concerned. Images connected with emigration and its attendant issues also began to be expressed through various art forms, especially through literature, in both Turkey and Europe. A striking example of one such work is Adalet Ağaoğlu's novel, *Fikrimin İnce Gülü* (*The Tender Rose of My Imagination*).

Settlement Abroad, Unification of Families, and Child Subsidies

This time of change symbolized the constant uncertainty about the future with which these immigrant workers lived. Although remaining faithful to the notion of returning home to fulfill their dreams, the news of continuing high unemployment and increasing violence and political instability meant that many postponed returning to Turkey until retirement. Thus, the dominant process became reuniting the family by bringing other family members abroad.

This trend towards family unification was indirectly encouraged by changes in child subsidy payments in West Germany, and a restructuring of work permit schemes for spouses and dependents. Until 1 January 1975, there was no distinction between German or foreign parenthood regarding the payment of child subsidies. However, in 1975 there was a significant monetary change to the payments based on whether children were resident with the parents in West Germany or living in Turkey. Taking into account the number of children in the family, payments of 10–70 German marks (DM) were made for each child remaining in Turkey, whereas subsidies in West Germany for all children, regardless of parentage, were 50–100 DM.

These changes, which had been instituted to reduce expenditures in social welfare, had exactly the opposite effect: Despite having the highest proportion of married workers among all foreign workers (86 percent), the Turks were, until this reform was instituted, among the least likely to bring their families to

TABLE 1.5.
Child subsidy payments to foreigners before and after 1975 (in DM)

No. of children	*1964–74 no difference*	*After 1975 for children outside Germany*	*After 1975 for children in Germany*
1	—	10	50
2	25	25	70
3	50	60	120
4	60	60	120
5	70	70	120

Source: *Metal Haberler,* (News from Metal Tradeunion), Frankfurt, December 1974, no 12, s.3.

Germany—only approximately 46 percent had done so. With the introduction of the reform, however, not only did family arrivals increase, but there was also a significant rise in births among Turkish families. Between 1974 and 1980 the number of young immigrant children in Germany increased by 129.8 percent; from 1978 to 1979 alone there was an increase of 15.7 percent.[20] This dramatic increase in the number of children added new a dimension to existing social problems.

The 1980s

Problems in Child Education

By 1980, 40 percent of Turkish immigrant communities in West Germany, Switzerland, Sweden, and Norway was under the age of eighteen, and it was becoming clear that lack of language skills, inability to cope with the complex rules of the various educational systems, and failure in social adaptation had left this younger generation isolated and withdrawn from the larger society, and inclined towards living a ghettoized life dependent on networks of friendship and family relationships. This situation had arisen despite the deep desire of their parents for their children to benefit from the success that would come with a complete educational experience. Successive West German governments placed the principle of equal educational opportunity high on their list of priorities, but the existence of a federal system of government meant that resolving educational and cultural problems was left to the discretion of state governments. The result was an unnecessarily complex system of educational models. In some cases this led to the children who were unable to follow courses in German being sent to what were known as *Sonderschule* (Special Schools), institutions that had in fact been established to cater to the needs of slow learners.

[20] Rinus Penninx and Leo Van Velzen, "Alternate Routes Abroad," in *Migration and Development,* eds Nermin Abadan-Unat et al. (Ankara University–NUFFIC, 1975), 180, table 5.2.2.1.

TABLE 1.6.
1970–80 Distribution of students in Germany by nationality and type of school (%)

Type of school	*Year*	*Turkish*	*Other foreigners*	*German*
8-year primary	1970	93.5	85.1	70.9
	1980	89.0	75.1	51.9
Private*	1970	2.3	2.5	3.7
	1980	4.1	4.7	4.1
High school	1970	1.7	3.5	9.7
	1980	2.4	6.2	16.0
Gymnasium**	1970	2.4	8.9	15.8
	1980	1.9	10.3	25.1

(*) schools for slow learners
(**) Schools for entry to university
Source: H.G. Kleff, 1984 *Vom Bauern zum Industriearbeiter, -Zur kollektiven Lebens-Geschichte der Arbeitsmigranten aus der Türkei.* (From Peasant to Industrial Worker- Collective Life-Stories of Immigrants from Turkey) Ingelheim: Manthano Verlag. Table 30, s.220.

It must also be kept in mind here that the German educational system of that time, and indeed until very recently, was rigid and elitist, and prevented as many as 90 percent of native German students from continuing on to a university.[21]

Only a small proportion of the children of Turkish immigrants managed to complete *Hauptschule,* the eight-year primary school cycle. Figures show that in the years following the reunification of families, 60 percent of children abandoned primary school prior to completion.[22] During this same period only 18 percent of the fifteen to twenty-one age group managed to gain entry to and complete courses in vocational education.

Thus, faced with such fundamental difficulties, many children of immigrants either abandoned their struggle—or were abandoned in their struggle—to cope.

The state of Bavaria began educating its young immigrants in Turkish, removing them altogether from most of the courses presented in German. This approach worked adequately for primary and secondary education but prevented youths from going on to tertiary education. In contrast, the Berlin model insisted on using German even in situations where native German students were a minority in the classroom. The result, for Turkish students whose par-

[21] Nermin Abadan-Unat, ed., *Turkish Workers in Europe 1960–1975: A Socio-Economic Reappraisal* (Leiden: E. J. Brill, 1976), 35; see also Nermin Abadan-Unat, ed., *Turkish Workers in Europe 1960–1975,* table 5, footnote 17, 314.

[22] Rist, *Guestworkers in Germany,* footnote 16.

ents had not mastered German, meant a distancing and alienation in parent-child relations.

Meanwhile, Turkish immigrant parents were also faced with the dilemma of choosing between sending their children to *Qur'an* courses or classes in Turkish culture sponsored by the Turkish government, which clashed with each other on Saturdays and Sundays. The situation was further complicated by the existence of different groups of teachers being given different tasks. On the one hand, the teachers were appointed by the Turkish government to teach Turkish history and geography at weekend courses in specific schools; on the other hand, a group of Turkish teachers were paid by the German government to teach German language. Only in the city of Berlin was Turkish on the curriculum as a compulsory foreign language at this time, which led to many young Turkish students losing interest entirely in their Turkish lessons at school. Another disadvantage was the fact that the German authorities decided not to monitor school attendance to the minimum age of sixteen among foreign students. This was especially detrimental to the young daughters of Turkish workers, many of whom were, as a result, left almost entirely without formal education. Most fulfilled the role of babysitter within the family, left to care for the younger children while both parents worked.

Growth of Associations

In the 1960s most Turkish workers' associations were financially supported by the authorities in the country of acceptance and, to a limited extent, functioned as unions and solidarity organizations. In 1963 there were 19 such associations active in West Germany. By 1974 there were 112, concentrated in Hamburg but also spread throughout the country, and a total of 44 in Switzerland, Austria, Belgium, Holland, and Denmark.[23] Over time, many of these associations became ideologically polarized. In larger cities, alongside organizations that had developed links with international leftist movements, there were equally as many extreme right-wing and religious groups, each and all seeking to increase their numbers. Many indeed had become nothing more than satellite organizations for radical political parties in the homeland. For example, as far back as 1973 the fascist Nationalist Movement Party had autonomous units in Berlin, Hannover, Cologne, Mannheim, Munich, and Stuttgart and had set up the *Bozkurt* militia movement. They were forced to cease their activities in November 1976 only following general outcry in the German parliament. In similar fashion, extreme conservative religious associations, not satisfied with simply supporting the National Welfare Party in Turkey, began establishing private schools in several larger cities for the purposes of pros-

---

[23] Wolfgang Bodenbender, "Zwischenbilanz der Auslaenderpolitik," in *Türkische Kinder in Deutschland,* ed. Franz Ronneberger (Nürnberg: Nürenberger Forschungsvereinigung, 1976), 9.

elytism. Indeed, by involving themselves in activities such as hunger strikes to draw attention to their criticisms of leaders brought to power in Turkey following the military takeover in 1980, many of the associations simply became the mouthpieces of Turkish political activists abroad. There still existed German state funding for these associations, and it was this and voluntary, and in some cases, involuntary, donations from Turkish workers through the local mosque that enabled the associations to carry on their activities. By this time, however, they constituted a serious problem in the field of international politics and were particularly active in the Kurdish separatist movement and in the formation of radical religious factions that were spreading the teachings of Ayatollah Khomeini.[24]

Rise in Demands for Asylum

Apart from the activities in associations, another unexpected development occurred during these years. As noted above, by this time European governments were already adopting policies that denied entrance to immigrants. When, after 1978, these policies became even more stringent, the West German government found itself faced with a dramatic rise in the number of individuals seeking political asylum. Some of these were undoubtedly simply economic immigrants who, with the assistance of German lawyers, hoped to take advantage of loopholes in German law that would allow them enter the country to seek employment. Their efforts were made easier by a clause in Article 16 of the German Constitution, originally written to facilitate entry to those fleeing socialist countries, which guaranteed the right of asylum to all. Potential immigrants from Turkey did not take long to discover this breach in the German defenses. In 1976, 809 individuals applied for asylum on the grounds of political pressure. In four years the figure leaped to 57,913.

In later years applications were mainly from individuals fleeing war-torn Bosnia-Herzegovina. These numbers quickly began to worry the German authorities, and it did not take long before they took measures to close the country's borders. After 1980, asylum-seekers were housed in special holding camps and were denied the right to work or to benefit from social security. The number of asylum seekers soon began to fall. After 1980, following the military coup, almost all European countries except England and Italy required Turkish citizens to obtain a visa to travel within their borders. This limited visits from immigrant-worker family members and was a source of tension between Turkey and her European neighbors.

---

[24] Nermin Abadan-Unat, "Die politischen Auswirkungen der Türkischen Migration im In-und Ausland" [The Political Impact of Turkish Migration within the Country and Abroad], *ORIENT* 20, no. 1 (1979): 22; İlhan Gülsün, *Sayılarla Yurtdışındaki Işcilerimiz ve sorunlarına ait istatistikler* (Ankara: IIBK, 1974), 59.

TABLE 1.7.
Annual number of asylum requests made to Germany by Turkish individuals

Year	*Number*	*(%)*
1976	809	7.3
1980	57,913	53.7
1985	7,528	10.2
1990	22,082	11.4

Source: Statistisches Bundesamt, (Federal Germany Statistics) Statistisches Jahrbuch, 1995, Table: 12.2

Political Parties and Migration Politics

Throughout its time in political power the German Social Democrat Party instituted a series of policies as part of an effort to engage second-generation immigrant youth in education and create greater social integration. In universities, courses on foreign pedagogy were introduced, and new educational models were tested in schools. The inherent virtues of the concept of "intercultural education" were extolled to teachers, who were actively encouraged to view the ethnic and religious diversity in their classrooms as an opportunity for educational enrichment. In short, the government attempted to bring into classrooms the tolerance primarily espoused by liberal and democratic values.[25]

Unfortunately, just as these efforts were beginning to bear fruit, the government changed. The elections of 1983 assured the CDU/CSU (Christian Democratic Party/Christian Socialist Party) a simple majority. Thus Chancellor Helmut Kohl, in coalition with the FDP (German Liberal Party), formed a new government.

The change was quickly reflected in public opinion. Indeed, when sixteen university professors in Germany put forward the fiercely nationalist Heidelberg Manifesto, which suggested that in order to protect the Christian values of Western Europe all immigrant workers must be repatriated, they found a responsive echo throughout Germany.[26]

Legal Incentives for Repatriation

Throughout the election campaign, Helmut Kohl's CDU focused on foreign workers as its primary theme and reiterated its aims, which were a halt to the

---

[25] Jochen Blaschke, "Islam und Politik unter Türkischen Arbeitsmigranten," in Jochen Blaschke and M. van Bruinessen, eds., *Jahrbuch zur Geschichte und Gesellschaft des Vorderen und Mittleren Osten* (Berlin: Parabolis, 1984), 295–300.

[26] Peter O'Brien, *Beyond the Swastika* (New York: Routledge, 1996), 66; Helmut Essinger and Achim Hellmich, eds., *Auslaenderkinder im Konflikt* [Migrant Children amidst Conflict] (Königstein, Germany: Athenaeum, 1981), 100.

migration of foreigners into Germany, incentives for those who wished to be repatriated, and social and economic integration for those immigrants long resident in West Germany.

Of course, Kohl's government was simply repeating what had been the aims of former CDU governments: Germany was not a country of immigration and thus would encourage neither the permanent settlement nor naturalization of foreigners.

Nevertheless, there were some courageous voices raised in protest from within the conservative camp. At the 1989 annual congress of the CDU, Barbara John, president of the Berlin Foreigners Commission, made this statement:

> There are approximately 54,000 babies born to foreign parents in West Germany each year, of which only 14,000 are given German citizenship. This is the smallest proportion among industrialized nations. This "third generation" will, in all likelihood, spend its entire life in Germany. It will speak German better than its native tongue and it will visit its native land for holidays only. Yet, in German law it will be forever labeled foreigner![27]

Unfortunately, despite the fact that they reflected reality, John's words—and all the problems they identified—went unanswered.

In 1984, the Green Party proposed a new law that would give full settlement rights to foreigners following a five-year residency period. This was rejected by the CDU, which insisted that immigrants had the right to choose their own destiny. This CDU principle was reiterated by Kohl in his first speech on the government's policy on foreigners. He insisted that foreigners in Germany must have the right to choose, but emphasized that the "right" was limited to either being repatriated or fusing completely with the German people.

As part of its immigrant project, the Kohl government introduced the "Foreigners Repatriation Incentive" law on 28 November 1983. The incentive was monetary, and the law established that any Yugoslavian, Turkish, Spanish, Portuguese, Moroccan, Tunisian, or Korean workers who elected to return to their homeland between 31 October 1983 and 30 June 1984 would, on fulfillment of specified conditions, be given 10,500 DM in state assistance and an additional 1,500 DM per child. The law also allowed that any pension contributions made by these workers during employment would be paid back in full at the time of return. This law led to a 5.4 percent fall in the Turkish immigrant population in 1984, as approximately 250,000 returned to Turkey.[28] Their return proved of little or no benefit to industrialization in Turkey, because the vast majority of returning workers chose to invest their savings in property and/or small businesses of their own. Only 23 percent applied to the state Employment Bureau

---

[27] *Die Zeit*, 26 December 1982.

[28] Christlich Demokratischen Union Deutschlands, *Bundesparteitag der Christlich Demokratischen Union Deutschlands: Niederschrift* (Bonn, Germany: Union, 1989), 374.

to work in industrial facilities. Thus, although Turkish migration did succeed in altering the social structure of Turkey, it never succeeded in fulfilling the expectations of the state planners who had seen emigration as a way of creating a skilled work force for Turkish industry. On the other hand, the repatriation law functioned as a kind of screening process for Germany, a "survival of the fittest" in which those who chose to return to Turkey and other countries were often elderly, unskilled, or incapacitated in some way and brought individual and/or family problems with them back to Turkey. In other words, the emigrant return movement symbolized failure for Turkey.

Meanwhile, back in Germany the entrepreneurial spirit of Turkish workers was leading to the establishment of more small independent businesses, including wholesale and retail businesses operating in food, goods manufacture, tourism, insurance, import/export, and office services. In 1985, 20,000 of these businesses owned by Turks created employment for a further 60,000 Turkish workers.[29]

The 1990s

The first years of the 1990s saw Turkish immigrant workers still engaged in the struggle to secure proper legal status for themselves, despite their thirty-year shared history with Germany.

1992 Foreigners Law

Although this law made the process of becoming a German citizen less complex for younger Turks, it also limited residency rights to those who had remained unemployed for long periods of time.[30] The law granted German citizenship to those between the ages of sixteen and twenty-three, subject to the following criteria: eight years of residency in Germany, school attendance of no less than six years, and, in accordance with Article 88 of the law, relinquishment of Turkish citizenship. Residency of fifteen years was required of those over the age of twenty-three. Article 46 allowed local authorities to deport individuals who, personally or in the name of a family member, had been dependent on state welfare payments for longer than three years. The article allowed authorities wide-ranging powers in order to specifically target large families that, without ever entering the labor market, survived entirely on state benefits of up to 3,500 DM per month.

In essence, it was possession of an *Aufenthaltserlaubnis* (right to residence) that prevented deportation. However, in West Germany, prior to obtaining an

---

[29] SOPEMİ, Report for the Continuous Reporting System on Migration (Paris: OECD, 1985), 22.

[30] Faruk Şen and Regine Erichsen, *Hinwendung zur Selbststaendigheit bei "Gastarbeiter" mit besonderer Berücksichtung von Türkei* [Tendency toward Self-Employment of "Guest Workers" with Particular Regard to Turks (Geneva, Switzerland: ILO, 1987), 14.

Aufenthaltsgenehmigung (residence permit) one had to be resident continuously for eight years, have an independent source of income, have paid at least sixty months of compulsory social insurance, and have no criminal record. Of the 566,994 Turkish workers employed in 1991, 89.7 percent had only residence permits. The law also imposed limits on retired workers.

Article 9 stated that any retired foreigner who spent more than six months of any given year residing outside Germany could lose his or her temporary or permanent residence rights, thus increasing the burden on Turkish families with members living in Germany. Each visit required a new visa, and they could not benefit from reduced cost flights.

Additional limits affected family reunifications. Second- and third-generation foreigners had to prove continuous residency in Germany for the preceding eight years and be of adult age in order to bring spouses to Germany. The spouses then had to be resident for five years prior to being granted independent residency permits or the right to enter the employment market. This was an especially harsh ruling for female Turkish immigrants. It meant that in the event of a divorce or the death of a spouse, they would have to leave Germany.

Finally, the law gave right of return to those between fifteen and twenty-one years who had been repatriated to Turkey by their parents, provided they had spent the required six years in school in Germany during their childhood, and had secured a living for themselves on return to Germany.

Thus, it is clear that German lawmakers had decided to maintain firm lines between foreigner and native. In this case they had Germany's welfare system in mind: they made it clear that they were interested only in keeping those foreigners who were good prospects in terms of integration and would not be a burden to the state. Indeed, Germany was almost unique among immigrant-accepting countries in its absolute refusal to allow dual citizenship,[31] insisting, despite everything, that citizenship must be based on *jus sanguinis* (blood ties).

The most recent amendment to this law was introduced on 1 January 2000. The amendment states that from that date, German citizenship shall be automatically granted to any child born in Germany into a family in which either the father or mother is German-born and has been resident in Germany during the ten years preceding the birth. This is valid until the individual reaches age twenty-three, at which point he or she must choose a citizenship. German lawmakers, it would seem, are determined to sever any ties their Turkish population may have formed with the country into which they were born, and

[31] For legal changes in 1990 to the laws governing foreigners in Germany and in comparison to other countries see Bülent Çiçekli, *The Legal Position of Turkish Immigrants in the European Union* (Ankara, Turkey: Karmap, 1998), 114.

TABLE 1.8.
Residency duration of Turks in Germany
(by year, in thousands, as of 31 December 2000)

Country	*Less than one year*	*1–4*	*4–6*	*6–8*	*8–10*	*10–15*	*15–20*	*20–25*	*25–30*	*30+ years*
Germany	33.1	187.1	149.1	138.4	151.5	308.5	174.9	318.7	348.7	189.0
Italy	16.3	53.1	37.3	29.3	27.2	71.1	55.1	76.5	87.2	166.0
Greece	8.7	29.0	20.8	19.0	26.0	54.5	21.5	27.1	56.9	102.0

Source: *Statistisches Bundesamt*, Table 10, s.30

to force those who insist on continuing to live there to be absorbed through integration.

Xenophobia

A development during the 1990s that would greatly influence the lives of Turkish workers was the rise in xenophobia. This became particularly prevalent following German reunification and spread throughout Europe during this decade. It had already raised its ugly head in the 1980s and grew more marked as Turks became more visible in the public space because of their persistent adherence to their culture, belief systems, and ways of life. According to Hans-Joachim Hoffman-Nowotny, "Wherever immigrants go they come to constitute a new *Unterschichtung* or underclass in the societies accepting them. This stratum is regarded as something alien or foreign and becomes the target of criticism."[32]

Figure 1.2. Turks Out!

This is what began happening in Germany, and with the passing of the

[32] The following are the primary sources for infomation on citizenship in other European countries: Yasemin Nuhoğlu Soysal, *Limits of Citizenship* (Chicago: University of Chicago, 1994); David Cesarani and Mary Fullbrook, *Citizenship, Nationality, and Migration in Europe* (London: Routledge, 1996); and Riva Kastoryano, *La France, l'Allemagne et leurs immigrées négocier l'identitée* (Paris: Armand Colin, 1996).

1973 law bringing a halt to labor migration, attitudes to foreign-worker populations who elected to remain in Germany became hostile and critical—a far cry from the welcome and praise that had greeted the first *Gastarbeiter* back in the 1960s. By 1982, 62 percent of West Germans believed that there were too many foreigners in Germany, and 50 percent felt that foreigners should be sent back to their countries of origin.[33] The permanent settlement in Germany of Turkish immigrant populations did not bring about any great change in German public opinion: in a 1990s opinion poll, only 34 percent of respondents replied positively to the question of whether a Turk born and raised in Germany may be considered German. And 46 percent of these positive replies came from sixteen- to twenty-nine-year olds.[34]

Negative attitudes became more widespread in the 1980s, and the Turk began to appear as an object of satire in cartoons and jokes. The graffiti saying *Türken-raus* (Turks out) or the more sinister *Erschlagt die Türken* (Kill Turks) could be seen scrawled on the walls in many cities. Anti-Semitic jokes from the Nazi era were resurrected and adapted to Turks.

The growing strength of extreme right-wing parties and the emergence of skinhead gangs helped to strengthen these prejudices, and the sudden increase in the refugee population, coupled with German reunification in 1989, led to debates on ethnicity and ethnic origin. Reunification of Germany brought many East Germans—called *Ossies* by the West Germans—and others from ex-socialist countries into the new Germany. West German attitudes to these groups were discriminatory from the start, which gave rise to even more severe exclusion of and negative attitudes towards Turks and others of Asian origin, who now became even more visible because of their cultural difference. Policies on foreigners became a significant part of the political agenda of the major parties, and the debate was broadened by the failure of the unified Republic of Germany to create a fresh and different ideological notion of what constitutes a nation. Without doubt, the efforts of those involved in trying to bring democratic order to the ex-communist East, and others calling for unity under the slogan of "*Wir sind ein Volk*" (We are one nation) brought a breath of fresh air to the German nation, but tensions between *Ossie* and *Wessie* continued.

However, with issues of identity on the agenda, it was almost inevitable that Germany's most populous foreign ethnic group, the Turks, would become the focus of open hostility. In 1989, as part of its political campaign in Hessen, the CDU told the electorate that each vote given to it could be counted as one against voting rights for foreigners. In particular, Helmut Kohl took it

---

[33] Hans-Joachim Hoffman-Nowotny, "A Sociological Approach towards a General Theory of Migration," in *Global Trends in Migration*, ed. Mary M. Kritz (New York: Center for Migration Studies, 1981), 74–75.

[34] Nora Raetsel, "Germany: One Race, One Nation?," *Race and Class* 32, no. 3 (1991): 31–48.

upon himself to speak out at every available opportunity on his party's commitment to the "nonsettlement" of foreigners, especially those seeking asylum. As a result, in 1992, the primary issue occupying German public opinion was not German reunification or the Gulf War, but plans to amend the German Constitution to halt the inflow of asylum seekers.

Although the attacks on refugees in Rostock took place before the elections of 1992, they made a deep impact on behavior. The public was implicitly encouraged in these attacks by inactivity of the security forces as the buildings were stoned and then burned to the ground. The response of the authorities was simply to bow to public pressure and transfer the refugees elsewhere. This served little purpose but to heighten the ferocity of various right-wing groups, and attacks on foreigners numbered 2,427 in 1991. Of these, 239 were directed against individuals, and 336 were acts of arson. In 1992, the number of incidents rose to 6,336, an increase of 160 percent.[35] Attacks against housing for foreigners took place in Rostock on 23–27 August 1992. On 23 November 1992, three Turkish women were murdered in their homes and eight Turks seriously injured by neo-Nazis. This was followed by an arson attack on a private house in Solingen on 29 May 1993 in which five Turkish women and one child died.[36] The ruling government of the time, instead of condemning these attacks outright as evidence of the rebirth of racism in Germany, chose to use the events as a excuse to legitimize the removal of Article 116 from the Constitution, which had given broad rights to those seeking asylum in Germany. Jürgen Habermas commented, "By using the arson attack in Rostock, and the killing in Mölln as a base for limiting an individual's right to political asylum, and thus implicitly laying blame for the attacks on the foreign victims, the German government cheapened republican and democratic values, and by political means, exalted the notion of ethno-nationalism."[37]

Response to these actions came in limited manner from German churches and unions. Many thousands of Germans took part in candlelight marches to express their desire for tolerance and belief in cultural pluralism. However, the marchers, in protesting directly against the individuals responsible for the attacks, and not the political context that allowed such attacks to happen, chose

---

[35] Elizabeth Noelle-Neumann and Renate Köcher, eds., *Allensbacher Jahrbuch der Demoskopie 1993–1997,* vol. 10 (Allensbach am Bodensee, Germany: K. G. Saur, 1997), 628.

[36] Stefan Gietl, Hans-Dieter Schwind, and Gabriele Zwenger, "Der 'non-helping bystander' Effekt. Wie kommıt es zu unterlassener Hilfeleistung," [The "Non-helping Bystander" Effect. How Did It Come to Denial of Help?] *Kriminalistik* 45, no. 4 (1991): 233–238; Ulrich Beck, "Biedermaenner und Brandstifter," *Der Spiegel,* 9 November 1992.

[37] Metin Gür and Alaverdi Turhan, *Die Solingen—Akte* [The Records of Solingen Trial] (Düsseldorf: Patmos Verlag, 1996). The trial continued for 125 sessions and the accused were sentenced to fifteen, ten, and three years imprisonment. Gülsün Ince (twenty-eight, married), Hatice Genç (eighteen, engaged), Hülya Genç (nine), Saime Genç (five), and Gülistan Öztürk (twelve) died in the fire.

to ignore the political element of racist violence. Erwin K. Scheuch, in comments during a European Parliamentary inquiry, expressed his belief that the roots of German hostility towards foreigners lay not in the low German birth rate, but in their fear of becoming a minority and their wish to protect their German identity.[38]

Political developments of recent years have shown that Germany, in its overriding desire to protect its historical heritage, is not yet prepared to recognize the necessity for political representation and citizenship rights for its foreign groups within a framework of cultural pluralism. Thus, Bavaria's Christian Social Unity Party, in its annual congress in November 2000, felt the need to express its belief that foreigners were obliged to adapt to the *Leitkultur* (dominant culture). The party went on to define this dominant culture as based on the values inherent in Western European Christianity, Enlightenment philosophy, and humanism.[39]

Foreigners and Identity Debates

Although German laws continued to adhere to rigid principles in regulating the status of foreigners, important changes in this area first began to emerge in language. Even prior to the end of the 1970s, the term *Gastarbeiter* had been abandoned in favor of *Ausländischer Arbeitsnehmer* (foreign employee) or *Einwanderer* (immigrant). Later, *Auslaendische Mitbürger* was pioneered by the Liberal Democratic Party (FDP) to refer to foreigners who had become a permanent feature of German life, and this became a widely used term.

The concept of integration became the main locus of state policies on immigrants after 1979. However, those using this concept accorded it various meanings, depending on their ideological position. For former CDU leader Helmut Kohl, "integration" simply meant living peacefully within German society without citizenship rights.[40] In other words, German right-wing thinking called for foreigners to live in society but forego the right to be a citizen.

On the other side of the debate were the Social Democrats (SDP) and others of the same mind (e.g., churches, unions, and foreigner associations) who, by identifying integration with "equal rights," called for "equal rights for different cultures." As the discourse of multiculturalism developed within the framework of political thinking, interest in and debates on ethnic and religious communities intensified. Increasing xenophobia had a twofold influence on the lives of Turkish communities: in strengthening their national ties it made them increasingly withdraw into the ghettoes in which they lived, but

---

[38] Jürgen Habermas, *Die Zeit,* 11 December 1992.

[39] *Frankfurter Allgemeine Zeitung,* 10 February1993.

[40] *New York Times,* 20 November 2000, 1.

it brought more attention to bear on their cultural differences. To this day, the German state continues to display an exclusionist understanding of citizenship, and consequently both federal and local governing bodies instead of facilitating citizenship acquisition have been encouraging foreign groups to organize themselves along ethnic and religious lines.

Transfer of Currency, Savings, and Turkish Social Welfare Laws

The savings potential of Turkish workers and the resultant flow of hard currencies into the homeland were factors that led the architects of the 1962–1967 First Five-Year Development Plan to organize Turkey's "labor export." Stephen Adler examined the effect of these savings on the Turkish economy during the years 1961–1980. Adler made a distinction between "consumption" and

Figure 1.3. His Only Goal: Saving

"investment," and suggested that a distinction also should be drawn between savings on macro, regional, and family/individual levels.[41]

There is no doubt that on the macro level the remittance of these savings affected the balance of payments in the Turkish state. Another important factor observed on the regional level was the indirect effect on local economies of the workers' growing wealth and spending power.[42] A comparison between family/individual levels of income and consumption and investment shows an increase in the purchasing power of both the immigrant worker and family members, especially female, remaining in Turkey. This situation may, in some cases, be attributed to conspicuous consumption.[43] On the regional level, Rinnus Penninx and Leo Van Velzen mentioned the disappointment on behalf of economists in relation to savings. Although the regions from where the workers came were the recipients of these savings, the region itself did not benefit from these transfers. The foreign currencies were channeled primarily to metropolitan cities such as Istanbul and İzmir, and their effect on the local level remained minimal.[44] However, despite any negative effects, the important part played by the foreign currencies sent from abroad never diminished. Indeed, since the early 1970s, immigrant workers' savings are estimated to equal Turkey's export revenue for the period of 1970 to 1980.

In 1964, a total of $45 million was sent home to Turkey in savings. The figure for the first seven months of 1981 was a staggering $2.078 billion. Following the military coup in Turkey on 12 September 1980, savings grew in volume. This reaction can be explained by the fact that after the coup, workers abroad considered the security of their home country as having increased. The amount of currency transferred to Turkey in savings in 1979 was $1.693 billion, and in September 1981 this figure was $2.476 billion. The generous interest rates—as high as 55 percent over six months—being offered especially for immigrant workers' savings by Turkish banks were another factor behind this increase in volume. These currency transfers continue to this day.

As can be seen in Table 1.9, during the 1980s currency transfers served to cover 60 percent of Turkey's trade deficit. This percentage dropped to 35

[41] Up to four thousand applications for work permits from sixty countries were made following changes to the migration policy which came into effect on 1 August 2000. Most applications were from India, Pakistan, Algeria, and Bulgaria. *Letter—Hochschule und Ausland,* Deutscher Akademischer Austausch Dienst (DAAD) [German Academic Exchange Service], no. 2 (June 2000): 12.

[42] Stephen Adler, *A Turkish Conundrum: Emigration, Politics and Development 1961–1980* (Geneva: ILO, 1981), 52.

[43] Rinnus Penninx and Leo Van Velzen, "The Economic Impact of External Migration on the District of Boğazlıyan," in *Migration and Development,* eds Nermin Abadan-Unat et al. (Ankara University: SBF Yayınları, 1986), 195–209.

[44] Nermin Abadan-Unat, "Implications of Migration on Emancipation and Pseudo-emancipation of Turkish Women," *International Migration Review* 11 (Spring 1977): 52.

TABLE 1.9.
Currency Transfers, GNP, Exports, and Trade Deficit, and the Share of Currency Transfers in Trade Deficit, Exports, and GNP (1975–2000) (in $ millions)

Year	*Transfers*	*GNP*	*Exports*	*Trade Deficit*	*Trade Deficit %*	*Export %*	*GNP %*
1975	1,313	47,452	1,401	−3,338	39.3	93.7	2.77
1980	2,071	63,391	2,910	−4,999	41.4	71.2	3.27
1985	1,714	66,891	8,255	−2,975	57.6	20.8	2.56
1992	3,008	158,122	14,891	−8,191	36.7	20.2	1.88
1993	2,919	178,715	15,610	−14,162	20.6	18.7	1.63
1994	2,627	132,302	18,390	−4,216	62.3	14.3	1.99
1995	3,327	170,081	21,975	−13,212	25.2	15.1	1.96
1996	3,542	183,601	32,446	−10,582	33.5	10.9	1.93
1997	4,197	192,383	32,647	−15,358	27.3	12.9	2.18
1998	5,356	206,552	31,220	−14,220	37.7	17.2	2.59
1999	4,529	185,171	29,325	−10,443	43.4	15.4	2.45
2000	4,560	201,188	31,375	−22,337	20.4	14.5	2.27

Source: Ahmet Icduygu, *Sopemi Report 2000,* Table: 10, s.26.

percent in the 1990s, a change that may be explained by liberalization of the Turkish economy as Turkey began to take its place in the world economy. Even during this period however, workers' savings still played their part in closing Turkey's trade deficit: in 1999, currency transfers equaled 43 percent of the deficit, and even as they decreased, currency transfers accounted for 2 percent of the gross national product (GNP).

It must be remembered that repayment of debt was not the only use Turkey made of the workers' transferred savings, and much debate focused on how this valuable resource could be best employed. The revenue was particularly important in efforts to relieve Turkey's energy shortages (i.e., in relations with oil-producing countries), and allowed for much of the importation of consumer products as well. In this context, a one-sided economic dependency emerged,[45] and in its efforts to correct this asymmetric relationship the Turkish government promulgated a series of laws pertaining to social welfare.

Relationship Between National and Foreign Credit

Prior to the 1980s and the explosion of interest rates after 2000, the dominant forms of investment among Turkish immigrant workers were the purchase of land, apartments, shops, and other real estate, and the establishment

[45] Rinnus Penninx and Herman van Renselaar, *A Fortune in Small Change* (The Hague, the Netherlands: Nuffic/Imwood Remplod Project, 1978).

of small private businesses. This trend changed in recent years for two reasons. First, the changes brought about by the 1973 decision of immigrant-accepting countries to halt further labor imports resulted in a growing tendency among Turkish workers to adopt a semi-permanent approach to living abroad, and thus engage in the purchase of apartments or houses overseas. Second, banks and bankers in the homeland, by being fiercely competitive in offering high interest rates, managed to attract considerable amounts of workers' foreign currency savings.

National Special Credit Allowances

Special laws such as Law 499, passed in 1964, were intended to encourage Turkish workers living abroad to send or bring their savings home. Law 499 provided special credit to emigrant workers opening foreign currency accounts in state banks:

- Emlak Kredi Bank offered mortgage-free loans to workers for a period of three years, providing they held an account with the bank in which they retained 40 percent of the loan sum agreed. This formula, however, failed to attract the attention of the workers.
- Ziraat Bank's special loans scheme offered overseas workers the opportunity to purchase land and/or farm machinery in Turkey. This scheme had no great success either in attracting any great numbers of investors.
- Halk Bank, originally founded in 1938 to help fund traders and artisans in setting up small industries, began in the 1960s to assist small businesses in the areas of business management and technology. In 1975, the bank developed a special credit plan for overseas workers in which it offered any worker opening a 20,000 DM account 1,250,000 Turkish lira (TL) credit after one year. However, even such an attractive offer was taken up by a mere 173 workers.[46]

Similarly, in 1972, an agreement between Turkey and West Germany was signed in July 1972. A special credit fund for Turkish workers abroad was created, and the West German Ministry for Economic Cooperation transferred 2.5 DM million to this fund in July 1972. In order to make use of the fund, there were two prerequisites. First, the worker was required to have made a decision to permanently return to Turkey and have plans to establish a small private enterprise there. Second, the worker had to participate in a West German educational program, followed by a business studies course in Turkey. The hypothesis of this project was that these processes would facilitate the integration of workers into the Turkish economy on his or her return. However,

[46] Johan Galtung, "A Structural Theory of Imperialism," *Journal of Peace Research* 8, no. 2: 81–117.

the project planners' were disappointed, because the number of Turkish workers who chose to return permanently remained far below estimates, even during periods of economic recession.[47]

After the 1970s, which followed the short-lived recession in Europe of 1968–1969 predominantly in the automobile section, governments in Turkey supported two different kinds of "participatory " investment models: Village Development Cooperatives and Worker Investment Companies.

VILLAGE DEVELOPMENT COOPERATIVES

The Village Development Cooperatives were created in 1962 by the Turkish Ministry of Rural Affairs and, as they grew, they received more attention from the government after 1970. It was assumed that through the creation of new employment opportunities in Turkey and the remittances of the migrant workers abroad, these cooperatives would secure their members a priority to go abroad and would help to meet future labor shortages abroad.[48]

Although the Village Developments Cooperatives were established in 1962, they only gained relevance after the recession of 1968–1969. At the beginning participation in a cooperative required a payment of 8,000 TL to be paid between the years of 1963–1965, of which 2,000 TL had to be paid as an initial deposit. During this first two-year phase, the cooperatives were used mainly as a grid to secure a preferential treatment for workers who were registered on the official waiting lists to go abroad. In 1965, following a critical evaluation, the Ministry decided to develop a labor force deployment project within these cooperatives.[49] This project was based on these principles: the 150 cooperatives that had been established in the three years prior to March 1966 would be responsible for securing 20,000 employment opportunities abroad for their members. Members to be sent abroad would make a payment of between 5,000–15,000 TL to their cooperative. In return for their personal contribution, the government would provide supplementary credit funding of up to 900 TL million for the workers abroad. Although the cooperatives would be responsible for the distribution of open jobs abroad that would be allocated to their members, the State Employment Bureau would monitor the members' fulfillment of their commitments. And a special department to deal with cooperatives would be established under the Ministry of Rural Affairs.

---

[47] Report of the Senate Investigative Commission into Problems of Turkish Workers abroad, *Cumhuriyet Senatosu*, no. 918 (October 1962): 24. The proposal remained in draft form and was never applied.

[48] Herman van Renselaar and Leo Van Velzen, "Public and Private Initiatives Aimed at Using External Labor *Migration* for *Development," in Migration and Development,* eds Nermin Abadan-Unat et al. (1975), 24.

[49] Nermin Abadan-Unat, ed., *Turkish Workers in Europe 1960–1975* (Leiden, Belgium: E. J. Brill, 1976a), 26.

There were 383 cooperatives in existence in 1964. By 1967 this number had risen to 1,349,[50] an impressive "success rate" that the Ministry of Rural Affairs had not foreseen. In reality, individuals were joining these cooperatives purely for the purpose of obtaining employment in Europe. At the same time, a number of politicians, as part of their efforts to increase their popularity among constituents, included information about the cooperatives in their campaigns and promised employment opportunities. However, after the general elections in 1965 in Turkey, the new ruling Justice Party (Adalet Partisi, AP) showed a lack of active support for the cooperatives, and, coupled with the 1966–1967 economic recession in West Germany, this slowed the growth of cooperatives. In fact, no new ones were established in 1967–1968. After the initial spurt of growth, their numbers eventually only increased from 1,349 in 1971 to 1,381 in 1972. Following the 1973 decision by European countries to halt all foreign labor imports (*Anwerbestop*), there were no attempts to form any new cooperatives.

Three factors played significant roles in hindering the success of cooperatives: (1) political and organizational inertia; (2) an unnecessarily complicated bureaucracy; and (3) limited resources put aside for the project by the Ministry of Rural Affairs.

From the start, the Village Developments Cooperatives were used as a means of "jumping the queue" to work abroad and they resulted in many disappointments. On the one hand, the development of Turkey was far from being the chief concern of cooperative members: Their minds were focused on emigration. On the other hand, there was the handicap of a serious lack of adequate technical and/or financial feasibility studies in the creation of these cooperatives.[51]

Later efforts to bring the cooperatives under a general umbrella organization such as KÖY-KOOP (Village Cooperatives) also failed. Consequently, it would appear that greater success for cooperatives was dependent on choosing projects that brought together industry and agriculture (i.e., agro-industrial projects); obtaining consistent state support; having adequate capital accumulation prior to project start-up; and having qualified managerial staff with the knowledge and leadership skills to oversee the projects.

WORKER INVESTMENT COMPANIES

For more than two decades, from 1970 to 1990, Turkish migration experts and social scientists debated the merits and shortcomings of the Turkish model of a "worker company." These workers' investment companies, which nowadays

[50] Penninx and van Renselaar, *A Fortune in Small Change*, 53.

[51] Sevim Osmay, *Türkische Dorfentwicklungsgenossenschaften* [Turkish Village Development Cooperatives] (Bonn, Germany: Bundesministerium für Wirtschaftliche Zusammenarbeit, 1975).

with very few exceptions have not been able to constitute, next to government and the market, a so-called "third economic sector," have been predominantly regionally oriented. They were founded by small groups and workers and had close ties with local individual leaders.[52]

These companies were conceived with the idea of securing open jobs for returnees as well as family members left behind. But as the years passed abroad, the desire to return vanished, and so did the operational capacity of these companies.[53]

Migration and Social Structure

Over the last fifty years more than 3.5 million Turks have moved to more than thirty different countries, and this has had a profound impact on the structure of Turkish society. Three of the most significant effects will be discussed below.

The Loss of Skilled Labor

With the exception of a ban preventing mining workers from Zonguldak province from going abroad to work, prior to 1973 Turkey did not have any criteria governing who could or could not go abroad. As a result, Turkey lost more skilled workers to the labor emigration process than any other labor-exporting Mediterranean country.[54]

During these years, 1961–1973, it is estimated that 17 percent of Turkey's skilled labor went abroad—and this figure does not include highly qualified technical and professional workers. Turkey's Second Five-Year Development Plan refers to skilled labor shortages of 337,000–885,000 between 1970 and 1975.[55] It is inevitable that such an intensive level of migration would have significant consequences for the national economy.

In fact, although this policy of unlimited migration was the subject of constant criticism from the State Planning Organization and the Turkish Union of

---

[52] According a German survey, ISOPLAN, in 1977 there were 125 such companies out of which 78 were active; an ILO study stated in 1978 there were 141 companies, 42 being operational. ISOPLAN, *Türkische Arbeitnehmergesellschaften in der B.D.R.* [Turkish Workers Investment Companies in West Germany] (Bonn: Saarbrücken, 1973).

[53] Workers' companies created a sharp polarization among Turkish and foreign researchers. Sociologists and migration experts such as Ali Gitmez, Rinnus Penninx, Herman van Renselaar, Susanne Paine, Stephen Adler, and Nermin Abadan-Unat share the opinion that these experiences had only a marginal effect on Turkey's employment problem. Sociologists such as İbrahim Yasa, Ömer Bozkurt, Sami H. Güven, and Nevzat Yalçıntaş maintained that these companies led to the founding of small- or medium-sized industries and were beneficial.

[54] Nermin Abadan, "Le non-retour a l'industrie, trait dominant de la chaine migratoire turque," *Sociologie du Travail* 3 (1972): 278–293.

[55] For more detail, see Susanne Paine, *Exporting Workers: The Turkish Case* (Cambridge: Cambridge University Press, 1974).

TABLE 1.10.
Percentages of skilled labor amongst labor sent abroad by State Employment Bureau

Year	*Numbers of workers abroad*	*Skilled labor %*
1964–66	152,106	35.4
1967	8,947	31.2
1968	43,205	28.1
1969	103,075	31.2
1970	129,575	27.0
1971	88,442	37.7

Source: State Employment Bureau 1964–71, *State Planning Organization 1973,* p. 676.

Chambers of Commerce, it was nevertheless supported because of the much-needed hard currency that flowed into Turkey as a result. Therefore, it may be said that it was the immigrant-accepting countries that, in the main, benefited from the emigration of Turkey's highly skilled labor force, as these emigrants played a major role in helping to realize those countries' development programs. The 1968 annual report of the Bundesanstalt für Arbeit (the German State Employment Department) states that, second only to Yugoslavian immigrants, Turks constituted the most highly qualified foreign labor force in Germany. Likewise, in October 1973, *Le Monde Diplomatique* highlighted the fact that Turks were the most skilled labor force among France's immigrant populations from Mediterranean countries.

Social Mobility

One inevitable consequence of the emigration movement was social mobility, both upward and downward. This paved the way for significant changes in Turkey's socioeconomic structure and in the stratification of Turkish society. Upward mobility was mostly intra-generational, and resulted in a move from agricultural to industrial-based work. This contrasts with the downward mobility experienced in West Germany by the relatively better skilled Turkish labor force there, a process that was observed mainly among white-collar workers who, upon arriving in Germany, took up blue-collar jobs; for example, teachers were employed as factory workers. According to estimates, between 1964 and 1973 a total of nine thousand Turkish primary school teachers were employed as industrial laborers. It must be remembered that in order to gain the opportunity to work abroad these individuals would not have revealed any details of their real profession.

Agricultural societies are, for the most part, characterized by upward and downward social mobility, which, following an awakening of status consciousness, may also lead to intense feelings of dissatisfaction with one's work. There has also been observed in Turkey what is referred to as "status inconsistency." This concept may be defined as an individual's confusion concerning which stratum he or she belongs to in a society.[56] This point is relevant because due to low pay and unsatisfactory working conditions, some white collar workers—such as clerks and teachers—are attracted by the high wages in the industrial sector abroad but are dissatisfied with the social status that defines such occupations. Status inconsistency is important because it indicates that in spite having achieved a higher social status, some people who were eager to accept a less attractive job abroad due to the more favorable material conditions.

*A New Element in Turkish Society: The One from Germany (*Almanyalı*)*

The Turkish emigration movement, which began with Turks going first to Europe, then to the Middle East, and finally to further shores such as the United States, Canada, and Australia, has become an established feature of Turkey's demographic structure. The movement gave birth to a new stereotype: as most Turks abroad live in Germany, those abroad are identified in the homeland as "the one from Germany."[57]

Immigrants to the Middle East, the Russian Federation, and the Turkic Republics are identified at home as "expatriates," and their numbers have been on the increase since 1995.

Both these types have bonds with their country of origin, Turkey, and the country in which they live: the former being their place of birth and where their heart lies, the latter offering employment and a means of living. There is no doubt that among those immigrants who go for a given period of time to the Middle East, the bonds with the home country are weaker, in that the exile is not felt so dramatically. On the other hand, the majority of workers living in Europe and working in an industrial institution have always, on return to the homeland, preferred to set up a small business or lead the life of a retired person living on a stable pension.

---

[56] İsmail Aydınoglu, "Manpower and Employment Policies under the Five Year Plans and Emigration," in *Turkish Workers in Europe 1960–1975,* 109–110; Nermin Abadan-Unat, "Turkish External Migration and Social Mobility," in *Turkey: Geographic and Social Perspectives,* Peter Benedict, Erol Tümertekin, and Fatma Mansur,eds. (Leiden, Belgium: E. J. Brill, 1974), 397.

[57] Statistics from 2002 reveal that among Turks living abroad, 1,998,534 of them reside in Germany. Source: Ministry of Labor and Social Security of the Turkish Republic, General Directorate of External Relations and Services for Workers Abroad [T.C. Çalışma ve Sosyal Güvenlik Bakanlığı, Dış İlişkiler ve Yurtdışı İşçi Hizmetleri Genel Müdürlüğü], April 2002.

CHAPTER 2

Turkish Migration to the Middle East and Russia

Figure 2.1. The Quest for Bread

Migration to the Middle East

At the beginning of the 1990s approximately 3.1 million Turks were living abroad. This number represented 5 percent of Turkey's population, and 6 percent of its labor force. The vast majority of Turks abroad had found employment in Europe, and of these almost 50 percent had chosen Germany as their destination. When, in 1973, European powers decided to halt foreign labor imports, another flow of emigration out of Turkey began, this time on a smaller scale and in a different direction, but that became constant over time. This time Turks were on the move to the oil-producing countries of the Middle East.

It is necessary here to outline the characteristics of labor force migration to the Middle East, because it differs in some important respects from the earlier migration that had taken Turks to Europe. In his detailed analysis, Gilbert Beaugé examines migration to the Middle East in the light of five main points. First, as opposed to the classic migration framework, migration to the Middle

East does not represent the movement of human resources towards areas of local capital. Instead, in the case of the Middle East, we see that both foreign investment and foreign labor move towards areas where profit may be made. The profit here, for the most part, creates nonproductive employment opportunities set aside for the native population. It is based on oil wealth and controlled by the state, which results in social bonds guaranteed by the state. Second, the migration model in petrol-producing countries that import foreign labor bears all the hallmarks of a temporary model. The immigrants are not given property rights, and all measures are taken to ensure the fast and unimpeded flow of currency savings to the homeland. Third, not only is migration to oil producing countries based strictly on "rotation," and therefore of a constantly changing structure, but it also accelerates and decelerates with fluctuations in oil prices in the world economy. Fourth, migration to the Middle East does not lead to any social dynamism in the local working class. Almost all employment involving actual labor is carried out by foreigners, with the result that they are to be found across the spectrum of the employment market. This, in turn, has led to the emergence of a hierarchy within the immigrant world itself, and a look at the pyramid from the top down reveals entrepreneurs, engineers, technicians, professors, doctors, and others involved in all forms of skilled and unskilled labor.[1] Finally, fifth, the structure of the employment market in oil-rich countries has specific characteristics:

- Certain areas of employment are reserved for the native work force. Positions in these areas are given to those close to the ruling house and those who have been educated abroad, and may be described as "sinecures."
- Laws that govern positions involving actual labor call for each immigrant worker brought in to the country to be sponsored by a native, who is answerable to the state for the sponsored worker's movements in and out of the country. The worker may not change jobs. This system of operation may be entitled "functional mediation." To prevent corruption in the employment of foreign labor there has been a kind of quota system in use since 1980.

There are, however, two important exceptions to this system of employment: one is for workers coming in from the Republic of Yemen, and the second is for workers who come as a "package deal."

Yemenis may enter the Gulf countries freely, change jobs or work as casual labor, as they wish. There are also foreign companies who reach agreement with a country—these are called "package agreements" in the gulf countries—

[1] Gilbert Beaugé and Friedmann Buttner, *Les Migrations dans le Monde Arabe* (Paris: Centre National de la Recherche Scientifique, 1991), 11–18.

by which large numbers of workers come as a group or "package." In this case, the company itself secures its personnel, decides what it will pay and is responsible for the workers in the package.

Certain changes occurred in the demographic make up of the Middle East following the 1990 Gulf War, one example being most Palestinian immigrant workers having to return to their homeland. Apart from these changes, the demographics of the region display the characteristics outlined in the following paragraph.

Demographic Characteristics of Middle East Countries

Migration to the Middle East, which became particularly intensive following October 1973, the date marking the beginning of the oil crisis, made evident existing differences among Middle East countries.

TABLE 2.1.
Distribution of labor in Middle East countries (1977) (%)

Country	*Agriculture*	*Services*	*Industry*
Turkey	64.0	27.0	9.0
Saudi Arabia	63.0	23.0	14.0
Morocco	55.0	28.0	17.0
Syria	49.0	28.0	23.0
Iraq	43.0	32.0	25.0
Tunisia	39.0	39.0	22.0
Algeria	30.0	53.0	17.0
Jordan	28.0	33.0	39.0
Libya	23.0	52.0	25.0
Lebanon	13.0	60.0	27.0
Kuwait	2.0	73.0	25.0

Source: *Changes in Labor Agreements and Social Security in Islamic Countries* (Ankara, Turkey: Statistics Center of Islamic countries, 1981), Table 4, s.81.

Population-rich countries of the Middle East possess the least of the natural resources in which the population-poor countries of the region are wealthiest. The countries are also significantly different in terms of technological development and labor resources.

J. S. Birks and C. A. Sinclair developed a typology for these differences, according to which the countries of the region are classified as follows: (1) countries that, for the most part, export skilled or vocationally trained labor (Egypt, Lebanon, Jordan); (2) countries that import large amounts of skilled labor (Kuwait, Saudi Arabia, Libya, the United Arab Emirates); (3) countries that export large amounts of unskilled labor (Algeria); and (4) countries that, being relatively self-sufficient, neither import nor export labor (Tunisia, Morocco, Syria, Iraq).[2]

The outbreak of the Gulf War in 1990 brought changes in the composition of foreign labor forces. A decrease in the use of labor of Arab origin was accompanied by a marked increase in imported labor from Asian countries such as India, Pakistan, Bangladesh, and Sri Lanka.

Another important difference between migration to Northern Europe and to the Middle East lies in the labor force distribution among sectors. In some Middle East countries, an important percentage of the labor force is engaged in industry and for the most part focused on the production of petrol and its by-products.

Another characteristic of labor-importing countries of the Middle East is that in some, such as Kuwait, Qatar, and the other Gulf states, imported labor accounts for more than 50 percent of the total employment force, and in the remaining countries it approaches 50 percent.

TABLE 2.2.
Citizenship status of labor force in the Middle East (1975) (%)

Country	*Numbers employed*	*Local (%)*	*Foreign (%)*
S.Arabistan	1,799,900	57.0	41.0
Libya	781,600	57.5	42.5
Kuwait	299,800	30.6	69.4
UAE	296,000	15.2	84.8
Oman	207,700	66.0	35.0
Bahrein	75,800	60.4	39.6
Qatar	66,200	18.9	81.1

Source: *Labor Agreements and Social Security in Islamic Countries* (Ankara, Turkey: Statistics Center of Islamic Countries, 1981), s.20.

As mentioned above, the 1990 Gulf War resulted in demographic changes in the region. However, apart from the data on Turkish immigrant workers in the region, there is none other available. These figures show foreign labor to be employed mostly in the construction and manufacturing industries. Indeed, it would seem that, as in Europe, construction work has been left almost entirely in the hands of foreign labor, with 60 percent of construction labor being done by foreign workers in Kuwait, 64 percent in Libya, 48 percent in Saudi Arabia, 82 percent in Qatar, and 96 percent in Abu Dhabi.

[2] J. S. Birks and C. A. Sinclair, *Arab Manpower: The Crisis of Development* (London: Croom Helm, 1980).

By 1975 there were 3.5 million immigrant workers spread throughout the Middle East in the oil-rich countries of Kuwait, Bahrain, Qatar, the UAE, Libya, and Jordan, 1.8 million of whom were in active formal employment, i.e. bound by contract—a figure that does not include the many household helpers and others who are not employed as part of a package deal (see below).

All the above-mentioned characteristics of migration to the Middle East served to create very different population structures to those of the immigrant-accepting countries of Europe. In some cases this migration has led to immigrant populations equaling the native population, and sometimes even exceeding it in number.

Other characteristics of this demographic worth mentioning here are that migration to the Middle East is almost exclusively male, with the teaching and health sectors being the only significant employment areas open to females. Except for the highly skilled foreign immigrants, no special provision is made for married workers, who are expected to work and live as single immigrants. And workers are employed on a group basis as a result of agreements that may be signed by companies in the country seeking workers, local agencies, private brokers, or personnel departments of international companies. As a result, employees are, for the most part, employed not as individuals but as part of a package deal.

Both residence and work permits are granted for the period of employment set out in the agreement. Permission to change one's job is granted only in exceptional circumstances. There is no tradition of agreements between states, and workers not in the category of "skilled or professional" have little if any chance of remaining in the country of employment for an indefinite period of time. There is no possibility of family unification, i.e., the worker bringing his family to the country of employment, but there are occasions when family members brought into the country on a pilgrimage visa to fulfill their religious duties remain after their visa has expired.

Turkish Labor Flow to the Middle East

Since 1961, the flow of Turkish labor has been mainly towards Western Europe, and by 1978, 1.6 million workers and their families lived there.[3] At that time, this figure equaled 3.5 percent of Turkey's total population, 5 percent of its active work force, 14 percent of its agricultural work force and 40 percent of numbers employed in the industrial sector.[4] With employment opportuni-

---

[3] Organisation for Economic Co-operation and Development (OECD), *SOPEMI* (Paris: OECD, 1979), 53.

[4] Adler, *A Turkish Conundrum*, 34.

ties in Europe becoming less available in the 1980s, those seeking employment began to look elsewhere, namely to the Middle East. The lack of reliable statistics makes it difficult to reveal the full extent of this second wave of Turkish emigration. According to Turkish Employment Agency reports, in 1980 there were between 130,000 Turkish workers employed in Arabic countries. Some 50 percent (60,000) of these were in Libya, 37 percent (45,000) in Saudi Arabia, 10 percent (12,000) in Iraq, and the remainder in the United Arab Emirates. According to the same data, Turkish workers comprised 4 percent of all foreign workers in Arabic countries. In Libya they constituted 14 percent of all foreign labor, in Saudi Arabia 3 percent, and in Iraq 2.5 percent. The total number of temporary migrant workers from Turkey to these Middle East and North African countries from the mid-1970s to the 1990s reached 500,000. It should be recalled that these migrant workers stay in the countries where they work on a temporary status with work permits valid for a few years, and following the expiration of their employment contracts, some of them return to Turkey and other countries after some time under similar employment contracts.

With significant numbers of Turkish businessmen and entrepreneurs entering the markets in these countries at that time, the Turkish authorities were expecting a marked increase in migration numbers, especially to Libya and Kuwait. However, these expectations remained unfulfilled with the outbreak of the first Gulf War, and 1999 data showed the following distribution of Turkish workers in the Middle East:

- Saudi Arabia: 115,000 workers; 12,700 self-employed
- Kuwait: 3,500 workers; 4,500 self-employed
- Libya: 2,600 workers; 500 self-employed[5]

These figures show that in the aftermath of the 1990 Gulf War there was a definite decrease in numbers of Turkish immigrant workers in the Middle East, and this was followed by a period during which the numbers have remained stable. The numbers dropped to less to 130,000 in the mid-1990s and diminished to as low as to 105,000 by the mid-2000s.[6]

Even though there was a constant increase in the numbers of Turkish entrepreneurs operating in the Middle East, the expected potential increase in migration of Turkish workers was limited by various factors. The primary factor was the new ethnic structure of the Middle East: as the numbers of workers of Arab origin decreased, there was a significant increase in the numbers of

[5] Labor Ministry, Foreign Relations Directorate, *1997, 1998, 1999 Annual Reports* (Ankara), 218, 237, 260 (respectively).

[6] Ahmet İçduygu, *International Migration and Turkey, 2007: The Country Report for Turkey for SOPEMI/OECD* (Paris: OECD), table 1.

Asian workers. In 1980, the proportion of workers of Asian origin increased from 25.6 to 33.7 percent, but during the same period Turkish worker numbers rose from only 0.5 to 3.1 percent.[7]

TABLE 2.3.
Numbers of Turkish Companies in Arab Countries

Country	*1979*	*1980*	*1981*	*1999*
Libya	17	30	38	25
Saudi Arabia	6	15	15	3
Kuwait	1	2	3	—

Source: Unpublished report, Labor Ministry, 1981; 1982 *Hürriyet,* 21.1.1982; 1999 Labor Ministry, *1999 annual report,* s.267, 225.

The main reason for the increase in the use of Asian labor was the relatively low labor costs: Asian workers were prepared to work for less than others. For example, a Turkish worker demanded at least $300 (U.S.) per month for working eight hours a day, six days a week; among Asian workers, Thais would do the same work for $225, Indians for $210, and Filipinos for $208.[8]

TABLE 2.4.
Turkish and foreign labor employed by Turkish companies in Saudi Arabia

Company	*Year*	*Turkish workers*	*Foreign workers*	*Total*
Yüksel Construction	1997	815	196	1,013
"	1998	1,210	248	1,458
"	1999	204	126	330
Gama Construction	1997	136	64	200
"	1998	130	35	165
"	1999	292	86	378
Tekfen Construction	1997	180	128	308
"	1998	366	375	741
"	1999	374	377	751

Source: Labor Ministry, Foreign Relations Directorate, 1997, 1998, 1999 annual reports, Ankara, s.210, 234, 211.

[7] Labor and Social Security Ministry, *Report about Migration to Oil-Producing Countries* (Ankara, 1981).

[8] Nermin Abadan-Unat, "Turkish Migration to Europe and the Middle East: Its Impact on Social Structure and Social Legislation," in *Social Legislation in the Contemporary Middle East,* eds. L. O. Michalak and J. W. Salacuse (Berkeley: University of California Press, 1986a), 325–369.

Social Security Laws in the Middle East

When discussing countries that import labor, the most important issue becomes the extent to which they apply their social security laws to foreign workers. Generally speaking, all Islamic countries have established some form of social security system to govern issues such as retirement, work accidents, death, and motherhood.

Besides this, Libya signed Equal Procedure Treaty No. 118, which governs various employment sectors.[9] It is also the only country from the region to have signed mutual agreements with Turkey, the first of which was signed on 5 January 1975. The agreement contained clauses concerning education to be provided for Libyan workers in Turkey and vice versa. In 1976, both countries signed a special social security agreement.

This guaranteed Turkish workers in Libya all the rights granted to the native work force, and also set out the conditions under which Turkish workers could remit their savings to the homeland. A coordination committee was also set up under this agreement.

An issue that gave rise to serious grievances concerned the compensation to be transferred in the event of work accidents, an issue covered in article 3 of the agreement. Conflict also arose over Libya's refusal to allow its Turkish workers to include employment periods in Turkey in their applications for Libyan state pensions. Complaints were also made about the unwillingness of some employers to provide a promised letter of recommendation to Turkish workers when they wished to leave Libya or change employment. This last issue was constantly on the agenda during state visits or other formal communications between the states.

The oil-rich countries of the Middle East that currently employ Turkish workers are all involved in policies that they hope will attract their own citizens into the employment market and make that market attractive particularly to their own youth. As part of these policies they offer amnesties to foreign workers whose visas and/or work permits have expired, thus encouraging them to return to their homelands. It would seem, therefore, that for the foreseeable future, Middle East countries will not be a great source of employment opportunities for Turkish labor. However, there are Turkish workers choosing to go to these countries. For the most part, these are individuals whose aim is to be self-employed, and the group is made up of a wide range of professionals—mainly doctors, engineers, and nurses, but also barbers, mechanics,

[9] The Statistical Economic and Social Research and Training Centre for Islamic Countries, *Report on Migration in Oil Producing Countries* (Ankara, 1981).

furniture makers, etc.[10] In recent years the number of Turkish workers sent to Middle Eastern countries indicates a medium growth in general and a visible increase in case of Saudi Arabia.

TABLE 2.5.
Number of Turkish Workers Sent Abroad by the Turkish Employment Office, 2001–2006

Countries	*2001*	*2002*	*2003*	*2004*	*2005*	*2006*
Libya	238	1,037	2,515	668	986	770
Morocco	0	69	182	279	330	368
Saudi Arabia	4,657	6,399	6,064	1,146	6,452	19,841
Sudan	0	14	29	18	107	469
Syria	9	21	2	0	0	0
United Arab Emirates	0	1	1	628	1,843	1,176

Source: Turkish Employment Office (TEO) http://iskur.gov.tr

Migration to CIS Countries and Russia

With the decline of manpower demand in Middle East countries, the former communist countries of eastern Europe and central and northern Asia became a new target for emigration after 1990. Whereas only 115 persons migrated from Turkey to the Commonwealth of Independent States (CIS; to date, Azerbaijan, Armenia, Belarus, Georgia, Kazakhstan, Kyrgyzstan, Moldova, Russia, Tajikistan, Turkmenistan, Uzbekistan, and Ukraine) between 1991 and 1995, this figure increased to over 65,000 during the 1996–2000 period and neared 90,000 between 2001 and 2005 (see table 2.6).

In 2007, while the proportion of those who found employment in Middle East countries was less than one-third of the total number of workers arriving in the Middle East, the proportion of those who found employment in the CIS countries was nearly half of the total who went to those countries (see table 2.7).

The migration to Russia went through three phases: the *initiation* period (1980–1990), the *transition* period (1991–2000), and the *consolidation* period (2001 and onward). Similar to the migratory movement towards Europe, in the case of Russia another dramatic change in the realm of foreign policy triggered a new migratory wave. Turkey abandoned a strongly unidimensional, Western-

[10] In 2001, The State Employment Bureau sent 238 workers to Libya, 4,657 to Saudi Arabia, 203 to Jordan, and 11 to Kuwait. There were no requests from Bahrain or the UAE. Labor Ministry, Foreign Relations Directorate, *BÜLTEN*, no. 1 (January/March 2002), 19.

TABLE 2.6.
Turkish Labor Migration by Destination, 1961–2005

Host Countries	*1961–1974*		*1975–1980*		*1981–1990*		*1991–1995*		*1996–20002001–2005*		*Total*			
	#	%	#	%	#	%	#	%	#	%	#	%	#	%
Europe	790,017	97.5	13,426	12.8	2,612	0.6	9,647	2.8	10,465	9.3	16,561	9.1	842,728	42.4
MENA Countries	2,441	0.3	74,181	70.6	423,208	97.7	208,274	60.4	32,195	28.5	57,974	31.9	798,273	40.2
Australia	5,806	0.7	2,647	2.5	2,478	0.6	1,324	0.4	515	0.5	176	0.1	12,946	0.7
CIS Countries		—		—		—	115	0	65,521	58.0	89,623	49.3	155,259	7.8
Others	12,235	1.5	14,792	14.1	4,875	1.1	125,238	36.3	4,256	3.8	17,533	9.6	178,929	9.0
Total	**810,499**	**100**	**105,046**	**100**	**433,173**	**100**	**344,598**	**100**	**112,952**	**100**	**181,867**	**100**	**1,988,135**	**100**

Source: Official sources: Compiled by İçduygu (2006), based on various statistics in Turkey

TABLE 2.7.
Number of Workers Sent Abroad by the Turkish Employment Office (TEO) 1997–2007

Receiving Country	*1997*	*1999*	*2001*	*2003*	*2005*	*2007*
European Union countries	1,814	2,419	2,685	4,299	1,710	9,393
Other European countries	13	10	219	237	176	2,367
The ME countries	9,500	5,896	5,156	10,189	24,798	24,401
CIS	16,980	7,092	8,019	16,330	28,663	36,404
Australia, Canada, US	400	396	116	93	94	261
Israel	4,300	1,485	3,917	422	417	277
Other	314	149	130	2,581	4,497	50,64
Total	**33,321**	**17,475**	**20,242**	**34,151**	**60,355**	**78,167**

Source: Turkish Employment Office (TEO), 2008.

oriented policy in the 1980s for a multidimensional alliance pattern aimed at improving multilateral cooperation. This affected the labor market and the pattern of emigration. The implementation of the 1984 Natural Gas Agreement and the $1,150 million (U.S.) export credit opened to the Soviet Union were the beginning, opening the Soviet Union construction market to Turkish contractors. The expansion of trade occurred almost on barter terms, with one party (the Soviet Union) exporting goods (natural gas), while the other (Turkey) balancing the trade by contracting some services (construction).

Under these terms Turkish construction companies such as STFA, ENKA, GÜRİŞ, and GAMA, which previously had undertaken major projects in the Middle East and North African countries, brought a high number of project-tied migrants and professionals to various regions in the Soviet Union. While in the period of 1970–1990 the share of migrant related projects in Libya fell from 71 percent to 15 percent, Russia's share, on the other hand, rose to 49 percent.

After the collapse of the Soviet Union, new migration situations were created. In this phase, the majority of labor migrants were short-term migrants, mostly from CIS countries, and they were involved in trading, building and repair industries, transportation, and other services. As for the labor migration from non-former Soviet states, registered inflows of migrant workers came from China, North Korea, and Turkey.

During this transition period Turkish construction companies enlarged the scope of their project-tied activities and gained experience and sophistication by focusing on low-technology projects in difficult locations in post-Soviet countries including Russia. Turkish businesspeople also got involved in different sectors such as tourism, textile, and food in Russia. Furthermore Turkish investors with small- or medium-sized capital established gift shops, cafes, restaurants, bakeries, or slaughterhouses in the newly emerging Russian market economy. During this period Turkish migrants were mostly attracted by the two cities of Moscow and St. Petersburg, which were migrant magnets. These cities not only received project-tied migrants but also small- and medium-sized investors.

During the third phase—defined as the consolidation phase—two major decisions affected the migratory trend. Beginning with the mid-2000s Russia attempted to tighten migration control. After 2005 an open-door policy was introduced. In the second half of the decade, the annual number of project-tied workers from Turkey in Russia reached 25,000 and the number of new projects leveled to around sixty per year, yielding annually a total value of $3,000 million (U.S.).

About 85 to 90 percent of the participants in these projects are project-tied migrants, and the remaining participants are professionals or small- and medium-sized investors. On the basis of a comprehensive field survey con-

TABLE 2.8.
Number of Workers Sent to Russia by the Turkish Employment Office (TEO) and Number and Value of the Turkish Construction Projects in Russia, 1989–2008

Years	*# of Project-tied Workers*	*# of Projects*	*$ Million*
1989	932		
1990	1,243		
1989–94	76,849	97	4,209
1995	35,792	33	1,055
1996	20,460	91	1,674
1997	13,195	124	717
1998	7,426	56	1,126
1999	2,215	80	732
2000	2,199	75	181
2001	4,190	31	165
2002	10,160	19	343
2003	10,816	38	428
2004	13,281	40	1,033
2005	19,540	70	746
2006	24,142	56	2,292
2007	23,118	59	3,605
2008	15,696	78	3,387

Source: Turkish Employment Office (TEO) and Moscow Office of the Commercial Counsellor.

ducted in Moscow 5–30 July 2008 by a team headed by Ayşem Biriz Karaçay,[11] information was gathered by respondents employed in the construction area. The interviewed migrants were all male, between twenty-three and fifty years old, with an average age of thirty-three. Due to the nature of employment—all projects were tied to a given date—all the migrants had left their wives and children at home. The major reason for working abroad was the desire to support the family, pay for children's education, and pay debts. In other words, the main motive as elsewhere too, was an economic incentive. The average salary of project-tied migrants usually ranged between $1,000 and $1,500 (U.S.), which was deposited into their Turkish bank accounts every month.

[11] All the information incorporated in this section concerning migration to CIS countries is based on an article by Ayşem Biriz Karaçay, titled "The International Migration System between Turkey and Russia: The Case of Project-Tied Migrant Workers in Moscow," and a paper by Ahmet İçduygu and Ayşem Biriz Karaçay, "The International Migration System between Turkey and Russia: The Case of Project-Tied Migrant Workers in Moscow," both of which were presented at the Migration Research Program at Koç University, Istanbul, 18–21 June 2009.

In such projects, when their contracts expire, the workers return to Turkey, stay for a while there, and wait for another project. With the exception of migrants with entrepreneur ambition, the majority does not take the permanent stay abroad as a serious option. Intermarriage occurs usually among the new entrepreneurs.

However, the interesting aspect of the Moscow survey is reflected in the fact that these project-tied migrants do not want to permanently return to Turkey. They prefer to be looked upon as a kind of circulating work force, or available manpower at large and determine their availability according their personal conditions. Although regularly recruited migrant workers benefit from all legal and social rights recognized by the CIS countries, similar to the situation in other migrant-importing countries, in case of illegal migration, severe problems of abuse on the workplace, exploitation, and bad living conditions are occurring.

The survey cited above reveals an important idea: the majority of Turkish migrant workers in Russia do not want to settle down there; they are not looking for family reunions. They cite cultural incompatibility, language barriers, and different religious practices as main obstacles to family unification. Thus it may be said that unlike the large-scale migratory waves in Europe, Turkish migrant workers in the CIS countries are not desirous of settling down permanently. Migrant worker-importing Middle East states—with exceptions in the case of highly qualified experts—prohibit family unification. In the CIS countries there is no legal barrier; on the contrary, Russia in particular encourages settlement, but for Turkish migrants cultural factors have so far been the major reason for leaving their family members at home. At present the outlook indicates that the rate of project-tied migration to Russia will continue and probably increase in the coming years.

CHAPTER 3

Empirical Research

Figure 3.1. Waiting for Remittances

Give up eating, Ahmets; give up eating Jales. Load your stuff on trains, Osman and Ayshes. Fly to Turkey. Your marks weigh little, but their value goes a long way. Fly home with your marks. Buy plots in our big cities. Even the cemeteries have been uprooted in recent years. These days, second-rate and third-rate cemeteries for those who had died of hunger are going for a song. For those who don't care for farming, there are some other fields of investment. Buy stocks and shares, buy into new industries. When you return to your country, you could become industrialists, no less. What's wrong with that? Haven't you worked long enough? In this mortal life, it should now be your turn to hire others, to put others to work.

—Bekir Yıldız, *Alman Ekmeği (German Bread)*
Translated by Talat Sait Halman

1963 West Germany Survey

Planning the development of the Turkish economy was one of the new elements of the 1961 Turkish Constitution. It was decided, as part of the First Five-Year Development Plan (which began in 1962), to implement a "surplus labor export" policy, which had the following goals: to decelerate population growth, reduce growing unemployment levels, ease social tension, and secure an educated, skilled labor force for state development. In its first labor exchange agreement with West Germany in October 1961, Turkey aimed to not only protect the rights of Turkish workers in West Germany, but also to use the agreement to help achieve these goals.

In 1960 there were only 2,700 Turkish workers in West Germany. By 1963, this figure had risen to 27,500, and it was not long before the situation of the workers involved in this incredibly rapid emigration began to draw the attention of the State Planning Organization. Aware that such a demographic movement would result in great social change, the Social Planning Department of the State Planning Organization gathered and analyzed empirically collected data in order to measure the extent of this movement.[1]

Characteristics of Workers Migrating to West Germany

The survey revealed that 51 percent of the Turkish workers in the sample had come to Germany from Turkish cities with a population of 100,000 or more, 7 percent from towns with a population of 20,000 to 50,000, 11 percent from towns of 2,000 to 20,000 inhabitants, and 18 percent from settlements of fewer than 2,000 people—in other words, villages. Although more than half of the sample gave Istanbul and Thrace as their place of origin in Turkey, it emerged that only 17 percent had actually been born in that region. This shows that many of the migrant workers had undergone a process of internal migration prior to their departure for Germany.

The finding of the research revealed that it was not, as commonly thought, the influence of radio and the press that had prompted the workers to migrate, but rather family connections, relatives, and other fellow citizens. Therefore, it may be said that the small role played by formal channels in providing reliable and objective information for individuals making a decision to migrate may explain the widespread disappointment felt by many of the workers on arrival in West Germany. Those workers sent abroad through the state Employment Bureau were given little if any time to examine the various contracts presented

[1] The details concerning the methodology used in this survey, the size of the sample, the cities chosen, etc., can be found in the Appendix.

to them for signature following their compulsory health checkup. The majority of workers received their only information from officials of the Employment Bureau, who spent fifteen to twenty minutes speaking to workers in groups of ten about the content of the contract, the pay, the type of work, the company that would employ them, and the city, town, or region to which they would be sent. Within two days of signing the contract, 55 percent of workers found themselves on trains bound for Germany.

The survey revealed that most of the male workers were of an age when their military service in Turkey would have been completed—most (67 percent) were between twenty-three and thirty-two years old. In comparison to later arrivals, these workers were comparatively better educated: 49 percent had completed primary school, 13 percent middle school, and 15 percent vocational schools. The females were better educated than the males: 24 percent were graduates of vocational schools, and 16 percent of high schools. Fifty-six percent of workers were married with an average of three children per family. Unlike the males, 18 percent of the females were divorced or widowed. At the time, only 17 percent of workers were living with their families in Germany.

Four-fifths of the sample of workers had been in employment prior to leaving the homeland. In other words, what prompted these individuals to migrate was not unemployment, but rather the higher wages paid overseas, the hope of making significant savings quickly, a desire to become more knowledgeable, and, finally, a sense of adventure and a desire to see the world.

Socioeconomic Status and Earnings of Turkish Workers

It was found in the survey that there was significant upward mobility among the Turkish workers. Although 39 percent of the male workers' fathers had been involved in agricultural work, only 9 percent of the workers themselves had been engaged in this prior to migrating.

The survey also revealed that a significant number of those migrating to Germany had been prepared to give up what would have been considered relatively respectable professions such as teaching, accounting, and sales and accept worker status. Lenski talks about this type of "status inconsistency" that may often be observed as a characteristic specific to newly industrializing countries.[2]

Fifty-five percent of the workers in the survey were employed in the manufacturing sector in construction and metallurgy, 19 percent in skilled trades, and 9 percent in mining. As they became older, workers tended to choose less physically demanding work. When asked what kind of work they would prefer, 27 percent answered by saying that they would like to be involved in the

---

[2] For detail on Gerhard Emmanuel Lenski's "status uncertainty," see Abadan-Unat, "Turkish External Migration and Social Mobility," 397.

TABLE 3.1.
Occupations of workers and their fathers in Turkey prior to going abroad

Occupation	*Fathers*	*Number %*	*Workers*	*Number %*	*Rate of Change %*
Small business owner	89	18.0	76	15.4	−14.6
Professional	19	3.8	26	5.3	+36.8
Civil servant/army officer	62	12.5	74	14.9	+19.3
Skilled laborer	76	15.4	209	42.3	+175.0
laborer	14	2.8	19	3.9	+35.7
Farmer	192	38.9	44	8.9	−77.0
Unemployed	14	2.8	1	0.2	−92.8
Other profession	5	1.0	32	6.4	+540.0
Indeterminate answer	23	4.6	13	2.6	−43.4
Total	494	99.8	494	99.9	

Source: N. Abadan, *Batı Almanya'daki Türk iscileri ve Sorunlar,* (Problems of Turkish Workers in West Germany) DPT, (State Planning Organization), Ankara, 1964, Table 48, p. 70.

manufacture of a product from beginning to end of the production process; 21 percent wished to work in a small workshop; and 12 percent expressed a desire to own a small business such as a retail outlet, a small workshop, a tailoring business, or taxi driving. The percentage of those who wished to continue in employment as an industrial worker was only 13 percent. These figures make it clear that the Turkish worker remained faithful to his or her pre-industrial habits and had a preference for work environments that would foster personal relationships and human contact.

As far as earnings are concerned, 67 percent of Turkish workers took home between 300 and 600 DM per month. Workers who had come to Germany on one- or two-year contracts were guaranteed accommodation and paid 34 DM per month towards the expenses of their lodgings. Most lived close to their place of employment and had few if any transport expenses. With monthly food costs averaging 157 DM, and other spending coming to 77 DM, it meant potential savings per annum of 3,000 DM for these workers, at that time.

In 1960, rather than using banks to transfer these savings at the official rates, 75 percent of workers were using other means, including buying Turkish lira on the open market and sending it home with a friend or acquaintance returning to Turkey on holiday; taking the money to Turkey and exchanging it for Turkish lira on the black market; and purchasing goods such as household appliances and cars in Germany to sell privately in Turkey.

Note that at this time it was illegal to buy foreign currency on the open market in Turkey. Following publication of the results of the survey, the government, seeing so much foreign currency disappear into the open market and realizing that it would go a long way towards helping them to close Turkey's foreign trade deficit, began to offer special exchange rates to migrant workers: the official exchange rate was then 1 DM to 2.25 TL, but workers were offered 2.85 TL for each of their DM. Over time, Turkey was able to use these savings, which constituted a huge part of the country's invisible income resources, in order to balance its foreign trade deficit. For example, in 1964 Turkish workers' savings amounted to $45 million (U.S.); by 1973 they were sending home $1.1 billion; and this figure had reached $2.476 billion by 1981.[3]

Workers' Living Quarters: Heim *(shared accommodation)*

At the time of the survey, 85 percent of the workers were living in the shared accommodation set out as part of the conditions of their contract. Fifty-three percent were sharing a room with four or five other workers.

TABLE 3.2.
Workers' housing types

Type of housing	*Number of workers*	%
Lodging provided by employer (heim)	417	84.0
Apartment shared with other workers	4	1.0
Lodging with a family	46	9.0
Rented apartment	4	1.0
No answer	23	5.0
Total:	494	100.0

Source: N. Abadan, *Batı Almanya'daki Türk İşçileri ve Sorunları,* (Problems of Turkish Workers in West Germany) DPT (State Planning Organization), Ankara, 1964, Table 83, p. 103.

Construction laborers especially were accommodated in particularly primitive conditions. Facilities in the communal housing and lodgings were generally far removed from those promised in the contracts signed with Turkish workers. Apart from construction sector employers, most employers provided a free or reduced-price hot meal to employees at lunchtime, although Turkish workers tended not to avail of this for fear of consuming pork or its by-products. Sixty-five percent of workers prepared their own meals but had problems in obtaining the necessary equipment to do so.

[3] Abadan-Unat, ed., *Turkish Workers in Europe 1960–1975,* 24, table 2; see *Milliyet,* 17 September 1981.

TABLE 3.3.
Numbers of workers sharing sleeping quarters

Rooms	*Number*	*%*
Single	9	2.0
2–3 person rooms	135	27.0
4–6 person rooms	259	52.0
7–10 person rooms	19	5.0
No answer	72	14.0
	494	100.0

Source: N. Abadan, *Batı Almanya'daki Türk İşçileri ve Sorunları,* (Problems of Turkish Workers in West Germany) DPT (State Planning Organization), Ankara, 1964, Tablo 85, s.105.

Turkish Workers' Attitudes to Industrial Life

Over half (55 percent) of the workers in the survey were employed in workplaces where their co-workers numbered between two hundred and one thousand. Complaints about working conditions were expressed mainly by those having to do dirty work (21 percent) and those having to work underground (12 percent). With many workers not having had the opportunity to examine their work contract in any great detail, it was only on arrival in Germany to the workplace of their prospective employer that they discovered they would be involved in mining work. From a psychological standpoint, this situation was particularly difficult for those from an agricultural background.

Almost half of those in the survey stated that it was primarily physical labor that was required from them, and consequently what employers looked for in a Turkish laborer was a strong, tough, healthy body.

The necessity for this is made clear by the following statistic: of the workers in the survey, 41 percent used no equipment and 45 percent were not involved in the operation of any machine; i.e., they worked with their bare hands. Seventy percent complained only of the physical exhaustion their work brought. Forty-one percent stated that they had learned all they needed to about their work in one day. Sixty-nine percent were on their feet constantly. The opportunity to sit down was afforded to 75 percent of female workers, but to only 23 percent of males.

The size of the workplace also had an effect on job satisfaction among the workers: 61 percent expressed satisfaction with workplaces in which five to ten Turks were employed. Satisfaction levels fell to 35 percent among those who were employed in places where great numbers of Turks worked. These were mainly in the motor and chemical industries, such as the Ford factory in Cologne, which employed more than one thousand Turks.

Execution of Contracts

Although 44 percent of workers in the survey accepted that the conditions set out in their contracts were being fulfilled, 34 percent had come to the conclusion that the contracts themselves carried little meaning or value anyway. An example from the survey clarifies this thinking: "We sign an agreement to come and work here through the State Employment Bureau in Turkey, but when we arrive here we are made to sign another contract, this time in German," said one worker. "This one is completely one-sided, with the Germans organizing everything to their own advantage."[4]

An example involved a mining shaft accident that occurred in the mine works near the town of Hamm, in which five workers were killed when a steel cable fell into the elevator descending into the mine. The contract signed by these workers with the construction company Heitcamp stated that they would be employed in construction. What the workers did not know was that the contract stipulated both surface and underground construction, and they were actually being put to work one thousand meters underground, laying a narrow-gauge rail track.

The workers had no idea regarding whom they should consult should they wish to voice a complaint about the type of work or pay. Some expected their work agreement to be controlled by the personnel manager, others by an interpreter. At this time, workers were making little use of the previously mentioned *Türk-Danış* or other consultative/advisory organizations, such as unions. In addition, the lack of necessary language skills or knowledge about what exactly their contract entailed meant that workers did not apply to labor tribunals in cases of work disputes.

Work Accidents

Of the workers in the survey, 24 percent had had accidents at work, a percentage almost twice that of their counterparts in Turkey. The highest accident rates were found in the chemical (37 percent), metal (28 percent), and mining (27 percent) industries. Turkish workers were subject to particularly harsh conditions in the mining industry. Mines were much deeper in Germany than in Turkey and workers had to operate at depths greater than one thousand meters down, in temperatures reaching thirty-eight degrees Celsius, on eight-hour shifts. For those who had been farm workers or shepherds in the homeland this was particularly torturous and resulted in suffering constant fear and nervous tension. Most accidents were a result of an object falling and crushing fingers and limbs.

---

[4] *Yeni Sabah,* 26 February 1964.

There was of course a direct relationship between probability of injury and the worker's past experience, and those who had no experience of laboring in industry paid a heavy price for their inexperience: 100 percent of those who came from a rural farming background suffered an injury at some time. The figure was 42 percent for those who had been in some form of nonindustrial paid employment, and 29 percent for those who had had low to middle level responsibility jobs in clerking. On 30 April 1964, however, Turkey and West Germany signed a social security agreement on that guaranteed workers compensation in the event of a work accident and pension rights.

In-Service Training for Turkish Workers

Generally speaking, those workers who were employed in industry hoped at some point to be promoted to a position that would bring them greater status and respect. Aware of the situation they were in, some were objective and knew that their lack of language skills, training, and education were obstacles to possible promotion, whereas others were more subjective and stated that it was German arrogance towards foreigners and their lack of respect for Turkish ideas that deprived Turks of promotion opportunities. This reaction is closely related to German companies' attitudes towards training their Turkish workforce. Turkey's First Five-Year Development Plan foresaw the return to Turkey of a skilled work force that it had sent abroad for training. However, it was not long before the government recognized that this was not going to happen. Only 30 percent of German companies presented any training or educational opportunities to their Turkish workers, and where such opportunities were available, they consisted only of familiarization or introduction to the worker's job. It is worth mentioning here how the workers in the survey themselves felt about the knowledge they had gained: 25 percent felt they were "learning quite a lot of new things"; 33 percent felt they were "learning some new things"; 5 percent felt they were "learning very little"; and 35 percent felt they were "learning nothing."

Those who felt they had learned a lot were, for the most part, among the better-educated workers and, in this group, female workers outnumbered males, with 43 percent of women saying they had learned many new things. This is not surprising because, at the time of the survey, most of the male respondents were semi-skilled workers, as opposed to the women who were, generally speaking, employed in jobs such as nursing or medical aid.

Turkish Workers' Relationship with Unions and Associations

New developments in industrial production, technological change, and increasing specialization resulting in greater division of labor all served to increase

Figure 3.2. Learning Nothing ...

conflict between the workers and management. Although management interests were focused on greater efficiency and an accelerated work tempo in the production units, the workers' demands centered on higher pay and improvement in working conditions. Thus, in the 1960s, at the time of this survey, it is clear that unions were playing an important role not only in Germany, but in the other major industrial countries. In our survey we tried to understand the attitudes of Turkish workers in Germany, given that the survey coincided with a time when workers in Turkey were being given benchmarking and strike rights. The data revealed that only 14 percent of workers in the survey were members of a union. At 87 percent, the highest union membership was among Turkish workers employed on the railways. Thirty percent of mining workers were unionized, as were 10 percent of metallurgy workers. These percentages are in line with those among the Turks' German counterparts in the same sectors. Low levels of union membership may be explained by the Turks' lack of both language skills and knowledge of unions, and their unwillingness to pay union membership fees. However, one bad experience was enough to change these attitudes among the Turkish workers. This occurred in the spring of 1963 in the Baden-Württemberg metallurgy industry, when a call to strike left many Turkish workers out on the street without employment. They quickly realized that had they been union members they would at least have been guaranteed financial support by their union in the course of the strike, and indeed, following this bitter experience there was a rush to join a union by many Turkish workers in the metal industry.

The Turkish workers' lack of interest in unions was reflected in a similar lack of activity on the part of *Türk-Danış,* the advisory institution established under *Arbeiterwohlfahrt,* the German government organization set up to monitor the rights of Turkish workers. *Türk-Danış* headquarters was in Bonn, and it had branches in Cologne, Frankfurt, Esslingen, and Munich. However, only 3 percent of Turkish workers were aware of its existence. At this point in time *Türk-Danış* was mainly involved in activities such as protesting against police attitudes, resolving contract disputes, and any other issues that, due to lack of time, personnel, or language skills, Turkish consulates, German unions, or Turkish workers were unable to deal with.

In granting financial assistance to *Türk-Danış,* the German government specified that the money was to be used by the organization in establishing associations among Turkish workers in an attempt to foster cooperation and solidarity. *Türk-Danış* undertook this responsibility with enthusiasm and thus began a time of intense association growth. By November 1963 there were associations in fifteen cities that had high Turkish worker populations, and the German government, in its desire to see these associations become federated, met the travel and accommodation expenses of association members who wished to be delegates at the founding meeting of the federation. Despite all these efforts, at the time Turkish workers displayed little or no interest in this federation. The survey revealed that 52 percent of the respondents were completely unaware of the existence of the federation, and a mere 8 percent were members. This situation was to change later.

Aydın Yüceler, the president of the Turkish Workers Association in the Karlsruhe region, undertook a piece of research regarding this lack of interest, and made the following statement in the *Haberleşme* bulletin in September 1963:

> In their mode of thinking, Turkish workers are not accustomed to association life. They are unaware of discussion methods. Insecurities and lack of tolerance show themselves. The individual's interests and wishes, which are incompatible with group interests, come to the fore. Tempers become frayed easily. In the material sense, the association management does not make adequate use of the resources available. There are delays in membership fee collection. Associations' headquarters are far from workplaces and hence travel expenses high. Existing resources are being used in an extravagant manner.[5]

Although the president and one or two members of each association were university graduates, the rest of the membership consisted of workers. As a result, the better educated had more authority within the association, and in cases where the president was also the representative of *Türk-Danış* in the region and received a generous salary, it is difficult to imagine any productive or harmonic relationship existing between such a president and association members from a different social class.

Turkish Workers' Leisure Time Activities

One defining characteristic of industrialized societies is the complex technical web within which the lives of individuals are played out. The working hours, private life, and leisure time of the individual is forever caught up in the embrace of activities involving production, transport, communication, social relations, and entertainment. Turkish migrant workers were often criticized for their unwillingness to avail themselves of or be interested in the opportunities presented by the industrialized society in which they found themselves. However, critics failed to see that a weekly workload of forty or more hours and the rest necessary to recuperate left these workers with approximately two or three hours of true leisure time. In our survey we tried to identify how and to what extent the workers adapted to the new culture in which they lived. The survey data revealed that the majority spent their free time engaging in what may be called "passive" activities: 34 percent simply strolled the streets, "checking things out"; 24 percent enjoyed going to the cinema; 22 percent rested; and 14 percent engaged in dance activities. The strolling activity mentioned here became a focus of attention in cities such as Frankfurt, Cologne, and Stuttgart

[5] Cited in Nermin Abadan-Unat, *Batı Almanya'daki Türk İşçileri ve Sorunları* (Turkish Workers in West Germany and Their Problems), (Ankara: Başbakanlık DPT, 1964), 168.

when large numbers of workers walked around on weekends in central railway stations. The waiting areas in these stations began to fulfill the function of Istanbul's Beyoğlu or Ankara's Atatürk Boulevard, and became places in which Turkish workers congregated, chatted, and generally "hung around."

At this time almost all workers lived in the communal housing set aside for them as part of the contract, and the management of these places found it strange that instead of making use of any of the facilities provided there such as the music room, sewing courses or table tennis, workers preferred to remain in their rooms. Three-quarters of the migrant workers viewed their time in exile as akin to military service, a time to be served, with the result that German language courses were only attended with any real desire and enthusiasm by a small percentage (17 percent) of the younger workers. It was noticed, however, in the course of the survey that there was a marked difference between the interest shown by males and females in German language courses, with 40 percent of females displaying genuine interest.

It also became clear in the survey that most workers viewed their housing facilities as an ersatz home, and this was an important factor in the distance that remained between them and German citizens and society. Seventy-seven percent of survey respondents had never visited a German family in their home. Further evidence of their isolation may be seen in the fact that in the six months prior to the survey, 24 percent of the respondents had not visited a German or foreign friend, nor indeed even a family member. The workers at this time were using the radio as their main means of obtaining world news and information from home. Indeed, the first purchase on arrival in Germany made by 80 percent was a transistor radio, which they mainly tuned to Ankara Radio. German radio and television were under state control at the time, with a certain level of state autonomy. However, for any broadcasts to be made in a language other than German there had to be a target population in excess of fifteen thousand residents in the state. Thus, at the time of the survey, there was one daily news bulletin in Italian, and weekly fifteen-minute programs for Spanish and Greek migrant workers. Radio signals from Turkey could not be received everywhere, so Turkish workers regularly tuned into a radio station called *Bizim Radio* (Our Radio), broadcasting in Turkish from East Germany. In the language of the time these broadcasts were considered a commentary from behind the Iron Curtain, and when it was understood that they were causing concern among Turkish authorities in Ankara, West German radio stations began to broadcast daily programs in Turkish. The workers could watch television in their lodgings, but with all programs in German, interest levels were not high: only 38 percent of respondents stated that one of the activities they pursued was watching television.

Most workers displayed great interest in the Turkish press, with 73 percent saying they read one or more Turkish daily newspapers. Although some had these newspapers sent from home, the majority bought them in Germany. It would seem therefore, that in addition to the topical issues that occupied their minds in Germany such as insurance, increases in child subsidy payments, and union membership, obtaining news from home was not only a priority for Turkish workers but, considering that the average cost of these newspapers would have been 1 DM, a priority for which they were willing to make inroads into their savings. The survey showed that the most popular Turkish newspaper was *Hürriyet*, read by 34 percent of respondents, followed by *Milliyet* at 22 percent and *Cumhuriyet* at 16 percent.

Turkish Workers and German Society

Turkish workers had come to Germany from a society that was only just beginning to break away from a rule of tradition and religion in which gender difference and distinction was firmly embedded. This was a source of no little distress to them in the new culture from the point of view of male-female relations, and according to reports in the Turkish press of the time, a significant number of Turkish workers, lacking both skills and in contact with German families outside their housing facilities, became involved in temporary relationships, more often than not in return for money.

In addition, there were other fundamental problems facing these workers in the social realm: with many German employers preferring to hire unmarried workers, many Turks chose to hide their real marital status, and only revealed this after they had gained the right to state child subsidy payments. Also, the German state did not forbid Greek and Italian workers from bringing their families with them, but did forbid Turks from doing the same. This proved problematic to many families, and made life difficult for the spouses left behind. Finally, in accordance with traditional patriarchal values, Turkish male workers attempted to maintain strict control over female workers coming from Turkey, but this only served to create insecurity among the females and drive them to develop friendships with German or American men.

Some male workers ended up living in complete withdrawal from female relationships, which caused many of them to have negative views of all male-female relations. For example, 78 percent of respondents did not have any friendships with members of the opposite sex. As expected, those in the twenty-three-to-twenty-seven age group, and/or from Turkish cities with a population exceeding one hundred thousand, and/or those who were graduates of vocational schools, were more positive regarding relationships between the sexes. Workers who came from Ankara, the capital, were accustomed to Western manners and behavior. They wanted to socialize, and thus the difference between younger, unmarried men and married ones seems evident. The latter were not anxious to have relations with the opposite sex. They did not speak the language and did not want to spent money. Furthermore, one has to take into consideration that Muslim workers coming from small towns and rural areas are often conservative and less open to Western values.

In contrast to the picture painted by some of the media, the survey revealed that Turkish workers were living extraterritorial lives on German soil, trapped within the confines of small workplaces and their living quarters. Evidence of this can be seen in the figures for marriages between Turks and Germans: of thirteen marriage ceremonies in Germany from 1964 to 1965 conducted between Spanish, Greek, Italian or Turkish male migrant workers and a German female, Turkish males were involved in the least amount of marriages.

During the same period, one hundred paternity claims were brought to the door of the German Embassy in Ankara. The survey data revealed a significant polarization in how workers evaluated male-female relationships. Fifty-one percent expressed the view that a male-female relationship had come to be considered the norm as a result of Western influences. Those from the northwest of the Marmara region, which was the most urbanized and industrialized part of the country, and in the twenty-three-to-twenty-seven age group, considered themselves more tolerant with respect to male-female relationships. However, 44 percent of respondents declared that such relationships, even those that involved little seriousness or involvement, were incompatible with religious or ethical norms. A sample of the personal statements made is sufficient here to reveal these value judgments: "Our religion forbids such things" (a thirty-three-year-old worker who had been employed in an iron foundry in Zonguldak, on Turkey's Black Sea coast); "I don't believe it is possible for a man and woman to maintain a friendship" (a thirty-three-year-old metal-worker, who emigrated to Turkey from Romania); "That kind of behavior is incompatible with religion and morals" (a twenty-three-year-old lathe operator from Diyarbakır in southeast Turkey).

Attitudes towards German family life reinforce the aforementioned tendencies: 70 percent of workers believed that Germans lived a different family life from Turks. Aspects of German family life considered positive were mixed gender employment, greater knowledge levels among individual family members, higher standard of living, better child care, and better use of time for work and play. The aspects considered negative were few ties among family members, extreme sexual freedom, and extreme materialism. Overall, 34 percent of Turkish workers made some negative comments when asked about German family life; 29 percent had wholly negative comments; and the remainder gave no replies.

On the other hand, Turkish females commended the social status of their German counterparts, and Turkish males noted the harmony and happiness of German couples' lifestyles. The study revealed that those critical of German family life came from both urban and rural environments in Turkey. This may be explained by the fact that some workers had already experienced internal migration in Turkey and moved to large cities such as Ankara, Istanbul, and Izmir, but continued to be bound by the traditional values of rural life.

Criticism of German females focused on the inadequacy of their ties to home and to their husbands, rather than their inadequacies as mothers. As Mübeccel Kıray pointed out in her Ereğli research in the 1960s, even in towns and cities in Anatolia, the female was always under the authority of the male, who was never to be questioned or disobeyed, and as a result did not share the same life.[6] Many male Turkish workers feared that the different way of family life in Germany was a threat to their traditional privileges, and it was this fear that lay behind their negative attitudes. Due to large-scale reforms carried out at the beginning of the Turkish Republic in the 1920s as well as exposure to Western value systems through migration, Turkey's social structure has been changing. But this change has also created a certain reluctance to accept new standards of behavior.

Turkish Workers' Religious Beliefs and Attitudes

From the perspective of sociology, religion—along with elements such as family, education, and government—constitutes a social institution within a culture. Because religious beliefs concern themselves with such value judgments as "evil," "goodness," "shame," and "merit," they play an extraordinarily powerful role in social control and have enormous influence on an individual's behavior and decision-making processes. This study did not have the workers' religious values as its main focus, and instead looked at their attitudes towards diet and working conditions. However, replies to questions on these issues did cast some light on the extent to which Islam is compatible with the tempo of modern industry, as well as the importance of religion in private life.

Formal Organized Religious Activities among Turkish Workers

At the time of the survey—the latter half of 1963—the Ford factories in West Germany, the German Railroad Authority, and some mining companies provided private rooms for Turkish workers to use for prayer. The Railroad Authority made two traveling wagons, complete with compass facilities, for use as mosques, and had these brought to where large groups of Turkish workers were employed. At this time, the Turkish General Directorate for Religious Affairs was not yet employing *imams* (religious leaders) to preach to workers

[6] Kıray, "The Family of the Immigrant Worker," 212.

in Germany, but the survey revealed that some individuals had taken it upon themselves to act as religious guides for the workers.

When asked about the social and individual need for a mosque, 39 percent of respondents stated that it was "very important," and 24 percent said that the absence of a mosque was a "significant loss" to them. When the data was further analyzed it became clear that the mosque's absence was felt equally by those coming from large urban environments as by those from a rural background: 41 percent of those from Istanbul strongly expressed the need for a mosque, as did 40 percent of those from villages. Most of those expressing the view that "one should be able to worship anywhere" were from Turkey's three largest cities: Izmir (47 percent), Istanbul (32 percent), and Ankara (29 percent).

Religious Attitudes among Turkish Workers

Although these workers greatly missed the presence of the mosque, a fundamental cultural element of the homeland, there was even less opportunity for them to fulfill another of the five precepts of Islam, namely the obligation to fast during the holy month of *Ramadan*.

Although 23 percent of respondents stated that they completed the fast, the number of those who stated that "fasting is not compatible with modern working life" was high, at 38 percent. Some German companies did make efforts to recognize and respect the religious traditions of their Turkish workers. For example, almost all mining companies in the Ruhr region put the workers on daytime shifts only to allow them to rest, and some other companies arranged the workers' annual holidays to coincide with the month of fasting.

The most highly observed religious custom among workers was their refusal to eat pork or its by-products. Although the accelerated work tempo, eight-hour shifts, strict discipline, and the heat, especially for those working in the mines, were all factors that, by causing extreme thirst, prevented them from fulfilling their fast obligation, the workers, almost without exception, remained faithful to the precept forbidding the consumption of pork. Eighty percent of respondents stated that they had never partaken of it. This resistance on their part had an important effect on their general health, with 30 percent of respondents stating that in reaction to the discomfort and doubt they felt, they had adopted a completely meatless diet. According to this group the meat of animals that had not been butchered and bled according to Islamic rules was unclean (*murdar*), and their wish was that someone would open a butchering facility that would sell meat prepared according to their religious custom. The survey revealed that on such deeply felt issues females were somewhat more liberal than males: as opposed to the 80 percent mentioned above who stated that they had never consumed pork, the figure was 73 percent for females.

The extent to which the rules of the Islamic religion occupied the minds of the workers may be seen in the following extract from a letter to the *Milliyet* newspaper:

> We are a group of Turkish workers in Kreuzthal in West Germany. We want the authorities to answer a particularly thorny problem for us: a) Is it a sin for us to consume the meat from animals killed here by strangulation?, b) Because of the lack of drinking water here we are forced to drink beer; is this religiously damaging?, c) If the same knife is used in the killing of cattle and pigs is the beef forbidden to us by Islam? d) Is it acceptable for one to keep the fast or pray if one has partaken of beer?[7]

As a result of avoiding pork and being generally worried about what they consumed, the diet of many workers became limited to a small group of foods such as onions, macaroni, cheese, and bread, and led to some workers contracting severe illnesses within a year or year and a half of their arrival in West Germany. The fact that only about 14 percent of workers availed themselves of the canteen food offered freely or at low cost by their companies may also be accounted for by the pressure of religious beliefs. Another factor that came to light in the survey was that in some cases an Armenian or Greek Orthodox Turkish worker working in a group of seven or eight Muslim Turks also refrained from eating pork in a show of solidarity.

Workers' Future Plans

There can be little doubt that in embarking on their journey to work in unknown lands, Turkish workers did so with the intention of fulfilling their hearts' desires at some point in the future. The survey revealed these desires to be the following: saving money (20 percent), guaranteeing their own and their family's future (19 percent), adding to their vocational knowledge and improving themselves (17 percent) and finally, owning a car (15 percent). What strikes one here is that although 47 percent of the workers appeared to have materialistic, concrete aims such as car or house ownership or the purchase of equipment useful to their job, and 23 percent had more undefined aims such as securing a better future, the remainder had been prompted to move abroad by more nonmaterialistic abstract desires such as seeing the world, improving themselves socially, or gaining some skills or education. In later years, this variety of targets would be reduced to that of simply making money, when workers came to the realization that being unskilled in the world of industry constituted an impassable barrier.

---

[7] *Milliyet*, 21 June 1964.

Of the survey respondents, 44 percent said they were achieving the target they had set, and of these, 49 percent expressed satisfaction with the amounts they were saving, and 24 percent felt they were improving their vocational skills. However, 52 percent voiced their disappointment in not realizing their hopes, citing various, rather vague reasons. When degrees of satisfaction were examined on a gender basis, it was found that females' complaints were mostly about low pay.

TABLE 3.4.
Unfulfilled expectations

	Number	%
Unable to avail of educational opportunities	29	11.0
Unable to make adequate savings	44	18.0
Not working in their field of training	24	9.0
Being misinformed/uninfomed	51	20.0
Expecting future plans to be realized	23	8.0
Newly arrived	45	17.8
No answer	41	16.0

Source: N. Abadan, *Batı Almanya'daki Türk İşçileri ve Sorunları,* (Problems of Turkish Workers in West Germany) DPT (State Planning Organization), Ankara, 1964, Table 225, s.213.

Almost all survey respondents had come to West Germany on one- or two-year contracts. Seventy-five percent stated that they had applied for extensions, of which 57 percent gave as their reason such factors as making money or saving more to make their target purchase.

Turkish Workers and the Homeland

A majority of the workers who traveled to West Germany in the 1960s were under the impression that on return to the homeland they would have little difficulty finding a job. In the survey, 57 percent said they believed this to be the case. Those who secured some form of sponsorship from the chambers of commerce and the like in the form of scholarships or training opportunities found work in West Germany in small workshops, repair shops, or the private sector that they felt would assist them in improving their vocational knowledge. Those whose only intention was saving money often planned to buy a car in West Germany and set themselves up as drivers when they returned to Turkey: it must be remembered that at the time, an automotive industry had not yet been established in Turkey. Unfortunately, for the workers leaving Turkey during these years, the Turkish government of the time had not been as

Figure 3.3. Dreaming of Owning a Taxi Cab

farsighted in its thinking as its Italian counterpart, and had not made it compulsory for Germany to provide training courses for Turkish workers. As part of a 1963 German-Italian agreement, 2,500 Italian workers attended courses in Germany in construction, metallurgy, and the hotel trade. These workers, on their return to Italy, had the benefit of such training and had little difficulty in securing employment.

At the top of the list of jobs in which Turkish workers wanted to become involved on returning home was the establishment of a small private enterprise or trade (31 percent). This was followed by such jobs as driving or setting up a trucking business. Only 19 percent wished to continue in employment as an industrial worker.

Findings of the Research

It was mainly Italy and Spain that sent their surplus labor into the more developed labor markets of Europe from the beginning of the 1950s. However, after the 1960s, openings in this market were left to Turkish and Yugoslavian workers to fill. This left the authorities in Turkey face to face with a tangled web of multifaceted and complex public administration problems.

Both the State Employment Bureau and the German Liaison Offices in Ankara and Istanbul found themselves understaffed in dealing with the requirements of the Turkish-German mutual agreements. Consequently, candidate migrant workers coming from all over Turkey to these central offices found themselves faced with an expensive wait of one to three weeks, during which, apart from undergoing the obligatory health checks, they were given little if any information concerning work and living conditions in Germany.

Work contracts were signed hastily in groups of ten to fifteen, with the workers having no opportunity to examine the contracts for specific conditions. Neither were they afforded any great information concerning pay, the sector or region in which they would be working, or housing. Most workers were chosen with little or no consideration being given to their area of employment prior to leaving which, for both employee and employer, left the way open for workplace disputes later.

Departure from Turkey by train usually took place within three days of signing the contract. With brochures in their hands, which most could not understand because of the needlessly abstruse language used in their preparation, the vast majority of workers left Turkey for foreign lands in a state of mind determined by subjective, one-sided information based, for the greater part, on hearsay.

All were almost completely uninformed of the situation in Germany, or in other European countries for which they were bound, regarding issues such as child subsidy payments, social security, or to whom they should apply in the event of an employer breach of contract or tax complaint. They were also uninformed of their legal rights, or of the fact that they could apply to the German authorities for assistance in finding new employment on cessation of their contract.

German employers, in putting their foreign labor to work doing the most undesirable, demanding, dirty and exhausting jobs, and refusing to offer any training, chose not to obey the conditions set out in the mutual agreements. This negative attitude among employers resulted in Turkish workers feeling psychologically excluded, and led to the realization that the Turkish Planning Organization was completely mistaken in its assumption that "emigration would secure a qualified industrial labor force for Turkey." Indeed, apart from learning to cope with the discipline entailed in working for large industrial companies, the workers learned little that would be of any benefit to them on their return to the homeland.

As far as foreign workers were concerned, labor unions in Germany made efforts only in the area of securing for them a wage commensurate with native workers, but the unions' primary aim was to guarantee better positions for their German members.

Laboring in a foreign country took Turkish workers away from their families. This was in contrast to the conditions of labor agreements Germany signed with Italy and Spain that, instead of discouraging family unification, contained clauses that actively promoted it. By delaying, and even completely blocking, the process of family unification, the German authorities deprived Turkish workers of this right.

The technical inability of Turkish radio stations to broadcast widely abroad in the 1960s resulted in many workers following Turkish broadcasts from radio stations in socialist countries. With broadcasts in their native tongue being provided for the other foreign worker groups, Turkish workers found it humiliating that they lacked such a facility.

Many Turkish workers at the time refused to send their savings home through normal banking channels at official exchange rates and, with these savings amounting to approximately $44 million, this deprived Turkey of a valuable source of much-needed foreign currency. The workers instead exchanged their money on the black market, or invested in purchases—e.g., automobiles, cassette players, record players—that they expected to sell at a profit in Turkey.

In their private lives and personal relationships the vast majority of Turkish workers remained faithful to their traditional values concerning male-female friendships, family life, and females in the workplace. Time spent in Germany resulted in little change to their ideas or mentality, a situation that may be explained by their leading marginalized lifestyles, and the lack of any creative efforts towards integration by the German or other state authorities.

1975 Boğazlıyan Research: Migration and Development

> Kazım is sending money home from Germany. So much money! If you worked for a year in the village you couldn't make it. His mother and father are making sure everyone knows about it, and his wife and kids are showing off too. Nothing but knives, forks and spoons now. Well, we understand forks and spoons. After all, times are changing. Wrapping rice in bread and dunking is for old timers. Young ones want spoons. And believe it or not some even want forks. But what on earth is a knife? And not only one, six of them! Kazım wrote about it in one of his letters. The knife is to be held in the right hand and the fork in the left. His knife

> and fork story got Hasan all hot and bothered. He took to the road on his own migration chase. They ripped him off like you would the skin off an onion.[8]

The State Planning Organization completed a field study among Turkish workers in Germany in 1963. The next research project, undertaken in 1975, was the cooperative effort of the Ankara University Institute of Housing and Urbanism, the International Foundation of Dutch Universities, and the Institute for Social Science Research in Developing Countries. Management of the project, which was called "Migration and Development: Research into the Effects of International Labor Migration on the Boğazlıyan District," was in the hands of Dr. Ruşen Keleş from the Faculty of Social Sciences at Ankara University, and Herman van Renselaar, who represented Dutch universities. The project's scientific team was headed up by myself, with Herman van Renselaar, Rinnus Penninx and Leo Van Velzen joining us from Holland, and Leyla Yenisey from Turkey. During the fieldwork phase we were also accompanied by Dr. Birsen Gökçe from Hacettepe University, Dr. Doğu Ergil from the Faculty of Political Sciences at Ankara University, and State Planning Organization representative Gül Ergil.

The research was conducted at a regional level, and in its investigation of the policies on migrant labor in the region, it focused particularly on two subjects: the effect(s) on regional development policies of both the emigration and return of workers, and the consequences of regional development and types of investment.

The district of Boğazlıyan in Yozgat province was chosen based on the following criteria: its high migrant worker population; its being categorized by the State Planning Organization as underdeveloped; its having exported labor to many European countries (e.g., Germany, Belgium, Holland); and the fact that its migrant labor abroad and its returned migrant population had invested their savings in a variety of ways (property, small businesses, village development cooperatives, and worker investment companies).

Theoretical Foundations of the Research

The research data was analyzed from two theoretical perspectives: the balanced growth theory, and the core-periphery or asymmetric growth theory. According to the former, in undeveloped economies the export of labor has a positive effect on economic growth. The worker is encouraged to use his savings for the purpose of domestic investment that, in turn, increases production and creates employment opportunities. This theory also foresees the active and successful integration of returned workers into the service sector.

The asymmetric model takes as its point of departure the fact that labor migration occurs as a result of the accumulation of capital in one center. Labor

[8] Yüksel Pazarkaya, *Oturma İzni* (Istanbul: Derinlik, 1977), 27.

recruitment then becomes necessary in order for optimum use to be made of this capital. This manpower results in further capital accumulation that, in turn, results in even more rapid development at the center. Development on the periphery cannot keep pace with that of the center and, over time, as the peripheral regions fail to keep up with the competition in industrial goods on the international market, they lose the power to compete altogether.

Upon completion, the research was published in Turkish as *Göç ve Gelişme—Uluslararası İşçi Göçünün Boğazlıyan İlçesindeki Etkileri Üzerine Bir İnceleme,* and in English as *Migration and Development: A Study of the Impact of International Labor Migration on the District of Boğazlıyan.*

Here will be presented a summary of the main aspects of this multifaceted and wide-ranging research, as we take a brief look at the following: the various channels through which potential migrants went abroad; public and private enterprise that hoped to benefit from emigration; the economic effects of emigration on Boğazlıyan; and the various ways in which workers invested their savings and the social effects of emigration on two villages in Boğazlıyan.

Effects of Emigration on the Local Economy

Channels Used in Order to Emigrate

As part of its plans to export labor, Turkey signed its first agreement in 1961 with West Germany. This was followed at later dates by similar agreements with other countries. The public institution made responsible for execution of the agreements in Turkey was the State Employment Bureau. From the beginning, the government placed no restrictions of any kind on nominal recruitment. The worker who had been recruited simply applied to the Employment Bureau with the documents proving that he or she had been accepted into the foreign country as an employee, and was then assisted by the Bureau in obtaining a passport. Records of the Employment Bureau show that between 1965 and 1975, a total of 238,255 migrants went abroad, having been nominally recruited. With this figure constituting only 33.8 percent of total migrant worker numbers for those years, it is clear that the Employment Bureau had a controlling role to play in the sending abroad of only one worker in three.[9] The Employment Bureau only functioned as the supervisor of the compulsory health checks, and also assisted with passport applications. The huge numbers migrating outside the control of the Employment Bureau make clear how "chain migration," i.e., migration through links with family or fellow citizens already abroad, became a fact of life, and also casts light on the process that, in later years, led to the emergence of ethnic communities.

[9] Abadan-Unat et al., eds, *Migration and Development,* 9.

Meanwhile the Employment Bureau set down specific rules in announcing and distributing information to those who wished to go abroad to work in jobs offered through the Employment Bureau's waiting lists, as opposed to through the mechanism of nominal recruitment:

- Preferential treatment was to be awarded to those applying from Turkey's least developed regions. This was in the form of the "two-year rule," which allowed these applicants to be placed nearer the top of the waiting list, as if they had applied two years previously.
- Fifteen percent of jobs available abroad were allocated to those applying through village development cooperatives. Workers applying through these channels were first required to become members of their local village cooperative, pay a specific amount to the cooperative, and also guarantee to send an agreed amount of their future savings to the cooperative.[10]
- Another 15 percent of jobs were allocated to those applying from regions in Turkey in which socioeconomic life was weakened as a result of natural disasters such as earthquakes, floods, or landslides, or had suffered economic losses as a result of crop disease.

Paths Chosen By Those Emigrating from Yozgat

The research survey revealed that 39 percent of those leaving the district of Boğazlıyan chose the safest and most economic route, namely, applying to the State Employment Bureau. Added to this figure must be the 11 percent who were nominally recruited from the district by the Bureau. However, the 1965 worker list issued by the Bureau shows that potential migrants faced a waiting period of up to one year. Just seven years later, in 1972, this had become a six- to seven-year wait, and consequently from 1968 onwards there is an increase in the numbers leaving as "tourists."

The survey also revealed that individuals who could not apply to go abroad through the Employment Bureau for a variety of reasons (they were too old, had inadequate funds to apply to the local cooperative, or a lack of contacts with relatives or friends abroad) prepared to go down the path of illegal immigration in order to seek employment. The fact that the numbers of such individuals constituted 42 percent of Boğazlıyan's total migrant population is evidence of the intense hold emigration, and all the expectations it brought with it, had at the time on Turkish people's imagination.

---

[10] For more detail, see State Planning Organization, *Dış Ülkelere İşgücü Göndermede Kooperatif Kuran Köylülere Öncelik Tanınması Projesinin Uygulanması Üzerine Bir Inceleme* [Study of the Realization of Recognizing Priority In Sending Farmers who founded cooperatives to foreign countries] (Ankara,1966).

TABLE 3.5.
How did you first travel abroad?

	Numbers going abroad		*Returnees*		*Total*	
	No.	*%*	*No.*	*%*	*No.*	*%*
Those sent by State Employment Dept. (IIBK), including from cooperatives	138	37.0	58	45.7	196	39.2
nominal recruitment through IIBK	45	12.1	10	7.9	55	11.0
As a tourist	158	42.4	54	42.5	212	42.4
Other channels	24	6.4	4	3.1	28	5.6
Unknown or invalid responses	8	2.1	1	0.8	9	1.8
Total	373	100.0	127	100.0	500	100.0

Source: N. Abadan-Unat et.al., Migration and Development, Table 5.2.2.1, p.180.

"Tourist" labor migration, or the process by which individuals entered a European country as a tourist in order to find employment, naturally resulted in various types of fraudulent activities. Corrupt individuals, prepared to exploit potential migrants' expectations and swindle them out of their savings, began organizing bus trips that attempted to enter West Germany by various routes such as through Italy or Austria, or by first "touring" Eastern Europe. Several striking examples of such fraud were uncovered during the Boğazlıyan research.

Case 1. Recollections of a Returned Migrant

> I applied to the Employment Bureau in 1965 in Yozgat. I waited three years but then in 1968 decided to go as a "tourist." I mortgaged twenty-five acres of land to cover travel expenses and the cost of getting a passport. With Ömer, a friend from the village, I went by bus from Istanbul to Yugoslavia. During the night, an Italian guide took us from Italy through the forest into Austria. For this we paid 900 lira per person to some international gang. We got into Austria, where an interpreter we met found us work. It paid 1,000 schillings per month. Later we found work on a farm. This lasted two months. They gave us food and accommodation and I got 3,000 schillings a month. After that, and again with the help of an interpreter, we found work in a timber yard. This paid 4,000 schillings a month. We were there for two and a half months. There were eight Turks working near there and with the extra work they found me I was able to put by about 5–6000 schillings each month.
>
> Later, along with the other migrants from my village, I went to Germany. I found work in Sigmar, in a big construction company. I was there for eight months. The work was hard and the pay was bad. I wrote a letter to cousins in Munich and they found me work. This lasted for a year and a half, but the work was very heavy

> and I became ill. I was in hospital for a while. In 1974 I became ill again. It was appendicitis, but they wouldn't operate. They just sent me home. This was the last straw! I decided then that it was time to come home to Turkey![11]

As may be seen in this example, workers going as tourists and working illegally had no access to social rights, union rights, or health insurance, and were subject to the worst kind of labor exploitation.

In the example below, a worker relates how, before he was able to save a penny, he lost all his money.

Case 2. A Seventeen-Month Adventure

> In 1966, a bus trip was organized by someone to take a group of forty of us to Europe. The group included fifteen from my own village. The bus was stopped at the Austrian border and wasn't allowed to continue. We went to Italy, and tried to get into Austria again, but we still weren't allowed in. Then we drove to Yugoslavia. We had a bad accident there. The bus went off the road and was written off. We stayed in a hotel for a few days, where we met an Arab who was involved in worker trading. He asked each of us for 100 DM and we gave it to him, but he never found us work. In the end we had to come back to Turkey.
>
> When I arrived back in Ankara, I met a German who promised he could find me work, so I obtained another tourist passport and set out for Germany with him. He disappeared when we were in Holland. I had relatives in Amersfoort, so I stayed with them for twenty-five days. One day I was caught by the police, who told me to leave the country. There were workers from my village in Belgium, working in the mines there, but they couldn't help me, and with not being able to speak the language I couldn't find work by myself. Then I went and stayed with others from my village in Austria. I found winter work in a holiday resort there, but only for forty-five days. After that I found work on a farm and then in a tile factory. In the factory I broke my arm when it got caught in a roller. They took me to hospital and I was there for three months. They were very good to me. The factory met all the bills, and gave me 1,000 schillings, by way of redundancy. It took five months for my arm to heal completely.
>
> I started to look for work again. I heard from someone that one of the employees, a woman, in the employment center would find you work if you bribed her. I gave her 1,000 schillings, but later she was arrested and appeared in court, so that was the end of that plan. After all this, I decided to come back to Turkey. I had eight thousand lira with me at that time, and there was two thousand left by the time I got home. That was the end result of my seventeen-month European adventure.[12]

This case reveals clearly just how little real or reliable information many of the individuals had about working abroad, and the dangers they faced from fraudsters ready and waiting to fleece them of their savings. In conclusion, one may say that the above anecdotes are evidence of just how limited a hold the Turkish state maintained over the manner in which its labor went abroad.

---

[11] Abadan-Unat et al., eds, *Migration and Development,* 186–188.

[12] Ibid., 199–201.

The period from 1968 to 1973 marks the time when migration was easiest. The possibility of nominal recruitment was high, and many of the villages of Boğazlıyan were populated only by males of "good economic standing." However, there was little groundwork done during these years by the Turkish authorities in the way of information provision or migration control that would have proved helpful in later years when migrant numbers increased dramatically. Indeed, just as a blind eye was turned to the existence of tourist workers, the state failed to take measures against those whom it knew were engaging in the fraudulent activities mentioned by the respondents in their stories, above. Twenty years later, in 1996, research done under the auspices of EUROSTAT revealed that many Turkish migrant workers still tended to travel to Europe as tourists with a view to remaining after their visa expired.

In earlier years many who chose to travel in this way continued to seek employment using their tourist passports until they finally gave way to despair and returned home, and as increasing numbers began returning in such a state of mind, after 1975 there was a decrease in the numbers choosing this route into Europe. From 1971 onward, spouses began to migrate as well, and this movement was still continuing at a steady rate in 1975—the year of the Boğazlıyan research project.

Public and Private Enterprise That Hoped to Benefit From Emigration

From 1964 onwards the State Planning Organization set about using emigration as a tool to develop Turkey. One result of this was the village cooperative schemes, set up by the Ministry of Rural Affairs. These allowed for the creation of a contingent supply of workers, and gave preference to cooperative members in the race to go abroad to work. The authorities' intention in promoting the establishment of these cooperatives was that they should play a significant role in local development, through the setting up and operation of such projects as air-conditioning plants, facilities for the purchase and use of farm equipment and machinery, irrigation facilities, dairies and farms. However, from the start these were perceived among those who became members as a new way to go abroad. Indeed, they came to be informally known as "Germany cooperatives" among the public.

When West Germany was hit by an economic crisis in 1967 and temporarily began to accept fewer foreign workers, many potential migrants in Turkey, in despair of never getting abroad, began to take a great deal more interest in the village cooperatives. Thus, in 1969, when foreign demands for Turkish labor grew again, the cooperatives began to multiply in numbers far exceeding expectations: in 1971 there were 2,263; in 1973, 4,514; and in 1974, 5,376. Membership at this time was approximately 960,000.[13]

[13] "Türk Sanayicileri ve İşadamları Derneği," *Görüş* 3, no. 5 (May 1975).

With respect to cooperatives, the reality exposed by the Boğazlıyan research project was that in Yozgat, and indeed in Turkey in general, they never really succeeded in fulfilling the expectations that had accompanied their establishment. The main reason was likely the members themselves, whose motive in joining was to use the cooperative as a springboard to emigration. In other words, their interests lay not in how the cooperative could play a role in Turkey's development, but rather in how it could play a role in their emigration. This is documented in individual cases in the research.

Case 3. The "Imaginary" Textile Factory (Yozkoop)

> Thirty-one small cooperatives in Yozgat decided to get together and operate as one large cooperative. The only visible result of this was a deserted half-built factory on a big site on the road to Sivas with a "security guard" at the front. Meanwhile, the president of the new cooperative set himself up as a publisher in a well-appointed office in Yozgat. The resulting publication, which came out monthly, carried news that a textile factory would be opening soon. He was the driving force behind the new cooperative, and later, when he was killed in a car accident, the cooperative, without having done a thing, became history.[14]

Similarly, during the Boğazlıyan research, machinery and other equipment, or what may be described as the remnants of such, were discovered in various factories and other industrial facilities in ten villages throughout Yozgat.

Case 4. Local Power Politics and a Flour Mill's Destruction

> For various reasons cooperatives wishing to become involved in more realistic ventures were also subject to failure. In 1972, migrant workers decide to form a cooperative for the purpose of building a flour mill. In this venture they were joined by local grain merchants. As share payments began to arrive from member workers in Europe construction of the mill was completed, and in 1973 actually went into operation for a period of three months. However, with the grain merchant partners charging high prices for the wheat they were providing, the mill soon began to operate at a loss. Finally, in 1974, the grain merchants decided to dissolve the cooperative, and the mill became a limited company.[15]

This case clearly demonstrates both the inadequacy of the government's structuring of these operations and the danger to the cooperatives themselves from those who were ready and willing to benefit financially from any difficulties cooperatives were faced with in their efforts to operate on the open market. It was recognized that many of the cooperatives' activities were inadequately supervised by the State Planning Organization. The failure of the Çandır sunflower oil extraction facility project provides a good example. This project was under capable leadership, had more than adequate founding capital, and was

[14] Abadan-Unat et. al., eds, *Migration and Development,* 238–239.
[15] Ibid., 240–242.

the subject of a detailed feasibility study prior to establishment. However, despite this, and the fact that the 2,657 cooperative members working in Europe continued to send their membership fees regularly, the project failed when sufficient quantities of sunflowers could not be supplied to the facility. This situation arose because the land available in Yozgat for the production of sunflowers was instead used to produce sugar beet, a more profitable crop. Consequently, the facility in Yozgat was forced to purchase its sunflower quota from Thrace in northwestern Turkey and, unable to compete profitably on the open market, later halted production.[16]

Emigration and the Inadequacy of Executive Coordination

It is evident from these cases that in becoming involved in the establishment of small agro-industries, migrant workers were desirous of bringing new industry and opportunities to their birthplaces. However, despite feasibility studies by the State Planning Organization and the advisory committees of various ministries, the lack of continuous and regular inspection, capital investment, and market analyses meant many projects were doomed to failure. Indeed, many other cases such as those outlined here were presented in the press of the time as failures of "worker companies" in what some social scientists called the "people sector."

Thus, as it slowly became understood by all involved that the state's hopes and expectations of regional development following naturally from its support of village development cooperatives and from the establishment of the worker investment companies would remain unfulfilled, migrant workers began to choose "individual" forms of investment for their hard-earned savings.

Investment Choices of Migrant Workers

Most migrant workers from Boğazlıyan, either before returning or on their return, chose to invest their money in land in the Boğazlıyan area. Research data shows that between 1967 and 1975 land prices rose by at least one-third. Workers did not look to agricultural production for their land purchases, but saw them rather as a monetary asset that could later be converted to cash.

Another popular form of investment was importing farm equipment and machinery, and there were some striking examples of this in the research analysis. Law 474 allowed for the importation of farm equipment at a reduced customs tax rate. This import activity, although it did serve to somewhat increase mechanization in agriculture, was more a source of improved status for the worker importing the equipment, and a source of profit for dealers in farm

[16] Ibid., 245–246.

machinery. Prior to the days of emigration, tractors could only be purchased through two state organizations, the Agricultural Equipment Organization or the Sugar Cooperative, both of which had a waiting list. When these organizations failed to meet the needs of farmers, a kind of black-market economy developed in farming equipment. On becoming aware of the existence of such an economy, dealers began to travel to Europe and buy from workers who were planning to return the rights they had to import such equipment. The workers exercised their import rights as table 3.6 shows.

TABLE 3.6.
Ownership of agricultural machinery in Boğazlıyan

	1966	*1975*
Total no. of tractors	299	967
Tractors owned by workers abroad	few	310
Harvesting machinery	0	116
Harvesting machinery bought by workers	0	23

Source: Köy isleri Bakanligi, *Köy Envanter Etütlerine Göre Yozgat ili,* 1968; *Migration and Development,* Table 6.2.4.2, p. 216.

Case 5. Everyone Satisfied

> The last two years I was in Germany, I met two dealers. They were looking for workers who were about to return to Turkey. One of them asked me to import a tractor. I didn't need a tractor. I had bought one the year before from the Sugar Cooperative. One of them asked me to bring in the tractor he had bought in Germany on my passport in return for 5,000 lira. There was absolutely no risk involved. The other one had bought a car and he gave me 15,000 lira to bring it in. I made quite a lot of money through little deals like that.[17]

There is no doubt that some of the workers bringing in tractors were intending to use them privately to work their own land, but a significant number did benefit from these deals on the open market and simply sold their rights to dealers. The saddest fact to emerge from all of this was that many of these tractors were of makes unknown or unfamiliar in Turkey, and with spare parts difficult, or in some cases impossible, to obtain, tractor graveyards began to appear, scattered here and there, full of unusable machines. Thus, much of the money invested in tractors and harvesting machines ended up back in Europe.

Transport was another area of investment, with a certain proportion of migrant workers choosing to invest in such vehicles as buses, trucks, minibuses, and jeeps. Imported automobiles were mainly used as taxis. However, housing was the area of greatest investment. Yet, many times, this only enriched those

[17] Ibid., 221.

outside the district since builders filled their labor needs by bringing in labor from outside. The fact that workers found housing the most secure form of investment may be explained by the lack of availability of other creative and profit-making investment opportunities and by their growing accustomed to consumer behavior while abroad.

It cannot be said that there was any significant productive development in the flow of goods or revenue into Boğazlıyan following the emigration of workers from there. The reduction in manpower led to a decrease in agricultural production. Savings sent home by migrant workers to local bank branches was automatically transferred to these banks' headquarters. Investment goods were, for the most part, bought in from outside the district. Indeed, prior to emigration from Boğazlıyan there was a balance between the agricultural products being "exported" from the district and its "imported" consumption goods. With emigration, Boğazlıyan found itself becoming a "dependent consumer"—dependent, that is, on external production. In other words, the growth that resulted in finances and the services and distribution sectors was artificial.

Emigration and the Social Life of Boğazlıyan

In order to determine the effects of emigration on the social life of the district, detailed studies were undertaken in the Boğazlıyan villages of Müftükışla and Yeşilhisar. It soon became evident that it was family structure that had undergone the most dramatic change. Prior to migration, the numbers of those living in the extended family structure were to a large extent matched by those living as nuclear families. Following emigration, however, and more particularly when the migrant worker abroad had saved enough to build his own house, nuclear family living became the general practice. As Mübeccel Kıray pointed out, the structure of the migrant worker family changed, and continued to change almost on a yearly basis, marked by the return of the migrant worker on holiday. With some family members leaving, some returning, and sometimes relatives or friends coming to stay for long periods, family configuration became subject to fluctuation.[18]

Another major change in family life was in division of labor and the freedom of decision-making that female family members gained. One particularly successful village wife wrote to her husband in Europe that there was no need to send money, so successful had she become in the business of rearing and selling sheep. Indeed, some of the village women had gained such enormous freedoms that they were fretful of what the return of their husbands would mean for their newly gained independence. Wives who had accompanied their husbands abroad expressed discontent with many things: village lifestyle, their

[18] Kıray, "The Family of the Immigrant Worker," 210–235.

being unable to dress as they wished, the gossipy atmosphere, and the criticisms to which they were subjected.

Emigration had a particularly negative effect on the children remaining at home. Although all migrant workers were completely devoted to the idea of educating their children, they firmly believed that a university education was for male children only. For their daughters, they considered the education offered at religious schools sufficient. Psychological problems were suffered by children left behind in the care of grandparents or other relatives, and those who, having been taken abroad with the family, failed to adapt to the education system in the country of acceptance.

Emigration made itself felt most in the area of consumer behavior. As symbols of their new social status, many workers built two-story houses containing as many as seven or eight rooms. For most migrant worker families the money coming from abroad was used in purchasing labor-saving home appliances, improving the family diet and, although not drifting too far from their traditional lifestyle, providing the family with a more comfortable standard of living. In some houses, however, there appeared household appliances that were simply not possible to use. One example of this consumption fever that overtook some is related in the following anecdote.

Case 6. Extravagance

> Şahap lived in a big house with his wife, five children, his daughter-in-law and two grandchildren. The parlor had been furnished with modern stuff from the city, none of which was ever used at all. The room also contained two electric blankets, two table lamps, a food processor, an electric knife sharpener, five or six clocks, a vacuum cleaner, a kind of electric heater used for easing rheumatism, a washing machine, a Turkish-made clothes drier, a refrigerator, and loads of Christmas decorations on the ceiling. At the time, the family was waiting for electricity to come to the village!

Extravagance was most obvious at weddings, on which workers spared no expense and often exceeded amounts spent by rich farmers.

Findings of the Research

As part of Turkey's First Five-Year Development Plan, the export of Turkish labor led Turkey into a dependent relationship with European states, particularly West Germany. Because of the conflict of interest that exists between what we may call the "periphery countries," i.e., all those exporting their labor, and the "core countries," or those who import this labor, this relationship may be defined as asymmetric. At the time of the Boğazlıyan research project in 1975, and in later years, this dependency had many unforeseen consequences, some of which are briefly touched upon in the following section.

International Migration and the Unequal Distribution of National Labor

In labor-exporting countries, intensive international labor migration has the effect of preventing the gradual move of the actively employed population from sectors of low productivity to sectors of high productivity. In other words, international labor migration, by perpetuating inequality in labor productivity among the various sectors, prevents balanced economic growth in labor-exporting countries and strengthens the dependency relationship between the "core" and the "periphery."

Demographic Changes in Rural/Urban Populations

The export of human resources brings about significant and clear-cut changes in the demographic structure of rural and urban populations and leads to the abandonment of various agricultural activities. Another consequence is the transition from male labor to physically weaker female labor. Furthermore, the loss of qualified labor, or what has come to be known as the "brain drain," slows down the development of national industry.

Misleading Forms of Investment, Weakening of International Competition

Investment in property, the establishment of small private enterprises in the informal sector, and unwillingness to participate in national industry, not only result in the inappropriate and ineffective use of migrant workers' savings, but also prevent the possibility for competition in the international economy.

Increase in Consumerism

Influenced by advertising, attractive credit possibilities, and the high levels of consumption they see abroad, workers prioritize car and house ownership. In directing their efforts towards achieving a better standard of life, they do not put their savings towards production.

Limited Political and Social Participation

The material well-being afforded by employment overseas leads to limited socialization and weak political participation among workers. With the accepting countries offering their Turkish foreign workers no possibility for political participation, and Turkey only allowing them to exercise their right to vote at border checkpoints, workers become a marginalized group, driven to feel politically and socially excluded.

Changes to Family Life, Differentiation in Individual Expectations

Fragmentation of family life and increased physical movement bring significant change to the traditional family order. Inconsistencies in social status, and the often-felt desire to migrate again on returning home, may result in egocentric behavior on the part of the individual.

Theoretical Commentary on the Research

When labor export was adopted as an integral part of Turkey's First Five-Year Plan little consideration was given to its possible consequences. This process of exporting labor to highly industrialized countries—a process that took 85 percent of all workers leaving Turkey to Germany—leads to high levels of dependency. Based as it is on a conflict of interest, the relationship that exists between the powerful, industrialized core countries and those on the periphery is asymmetric in character. This dependency relationship had fundamental long- and short-term effects on Turkey's development. In trusting resolution of its unemployment problems, even in part, to the export of labor, a country places itself in a position of economic dependency. When looked at from this perspective, the hypotheses of the "asymmetric development" model, which the Boğazlıyan research project took as its point of departure, would seem to have been proven, and it is possible to summarize the general trends under the following headings:

Limited Effects of Labor Migration on Employment

Should the majority of migrant workers be unemployed, invisibly or otherwise, prior to migration, and be expected to return to the homeland with new industrial skills, labor migration could be said to have beneficial uses. However, among Turkish workers abroad, only limited numbers had been unemployed or working in the agricultural sector. As a result, it may be said that, in Turkey's case, emigration, on a national scale, or indeed on a local scale such as that of Boğazlıyan, played little or no role in Turkey's industrial development.

Effects on Industry of Workers' Savings

The research revealed that workers' savings sent home either through the mechanism of the village development cooperatives or the worker investment companies played little if any role in the process of industrializing Turkey.

The Economic Role of Returning Migrants and Their Investment Choices

When the Boğazlıyan research project was being carried out in 1975, numbers of migrants returning permanently were limited. Those who had returned, by electing to use their savings for the establishment of a small business such as a retail shop, were investing in an already saturated sector, and therefore created no new conditions that would help move Turkey towards industrialization. The accumulated money and later, the accumulated labor power, gravitated towards the industrial center of Turkey, the northeastern Marmara region. Consequently, it is impossible to refer here to a "balanced growth" model.

The Role of the State in Regional Development

The state's efforts to encourage the flow of investment towards its underdeveloped and developing regions in the form of reduced custom tax rates and other import amnesties failed to produce the expected results. An examination of the Industrial Development Bank's investments for 1974 reveals that regions of capital accumulation, more than what might be termed rural regions, had reaped the benefits of investment. The credit policies of Turkish banks helped to further delay economic growth in Turkey's underdeveloped regions, especially during the 1970s. Branches that distributed credit were to be found in areas in which the credit would secure most profit.

Savings and Turkey's Foreign Trade Deficit

It must be remembered that huge sums of money entered Turkey in the form of migrant workers' savings. Without a doubt, this money played a part in improving the lives of some Turkish citizens. But whereas it also helped to lighten Turkey's foreign debt and encourage consumerism, it was never directed towards investment that would play a part in invigorating production. The fact that workers' savings were used to help clear Turkey's foreign debt, without, at the same time, any consideration being given to the inflationist effect the savings were having on the economy, served only to increase the volume of the service sector.

Labor Migration and the Structure of Turkey's Labor Force

Throughout the emigration years much skilled Turkish labor leaving Turkey's shores chose to conceal its knowledge and qualifications in order to qualify and apply through legal channels for employment abroad, a situation that must be understood as the transfer of invisible capital. There is, after all, cost involved for any state in the nurturing, education and training of a skilled work force. It was the countries of acceptance that benefited from the skills of these workers, and the hypothesis that stated that an unskilled work force would be sent abroad only to return with much-needed skills remained unproven. In fact, most Turkish workers abroad were put to work doing the filthiest, most monotonous, and heaviest tasks.[19]

Increase in Turkey's Economic Dependency

Turkish labor export was governed completely by the labor demands of the accepting countries, both with respect to numbers and skills. In 1973, European countries, in addition to halting their labor imports, began, in some cases, to offer monetary incentives to those deciding to return, in order to actively discourage family unification and encourage return migration. In this context, Turkey may only be considered as a dependent business partner. In its desire to reduce its foreign debt and increase exports, it found itself becoming more dependent on the revenue entering the country in the form of workers' savings. The outcome of this, of course, was the strengthening of European capital since, without much delay, the workers' savings reentered the coffers of Europe, to be added to the Turkish worker savings already deposited in banks there.

Limited Involvement in Social and Political Life

One natural outcome expected from the state-planned export of Turkish labor was that the migrants' experience of living in a multiparty democracy and becoming accustomed to the functioning of labor unions would result in both phenomena becoming more deeply rooted in Turkey. In reality, this too failed to come about. At the time of the Boğazlıyan research project, migrant workers were looked on as a temporary phenomenon, a group to be marginalized both socially and politically. Their lives, lived out in ghettoes throughout Europe, were remote from being of a quality that would foster social change. With their native country only granting them the right to vote at its border checkpoints, it is not surprising that in Europe, in their countries of settlement, their rights extended only to taking part in local government. The root cause of all these developments must lie in the fact that when Turkey adopted the policy of labor exportation it did so without simultaneously developing any future-oriented migration policies.

---

[19] Paine says that among all skilled workers coming from Meditarranean countries—excluding Yugoslavia—the highest numbers came from Turkey (46.3 percent). See Susanne Paine, *Exporting Workers,* 82.

CHAPTER 4
Social Processes: Migrant Women

Figure 4.1. Women Entering Industrial Life

Different cultures generate different explanations as to why people become sick and die, why the rain destroys the harvest and why a house is destroyed by fire. The philosophy of the Kulu women provides alternative ways of explaining events that occasion anxiety, disorder or threats. … When a child falls ill in the cold of winter or heat of summer, a Kulu woman reasons that an unmediated force—that is to say, the cold or the heat—has entered the child, causing it to be ill. … The evil eye has been transmitted by someone to the child, making it susceptible to the cold.

—Lisbeth Sachs, *Evil Eye or Bacteria: Turkish Migrant Women and Swedish Health Care*

In this chapter I will attempt to show how the emigration of Turkish women caused serious changes in their status, which in turn led to changes in their ability to enter the workforce, in gender relations among spouses and within the family, and to educational problems for the second and third generations. I will also show the impact of industrial work on Turkish women during the period of the *Gastarbeiter* program.

The appearance of migrant women during the years from 1962 to 1974 in the highly organized Turkish society was a major novelty. The most relevant aspect of this movement was the fact that the decision of Turkish women to migrate was imposed, or at least encouraged, to a large extent by the male members of the family. The demands of the economies of Western countries opened a door for women who had never thought of living abroad and working in an unknown place. Their experiences and reactions represent a different perspective from those who, after the economic crisis in Europe of 1967–1968 and the end of recruitment in 1974, asked for family reunions and rejoined their spouses. I will try to show how Turkish migrant women reacted and performed in an unknown milieu, the impact on their saving and spending habits, and why they faced the fragmentation of the family. In the second part of the chapter, I will examine the evolution of their decision to settle down, choose a vocation, and become partners in family enterprises. In the final section, I will address the problem of the education of the second and third generations.

Turkish Migrant Women Enter the World of Industry

In Turkey in the 1950s due to the introduction of modern agricultural technology and rapid population growth, a significant proportion of the rural population started to move to the cities. The phenomenon of "de-peasantization" began. At the beginning of the 1960s, with the increase of job-seeking new urbanites, a brand-new solution was adopted by the State Planning Organization. The new policy was called "the export of surplus manpower." Thus like other southern Mediterranean countries such as Italy, Spain, Greece, and Yugoslavia, Turkey started to send its citizens to Europe. This policy was built on a series of bilateral agreements that secured the social rights of foreign and national labor. The famous *Gastarbeiter* program was intended to be based on a yearly rotation principle, with returning workers and fresh replacements. But almost immediately both employers and workers opted against this turnover, and within a short span of time the number of Turkish migrants abroad swelled to almost 1 million.

At the beginning this migration was selective, consisting solely of young male adults, and was predominantly directed toward West Germany. Thus the

TABLE 4.1.
Numbers of male & female Turkish workers in West Germany (1960–74)

Year	*Female*	*Male*	*Female workers (%)*
1960	—	2,527	6.8
1961	430	6,370	6.7
1962	1,563	17,283	9.0
1963	3,569	29,395	11.1
1964	8,045	77,127	10.4
1965	17,759	115,018	15.4
1966	27,215	133,735	13.4
1967	25,456	105,853	16.9
1968	34,257	118,648	19.4
1969	53,573	190,762	22.4
1970	77,405	276,493	21.9
1971	97,358	355,787	21.5
1972	100,763	348,913	20.2
1973	128,808	399,606	20.4
1974	159,984	457,547	25.9

Source: Auslaendische Arbeitnehmer 1971, Nürnberg 1972, 19; Auslaendische Arbeitnehmer 72/73, Nürnberg 1974, 70–71; Amtliche Nachrichten der Bundesanstalt für Arbeit, Mart 1976, 277–278.

dirty, tiresome, unpleasant, and low-prestige jobs were carried out by the migrants, permitting the national labor class to become upwardly mobile.

During the initial phases of this migration, female participation was extremely low. But over time it increased, due to two factors: the explicit migratory policies of the host country, and the voluntary or imposed demands of potential women migrants.

The coal and steel industries and the docks on the Northern Sea requested physically strong workers at the beginning, and the automobile, textile, electronic, chemical, food, and packaging industries followed, demanding workers with manual dexterity. This situation produced a new challenge for Turkish women and men. Given the fact that during this period over 1 million Turks were registered for work permits and contracts at the Turkish Labor and Employment Office, the chances for men at the bottom of the list to get a contract were low. However, when it became evident that women were in demand and, if they were recruited, employed women could, after a certain period of time, claim for family reunion, a silent but relevant change in the minds of average Turkish men took place. The idea that via family reunion Turkish men would also be able to migrate to Europe created in the mentality of a great number of conservative men a radical change. Women of rural background or those living in shanty towns of the big cities, who were traditionally socialized, mentally unprepared, and to some degree, unwilling, were strongly urged by their fathers, husbands, or other relatives to take up industrial or service jobs in foreign countries in order to secure for their male relatives the possibility of obtaining lucrative jobs. Thus, a great number of Turkish women entered industrial jobs without having been exposed to city life, disciplined working hours, or production norms. For some, their journey to faraway places was akin to military service: a temporary period to be endured. For a minority of these women it meant personal liberation from family control. As far as the employers were concerned, female migrants were considered docile, passive, and uninterested in trade union activity, and so represented a cheap labor source.

The astronomic rise in the number of female migrants abroad represented a great discrepancy with the position of the female industrial workers in Turkey.[1] Initially, Turkish women consoled themselves with the thought that emigration was a temporary phenomenon, serving only to satisfy the dreams of their husbands to work in the West. However, as the current of emigration became stronger, the situation changed utterly, and individuals found themselves in uncharted waters. Many of the women who were forced to adapt to work in the alien world of industrial facilities continued to do so after their husbands had joined them, also as employees, bringing radical change to the lives of their families.

Looking at the characteristics of Turkish migrant women during this early period, several traits can be discerned. First, they represented a relatively young population group: 56 percent were twenty-five to thirty years old. Like other migrant women in Europe of that period, 76 percent of the Turkish migrant women were younger than thirty-five years old. Two-thirds (64 percent) of these women were married, and 58 percent of those married lived with their husbands in Europe.

The highest fertility rate belonged to Turkish families; 50 percent of Turkish women had two children; 21 percent had three to five children; and 10 percent had more than five children.

The educational level of Turkish migrant women reflected two distinct groups. The first group was comprised of those women who did not attend school at all; these were slightly more numerous than the uneducated male migrants (10 percent versus 7 percent). Sixty-one percent of women attended only primary school, as did 70 percent of men. The second group was rep-

[1] In 1965 only 5.9 percent of the female workforce worked outside agriculture, and this figure rose to 10.1 percent in 1970 and 11.6 percent in 1975. In West Germany alone the percentage of Turkish migrant women shot up to 159.984 (25.9 percent) in 1974. See SOPEMI, Continuous Reporting System on Migration (Paris: OECD, 1979).

resented by those women who attended secondary or professional schools. More women had a higher educational level than men (38 percent versus 21 percent).

The female migrant workers were mostly employed in jobs requiring no qualification (50 percent); out of 81 percent in production jobs, 26 percent were in the metal branch, 19 percent in textiles, 9 percent in food industry, and 9 percent in the chemical industry. The remainder worked in the service sector. In Scandinavian countries the majority of Turkish female migrants were only employed in part-time jobs.

A final trait of Turkish migrant women was their primary motivation for migrating abroad. Fifty-five percent of female migrants indicated the desire to join their families, whereas another 45 percent wanted to save money.

Working Conditions and Adaptation to Industrial Labor

It would be assumed that with many of these women being completely inexperienced in the ways of industrial life, being placed in industrial workplaces in a relatively short period of time should have led to some adaptation problems. However, the results of their being in the workplace reveal that in fact the opposite is true: no significant problems were encountered in what was, for the most part, the completion of repetitive, basic, and monotonous tasks.

Turkish female labor was concentrated in the areas of textiles, tailoring, electronics, and food packaging. From a physical perspective this was not particularly tiring work, given the technological developments in these areas of industry. As mentioned before, my research in 1963 revealed that 74.5 percent of women were offered the opportunity to be seated while working. The industrial accident rate was very low among female workers: males suffered three times as many injuries as females.[2]

The greatest source of dissatisfaction among female workers was rates of pay. The aforementioned research conducted in 1963 showed that only 30 percent of females reported satisfaction with their remuneration. Dissatisfaction increased in proportion to education levels: Although 44 percent of primary school graduates expressed displeasure with their pay, this rose to 58 percent among those who had undergone education to the middle school level.[3] Female workers were also more vocal than males in their criticism of workplace supervisors: 18 percent compared to 11 percent. It is likely that never having worked in an industrial atmosphere before, female workers had internalized feelings of hostility.

---

[2] Nermin Abadan-Unat, *Batı Almanya'daki Türk İşçileri ve Sorunları* [Problems of Turkish Workers in West Germany], (Ankara: Başbakanlık DPT, 1964), 120, table 106.

[3] Ibid., 125, table 113.

It is possible to explain the relative ease of adaptation among female workers in terms of the socialization process they would have undergone as young children in Turkey's rural regions. Among the rural population, girl children were often called "guests," a term arising out of the fact that sooner or later they would be leaving the family home. These girls were constantly being prepared for the situation in which they would be daughters-in-law, subject to acceptance of parents-in-law and adaptation to what would be an unfamiliar environment.

The fact that most of these women had never worked in an industrial environment before, that they came from a different social stratum, and their being settled in different housing accommodations are all factors that explain why females experienced greater degrees of loneliness than males, and why solidarity among them was weaker compared to that among males. In 1963 it was revealed in their responses to situations that called for mutual aid and support: Only 5 percent of males refused to go to anyone for help during working hours, as opposed to 25 percent of females. Likewise, 80 percent of males expressed the view that solidarity was a positive influence in their working lives, whereas only 65 percent of females said that such solidarity existed.[4]

The doubts and fears that resulted from loneliness experienced at work were somewhat eased among females by maintaining friendships outside of work: 41 percent of male workers, as opposed to 60 percent of females, met with work colleagues during leisure time.[5] Communication and sharing of ideas was especially strong among women who had undergone some vocational training: 50 percent of these shared leisure time with fellow workers.

Another interesting point to emerge from the research was the expression by the workers of their attitudes to workers of other nationalities. Although both males and females expressed as their first priority friendships with natives of the country in which they were resident, as their second preference, 9 percent of the males gave Italians, and 6 percent of the females said Greeks.[6] Thus, negative stereotypical ideas, formed within the frame of reference of similar social conditions, were becoming less influential.

The fact that Turkish female workers were subject not to physical but psychological stress is evident in situations concerning their loneliness. Almost twice as many females as males (43 percent versus 22 percent, respectively) expressed a desire to have the opportunity to speak and exchange ideas with their supervisor. The data from the research reveals that the females felt they had gained much new knowledge with entry into the world of industry. This was shown primarily in their intense interest in learning language: twice as

---

[4] Ibid., 131, table 121.

[5] Ibid., 132, table 124.

[6] Ibid., 136, table 130. It must be remembered that these figures predate the 1974 Turkish invasion of Cyprus.

many females as men participated in the available language courses. Indeed, it may be said that the lack of desire to learn the language of the country of acceptance lies at the origin of the "ghetto" living of many Turks, who conducted all the business of daily living in their native language.

In conclusion, it must be said that the industrial work undertaken by these women, and especially from the perspective of those coming from rural backgrounds in Turkey, did little by way of providing them with new or multifaceted skills. On return to the homeland, they did not participate in the industrial life of Turkey, and the regions from which they had migrated would have had few if any large industries at the time. During their time in industrial labor they would also have been confronted with such concepts as work discipline, punctuality, and the value of time, and services provided by social security and unions, all of which they would have come to understand and adopt to a greater extent through urban living and the availability of mass communication.

Thus, we may say that economic independence, a more satisfying income, and the possibility for saving that these created were elements in emancipating these women, but the important issue to be considered here is that in their adaptation to an urban environment and work, the two greatest challenges that female Turkish migrant workers faced were the changing social roles within the family and their children's education.

Changes in Family Structure, Abroad, and at Home

Social scientists dealing with Middle Eastern family structure have generally defined it as being extended and patriarchal. However all researchers who studied the family structure in general in Turkey either on a national scale (Timur, 1972) or in isolated villages (Yasa, 1955; Stirling, 1965; Kıray, 1964; Erdentuğ, 1968) show that more than 60 percent of families were nuclear families.

With the change in agro-economic life and fast population growth, an additional increase in the proportion of nuclear households emerged. External migration produced a further escalation in nuclear households and had a deep effect on women's status and marital roles. Furthermore, the policies of the receiving countries, their restrictive policies on work permits and family unification, and the tendency among migrant workers to increase their savings produced new forms of family fragmentation. Thus internal and external dynamics played a determining role in families, and the result was a new type of nuclear family. Kıray puts it best: "[M]igration to foreign countries rejects every rule and pattern about the family and shows that the dispersal and composition is really a *kaleidoscope* where the pattern changes every year or with every vacation the man has."[7]

[7] Kıray, "The Family of the Immigrant Worker," 220.

Migration, in deeply affecting family life and in playing a partial role in the process of female emancipation, also placed extra burdens on the shoulders of both the women going abroad and those remaining in the homeland.

Until the middle of the 1970s, families wishing to engage in migration had to choose from among the following: (1) the head of the household emigrating; (2) one spouse going and seeking employment for the other later; or (3) leaving as a couple with the children staying behind. These choices are the dominant factor in fragmentation, and in other words mean that it was considered acceptable at the time that members of the family unit remain separate for what could be years at a time.

In Turkey, this readiness to accept such a situation was undoubtedly an extension of an already existing tradition or practice. It was traditional, as a rule, for a man to leave his family in the care of others during times such as military service, seasonal labor, or at the time when internal migration first began in Turkey. As a result, it was not uncommon for family members to be apart temporarily. However, until recent times the wife and children would have lived with or near family relatives. The transformation ushered in with emigration was that the movement this time included single and married women leaving

Figure 4.2. The Power of Tradition

behind families or children and going to work abroad. Also new was the situation whereby some of the women left behind continued to live and manage their lives and families alone. It was these women who determined what happened to the savings being sent home by their husbands abroad.

In the 1970s the right to unify the family was based on one spouse being in permanent employment in West Germany and able to secure adequate living accommodations for the family. In situations where the female spouse had been the first migrant, the husband was considered to be entering the country under her protection, and in doing so, to be accepting that he had to learn from his wife. By the time this process had been completed, relations between man and wife had irreversibly altered. In this situation, the wife had in effect also become the family breadwinner, and the husband, the child-minder. Indeed, during these years no small number of male Turkish migrants abroad petitioned local Turkish representatives and Turkish governments to ban the export of female labor. Inasmuch as these petitions may be seen as the desire of individuals, they may also be seen as the result of the propaganda of religious or conservative political parties.

Of one fact there can be no doubt: extraordinary changes came about in the lives of women who engaged in the process of migration, whether from rural or urban backgrounds, and these changes continue to this day. The beginnings of these changes take us back to 1963, the year when the migration movement began to accelerate. In my research of that year, female migrant workers revealed their envy of the status of German females in the family, and their equal rights with their husbands and in the workplace. Almost 39 percent of female respondents expressed the belief that because German women were better educated, they brought up their children better. In the same research, however, 27 percent of male respondents were of the opinion that the German family structure was wrong and deserving only of contempt. The Turkish females, however, admired the structure and came to the conclusion that it was female freedom within the family that made the German family model so successful. More than 29 percent of those from towns and 25.4 percent from villages were of the opinion that better care of children and more compatible female-male relations were closely linked to the status of the women.[8]

In general, it may be said that Turkish female workers adapted more easily than males to what were, for them, the extraordinary and often intolerant surroundings in which they found themselves abroad. One reason for this, as mentioned above, may be that the women had been brought up in traditional family surroundings, in situations which had always called for the skill to adapt.

[8] Abadan-Unat, *BatıAlmanya'daki İşçileri ve Sorunları*, 202–204.

Figure 4.3. On the Way to Integration

Women's Economic Participation and Control of the Family Budget

Apart from the women's openness to new values and rules, their participation in the economy also affected the structure of the migrant family. Although the decision as to who would be invited for long or short visits from the homeland had always been determined by the husband in traditional families, ever greater numbers of those women who were in full-time employment began to avail themselves of their legal right to bring whichever family member they wished to the country of settlement, regardless of their husband's wishes in the matter. Indeed, some women took in individuals from outside the immediate family in order simply to save on rent and other living expenses. It must be remembered that all these activities by women meant that many traditional rules were being turned on their heads.

Among Turkey's lower income urban classes the head of the household is usually the male. In rural areas, although the women are expected to participate fully in production, it is the husband only who communicates between the family and the market. Cracks began to appear in this structure when females began to engage in emigration. In a 1975 research project completed in Berlin by Ayşe Kudat, the chief source of argument between working husbands and wives was the manner in which the family income would be spent.[9] Another source of conflict was the opening of separate bank accounts. Women applying to the accounts department in their place of employment to have their pay transferred to separate bank accounts proved to be an enormous shock to their husbands' authority, and this internal change in the power structure of the family more often than not led to friction.

The usage of money in shared savings accounts also led to attrition and misunderstanding, and serious conflict arose from the husbands behaving according to tradition and registering only in their own name property or other assets that were acquired using this money.

All these forms of conflict led the way to changes in the structure of marriages, out of which emerged new types of families in which the women, according to their degree of emancipation, desired to participate in any problems or challenges facing the family and in the creation of solutions.

Girls Becoming "Surrogate Mothers"

For separated families the greatest concern of the parents was the children left behind with family relatives or in social care facilities, while for families who were together, the children's care fell to the older daughters. It may generally be said that those who lost most in this situation were these girls of school-going age who, with both parents working, became the full-time minders of the younger family members. This of course meant that they were deprived almost completely of any opportunity to participate in formal education. In situations where either parent had gone abroad and was not in a position to provide the family with income, girls of eleven or twelve—and sometimes even younger—found themselves shouldering all the responsibilities that had hitherto been their mother's in rearing younger children, often in an alien environment. Living with such a burden at an age when they were neither physically nor emotionally ready to do so brought great psychological pressure to bear on these girls, many of whom, even though they were in the homeland, received little of the support or help that would have been expected from neighbors or family.

Mehrlaender[10] tells us that among foreigners in West Germany the largest families were to be found among the Turks: 18 percent of Turkish families had two children, 29 percent had three, 16 percent had four, 10 percent had five,

[9] Ayse Kudat, *Stabilitaet und Veraenderung der türkischen Familie* [Stability and Change in the Turkish Family at Home and Abroad: Comparative Perspectives] (Berlin: Wissenschaftszentrum, 1975), pre-print series nos. 75–76, 87.

[10] Ursula Mehrlaender, *Soziale Aspekte der Auslaenderbeschaetigung* (Bonn: Verlag Neue Gesellschaft, 1974), 207.

and 6 percent had six or more. This situation changed dramatically when the West German government amended income tax laws and decided to make child subsidy payments in equal amounts to all German residents regardless of national origin. The oil crisis of the early 1970s and the resulting halt to foreign labor imports had been expected to slow down and even decrease foreign worker population growth, but the result was entirely the opposite, and the changes to the law and increasing family unification brought about what can only be described as a "child rush."[11] One result was even more responsibility being placed on the shoulders of the older daughters of the family, with parents often deliberately not sending them to school so that they could be the caretakers in families that were growing larger.

At this point we must also add that other changes were occurring in the norms governing girls working outside the family. Although in Turkey, families from the lower economic classes would not consider sending their young females out to work for fear of dishonor or shame being brought on the individual herself and thus on the family, and such jobs as cleaning or factory work would be done by the mother, abroad, this rule was cast aside as soon as a relatively well-paid job could be found for the young females. The young women going out to work—these were generally aged between eighteen and twenty-five years—are in a different category than the younger girls taking care of siblings, yet there is an important similarity between the two: For economic reasons the young girls and women of both groups gave up on formal schooling at an early age and found themselves living in highly industrialized societies in which much importance was placed on education. This new situation of young women entering employment abroad naturally became a mechanism in the breaking down of the tradition that young unmarried girls remain inside the home.

As it became clear that young women's savings amounted to not insignificant sums, some rural Anatolian families found it acceptable for their young daughters to emigrate. It is easy to understand why some of these young women suffered from personal problems in the new relaxed environment abroad, when one considers that they were leaving a society in which their lives were under strict social control and where they were not permitted to go outside the home unaccompanied. However, given that almost all of these young female foreign workers were housed in communal living quarters (*Heim*), where their relationships with males outside work were strictly controlled, it would be overly optimistic to think that individual freedom granted them more independence of character. Although it is true to say that communal living and

[11] Abadan-Unat, ed., *Turkish Workers in Europe 1960–1975,* 35. The reason for amendments to the law was that in 1973, 60.3 percent of all child subsidy payments were being made to Turkish migrant worker families. From 1975 onwards, payments for children resident outside Germany were set between 10–75 DM per month and payments for children in Germany at 50–120 DM per month.

working in industry brought great changes to the lives of these young women, these were not of sufficient duration to bring about any lasting mental process of emancipation. Today, *Heims* no longer exist, but social and family pressures linger on in the lives of young Turkish women.

There is one more issue that must be taken into account here. In situations where pathways to communication within the family are more open, it is easier for both younger and older members to come to accept changes in social rules. In societies in which gender-based difference is at the fore and especially

Figure 4.4. Migrants Are Consumers

where the natural pathways to communication among family members are inadequate, intergenerational conflict becomes more pronounced. For some of the young women leaving Turkey, it is little surprise that their inability to express their problems in either Turkish or the language of the accepting country should have led to unhappiness. Migration then was responsible for laying obstacles in the way of personal interaction, or, in other words, for blocking the channels of communication within the family.

Savings and Investment Preferences

In 1970, detailed research of the State Planning Organization indicated that migrant women of urban origin showed the least preference for saving money (35 percent). Age played also a role: women over thirty-five were saving more (53 percent), and in terms of education, the illiterates (56 percent) had the highest rate of saving. In terms of consumption, female workers (38 percent) put their savings into the purchase of a car with the intention of obtaining the right of import and then later reselling it on the market. This consumption pattern changed as soon as an automobile industry began to develop in Turkey in the mid-1960s.

These trends shows that female workers tended to invest in what was most easily and readily available, and had as their main aim fulfillment of their immediate wishes. It was through conspicuous consumption that they provided evidence of their upward mobility. This accounts for their relatively low levels of savings compared to male migrants. It also reveals that their interest in working abroad lay not in having the opportunity to save, but also in the chance to provide a better standard of living for themselves. Women, in speaking of the opportunity to enjoy themselves and travel—desires hardly ever expressed by male workers—were expressing also a growing feeling of self-confidence.

Today the second and third generations of migrant workers do only partly invest in their birthplaces. If any investment in housing occurs, the location is rather the nearby town or preferably the capital of the district they come from. Research on saving and investment patterns indicates that the majority of Turkish migrants in Europe, after having decided to settle down abroad, are opting for an investment in housing where they work and live. Investment in Turkey is now oriented toward second home purchases in tourist seaside regions along the Mediterranean or the Black Sea.

The Effect of Migration on Women in the Homeland

External migration entails a new form of living, and this irreversible process presents challenges not only for those engaging in migration but also for those left behind in the villages and towns. Although migrant workers are viewed as marginal groups in the countries of acceptance, in the homeland they are regarded as having successfully engaged in a process of social mobility, and as a result their status in the community has altered. In the 1975 research completed in Boğazlıyan and other villages in Yozgat, of 127 migrants who had returned permanently, 18 percent considered themselves members of the upper lower class; 44 percent, members of the middle class; and 18 percent, members of the upper middle class. Sixteen percent felt that emigration had afforded them no opportunity for upward social mobility. There can be little doubt that such consciousness of new social status must also have affected the family members remaining in the villages and towns whose family members were abroad. One woman, interviewed in the course of the Boğazlıyan research, who had two sons working in Holland, said: "I could never have gone into the grocery shop in the village. Now, if I wanted to, I could buy anything they have."

Today intra-European and even intercontinental migration movements have one important characteristic: in comparison to previous centuries when millions left their homelands never to return or, in many cases, make contact again, today's migrant workers maintain contact with their past. This, of course, has become much easier for those involved in growing migrant worker movements because of the rapid growth of mass communications and transport, especially in the post-World War II period. In the Boğazlıyan research it was discovered that of 113 workers who had been abroad for seven years or more, eighty-four had visited their village at least five times—evidence of how international migrants succeed in maintaining strong ties with family.

In all village and towns subject to high levels of emigration, new social divisions were evident. All family members working abroad, regardless of country, were "ones from Germany," and those staying at home were "locals." The former generally resided in relatively big houses, often brightly painted, which they had built themselves on the outskirts of the town or village. These houses were also distinctive in that their gardens were surrounded by metal railings and the windows had either iron grilles or shutters. Thus, they were easy to distinguish, and were also evidence of the extent to which the concept of property occupied the minds of their owners.

Decision-Making and Authority

The decision-making process in villages generally centered on a number of known subjects such as choice of crop and livestock, cash spending, and marriage. Until recent times, in Turkish village families, of a nuclear or extended structure, tradition dictated that the husband had the final word. This supremacy, an expression of a hierarchical structure, was first and foremost awarded to the eldest male member of the family, followed, in his absence, by the eldest son. Migration, of course, brought major change to this structure, and placed many women with little or no education or experience with such a world in positions of authority.

In local post offices and banks, as the natural head of the now fragmented family, they became the primary handlers of the money being sent home from abroad. As family needs dictated, they would withdraw either all or part of the money from savings accounts. This marked the beginning of a period of new and important interactions in their lives, with many coming into contact with state institutions for the first time through their dealings with the local post office or through applying for official identity papers. They would never have had to participate in such areas of activity in their previous lives. For families with land it was these women also who now had to decide what was to be done and by whom. Furthermore, in the case of nuclear families, their authority over the children was no longer a subject to be disputed by other members such as husbands or mothers-in-law.

In the extended family, women's contact with the outside world was rare and education was considered to have no function in women's lives. These women, however, suddenly burdened with the new role of head of the house

TABLE 4.2.
Involvement in decsion-making processes in Boğazlıyan according to typology of family (%)

	Nuclear family	*Extended family*	*Total families*
Financial decisions			
Household male	7.0	34.0	17.0
Male outside household	7.0	2	5.0
Senior female in family	5.0	18.0	10.0
Wife of migrant	68.0	28.0	54.0
Other	6.0	11.0	8.0
Invalid responses	7.0	7.0	7.0
	100.0	100.0	100.0
Other important decisions			
Household male	9.0	43.0	22.0
Male outside household	28.0	8.0	21.0
Senior female in family	6.0	23.0	12.0
Wife of migrant	50.0	20.0	39.0
Other	4.0	2.0	4.0
Invalid responses	2.0	3.0	3.0
	100.0	100.0	100.0

Source: N. Abadan-Unat et al., *Göç ve Gelişme* (Migration and Development). Ankara, Turkey: SBF, Table 9.1.1, 1975, 358.

while their husbands were abroad, became aware of the importance of literacy and education and began to voice their desire for their daughters to have an education.

Other important areas of decision-making such as choice of school and the right of exercising the vote gradually became the monopoly of the wives in the homeland. It is worth noting that in the Boğazlıyan research, of 373 family members left at home, 293 (78 percent) were female, and of these only 16 percent consulted with other family members or neighbors in school registration for their children. Likewise, it's worth mentioning the educational desires that mothers who had been in formal education themselves had for their daughters:

TABLE 4.3.
Preferences for girls' education among families remaining in Turkey (%)

Primary school only	23.0
Qur'an courses only	—
Middle school and vocational school	13.0
University	18.0
According to the girls' wishes	23.0
Lack of any necessity for girls to be schooled	1.0
	100.0

Kaynak: Bogazliyan field research, 1975, unpublished findings

Another interesting revelation of the research was that at election time only 7 percent of husbands were sending orders home by post concerning the family votes, and 84 percent of the women decided for themselves as to which political party would get their vote.

In both rural and urban regions of Turkey, the most visible effect of the migration movement was the importance placed on conspicuous consumption. As Thorstein Veblen pointed out, "not a single social class, even the poorest, was willing to give up on the tradition of conspicuous consumption."[12] Data gathered in social research reveals that for women who had a regular income at their disposal, independence in decisions as to the disposal of that money constituted the greatest of the new freedoms that entered their lives. It is precisely in this context that we may to refer to the concept of "pseudo-emancipation," meaning that instead of constituting any real emancipation, this money and the disposal of it simply represented a kind of escape mechanism. This is closely related to social mobility. Family members of those who

[12] Thorstein Veblen, *The Theory of the Leisure Class: An Economic Study of the Institutions* (New York: Penguin, 1979), 89.

had migrated greatly desired to create an image that would reflect their new wealth and higher status in the community. This resulted in such things as the appearance in village homes of hitherto unknown "parlors," furnished in imitation of urban life, and the purchase of televisions and other electrical appliances and tools in villages that had no electricity. Also added to the list would have been other cheap and gaudy furniture and carpet purchases. Machine-made wall hangings imported from Europe became objects of preference whereas the traditional arts of hand-weaving carpet and *kilim* making were left to extinction.

Accompanying this trend of conspicuous consumption was a growing avoidance of time- and energy-consuming farm work, for example rearing sheep. Young girls of marriageable age continued with the tradition of preparing their dowry chest, but the once-treasured handcrafted clothing and house decoration were replaced almost entirely by synthetically made, purchased items.

In conclusion, the movement of female workers from regions in which high structural unemployment existed into urban workplaces of industrialized countries did not always give rise to a gradual movement towards emancipation. The alternatives adopted by migrant women at home or abroad were not exclusively taken on the basis of individual or familial preferences, but as a by-product of the policies shaping the international migration process. Furthermore, female emigration resulted in widespread breakdown of the extended family structure and a marked increase in nuclear family living. In the event of permanent return to the homeland, this situation brought about certain changes in important duties such as income generation, savings, investment, and spending. These changes in family life may also be observed in the enormous transformation in the attitudes and value judgments of young women towards education. This was often the cause of tension within the family and, in becoming open conflict, sometimes resulted in separation. Without doubt the older female children were affected by this process the most, as they had to take on the responsibilities that would naturally have belonged to the mother. The high levels of mobility (both male and female) and family fragmentation seen in migrant families meant that males and females had to cooperate in the decision-making process. This cooperation reached its highest level in family enterprises abroad, where husband and wife were acting like partners. This cooperation generally came to an end with permanent return to the homeland, where women preferred to act as housewife. (However, the number of women with vocational training and higher education in Europe is constantly increasing. This new type of woman is no longer the female migrant but a citizen of the respective country, with an outspoken individual outlook.)

The participation of women in the industrial and service sector, particularly those from rural backgrounds who had been subject to a traditional upbringing, in some cases resulted in their isolation and a strengthening of their traditional values and judgments: women working as part-time cleaners especially had little if any contact with anyone in their work environment. Factors such as full-time employment and union membership constituted important variables in terms of social interaction in the workplace.

Migration does not logically lead to emancipation of women, understood as liberation from social pressures that hinder individual independence and self-realization. Emancipation requires increased redistribution of roles and role-sharing within the family and during leisure time. As a dimension of modernization, migration had a dual effect: Although it contributed to emancipation of the female, it also created a climate of "pseudo-emancipation," represented by an increase in purchasing power only. Limited structural change is therefore reflected in the limited change in the spectrum of individual behavior.

The attitudinal changes detailed above apply to the period of 1970–1990. Later Turkey's fast program of industrialization led to the shrinking of the agrarian sector and the role villages played in the economy. Nevertheless the position and preferences of women with regard to migrating retained a continuous character. Women were eager to achieve a greater degree of independence and hoped to consolidate this freedom by moving to Europe. In recent years, the completion of integration courses and language courses in French or Flemish before getting permission to move to Belgium has become compulsory for newly married non-European couples.[13] This obligation has motivated more ambitious and training-oriented young women to go abroad, whereas young men who marry a girl abroad usually are more eager to obtain a job than to integrate into the new society where they now live.

Migrant Women of the Second and Third Generation

Although the major characteristics of migrant women during the years following the halt in 1974 of recruitment tended to indicate a uniform aspect of women with a rural background, most of them uneducated, lacking professional skills, and having no language knowledge, the situation after the millennium has remarkably changed. The situation has become differentiated, both among the generations and even within one generation. At present, in all European countries with large immigrant populations, there are well-educated migrant women with adequate incomes as well as migrant women without schooling and occupational qualifications. This last group, which has no chance to enter

[13] Christiane Timmerman, "Gender Dynamics in the Context of Turkish Marriage Migration: The Case of Belgium," *Turkish Studies* 7, no. 1 (2006): 125–143.

the labor market, has little hope for improving their situation. Likewise there are numerous migrant women who are intensively participating in the associative and political life of the receiving country, but again there are others who are deliberatively isolating themselves, retreating into their respective ethnic group.

Although the second and third generations of Turkish women who grew up in countries such as Germany, the Netherlands, and Belgium have specific and diversified demands on the government of their new country, such as mother tongue education, recognition of their mother tongue as secondary foreign language, and more, European public opinion still retains its prejudices concerning Turkish women. They are considered as being subjugated by their fathers or husbands, uneducated, and devoid of personal independence. But this stereotyped picture is inadequate. A comprehensive study carried out in Nordrhein-Westfalen, where over 627,000 Turks and 228,000 naturalized Turks are living, and which is thus a representative sample for other European states as well, illuminates the following new information:

- Thirty-three percent of young women between eighteen and twenty-nine have a profession; 50 percent are unmarried; and two-thirds are disposing of a regular personal income. The percentage of professional, educated Turkish women (22.7 percent) is higher than their male counterparts (15.7 percent). Nearly 21 percent are in training, and 7.4 percent are attending university. These percentages show that young Turkish women are more oriented toward educational performance and acquisition of language. Two-thirds of women under thirty are conversing with ease in German. Their inclusion in the labor market indicates that 20 percent are full-time, 13.6 percent part-time, and 5.2 percent occasionally employed. However, there are still 60.6 percent of women who are outside the labor market, being solely housewives.
- Again, young Turkish women are up to 92.3 percent highly satisfied with their new country. In regard of their future-oriented plans, 57 percent do not want to return to Turkey; 11 percent are undecided; and only 32 percent think about a return. In terms of self-definition, up to 6.7 percent of Turkish women under thirty consider themselves as traditional, 58.3 percent as belonging to two cultures, and 35 percent as being modern.
- Half of these young women have steady contacts with German coworkers, friends, and neighbors. Only one-fifth (21 percent) are living in predominantly Turkish sections of their city of residence.
- The political preference of the second and third generations both among men and women is clearly in favor of the Social Democrats (66 percent) and the Greens (22 percent) in Germany. Again the young generation

acquires up to 90 percent of its political information from national and Turkish media.[14]

Summing up, it can be stated that depending on the economic situation in different European states, young Turkish women who achieved an adequate education are indicating a better score of achievement in comparison to their male cohorts. Fewer are working in industry, which indicates a higher percentage of women in the white-collar category. Furthermore, a large portion of unpaid work in family enterprises is performed by women. The major shortcomings are a significant percentage of nonattendance of preschool, insufficient professional education, and poor housing. A dominant trait of the young Turkish women is their attachment to a double or mixed identity. Today, Turkish migration can no longer be seen as a fixed move from one point to the other. The formation of transnational communities enables the maintenance

Figure 4.5. Marriage Migration

[14] Andreas Goldberg and Martina Sauer, "Die Lebenssituation von Frauen und Maenner türkischer Herkunft in Nordrhein-Westfalen," *Ergebnisse der sechsten Mehrthemenbefragung, im Auftrag des Ministeriums für Gesundheit, Soziales, Frauen und Familie des Landes Nordrhein-Westfalen,* (Universität Duisberg-Essen, 2004). This study contains an extremely detailed bibliography in German.

of vibrant relations between the migrant society and the country of origin. This process contributes to the transmission of existing sociocultural traditions concerning gender relations.

Arranged Marriages, Domestic Violence

The large-scale migration movements we see in the world today often involve individuals from entire families, communities or even regions moving to new lands. This particular phenomenon, described as "chain migration," which results in individuals of the same ethnic or religious origin concentrating in specific localities within cities gives rise to an atmosphere of intense social control. This, in turn, strengthens the tenacity with which the group maintains its hold on traditions brought from the country or region of origin, and becomes a form of self-defense against a modernity that is frightening to the newcomer. This tendency, combined with the extraordinary importance attached to female virginity in the Islamic family structure, impels many families to arrange marriages for their children. In their rejection of arranged marriages some Western feminists have been prompted to liken the procedure to the sale of daughters, and the repercussions for the bride in the cases where she is not virginal, such as examination by a doctor or her being returned to her father's household, are the subject of constant criticism by women's rights organizations. This practice is not only conducted in the much criticized "imported brides" custom, whereby suitable young men or women are chosen as spouses from the homeland; there are also cases where young women born and raised abroad are sent home to Turkey as brides. The resulting unions, based on neither understanding nor love, more often than not result in the woman becoming the victim of physical violence and, amongst many, are considered violations of basic human rights. The continuation of traditional lifestyle by its very nature means the continuance of the patriarchic family structure, and for some women involved in these arranged marriages and their often violent consequences, the end may be suicide or honor killings. Difference in values and religion are both factors that compound the problem of violence towards women, with many males taking as their understanding of multiculturalism the right to apply practices from the country of origin such as polygamy, female circumcision, and unilateral divorce.

Marriage Migration

Arranged marriages are usually preferred by conservative families, who believe that brides from the homeland are culturally "pure" and thus capable of raising "better educated" children. Recent surveys indicate that 48 percent of French-Turks, 40 percent of German-Turks, and 35 percent of Belgian Turks are not against the idea of arranged marriages. It is estimated that each year 17,000 brides and bridegrooms come from Turkey to Germany and 1,300 to Belgium.[15] Şebnem Akçapar lists the major reasons as including: (1) increasing restrictions on family unification in the West since the 1970s; (2) continued arranged marriages and endogamy within Turkish society; (3) continued solidarity networks between transnational subjects and their kin in the homeland; (4) the high number of young men expecting a better life abroad as well as parents who are willing to benefit from marrying their daughters to a young man residing abroad; and (5) concern about raising new generations within a pure culture—something that imported brides are expected to bring with them from Turkey.[16]

Female newcomers in particular find themselves completely dependent on their husband and/or his family because their traditionally dependent role is further enhanced by their lack of knowledge of the host society. However, often these women from Turkey came to Europe with the expectation of realizing their hopes for more independence. This urge for more freedom can also be detected in the preference of young Turkish women in Europe who desire to escape the too tight control of their families at home. They opt for a partner who is raised in Turkey because they expect that this will give them more independence: the parents-in-law will stay behind and the husband will depend on the woman for orienting himself in society.[17] In many cases the mutual disappointment of the partners and their difficulty in adjusting ends in divorce. Next to the practice of realizing "planned family formation," there are also cases where women are abused, or are subject to physical, sexual, or psychological violence.

Finally the same scheme is used for "fake marriages," where the only goal is to obtain a residence permit. In such cases people often later prefer to annul their marriage, a procedure that is less expensive than a divorce.

The ongoing marital conflicts and the difficulty newcomers face in adapting to the new home country have led to major, radical changes in the ad-

---

[15] Ayhan Kaya, *Islam, Migration and Integration* (New York: Palgrave/Macmillan, 2009), 149; Hayrettin Aydın, "Heiratsmigration bei Türkinnen und Türken," in *Migrationsbericht der Stiftung Zentrum für Türkeistudien,* eds. Andreas Goldberg, Dirk Halm, and Martina Sauer (Hamburg, Germany: LIT Verlag, 2003), 227–299.

[16] Şebnem Akçapar, "Batı Avrupa'da Yaşayan Türk 'ithal' Gelinleri ve Entegrasyon Sorunları: Belçika Örneği" [Turkish "Import" Brides in Western Europe and their Integration Problems: The Case of Belgium] in *Kökler ve Yollar* [Roots and Routes], eds. Ayhan Kaya and Bahar Şahin (Istanbul, Turkey: Bilgi University, 2007), 401–421.

[17] Christiane Timmerman, "Gender Dynamics in the Context of Turkish Marriage Migration: The Case of Belgium," in *Turkish Immigrants in the European Union,* eds. Refik Erzan and Kemal Kirişçi (London: Routledge, 2008), 121–139.

mission procedures of family reunification and family formation in almost all European countries, particularly in Denmark, Belgium, the Netherlands, France, Germany, and Austria. These new legal rules, requiring attendance of language courses and integration programs as well as successful completion of citizenship tests, will be discussed in the chapter on citizenship and migrant rights.

Internationalization of Honor Killings

As we have mentioned above, arranged marriages whereby two individuals marry not of their own free will but according to the wishes of a family "council" composed of the extended family have been known to result sometimes in what are called "honor killings." These killings, heavily criticized both in Turkey and abroad, are considered among the gravest violations of basic human rights. They have recently received much attention from Turkish social scientists[18] and been the subject of a special investigative commission set up by the Turkish National Parliament.[19] Western anthropologists and sociologists, however, are faced with a dilemma in their attempts to scientifically explain such practices as the killing of female children, female circumcision, rape, and the forcing of prepubescent children into sexual relations. Those who adopt extreme right-wing racist ideology view such practices as the part of the "barbaric" culture of the incoming migrants. The same ideology also perceives Turkish, Kurdish, and Arabic cultures as possessing a patriarchal family structure based on violence and degradation of the female. Social scientists who use cultural relativism in order to explain violence against women refer to the fact that it is a universal phenomenon and is triggered by premodern structures. They also believe that some traditions based on violence must be viewed tolerantly.

It is useful here to examine how European public opinion is reacting to the violence faced by young migrant women EU countries such as Sweden, the Netherlands, Belgium, and France. Social scientists in these countries and their Turkish counterparts are attempting to explain these events in different

---

[18] Pınar Ilkkaracan, ed., *Women and Sexuality in Muslim Societies* (Istabul, Turkey: Kadının Insan Hakları Projesi Yayını, 2000); Nükhet Sirman, "Kinship, Politics and Love: Honour in Post-Colonial Contexts—The Case of Turkey," in *Violence in the Name of Honour,* eds Shahrzad Mojab and Nahla Abda (Istanbul: Istanbul Bilgi Üniversitesi, 2004), 39–56.

[19] As leader of the Parliamentary Commission established to investigate honor killings, Justice and Development Party member of Parliament Fatma Şahin held discussions with clan leaders Kuran, Karakeçili, Pijan, Şihanoğlu Binyıldız, and others. The results of the Commission's work was the mapping out of these killings in Turkey, and amendments being made to Turkish law which put these killings into the category of first-degree murder.

ways.[20] Western social scientists are trying to formulate their explanations in a framework of ethnicity and religion in relation to Turkish and Kurdish victims and are trying to reach broader theoretical explanations. For example, they are elaborating on the topics of a non-Western perspective, the value judgments that are a legacy from colonial times, underdevelopment, poverty, and anti-Islamism. In contrast, Turkish researchers in Europe are trying to explain issues such as imported brides, dowry practices, forced marriages, blood feuds, and honor killings by blaming the hostility they see being expressed against Turkey and Islam and examples from their own personal experiences.[21] Marrying someone from Turkey points to the willingness of migrant families to stay in touch with Turkey, as well as to protect cultural values such as honor. Honor is not only an individual value, but also something social and communal. Cultural values such as honor become a source of distinction and difference in a remote land where the diasporic individual encounters the other. Those cultural values can sometimes be considered a resistance against assimilation.

[20] Mary Elaine Hegland, review of "Crimes of Honour" and "Our Honour and his Glory," *Middle East Women's Studies Review* 15, nos. 1–2 (2001); Clementine van Eck, *Purified by Blood: Honour Killings amongst Turks in the Netherlands* (Amsterdam: Amsterdam University Press, 2003).

[21] Necla Kelek, *Die Fremde Braut—Ein Bericht aus dem Inneren des türkischen Lebens in Deutschland*, 4th ed. (Cologne, Germany: Kiepenheuer und Witsch, 2005); Ateş Seyran, *Grosse Reise ins Feuer. Die Geschichte einer deutschen Türkin* (Berlin: Rowohlt, 2003).

CHAPTER 5

Education of Second- and Third-Generation Migrants

Figure 5.1. Educating the Young Generation

> I'm not doing too badly, Kazim; I get close to 1800 a month into my hand. Two of the boys are in a bakery and the other one works with me so theirs is thrown in as well. The eldest one has delusions about educating himself. Go to school and then what? … Wave a red flag in the government's face. He's earning 700 marks at his age. If he goes to school we'll lose that and have to pay his expenses. We're not here to stay anyway. Schooling is for the rich!
>
> —Aras Ören, *Niyazi'nin Naunyn Sokağı'nda İşi Ne?*

The problem of the education of migrant children has remained a permanent item on the agenda of decision-making authorities in Europe since the recruitment stop in 1974 and the increase in family reunions. Until the beginning of the 1990s, Germany as well as other EU members assumed that their migrant workers would return to their homeland, and thus the direction of the education of their children needed to facilitate their reinsertion into the homeland. However, the guests workers remained. The decision to establish themselves in Europe obliged the different EU members to modify their legislation. This became particularly important in Germany, which has the largest number of Turkish citizens. Following the sharp dictum of the Kohl years—"We are not a country of immigration"—the coalition government of the Social Democrats (SPD) and the Greens, which came into power in 1998, drastically changed the country's approach to foreigners. A new Alien Law was ratified in 1999,which is partially based on the principle of *jus soli* (the right to acquire citizenship according to the place of birth). Accordingly, foreign children born on German soil after 1 January 2000 automatically acquire, until the age of twenty-three, German citizenship as well as the citizenship of their parents. However, dual citizenship is only temporarily allowed. These youngsters have to make their final decision between the ages of eighteen and twenty-three. At present almost every second foreign student in Germany holds a Turkish passport. The number of migrant children benefiting from this rule is about 35,000 to 40,000 each year.[1]

It is in this light that the school performance of children needs to be analyzed; however, it seems useful to discuss briefly certain relevant theoretical concepts that will help locate the social position of migrants and their siblings in the receiving society. This exercise is necessary because of recent attempts to explain the academic deficiencies and shortcomings of these children by simply stating "they are from a different culture." Adaptation and integration problems cannot be explained solely with cultural factors, predominantly those pertaining to religious practices. As Elizabeth Beck-Gernsheim rightfully reminds us, the social stratification, school system, and discriminating evaluation of teachers are equally relevant in interpreting the achievement or failure of second and third generation youth.[2]

One important theoretical concept is Hans-Joachim Hoffmann-Nowotny's concept of "structural marginalization."[3] According to Hoffmann-Nowotny, migration produces in receiving societies a new underclass, which he defines as a process of "undercasting": The emergence of this new class enables the native population to move up the social ladder and thus acquire a new status and prestige, whereas the new migrants remain at the edge of societal life. As long as foreigners remain at the lowest level, the children of the indigenous population become the main beneficiaries of the available educational opportunities. It would be erroneous to postulate that this kind of structural marginalization remains an unchanging element of the social fabric. On the contrary, this process has its own dynamic and undergoes constant change, but a marginal

---

[1] Janina Söhn and Veysel Özcan, "The Educational Attainment of Turkish Migrants in Germany," in *Turkish Immigrants in The European Union,* eds. Refik Erzan and Kemal Kirişçi (London: Routledge, 2008), 99.

[2] Elizabeth Beck-Gernsheim, *Wir und die Anderen,* (Frankfurt: Suhrkamp, 2007), 92.

[3] Hans-Joachim Hoffmann-Nowotny, "A Sociological Approach," in *Global Trends in Migration,* 74–76.

section remains in each phase. In spite of the growing number of professionals and university graduates among Turkish youth, public opinion leaders in Europe continue to stigmatize this population, insisting they are unable to integrate. In this respect, Islamophobia plays a determining role.

A second concept focuses on "cultural identity." The consciousness of being different, of having different values and preferences, shapes one's personality. Accepting this cultural identity requires people who have opted to live in a given country to recognize that they are entitled to equal rights and opportunities if integration is to be successful. The first wave of Turkish migrants did not aspire to be integrated. In spite of their low status, they considered themselves fortunate to have been able to improve their material conditions. Returning home was their first aspiration. However, as the dream of returning home vanished, and as growing consciousness of discrimination started to permeate the thinking of the second generation, the decision about which identity to choose became crucial. These youngsters had three choices: (1) they could partially or completely assimilate themselves into the mainstream society and thus escape discrimination; (2) they could strongly underline the tradition and habits of their parents and adopt them, eventually using these assets aggressively against the system, e.g., misbehaving in discos, using physical intimidation; or (3) they could remove themselves from mainstream society and live in what is now referred to as a "parallel society" (this used to be called a "ghetto").

Finally, the role of language deserves special attention. Again the indecision of the first generation about returning to the home country or settling down in the new country played an important role in this regard. Members of that generation did not feel the need to learn the language of the host country. Later, the emergence of ethnic enclaves or "little Turkeys" (e.g., Kreuzberg and Wedding in Berlin and Südstadt in Cologne) created a haven for those uninterested in integrating, and at the same time seemed to secure an alternative place that could generate a job for someone who then didn't have to master the dominant language of the country.

In the near past, migrants overcame their lack of linguistic skills by relying on intermediaries, who were often informal channels for information such as visitors, translators, and established Turks. Nowadays the situation has changed. Europe is covered with satellites with a high number of Turkish television channels, which reinforce the role of the original language. Here the new generation plays a determining role. For them, German, Dutch, or French is the main language, whereas their knowledge of their mother tongue is incomplete. In cases in which both parents work, teaching the mother tongue becomes difficult, if not impossible. Thus migrants are faced with difficulties not only concerning communication with the host country, but also in creating an understanding among the members of the family and the different generations.

The degree of successful integration depends heavily on the school system the host county offers, together with the chances of employment. It is with the help of these above summarized concepts that I propose to describe the educational problems that Turkish migrant youths are facing today. The findings of broad comparative studies (e.g., Program for International Student Assessment, or PISA, reports[4]) as well as single studies all confirm the decisive impact of the school system, particularly if it carries a segmented character, the language knowledge of parents and children, and the socioeconomic status of the parents (i.e., class belongingness). In addition, the fact whether children entered the country after their parents arrived or were born in the country did play a relevant role in the past. In the years between 1980 and 2000, three different categories of children existed. The first category is children born in the host country or taken there at very young age, and who had the experience of preschool education had the opportunity to be fluent in the language of the host county. Their problem was their relationships with their families.

The second and largest group consisted of those born abroad or taken there at a very young age, but who were not given the opportunity of preschool education in the host country. These children began their school years at a great disadvantage in terms of language. In research completed in 1977,[5] 19 percent of children five to six years old and 52 percent of children seven to fourteen years old were being raised by older sisters or other relatives or were more or less left to raise themselves. In homes where the mother was present, the child's lack of language skills resulted in poor communication and prevented her from assisting the child with schoolwork. This group represents a high number of dropouts.[6]

The most problematic Turkish children were those who were brought to West Germany from the homeland in order to reunite the family; they represented the third category. At first, the German authorities put an upper age limit of eighteen on children who could be brought from the homeland. Later this age was dropped to sixteen. As was only to be expected, many of the children in this group, having been born in Turkey and gone through the education system there prior to coming to Germany, suffered a great many problems in adapting to the education system of their new home. In 1981, in an attempt to ease social adaptation for these young people and to give them the opportunity to learn a trade, the Vocational Preparation and Social Adaptation

[4] OECD, *Learning for Tomorrow's World* (Paris: OECD, 2004); M. Crul and H. Vermeulen, "The Future of the Second Generation: The Integration of Migrant Youth in Six European Countries," *International Migration Review* 37, no. 4 (2003): 979.

[5] Ziya Öztekin et al. "Health Problems of Turkish Migrant Workers' Children Living in West-Berlin," (paper presented at International Conference on Migrant Children, Ankara 1977).

[6] Deutsche Bundesregierung, "Weiterentwicklung der Auslaenderpolitik," *Beschlüsse der Regierung vom* 19, no. 3 (1980).

Figure 5.2. Waiting for Mother

Measures (MBSE) project was undertaken. Unfortunately, in the establishment of classes for the training of these young people no account whatsoever was taken of their previous educational experience, only their level of German language. As a result, the project failed in its aims and ended after two years. It is also worth noting here that when it was found that German language skills among this group were inadequate, some of the children were placed in *Sonderschule,* public establishments set up to assist slow learners among the native population. Many young individuals in this group had been brought to a foreign country at a relatively late age, but despite this many were also hopeful of being able to fulfill the high expectations they had for themselves. Sadly, for many of them, the process whereby they would learn a foreign language and adapt to the culture and norms of the host country proved too much, and they became "migrant travelers between two worlds." The case outlined here is a good example of such a life:

> Bülent's father was nominally recruited to work in West Germany in 1969. Bülent had been born in 1960 and went to live with his parents in Germany in 1971 in West Berlin, where he was put into a fifth grade class. In 1972, the family moved to Ulm, where again Bülent was registered to a fifth grade class. When his parents divorced Bülent was sent to Turkey and began working in a restaurant. Following the divorce his mother moved to Munich, and this time Bülent moved there. By this time he was 13 years old, bright and ambitious to learn, but found himself yet again in a fifth grade class. Four months later he decided he could not go to school any more and returned to Turkey. He worked this time in a soft drinks production plant as a driving assistant. In the spring of 1977, he returned to Germany once more. By this time his formal education was badly deficient, but he was oriented towards becoming a technician in the area of automobiles or electrics. His plan, at this time, was to remain in Germany and study.[7]

Family Reunification and Children Allowances

Following the 1973 decision by West Germany to cease importing labor, the issue of family reunification became the subject of heated debate among the German public. At the center of this debate were the topics of education and child subsidy payments. In order to benefit from changes to these payments in 1975, Turkish parents began to bring all or most of their children from Turkey. Until that date the West German government had paid child subsidies in equal amounts to all residents, regardless of nationality. However, in 1975, having had doubts for quite some time about the existence in Turkey of some of the children for whom signed and stamped identity papers were being presented, the government amended the law in such a way that smaller payments would be made for children who had been left in the homeland, whereas payments for children resident with their parents in Germany would continue to remain on a par with those made to native German families.[8] Following this, Turkish parents seized upon the opportunity for added family income without prop-

---

[7] Gewerkschaft, Erziehung und Wissenschaft (GEW) [Teachers' Trade Union], *Blickpunkt; Auslaendische Schüler—keine Chance für Auslaender* (May 1979): 29. No further information is available on Bülent's later life.

[8] Abadan-Unat, ed., *Turkish Workers in Europe 1960–1975,* 35, table 5.

erly thinking through the expense involved and began bringing their children to Germany. With the average German family having 2.1 children, it was not long before numbers among foreigners, and especially Turks, began to exceed this average. So, in this group there were many young people, brought to Germany for family financial gain, whose educational life was interrupted, and who were able, in their observations of life around them, to quickly come to the conclusion that both their lack of German language skills and the strict regulations governing work permits meant that the jobs left for them to do were those least desired and requiring the least skill. In other words, despite the hopes and expectations they may have carried with them on arrival, they were rapidly disillusioned in finding that they too had to undertake the same work as their fathers. Indeed, some suffered severe psychological problems as a result of their deeply felt disappointment and frustration. Some took the road to teenage violence and vandalism, expressing their frustration through aggression; others sought solace in narcotics; and others fell into the clutches of international prostitution gangs.

In general, the girls fared better than the boys, and were more positive in their attitude. For most of them, any job, however monotonous and undesired, meant freedom from the home. However, there were girls among this group whose experiences following their arrival in Germany would later lead to psychosomatic disorders such as anxiety and depression. Among these experiences were marriage at a relatively young age (an event itself which often brought family misunderstanding and conflict in its wake); loss of a work permit in the event of marriage failure; constant submission, first to family and then to husband; and lack of language skills, which in turn led to feelings of isolation and helplessness. The kinds of illnesses that result from these experiences are described as "migrant worker syndrome" among the medical profession in Europe.[9]

Almost without exception, the socialization process among all younger generations of migrants was, to a greater or lesser extent, made difficult by conflicts and contradictions. On the one hand was their family, who wished to transmit to their children traditional values and morals regarding patterns of behavior between the genders, whereas at school and in other areas outside family life, they found themselves faced with different sets of values. This situation was particularly traumatic for those going through the important developmental years of puberty.

Changes have been brought about in the situation of such children and their families over the last twenty years, with the number of foreign children not attending school cut in half, but it must be said that although a significant

[9] H. Benhert, L. Rorn, and H. Fraistein, "Psychische Störungen bei auslaendischen Arbeitnehmer," *Nervenarzt* 45 (1974): 76–87.

number of children of migrant families, regardless of country of origin, attend and graduate from the school system, statistics from 2000 reveal that 19.9 percent still abandon school before graduation. The percentage among the native population is 8.3 percent.[10] This discrepancy, which was highlighted in the PISA report of 2003, has not diminished.

Actually, Turkish parents who migrated in the 1960s and 1970s did have rather high expectations concerning education for their children. The author's research in 1963 showed that although Turkish workers did somewhat distinguish between the sexes, they were very much in favor of all their children benefiting as much as possible from all levels of education. However, they seemed to have assumed that this would not call for any effort on their part in encouraging the discipline and preparation necessary for success in school.

Over the years, as Turkish youth gain access to more skilled vocational training and more of them continue on to higher levels of education, a section of their population will undoubtedly become a highly skilled, dynamic workforce. However, data reveals that in the education process, which opens up employment opportunities in private or the public sector, only a limited number of young Turks have been able to obtain a university degree. In Germany, in 1999–2000, there were 23,762 Turkish students attending German universities. This figure had only increased minimally by 2003.

TABLE 5.1.
Figures for Turks and other foreign populations continuing in third-level education

Year	*Foreign students*	*Turkish students*
1999/2000	175,065	23,762
2000/2001	187,027	23,640
2001/2002	206,241	24,042
2002/2003	224,591	24,114

Source: Bundesministerium für Bildung u.Wissenschaft, *Grund-und Strukturdaten 2003/2004*, Wiesbaden, Germany: Statistisches Bundesamt, 2004. Due to an increase in naturalization separate figures for the Turkish nationals is no more given in official statistics.

Diversified School Systems and Their Problems

There are two main reasons for this relatively low attendance by Turkish students. In many states in Germany the education system calls for students to

[10] Max Planck Institute for Demographic Research, *Migration und Bevölkerung*, February 2002, www.demographie.de.

be chosen as early as the fifth year in primary school to enter the exam that allows attendance to *Gymnasium*, the only type of school at the secondary level that specifically prepares its students for the *Abitur* (university entrance examination). In this selection process, the primary criteria are knowledge of the German language, attendance at preschool and the class teacher's belief in the student's capabilities. In other words, those whose destiny it is to attend university are chosen at a very young age and their teacher at the time plays a determining role. There can be little doubt that the student's identity also looms large in this process. In some states, such as Baden Württemberg, and in the city of Hamburg, the system is different and it is the parents and not the teacher who exercise the preference, but still a lack of in-depth knowledge of the German language and low grades prevent entrance into *Gymnasium* and subsequent success in the *Abitur* examination.

A detailed study is providing insight into the results of this selection process. Although almost a quarter of all Turkish students attend *Hauptschule* (the lowest track of secondary education), only 13 percent of West German students do so. The situation is the reverse with regard to *Gymnasium*: almost a quarter of the German children attend this most advantageous type of school, whereas only 6 percent of Turkish students do so.

TABLE 5.2.
Distribution of Turkish Students across Different School Types in West Germany: 2003–2004 (by percentage)

Selected School Types	*Turkish Students*	*All Students*	*Difference*
Primary School	40	34	+6
Lower Secondary School (*Hauptschule*)	23	13	+10
Medium Secondary School (*Realschule*)	10	15	–5
Higher Secondary School (*Gymnasium*)	6	23	–19
Comprehensive School	8	5	+3
Special Education (including learning disabilities)	7	4	+3
Other Types of School	5	6	–1

Source: Statistisches Bundesamt, *Bildung und Kultur. Allgemeinbildende Schulen. Schuljahr 2003/48* (Education and Culture, General Schools, School Year 2003/04), Fachserie 11, Reihe 1

One of the most important aspects in migrant children's education is their attendance of *Kindergarten.* Among German children there is no clear correlation between *Kindergarten* attendance and later school success, whereas this does not hold true for non-German children. According to a recent study

Figure 5.3. Eager to Learn

of foreign children who had attended *Kindergarten,* 51.4 percent succeeded in entering intermediate or higher secondary school tracks. In contrast, only 21.3 percent of the children who had not attended *Kindergarten* reached the same school level.[11] It seems that German children acquire certain abilities and knowledge through family socialization that non-German children can only attain in *Kindergarten,* above all the acquisition of the German language.

To improve the educational level of Turkish youth all over Europe, three categories of factors have to be overcome. First, migrant parents' familiarity with the local school system—their knowledge about "good" and "bad" schools and about the long-term consequences of certain decisions—is important. A qualitative study about Turkish, Spanish, and Portuguese youths in the Netherlands indicated that Turkish mothers who had informal contact with Dutch parents learned to choose better (i.e., less ethnically segregated) schools for their children.[12]

Second, proficiency in the societal language is essential for a child's academic advancement. And third, the parents' education carries primary significance. Class bias is one or even the major reason why a majority of students

[11] C. Katharina Spiess, Felix Büchel, and Gert G. Wagner, "Children's School Placement in Germany: Does *Kindergarten* Attendance Matter?" *Early Childhood Research Quarterly* 18, no. 2: 255–270.

[12] Flip Lindo, "Does Culture Explain? Understanding Differences in School Attainment between Iberian and Turkish Youth in the Netherlands," in *Immigrants, Schooling and Social Mobility,* eds. Hans Vermeulen and Joel Perlman (London: MacMillan, 2000), 213–214.

TABLE 5.3.
Educational status of Turkish and other foreign children in Germany, 2003–2004

School	*Foreign students*	*Turkish students*	*Turkish—previous year*
Elementary education Preparatory class	4,817	1,999	2,235
In-school kindergartens	8,595	4,267	5,083
Primary schools	377,827	170,236	184,770
Elementary education schools	235,791	111,237	103,293
Multi-educational schools	9,538	2,942	2,389
Middle schools	87,505	38,787	34,590
High schools	90,237	22,792	22,333
Mixed schools (*Freie Waldorfschulen*)	69,899	34,515	33,043
Evening school & colleges	9,316	3,132	2,941
Special learning schools	67,846	28,211	26,489
Vocational schools	194,327	78,051	84,782
Total	**1,155,708**	**496,169**	**501,948**

Source: Bundesministerium für Bildung u.Wissenschaft, *Grund und Strukturdaten*, 2003/2004

of Turkish background fare so poorly at school. As most migrants of Turkish origin are of low socioeconomic status, children of these parents have to bear the brunt of the German education system's tendency to reproduce social inequality more strongly than any other OECD country.[13]

Recent statistical data reveals that the greater majority of Turkish youth are involved in compulsory education only, which offers little by way of vocational training. Many EU countries, and especially Germany, are engaging in efforts directed primarily at parents, many of whom are very distanced from education, to persuade them to allow these young people to become more informed and productive through education. Most employment in the information age in which we now live calls for very developed language skills, which cannot be attained by only sitting at school desks, but must be built throughout daily life as well.

Thus, it is clear that the greatest obstacles facing Turkish youth as they try to enter the employment market in a Europe that is fast becoming an information society are completion of vocational training and proficiency in language skills. The main responsibility for removal of these handicaps must lie with employers and, in recognition of this, on 16 June 2004 the "Vocational Education Pact" was signed by the German government and representatives of

[13] Janina Söhn and Veysel Özcan, "The Educational Attainment of Turkish Migrants in Germany," in *Turkish Immigrants in The European Union*, eds. Refik Erzan and Kemal Kirişçi (London: Routledge, 2008), 110.

German employers.[14] According to this pact, employers and the government respectively committed themselves to making available training opportunities by opening new workplaces. In 2010, out of a total of 58, 400 training places, 36, 200 were newly created.[15] Because these employment opportunities are open to all youths, young German-born Turks face stiff competition in the battle for success, and those who fear this are for the most part employed in an unskilled capacity by Turkish-owned private enterprises.

The result is that young Turks are for the most part represented in certain branches of the vocational school system, and to a lesser extent are gaining entrance to university: from 1999 to 2000, the total foreign student population in German universities was 175,065, of which 23,762 (13.5 percent) were Turks. Of the total foreign student population, 18,988 (10.8 percent) had gained their place by passing the *Abitur* exam, or in other words were *Gymnasium* graduates. In the same year 51,944 young Turks were registered in various institutions offering vocational education through the Dual System, in which they constituted 42.5 percent of the foreign student population.[16] The ten most popular areas of vocational training chosen by foreigners were sales, hairdressing/barbering, motor mechanics, medical technician, secretarial/office work, painting/decorating, dental technician, electronics, wholesale market sales, and plumbing.

As can be seen, preferences are towards what are called "intermediate occupations," those that do not require a great deal of specialization.[17] However, when we consider that in recent years more than 450,000 Turks have chosen to adopt German citizenship, it would appear that the third generation has to some extent, and despite the discriminatory nature of the education systems in Europe, begun to overcome the obstacles in its path. Still, those who have gained entry into the elite are a small minority.

---

[14] T. C. Çalışma Bakanlığı, *2004 Report* (Turkish Ministry of Labour), 48. The original title of the agreement is "National Pakt für Ausbildung und Fachkraftnachwuchs in Deutschland," [Vocational National Pact in Germany].

[15] Nationaler Pakt für Ausbildung und Fachkräftenachwuchs, 2010 (Zwischenbilanz 7. Paktjahr 2010–2014), available at http://www.bmwi.de/BMWi/Navigation/Ausbildung-und-Beruf/ausbildungspakt.html.

[16] Stastistisches Bundesamt, Bildung und Kultur, 1999–2000 statistics, 39, table 18; 42, table 21.

[17] Ibid., 47, table 23.

CHAPTER 6
Civil Society and Islam

Figure 6.1. Civil Society and Islam

> The project known as "Germanizing Islam" wishes to equate the foreigner with Islam, brings religious identity to the fore and, above all, plays with foreigners' identities. Germany has forgotten the Turk and adopted the Muslim. There is an insistence that Turkey become a "mosaic," while the German "mosaic" is being discounted and destroyed.
>
> —Hikmet Çetinkaya, "The Organization of Radical Islam in Europe"

In European countries prior to the 1960s, Islam was primarily viewed as an area of academic research, conducted mainly by scholars in such disciplines as philosophy, theology, and linguistics. From the late 1950s onwards, labor agreements between countries meant that guest workers began to arrive in Europe. At that time, these new arrivals were remarked upon only because of their different physical appearance and race, with little or no mention made of any cultural or religious difference. Initially, among the workers themselves there existed no great or urgent desire to recreate in the host country the social and religious environment they missed, because the vast majority were of the opinion that their stay abroad would be temporary. In order to forget the painful years of fascism and Nazism, Europe at the time was strengthening its civil society, but the migrants were unaware of the possibilities this society would present to them. Aras Ören noted that they indeed failed to take into account that their stay in Europe could be anything more than just a visit or going to work.[1]

In Germany in the 1960s, Turks employed in the same factory or neighborhood stayed in communal housing (*Heim*). The first mosque associations were born out of their demands that one of the rooms in this housing be converted into a place of prayer. These were called *Hinterhof Moscheen* ("backyard mosques"). Within just ten years the situation changed dramatically, however. In 1963, Turks numbered just 27,000 among foreign populations, placing them fifth behind the Italians, Spanish, Yugoslavians, and Greeks. By 1973, however, their numbers had risen to 615,827, and they constituted Germany's largest foreign population. These figures are proof that during the intervening ten years people of the Islamic faith had become a new demographic element in Europe, particularly in Germany and France. Public sensitivities towards this group increased as their presence became ever more visible in changes to the demographic structure of many large cities in England, France, and Germany (in some cases Muslim populations represented as much as 4 percent of the city population), in the ghettoes where they lived, and in the lifestyles they favored. The foreign labor issue then was the means by which Islam became a primary focus of public debate in Europe—a debate that still continues today.

From Transience to Permanence

Following the halt of imports of foreign labor as a result of the energy crisis in 1974, the structure of the Turkish migrant population underwent significant change, influenced primarily by four factors: (1) an increase of their number to 2 million, through family unification; (2) greater numbers of Turkish migrants choosing to stay permanently in Germany; (3) more and more women and children making what had heretofore been an almost exclusively male population more heterogeneous in structure; and (4) the rules of Islam coming to the fore in the private lives of the migrants.

Islam revealed itself in the intense period of association establishment in the 1970s, and became significant in activities directed more towards the homeland than Germany or other European countries. Faced with this situation, political parties in the homeland at the time recognized the opportunity it presented for new platforms of debate. Although the basic rights and freedoms granted by constitutional law in Europe did not extend to giving migrant workers the right to vote, they did allow for the formation of associations, protest activities, and

[1] Aras Ören, *Detschland, ein türkisches Maerchen* (Düsseldorf: Classen-Verlag, 1994).

the right to broadcast, and political parties in the homeland who had adopted a stance in opposition to the secular and unitary principles of the Turkish Republic were quick to seize the opportunities offered by these omissions. Parties of the extreme left in Europe also found support among the Turkish workers abroad, but most interest focused on ties being made with the homeland. Thus, in the 1970s, political parties such as Necmettin Erbakan's *Milli Nizam* (National Order), which was followed by *Milli Selamet* (National Welfare), followed in turn by *Refah* (Welfare), and Alparslan Türkeş's *Milliyetçi Hareket* (Nationalist Movement) all placed great importance on establishing organic relationships with organizations abroad that had adopted an Islamic program.

TABLE 6.1.
Turkish labor and Turkish citizens abroad (1973–2000)

Year	*Population of Turkey (1)*	*Turkish citizens abroad (2)*	*(2)/(1) %*	*Turkish labor (3)*	*Turkish labor abroad (4)*	*(4)/(3) %*
1973	38,072,000	948,531	2.29	14,670,000	735,363	5.01
1980	44,736,957	2,018,602	4.50	17,842,451	888,290	4.98
1990	56,473,035	2,539,677	4.49	20,163,000	1,149,466	5.70
1991	57,326,000	2,857,696	4.98	20,145,000	1,250,964	6.20
1992	58,584,000	2,869,060	4.89	20,073,000	1,313,014	6.54
2000	62,865,574	3,603,000	5.73	22,925,000	1,180,420	5.15

Source: Ahmet Içduygu, *Sopemi report,* OECD 2000, Table 9.

Meanwhile, the Turkish population in Europe had considerably increased. Indeed, at present the Turkish population exceeds 2.5 million.

TABLE 6.2.
Turkish Migrant Stock Abroad in mid-1980s, mid-1990s and mid-2000s

	Mid-1980s		*Mid-1990s*		*Mid-2000s*	
	#(x1000)	*%*	*# (x1000)*	*%*	*#(x1000)*	*%*
Austria	75.0	3.1	147.0	4.4	127.0	3.8
Belgium	72.5	3.1	79.5	2.4	45.9	1.4
France	146.1	6.2	198.9	6.0	208.0	6.3
Germany	1400.1	59.3	2049.9	62.0	1912.0	57.9
Netherlands	156.4	6.6	127.0	3.8	160.3	4.9
Scandinavian Countries	41.2	1.7	73.0	2.2	51.6	1.6
Switzerland	51.0	2.2	79.0	2.4	79.5	2.4
Other European Countries	42.0	1.8	87.0	2.6	130.0	3.9
Total Europe	1984.6	84.0	2841.3	85.9	2714.3	82.1

Source: Figures are compiled by İçduygu (2006) from various sources of OECD and Eurosat

Figure 6.2. Praying in a Train Wagon

Many of the individuals who fled Turkey for political reasons following the 12 March 1971 military coup and entered Europe as asylum seekers sought assistance primarily from these Turkish associations. As a result, the Islam-oriented associations took on more of a political character, and the existence in Europe today, and particularly in Germany, of such a diverse range of Muslim groups is evidence of this.

Major Religious Associations and Communities in Germany/Europe

Over the years the Turkish diaspora established a large number of Islamic associations in Germany. Given the fact that they enlarged their field of activity to other European countries and maintain a dense network, they deserve to be explicitly described.

Union of Islamic Culture Centers (Verband der Islamischen Kulturzentren)

Founded in 1973 and federated in 1983, the Union of Islamic Culture Centers (VIKZ) is one of the oldest religion-based associations. Its ideology is based on the teachings of the Nakşibendi sect, which dates from the fourteenth century. In accordance with its Sufi teachings, members express their allegiance to the association's founder, Süleyman Hilmi Tunahan (1888–1959), with a special ceremony called the *rabıta* (affiliation).

This community chooses not to disclose its goals. Politically, it aims towards establishing a religious state in Turkey. It is strictly forbidden for its members to dress like Christians or take part in any Christian festivals. Its center of activities outside of Turkey is Hamburg.[2] The association is highly centralized, especially in its decisions concerning activities such as opening of branches in other countries. VIKZ is also a member of the *Islamrat der Bundesrepublik Deutschland* (Central Council of German Muslims, or IR).[3]

The Nur Community (Islamische Gemeinschaft Jama'at un-Nur)

The Nur Community has been in existence since 1967. It primarily targets the intellectual or educated. The teachings are based on the Qur'an and the *Risale-I Nur*, the compiled writings of the sect's founder, Said-i Nursi (1877–1960). The sect aims to prove that Islam can be harmonized with modern life. It differs from the other sects and Islamic foundations in that it engages in no mosque establishment and does its teaching instead through educational centers. It acts more like a missionary organization in that it tries to spread the Islamic word. Their German magazine, *Nur*, is also popular among Turkish migrant women as it permits them to enter into religious debates, in contrast to the mosque, which give no voice to females.[4]

The Union of Islamic Communities and Associations

The founder of the Union of Islamic Communities and Associations (ICCB), Cemalettin Kaplan, was sent to Germany by Turkey's Religious Affairs Di-

[2] Ursula Mıhçıyazgan. *Moscheen türkischer Muslime in Hamburg* (Hamburg: Behörde für Arbeit, Gesundheit und Soziales [Department of Labor, Health and Social Services], 1990), 25.
[3] David Westerlund and Ingvar Svanberg, eds. *Islam Outside the Arab World* (New York: St. Martin's Press, 1999), 330.
[4] Werner Schiffauer, "Religion und Identitaet," *Schweizerische Zeitchrift für Soziologie* 10, no. 2 (1984): 485–516.

rectorate to ease the ideological conflicts emerging within the National View organization. Due to his extremely authoritarian, uncompromising, and fundamentalist approach, he distanced himself from Turkey and created his own organization. Kaplan's severe and vocal criticism of governments in Turkey led to his citizenship being revoked in 1984. He was single-minded in his aim of declaring a holy war (*jihad*). He wanted to establish an Anatolian Islamic Federation and spread Islam throughout the world. As far back as 1992, Kaplan declared himself president and caliph of an Islamic Turkish state. Following Kaplan's death in 1995, his son Metin was imprisoned after a trial for involvement in the murders of some members of the organization. After the 11 September 2001 attacks in the United States, Germany's Internal Affairs Ministry declared the organization to be "a threat to constitutional order and world peace" and terminated all of its activities on 8 December of the same year.[5]

Religious Affairs Turkish Islamic Union (Diyanet İşleri Türk İslam Birliği)

The Religious Affairs Turkish Islamic Union (DİTİB) has the highest membership of any of these associations in Europe and functions as an umbrella organization directly linked to the General Directorate of Religious Affairs in Turkey, which is attached to the Prime Minister's office. It has been in operation since 1984 and was founded in reaction to the activities abroad of certain religious associations, engagement with which, according to the articles of the Turkish Constitution, was forbidden within Turkey. DİTİB considers itself the official representative of Turkish citizens in Germany. Its activities are coordinated by the Turkish embassy and consulates, and in 1999 it was operating through 776 branches. Member numbers at that time were estimated at 110,000, and in its efforts to cater to the religious needs of its members, the establishment of mosques was one of its main priorities. Most recently it was responsible for the construction of mosques in Mannheim, Pforzheim, Wesseling, and Neuss. In 2008 it was managing 800 mosques in Germany alone.[6]

Imams who work in these mosques are considered to be employed by the Turkish state and are appointed for periods of five years. They numbered 414 in 1993, and over 700 by 2008. The greatest problem facing DİTİB in its relation with these imams is their lack of adequate education and foreign language skills: the majority do not speak German and are given little if any prior information about the problems that Turkish citizens must deal with in the course

[5] Werner Schiffauer, *Die Gottesmaenner, Türkische Islamisten in Deutschland* [The Men of God: Turkish Islamists in Germany] (Frankfurt: Suhrkamp, 2000); *1995 Bericht* [1995 Report], Bundesamt für Verfassungsschutz [Federal Organization for the Protection of the Constitution] (Bonn, 1996), 10–11.

[6] Gökçe Yurdakul and Ahmet Yükleyen, "Islam, Conflict, and Integration: Turkish Religious Associations in Germany," *Turkish Studies* 10, no. 2 (June 2009): 218.

of their everyday lives in Germany. Thus, they are not in position to engage in much constructive dialogue with the German authorities. Beginning in 2007, a German language program for the Islamic personnel of DİTİB in Germany was undertaken in collaboration with the Goethe Institute.

The DİTİB also supports the establishment of cultural, parent-teacher, and sports associations and aims to bring these under its legal control. In formally representing the Turkish state, the union also sees itself as the guardian of the Turkish Constitution, but it emphasizes its independence of action in its contacts with the German authorities. As in Turkey, the DİTİB promulgates only Sunni teachings and views and has, in recent years, concentrated its greatest efforts in areas and issues concerning women and children.[7]

Islamic Society National View (Islamisch Gemeinschaft Milli Görüs)

The Islamic Society National View (IGMG) was founded in 1976 by Yusuf Zail al-Abidin, who is of Iraqi origin and closely connected to Hasan al-Banna, the founder of Egypt's Muslim Brothers. It was then known as the European Turkish Union. In 1985 it became known as the National View and was known to be closely involved with Necmettin Erbakan, the Turkish politician who became, in turn, the president of the National Order, National Welfare, and Welfare political parties. In a work published by Erbakan in 1973 entitled *Milli Görüş ve Anayasa Değişikliği (National View and Constitutional Change,* he writes of the existence of three political approaches in Turkey: leftist (Communist), liberalist (market-oriented, colonialist), and nationalist (right-wing, Muslim, moderate). He also wrote that of the 2,200 mosques in Germany at the time, 539 were under his control. At the IGMG Congress on 15 April 2001 in Hagen, Sabri Erbakan, who is a nephew of Necmettin Erbakan, was chosen as president.

Following the closure of the Welfare party by the Constitutional Court in Turkey, the European National View Community (*Avrupa Milli Görüş Topluğlu,* or AMGT) reorganized in 1998 as the IGMG. All properties throughout Europe owned by the former AMGT were transferred to the European Association for the Support of Mosques (*Europäiche Moschee und Unterstützungsgemeinschaft,* or EMUG). Thus, the IGMG found itself responsible for the religious and social welfare of its 27,500 members in Germany. The association broadcasts two publications, *Milli Görüş & Perspektive* and *Milli Gazete.* Its headquarters are in Cologne and the majority of its members reside in the state of North Rhine-Westphalia. Today the IGMG, next to DİTİB, has the broadest base among

[7] Westerlund and Svanberg, *Islam Outside the Arab World,* 329; M. Gür, *Türkische-Islamische vereinigungen in der BRD* (Frankfurt: Brandes und Apsel, 1993).

the Turkish religious organizations in Germany. The Berlin branch, with the support of the local senate, operates a television channel, various publications, schools, and hundreds of businesses. One main focus of its operations is the organization of youth holiday camps and courses on the Qur'an, and it also operates two women's organizations, one of which is engaged in activities for women of Turkish origin and the other for German Muslim women. Activities and publications for the latter are conducted in German.[8]

With its reorganized structure the IGMG appears to have chosen to use the "legal" path in its methods and hopes to reach its target by changing institutions from the inside. The IGMG was closely connected with Recai Kutan's *Saadet* (Happiness) Party in Turkey. At present, the *Saadet* Party is headed by Numan Kurtuluş, an academician, elected in 2008. The demands of the IGMG, as with the former AGMT, are directed towards Turkey, as it tries to work towards the establishment of a Muslim state there. Since 1992, it has been working in cooperation with MÜSIAD, the association of Muslim entrepreneurs in Turkey.[9] IGMG leaders, who have said that they wish to achieve their target through persuasion and increased membership, maintain contact with and seek the support and cooperation of various church representatives and other NGOs in Germany. Some German media insist that the IGMG is not sincere in its Christian-Muslim dialogue and has other interests at heart; the IGMG is listed by the German Intelligence Service (*Bundesverfassungsschutz*) as a "threat to German democracy." The IGMG is considered part of a political Islam that prevents immigrants from achieving full integration in German society, and the German Intelligence Service cites anti-German and anti-Semitic statements in IGMG's newspaper, the *Milli Gazete.*[10]

The Berlin branch of IGMG, *Islamische Föderation Berlin,* undertook a legal action that lasted fourteen years, but that, in 2002, obtained the right to teach Islam as a religious course in public schools. In 2002–2003 these courses had 1,607 students, and in 2007–2008 this number had grown to 4,600. At that time the association was controlling 514 mosques in Europe.

The major distinction in terms of integration politics between DİTİB and IGMG is their interpretation of Muslim life. DİTİB claims to campaign for intercultural and interreligious dialogue, whereas IGMG wants to integrate specificities of Muslim life into the German sphere. In fact, the IGMG has introduced the following legal court cases:

---

[8] Gamze Avcı, "Religion, Transnationalism and Turks in Europe," *Turkish Studies* 6, no. 2 (June 2005): 201–213.

[9] Yasemin Karakaşoğlu and Gerd Nonneman, "Muslims in Germany with Special Reference to the Turkish-Islamic Community," in *Muslim Communities in the New Europe,* eds. Gerd Nonneman. Tim Niblock, and Bogdan Szajkowski (Berkshire: Ithaca Press, 1997), 257.

[10] "Organization for the Protection of the Brandenburg Constitution," *Verfassungsschutzbericht Brandenburg* (2001): 145–146.

- the right to ritual slaughter (decided positively in 2002)
- Muslim teachers' right to wear religious attire in schools (decided negatively in 2003)
- the right to have religious education (decided positively in 1984)
- Muslim girls' right to withdraw from swimming courses when both sexes are present (decided positively in 1993)
- the right to add Muslim names in conversion to Islam (decided positively in 1992)
- the availability of Muslim services in social and medical institutions (under discussion)
- the right to burial according to Muslim rituals (under discussion)
- the right to the announcement of Islamic prayer (*ezan*) with speakers (not yet in court)
- and the right to receive permission from the employer for daily prayer times (*namaz*) and for religious holidays (*dinî bayram*) (not yet in court)[11]

A split between conservatives and innovators within IGMG has been observed throughout Europe. This split is also a reflection of the political scene in Turkey itself. The innovators, represented by the present party in power (the Justice and Development Party, or AKP), are underlining the necessity to be flexible and to adapt to German realities.

The German state wishes to deal with a unified body of Muslim organizations, and since 2006 has organized three conferences and created an umbrella organization called the Coordination Council of Muslims (*Koordinierungsrat der Muslimen*, or KRM). The four organizations that have been invited to participate are DİTİB, VIKZ, IR, and ZMD. Given the fact that Muslims have no hierarchical clerical organization, the existing diversity in Europe is not reflected in the new council. It remains a fact that Muslims do not have one voice and are divided by religious-theological, ideological-political, institutional-social, and ethnic-national issues. According to the most recent report of KRM, the composition of Muslim denominations in Germany are as follows: 74 percent Sunni, 7 percent Shi'ite, 13 percent Alevi, and 6 percent other.[12] The newly created coordination council has not incorporated the Alevis, Shi'ites, or Ahmadiyya members, nor are there any representatives for secular Muslims. Finally, it has to be mentioned that radical Islam is shunned from all kinds of formal institutions.

---

[11] Yurdakul and Yükleyen, "Islam, Conflict and Integration: Turkish Religious Associations in Germany," 225; see also IGMG's website, www.igmg.de.

[12] *Muslim Life in Germany*, Federal Ministry of the Interior (Deutsche Islam Konferenz, 2008), figure 2.

Federation of European Alevite Unions (AABF)

Although there is sharp competition between the two major religious organizations in Europe, DİTİB and IGMG continue to operate as a dense transnational network. Migration to Europe has also produced the emergence of new religious identities, which until recent years remained silent and undercover. The increase of political demands on behalf of Muslim immigrants in Europe brought to the fore the existence of a vibrant Alevi community.[13]

Many scholars define Alevis as a heterodox Muslim group with roots in Turkey. Alevi belief is marked by a mystical understanding of religion, the belief in a deeper spiritual message in the Qur'an, an overwhelming love for Ali, Muhammad's cousin, who is revered as the keeper of mystical knowledge, and practice of a communal ritual (*cem*) in which both men and women participate. These distinct features were formed through syncretistic integration of Central Asian Turkish shamanistic beliefs, mystical Islam, and local religions in Anatolia.[14]

Although Alevis constitute somewhere between 10 and 30 percent of Turkey's population—13 percent in Germany—they do not receive any services from the DİTİB. The nationalist and secularist ideology of the Turkish Republic resulted in support of a homogeneously Sunni interpretation of Islam.

Because Alevis live in more isolated parts of the country, they have been eager to move to Europe, and in the 1970s the great majority of Alevis were influenced by socialist ideals. Alevi identity in Europe was quite latent until the late 1980s. After the military junta came to power in 1980, Turkey began to persecute leftist activists. As a large number of Alevis applied to be accepted as political refugees in Europe, they began to organize exclusive Alevi organizations. In 1986, the European Parliament decided to subsidize associations that promote immigrant cultures and identities across Europe. This permitted Alevis to coordinate their activities at the European level. Benefiting from the freedom of opinion and publication, particularly after 1990, Alevis established dozens of Alevi websites and published books. Their impact on Turkey has been remarkable. Today some see Alevi beliefs as a Turkish interpretation of Islam (*Cem Vakfı*); others see them as a Shi'ite interpretation (*Ehl-i Beyt Vakfı*); and still others look upon them as part of a socialist resistance movement (*Pir Sultan Abdal Derneği*).

---

[13] An interesting look at Alevism from a German perspective is contained in Karin Vorhoff, "Die Aleviten, eine Glaubensgemeinschaft in Anatolien," *Pera Blaetter,* no. 1 (1995). Also see Thomas Lemmen, *Islamische Organisationen in Deutschland* (Bonn : FES Library, 2000), at http://library.fes.de//fulltext/asfo/00803toc.htm.

[14] Irene Melikoff, *Hacı Bektaş: Efsaneden Gerçeğe* [Hacı Bektaş: From Mythos to Reality] (Istanbul: Cumhuriyet Kitapları, 2004).

Alevis living throughout Europe became religiously and culturally organized much later than their Sunni counterparts, and in their organizational efforts a major role was played by the city of Berlin, which was at the time trying to bring to life its policy of multiculturalism. Violence against Alevis erupting in the Turkish province of Sivas in 1993 and in the Gaziosmanpaşa section of Istanbul in 1995 left Alevis in Berlin with a desire to more openly display their identity. Strengthened by support from the Berlin Senate, various Alevi associations began to use the media space accorded to them as a means of elaborating on the history of Alevism in Anatolia and explaining how they differed from Shi'ites on matters of faith. The Federation of European Alevite Unions (AABF) expresses its aim as being the perpetuation of the cultural identity and religious values of the Alevis. To this end, it supports the establishment of associations and seeks to have Alevi teachings adopted as part of school curricula.[15]

As Alevis began to organize in Germany, they found that the particular characteristics of their faith—e.g., not going to the mosque, not praying five times a day, men and women praying together, women not covering their hair—was looked upon by Germans as progressive and tolerant. In 1989 the Alevis produced a manifesto. This document defined Alevism as a branch of Islam and aimed to make the demands of Alevis publicly known. In 2005 the European Federation was organized, with nine countries and 184 affiliated organizations. Since 2002 the local government of Berlin recognized Alevism as an official religion and gave the Alevi community the right to teach Alevism in schools. In Austria, where Islam is recognized as an official religion, and because they do not feel that they are part of the Sunni community, the Alevis applied to be recognized as a separate religious community in 2004.

The interconnectedness of the Alevi movements in Europe and in Turkey demonstrates that the European context and sociopolitical forces shape the identities, beliefs, practices, and political agendas of its Muslim residents.[16]

Accommodation of Islamic Claims

State accommodation of Islam has become a pivotal political issue across western Europe. Around 20 million Muslims currently live in European countries, and Islam is now the third largest religion overall in Europe.

---

[15] Tahire Erman and Emrah Göker, "Alevi Politics in Contemporary Turkey," *Middle Eastern Studies* 36, no.4 (2000); Tord Olsson, Elisabeth Özdalga, and Catharina Raudvere, eds., *Alevi Identity: Cultural, Religious, and Social Perspectives* (Istanbul: Swedish Research Institute, 1998), 69–87.

[16] Esra Özyürek, "The Light of the Alevi Fire was Lit in Germany and Then Spread to Turkey: A Transnational Debate on the Boundaries of Islam," *Turkish Studies* 10, no. 2 (2009): 233–253.

Germany only recognizes three religions, Catholicism, Protestantism, and Judaism. They are organized in the form of legal entities and benefit from a church tax that is redistributed by state authorities. The Muslims do not have a legal personality and therefore do not benefit from any such financial help. Furthermore, the Christian Democrats in power are inclined to reduce migrants and their children to their religious affiliation, a tendency that is sharply criticized by the Turkish communities.

The training of Turkish imams who will work in Germany is performed in Turkey. However, the Goethe Institute contributes to the teaching of German for these imams, and the Universities of Frankfurt and Münster offer a master's degree in Islamic religious education.

The above-mentioned Coordination Council brings together representatives of the Federal government and of the *Länder* and the local councils, and representatives of some of the Islamic communities. Subjects discussed include religious extremism, the question of sermons in German, religious classes in state schools, training of imams, the role of women in Islam, the relationship between the state and religious communities, and the economic situation of Muslims in Germany.[17] Because Muslims are more heterogeneous and without any clerical organization, this new agency favored by the German state is not considered representative.

The subject of religious education in schools has long been a subject of debate in Germany. Article 7 of the German Constitution sets out that religion shall be taught in schools, which grants publicly incorporated churches the authority to teach in public schools. Religious education is compulsory until the age of twelve. According to the conditions of the first labor agreements between Germany and Turkey, migrants were provided with the opportunity to have their children voluntarily attend religion lessons given by teachers seconded from Turkey. In practice, this opportunity varied from state to state within the federal system that operates in Germany, and in Baden-Württemberg, Berlin, Bremen, Saarland, and Schleswig-Holstein, these lessons were provided outside school hours by Turkish language teachers appointed from Ankara. In contrast to this, in the states of North Rhine-Westphalia and Hessen as well as the independent city of Hamburg, financing for lessons in the Turkish mother tongue came from the state budget and the teachers were considered employees of the state. Apart then from religion being taught as part of extra lessons

[17] The German Islamic Conference (DIK) was established in 2006. One of its first outcomes was the Foundation of the Coordinating Council of Muslims (KRM), an association of the four largest Islamic organisation in Germany. KRM is not a central umbrella oranization; it only represents roughly 9 percent of the Muslims in Germany. The Federal German Agency for statistics (Statistisches Bundesamt) does not provide any data about the religious orientation of the population in Germany. For more details see Islam Institute Soest, Frühjahrsumfrae: Neue Daten und Fakten über den Islam in Deutschland, 1/2006 (Soest, 2006).

given in the mother tongue, lessons on Islam as a religion were nowhere a part of school curricula. One main reason for this was the lack of any one Islamic institution, among the many that existed, that could have been said to represent all Muslims in Germany. Finally, however, the many Turkish and German associations, foundations, and centers outlined in detail above decided that this issue should be brought before the courts in Germany, and thus it was that the IGMG (see above), brought its case to the Berlin Administrative Court. The court's decision, handed down in 2002, stated that regardless of whether it was a legally incorporated body or a private association at the time of its founding, the IGMG was capable of being a representative institution to the degree that it had created "like-mindedness on the issue of religion." In response, the Berlin city government appealed this decision to a higher judge on the grounds that the IGMG's close connections with a political party meant the decision did not comply with the rule of neutrality set out in the German constitution. On 23 February 2000, the case was finally settled, with Berlin's appeal being denied and the IGMG being given the authority to teach compulsory religion lessons in schools in Berlin. The result of this decision is that this one institution, whose political stance is clear, has been able to strengthen itself enormously through the use of religion, and to gain financially because it too is able to avail itself of state funding in its teaching activities.

The decision was widely criticized throughout Germany and led to a new approach being put forward, namely that lessons on Islam be presented not in the native language of Turkish but through the medium of German by teachers prepared especially for the subject. With approximately 350,000 Turkish children in German schools, the subject caused heated public debate.

France regulates the relations between the state and religions through a traditional system of separation of state and religion, with some exceptions. Religious education is not provided in public schools. France has not accepted the establishment of a Muslim representative authority. However, since 2000 there has been a French Muslim Council, the *Conseil Français du Culte Musulman* (CFCM). The Council, which is comprised of regional councils and a national executive, represents an attempt to unify all the religious and political tendencies existing in the Muslim population in France. Its performance has been sharply criticized.

Like Germany, France signed an agreement with Turkey in 2005 that required the offering of French language courses to future religious officials.[18] The *Institut Français d'Etudes et Sciences Islamique* (French Institute of Islamic Studies and Sciences, or IFESI) offers a five-year study program.

---

[18] For more details on "Rapport Machelon" see US Department of State, Bureau of Democracy, Human Rights and Labor, *France: International Religious Freedom Report 2007,* availale at www.state.gov/g/drl/rls/irf/2007/90175.htm.

Belgium officially recognizes and subsidizes six religions (Catholic, Protestant, Anglican, Christian Orthodox, Jewish, and Muslim) as well as non-religious philosophical communities such as *Laicité organisée* (organized laity). The Muslim community undertook some negotiations to resolve the relationship between the Belgian state and Islamic associations. As a result, elections were held among the Muslim community in Belgium. At the first election in 1999, the representatives elected resulted in a dominance of Moroccans—there were twenty-one Moroccans, twelve Turks, nine other, and eight converts. The second election in 2005 yielded a composition in which the Turks dominated, with forty Turks, twenty Moroccans, six others, and two converts. The profile of these two assemblies indicates that Moroccans and Turks have conflicting interests and are far from setting up a representative entity. The Belgian state does not provide Muslims with any training activities for their imams; this task is shouldered by non-profit associations and some universities.

In the Netherlands, religious organizations are recognized in the form of private-law civil entities. However, the state has not had any financial obligation towards them since 1983. The Universities of Amsterdam and Leiden offer degrees in Islamic studies.

The Headscarf Issue

In France, a heated discussion about the right to wear the customary Islamic headscarf in class produced a sharp controversy. The issue erupted at three separate moments in 1989, 1994, and 2003. In October 1989 the headmaster of the school in Creil, a town thirty miles outside of Paris, refused to permit three Magrebian girls to come to school wearing their headscarves on the grounds that this would contradict the republican principle of *laicité* (the French version of secularism). The Minister of Education at the time, Lionel Jospin, intervened and overturned the suspension order. Eventually the issue became an electoral instrument. In 1993, Jospin, who had become a deputy of the rightist party *Raillement pour la République* (RPR), offered a bill that would ban all "ostentatious" signs of religious affiliation. One year later the Minister of Education followed this by issuing a decree forbidding the display of religiously motivated "ostentatious signs." This decision was sharply contested. In the public debate, the headscarf issue was presented as a fault line between modernity and tradition, between modernization and Islamic fundamentalism, and between *laicité* and Islamism. In 2003, the French Assembly created a special investigating commission headed by Bernard Stasi; the report of this commission called for a full respect of spiritual diversity. In spite of the recommendations for a more tolerant approach, in December 2003 President Jacques Chirac introduced a law proposing the prohibition of the wearing of any signs of religious affiliation in public schools. This bill was adopted on 15 March 2004. For lawmakers, the headscarf was an endorsement of submission, an abandonment of individuality, and a declaration of one's primary allegiance to communal standards, which was interpreted as an open opposition to the republic.[19]

Opposing views that emerged after a series of interviews with many young Muslim women revealed that for many young girls and women the choice to wear a headscarf was an autonomous one taken not for militant, political, or religious reasons, but as an affirmation of identity, an attempt to break up the restrictive patriarchal norms and to become a part of the French public space, combining French and Islamic identity. In their analysis, Gaspard and Khosrokhavar[20] treat the veil not as a symbol of oppression, but rather as a tool for emancipation used by Muslim women to move out of segregated living spaces while observing the basic moral requirements of separating women from men who are not relatives.[21]

Similarly, the debate on wearing a headscarf to school as a pupil or teacher in Germany also resulted in special legislation. The request of a naturalized teacher originally from Afghanistan, Foreshte Ludin, to be permitted to teach with a veil was turned down by the Federal Administrative Court in 2004. An appeal to the German Constitutional Court resulted in a ruling that restrictions on religious dress are only permissible if explicitly laid down by law. Because of this ruling, half of West Germany, namely Baden-Württemberg, Bavaria, Lower Saxony, North Rhine-Westphalia, Saarland, and the independent cities of Berlin and Bremen, have passed laws prohibiting civil servants from wearing dress indicating their religious denomination.[22] However, school pupils are not subject to these restrictions. Since the 1990s in Turkey, the female members of the new Muslim bourgeoisie have been eager to display a new Islamic identity by remaining fashion-oriented while covering their heads. Their choice no doubt is influencing their counterparts abroad.[23]

Islamophobia and Euro-Islam

Migrants moving to Europe after World War II for economic or political reasons contributed greatly to the development in Europe of democratic thinking

[19] Joan Wallach Scott, *The Politics of the Veil* (Princeton: Princeton University Press, 2007), 89.

[20] François Gaspard and Farhad Khosrokhavar, *Le foulard et la république* (Paris: La Découverte, 1995), 204.

[21] For the most extensive analysis about veiling and the behavior of Turkish women in Europe consult Ruth Mandel, "Veiling Modernities," in *Cosmopolitan Anxieties: Turkish Challenges to Citizenship and Belonging to Germany* (Durham, NC: Duke University, 2008) 294–325.

[22] Human Rights Watch Report, 26 February 2009.

[23] For a detailed discussion about the situation in Turkey see Ayşe Saktanber, "Cultural Dilemmas of Muslim Youth: Negotiating Muslim Identities and Being Young in Turkey," *Turkish Studies* 8, no. 3 (September 2007): 417–434.

based on the principle of respect for difference within unity. Unfortunately, as the present century arrived and millions of people of the Muslim faith became a permanent feature on the European landscape, consensus on this issue was greatly undermined and disquiet concerning Islam grew. This concern reached new levels following the 11 September 2001 events in the United States and the 2005 bombings in London and peaked following the cartoon crisis in September of the same year. A product of a Danish cartoonist, the cartoons showed the Prophet Mohammed as a terrorist. Intense protests and flag burnings took place all over the world as a result, and in the minds of the Western public ordinary Muslims became one with fundamentalist Muslims.

Today, it is possible to speak of an open "Islamophobia" in political institutions of the EU and the United States. At first, this term was used primarily in the printed media, but in 1997 a report on Islamophobia was published by the Runnymede Trust. According to this report, for those using this term, Islam has the following characteristics: (1) monolithic, one-dimensional; (2) separate from other cultures, no shared aspects with other cultures; (3) inferior to the West, barbaric, irrational, and sexist; (4) leading cause of clash of civilizations, open to violence and aggressive; (5) a religion that is used as a political ideology.[24]

These stereotypical ideas may be considered a legacy of the Crusades. Several influential factors created such a negative climate regarding Islam. The Republican Party in the United States places extreme importance on the views of its evangelical wing of Protestant sects. These groups and their affiliated associations are highly organized politically and constitute what has been called the "moral majority" in that country. They see an organic relationship between terrorism and Islam. By contrast, the level of importance attached to religion in Europe is much lower: regular churchgoers account for no more than 20 percent of the population, and are only 10 percent in Scandinavian countries. However, right-wing parties in Europe, as in the United States, are using anti-Islamism as part of their populist discourse in order to win votes. Public opinion in the Netherlands became overtly anti-Muslim following the assassination of Pym Fortuyn, the leader of a political party, despite it being proven later that the killer was in fact an environmentalist. A year later, the murder of Dutch film director Theo van Gogh by a Moroccan migrant following the showing of a film made by him that criticized Islam's treatment of women resulted in further reaction against Islam, particularly among those who consider sexual preference to be a human right. Dutch reactions were echoed throughout Europe and gave greater impetus to the growing Islamophobia.

[24] The Runnymede Trust's report consisted of a summary of research completed in fifteen EU countries on the subject of Islamophobia. See Chris Allen and Jorgen S. Nielsen, eds., *Summary Report on Islamophobia,* EU Monitoring Centre on Racism & Xenophobia (Vienna, 2002); see also Chris Allen, *Islamophobia: Its Meaning and Manifestations in UK and Europe* (Switzerland: University of Friburg, 2005).

However, looking at these events from a broader perspective, it is clear that what lies behind Islamophobia is the failure of Europe's integration project rather than any clash of religions. Tensions reached their peak following the cartoon crisis.[25] Although those publishing the cartoons claimed that their intention was to test the limits of freedom of opinion, it is clear that their intention was otherwise. There are specific moral codes that govern the limits on freedom of opinion in Western countries, as may be seen in the fact that it is considered a crime to claim that the Holocaust never occurred. Presently, however, it is not a crime to promulgate anti-Islamic views. Consequently, it may be said that the cartoon crisis is evidence that the West still maintains a prejudiced view of Islam and perceives it as an "object."[26] The West claims that this position is a logical result of the freedom of opinion, while the Islamic world considers it a denial of the freedom of belief. The cartoon crisis also revealed the organizational power of diasporas and their effective use of communication technologies, although it also showed both the power of international politics as well as its weakness in the prevention and suppression of violence. As Oliver Roy has said, reconstruction of communities is occurring along supranational lines.[27] European Islam and its institutions, which are attempting to organize around both moderate and fundamentalist ideas, are appearing simultaneously on local, national, and international platforms. The direction is not towards, but outwards from western Europe, and migrant groups of similar origin are coming together on a global scale and establishing and maintaining relationships that transcend ethnic and national borders. According to Roy, the Salman Rushdie affair[28] played an important role in the

[25] The crisis began with the publication on 30 September 2005 of a series of twelve cartoons in the *Jyllands-Posten* newspaper published out of Aarhus in Denmark. The cartoons ridiculed the Prophet Mohammed and portrayed him as a terrorist. Following their publication the ambassadors of ten Islamic countries requested a meeting with Danish Prime Minister Rasmussen. Their request was refused, with Rasmussen stating that he was unable to interfere because of freedom of the press. The leaders of Muslim associations active in Denmark then went abroad on a series of visits to Middle Eastern countries and asked for their support through protest. Boycotts of Danish products began in several countries, following which, the newspaper that had originally published the cartoons publicly apologized to Muslims on 20 January 2006 and placed the journalist responsible on leave. On 1 and 2 February, however, newspapers in England, France, Germany, Spain, Italy, Belgium, Portugal, and Switzerland published the cartoons again in support of freedom of opinion. Events then spun out of control and became a global phenomenon. Protests were held in Damascus, Cairo, Jakarta, Karachi, Tehran, and Istanbul. In many Muslim countries (excluding Turkey), Danish, Norwegian, and French embassies were attacked and their flags burned.

[26] Burak Erdenir, "Avrupa İslam korkusunu aşamıyor" (Europe Cannot Overcome Its Fear of Islam), *Cumhuriyet-Strateji,* 21 February 2006.

[27] Olivier Roy, "Euro-Islam: The Jihad Within?" *National Interest* (Spring 2003), 63.

[28] The Salman Rushdie affair broke out after the publication of Rushdie's book *Satanic Verses.* This book reinterprets the Quran. Violent disputes took place because of his allegations throughout

growth and spread of this global network, because it marked the first point at which a diasporic issue was transformed into a global phenomenon. The organizers of the 11 September attacks in the United States were educated and socialized in Europe. They were not the product of provocation from an external power, but like U.S. evangelicals, would describe themselves as "born-again" Muslims. They may be compared to groups like Germany's Baader-Meinhoff, Italy's Red Brigade, and France's Action Directe, which held Europe hostage in the 1970s. Muslim youth involved in violence are seeking consolation from what they see as the materialistic values of ruthless capitalism, forms of secular behavior, and discomfiting modernity. Meanwhile, the apparently never-ending conflict between Israel and Palestine, the United States' insistence on maintaining its role as commander in chief of world affairs, and the baseless war in Iraq all serve only to further strengthen fundamentalist Islam.

Despite all these negative developments, it has been shown time and again by public opinion polls that the majority of Europeans condemn provocative publications such as the Danish cartoons, and support the values inherent in tolerance, multiculturalism, and respect of difference. However, such publications, by blaming the "other," cater to the needs of political parties espousing right-wing ideologies. For example, following the cartoon crisis, the governing party in Denmark increased its vote in the next elections.[29] Islamophobia is undoubtedly an essential element in the resurgence of nationalism that is now happening in Europe. Indeed, in response to growing negative attitudes towards the existence of Muslim communities, some governments are moving towards obtaining more of the labor force they need from such countries as Argentina, Mexico, and Romania.[30]

Any debates on misunderstandings and conflict concerning Islam today in Europe are accompanied by parallel debates on "Euro-Islam." This concept has two very distinct interpretations. First, according to Bassam Tibi, in order for Muslims to live peacefully in Europe they must adapt to the *Leitkultur* (mainstream culture), the logical conclusion of which is that Muslims abandon concepts such as the *jihad,* the separation of the world of Islam (*Darül Islam*) and non-Muslim world (*Darül Harb*), and move towards the principles of democ-

---

Europe, particularly in the UK. The Iranian Head of State at the time, Ayatollah Ruhollah Khomeini, issued an order asking for the murder of Rushdie. The writer was obliged to live for years under special protection.

[29] According to a public opinion poll carried out in Denmark on 6–8 February 2006 by Ramböll Management, votes for the extreme right-wing Danish People's Party (PPD), a partner in the liberal-conservative coalition, increased from 13.3 percent to 17.8 percent. *Cumhuriyet Strateji,* 20 February 2006.

[30] Stepan Trokhymchuk and Solomiya Zinko, "Muslim Migrants in Europe: A Challenge to a Social Policy of a State," in *Proceedings of 4th International Immigration Conference,* Warsaw, Poland: Independent University of Business (21–23 November 2004), 75–92.

racy and human rights.[31] Tibi's proposals have been the subject of intense debate, and those who reject them consider him to be calling for assimilation. It must be said that it would appear impossible to realize the conditions Tibi sets forth for Euro-Islam, and such a Euro-Islam has not yet organized in Europe.

The second interpretation of Euro-Islam has been proposed by Tariq Ramadan, according to whom the "migrant Islam" constructed by migrants in Europe must become part of the wider *umma,* or community of the faithful. In this adaptation process, migrant Islam must survive in Europe without compromising on its basic principles and by maintaining its interpretation of the world as divided into *Darül Islam* and *Darül Harb.* At the core of Ramadan's proposal is the "Islamization" of Europe. According to Ramadan, the rights and freedoms espoused by Islam are universally valid. Through Islamization, Ramadan believes that Muslims can free themselves from their "double inferiority complex."[32]

When we consider "Euro-Islam" as a project that is in fact being discussed along the axis of European identity, it is clear that such polarized debate must closely interest Turkey.[33] In essence, this concept emphasizes the idea that an Islam that develops in Europe must be shaped by European values and originate from within Europe itself. Commentators who discuss this issue from Turkey's perspective claim that Islam cannot be confined to a single area or culture.[34]

Only future years will show how the different Islamic sects and groups position themselves in relation to "Euro-Islam." For the moment, it seems that some European countries, in taking a step towards expanding a belief system that is closer to basic European values, will include lessons on Islam in primary and secondary schools through the medium of the language of the country of settlement.

Institutionalization versus Individualization of Islam

Attempts to institutionalize Islam in Europe have consolidated the class of Muslim functionaries who have a vested interest in the creation of religious institutions. Some authors such as Olivie Roy are calling this process the "Churchification of Islam."[35]

In recent years religion no longer has an essentialist stance but rather a symbolic meaning for the third and later generations of the Muslim diaspora. It looks as if this process will accelerate the spreading of secularization.

---

[31] Bassam Tibi, *Political Islam, World Politics and Europe* (New York: Routledge, 2008).

[32] Tarıq Ramadan, *Être Musulman Européen* (Lyon: Tawhid, 1999).

[33] For commentary on Islam as France's second-largest religion see Yves Charlles Zarka, Sylvie Taussig, and Cynthia Fleury, *L'Islam en France* (Paris: Presses Universitaires de France, 2004).

[34] Necdet Subaşı, "Gecikmiş bir Kimlik Tartışması: Euro Islam," *Karizma* 6, no. 24 (2005): 91.

[35] Olivier Roy, *Globalized Islam: The Search for a New Umma* (New York: Columbia University Press, 2004).

CHAPTER 7

Ethnic Communities and Ethnic Business

Figure 7.1. Ethnic Business

Social policies formulated to deal with foreigners end up creating what may be termed an "ethnic" market. As with all markets, in this ethnic market actors compete for the commodities which, in this case, consist of identity and culture on the one hand, and, on the other, the financial resources made available for the development of these. However, the usage of culture here opens the way for other divisions within the group.

—Riva Kastoryanu, *Identity Bargaining*

The ongoing and spreading transnationalization of meanings and symbols through social and symbolic ties in transnational social spaces helps to keep up multifold transactions transversing borders. Under propitious conditions—such as modern technologies (satellite or cable TV, instant mass communication, personal communication bridging long distances via telephone and fax, mass affordable short-term long-distance travel), liberal state policies (polyethnic rights and anti-discrimination policies) and changing emigration state policies … transnational syncretism of culture finds a fertile breeding ground.

—Thomas Faist, *The Volume and Dynamics of International Migration and Transnational Social Spaces*

Migration and Changing Paradigms

In the 1960s researchers in the field of migration for the most part concentrated on the interpretation of the economic theory of cost-profit, which evaluates the results of migration solely by calculating the monetary gains and losses of the individual migrant. In the 1970s, their interest centered on the issues of assimilation, adaptation, and integration, whereas in the 1980s the main focus was on ethnic enclaves, collective organizations, and the interaction the migrant groups engaged in among themselves and with their home countries and their countries of settlement. The fall of communist regimes that began in 1989 resulted in new paradigms entering the realm of western European thought. The search for new models of modernization in the wake of the modernity crisis, the increase in numbers of transnational organizations, the liquidation of the former Soviet Union, and the disintegration of states such as Yugoslavia and Czechoslovakia gave impetus to the debates surrounding conflicts among communities. The extension of markets and the spread of communication networks led to greater interaction among groups representing these communities, and escalated competition among them. This, in turn, influenced migrant attitudes and led to migrant groups undertaking autonomous initiatives and creating collective organizations, and to the emergence among these migrant groups of new networks based on ideology, religion, and ethnicity.

Ethnic Communities

Both ethnic communities that, due to dense concentration, become visible and are engaged in economic activity and ethnic communities that are smaller and less dense and that engage in different organizational forms are playing an increasing role in the restructuring process that is occurring within migrant-accepting countries. These communities' willingness to integrate, or not, plays an important part in continuing conflict between native and foreign populations and discrimination against foreigners. The question of their potential ability to integrate must be approached from two perspectives, the parameters of the policies pursued by the migrant-accepting country and the synthesis of the migrant community. The makeup of the latter is influenced by the type of migration, spatial density, and ethnic and religious differences. The social institutions and the dense patterns of informal communication that developed among migrants as they exercised the democratic rights available to them in Europe merit close examination. These formations may be partly explained by the conditions that brought about migration. Our examination of the Turkish migration movement revealed that, at the beginning, it was based on the principles of rotation and temporary labor agreements.[1] The initial wave of migration consisted almost exclusively of males, the great majority of whom came from Istanbul, Ankara, and Izmir as a result of previous internal migration.[2] Later, however, in Germany and other European countries these laborers who had been accepted only for a short period of time were presented with the possibility of not only extending their own residence permits but also bringing family members, friends, and other citizens into the country through the mechanism of nominal recruitment. At the same time, in Turkey, on the official waiting lists for working abroad, preference was being given to those from rural areas and areas subject to natural disasters. With all these factors being linked to geographical conditions, it was not long before a number of individuals from the same village or region found themselves working for the same company or living in the same city abroad. This form of chain migration was particularly prevalent in Sweden and Denmark and was the reason for the appearance there of kinship-based social networks. Gitmez and Wilpert give many striking examples of such networks in Berlin: a group of 180 individuals from villages in Malatya in southeastern Turkey, comprising 35 families (200 families from the same group had settled in Stuttgart); a group of 550 individuals from one village in Erzincan in eastern Turkey, comprising 100 families; 140 families, made up of 1,050 individuals, from six villages in Şanlıurfa in southeastern Turkey; a Kurdish group from Siirt in southeastern Turkey, consisting of 1,850 individuals in 250 families; and 140 Circassian, Kurdish, and Laz families, all from villages in Samsun in northern Turkey.[3]

Köksal and Alpay's research in Rinkeby, a neighborhood in Stockholm, Sweden, which sheltered more than half of all Turkish migrants in the city, noted that the majority of Turks in the neighborhood came from the town of Kulu in central Turkey.[4] Participating in chain migration not only allowed the old family and neighborhood networks to be maintained abroad, but also meant that the population remaining in the village in the homeland continued to exercise social control on those abroad. The relationships that emerged out of these networks were the vehicle for all support and socioeconomic mobility,

---

[1] Abadan-Unat, ed., *Turkish Workers in Europe 1960–1975*, 17; R. Weber, "Rotationsprinzip bei der Beschaeftigung von Ausländern," *Auslaendskurier*, 5 October 1970, 10.

[2] Abadan-Unat, "Turkish External Migration and Social Mobility," 371, table 4.

[3] Ali Gitmez and Czarina Wilpert, "A Micro-Society or an Ethnic Community? Social Organizations and Ethnicity amongst Turkish Migrants in Berlin," in *Immigrant Associations in Europe*, eds. John Rex, et al. (Aldershot, England: Gower, 1987), 95.

[4] Sema Köksal, *Refah toplumunda "Getto" ve Türkler* ["Ghetto" in the Welfare Society and Turks] (Istanbul: Köksal, 1986), 126, table 22; see Alpay, Şahin and Halil Sarıaslan, *Effects of Emigration: The Effects on the Town of Kula in Central Turkey of Emigration to Sweden* (Stockholm: EIFO, 1984).

and the means by which difficulties were surmounted. At the same time, inasmuch as these close ties opened new horizons for migrants and altered their orientations, they also encouraged the formation of an identity based on region, culture, or religion. The identity problem was most visible in the process of the formation of new families. There were clear lines drawn between Turk and Kurd, Sunni and Alevi, even to the extent that members of the same group, but not of the same sect, did not engage in marriage. Even today, marriage by arrangement remains common, as shown by case studies from France.

Riva Kastoryano researched three different Turkish communities in France: Bellegarde, Metz, and Strasbourg/St. Denis in Paris.[5] Bellegarde is a small town in the province of l'Ain, and had a population of 11,690 at the time of the research. The town's Turkish population of 554 was concentrated in a few streets in the oldest part of the town. They had organized themselves and developed strong ties of solidarity, and local social service workers in Bellegarde spoke of the difficulties of trying to gain entry into the small world these Turks had created for themselves.

Metz is a medium-sized city of about 120,000, of which approximately 3,000 were Turks. Two hundred Turkish families lived in low-cost housing (HLM) in the Borny-Metz neighborhood near the Citroën factory. The high density of housing reflected the characteristics of ghetto living. The existence of these Turks was made more noticeable by their lifestyle: In front of the apartment buildings the females of the families dressed in traditional clothing and could be seen spending their time sharing news of different families while knitting or carding wool from fleeces. The men's leisure time was spent in the corner café, and all three local shops in the neighborhood sold *halal* meat and meat products.

Thus it would appear that migrants faithfully reproduced the environment of their previous rural lives. Another Turkish community, in the Chamards neighborhood of Dreux, was the subject of research by Yıldız Sertel, and the data revealed much the same tendency.[6] Be it in Bellegarde or Borny-Metz, the close social ties among migrants proved a stumbling block to better interaction with the country of acceptance, which in turn served to reinforce their isolation. At the same time, the fact that the Turkish communities in these two towns were of different ethnic origin brought about polarization in the associations established by each. In some, religious problems were of primary importance, whereas for others social and cultural issues came to the fore, and their ideological differences were revealed in the discourse they practiced. The leaders of

[5] Riva Kastoryano, "La présence Turque en France," *Hommes et migrations* (1994): 72–78; Hamit Bozarslan, "Une communautée et ses institutions: le cas des Turc en RFA," *Revue Européenne des Migrations Internationales* (1990): 63–81.

[6] Yıldız Sertel, *Nord-Sud: crise et immigration—le cas Turc* (Paris: Ed. Publisud, 1987), 134–35.

these associations, by choosing to emphasize either "Turkishness" or "Kurdishness," were attempting to prioritize either religion or nationhood.[7] Whether these migrants formed part of the working class or another altogether distinct subgroup has been explored by other social scientists, particularly R. Lissot.[8]

When we come to examine what is known as the Turkish district of Paris—St. Denis—we find that the powerful social control mechanisms operating in Bellegarde and Metz no longer exist: instead of a spatially dense ethnic community, there exist "ethnic enterprises." Turkish labor in Paris is employed in ateliers that operate for the ready-to-wear and haute couture industries. Only 48 percent of Turkish migrant workers live in the neighborhood in which they work, with the remainder scattered throughout various neighborhoods on the outskirts of the city. However, this geographical distance has not brought with it any subsequent loosening in social ties among families, and if anything has rendered these relationships more complex. Although the Turkish associations in Metz and Bellegarde, in their efforts to find a solution to the educational problems of the second generation, make some effort to participate in activities that encourage integration, activities in Paris are purely of an economic nature. Turks living in Paris, in availing themselves of the network of anonymous relationships provided by a metropolis, draw a definite line between their private and public lives. While preserving their identity and culture in the home, they are particularly diligent in avoiding any friction or conflict with their employers. With respect to political activity, the associations here, instead of actively trying to exert some influence over the policies of the country of acceptance, find themselves trapped within their ideology. They conduct political activities only within the framework of the homeland or international organizations such as the Council of Europe and the United Nations. During most recent times, their activities have centered on searches for identity based on a politicized ethnicity, nationalism, or religion.

Social scientists have also worked on analyses that would explain the nature of the ties within migrant communities. Clifford Geertz[9] has called these ties "primordial attachments." In this framework, blood ties, language, and customs create extraordinarily strong behavioral compulsions. Other social scientists define these ties as arising out of the situation itself or as structural developments. Any or all of these theories may assist us in our understanding

[7] Riva Kastoryano, *Etre Turc en France: reflexions sur famille et communautée* (Paris: L'Harmattan, 1987).

[8] For more detail, see R. Lissot, Nadir Boumaza and Ghislaine Clement, *Ces migrants qui font le proletariat* (Paris: Meridian, 1994), 93–104.

[9] Clifford Geertz, *The Interpretation of Cultures* (New York: Basic Books, 1973), 259. See also Pierre Bourdıeu, *Outline of a Theory of Practice* (Cambridge: Cambridge University Press, 1977); Jack David Eller and Reed M. Coughlan, "The Poverty of Primordialism: The Demystification of Ethnic Attachments," *Ethnic and Racial Studies* (February 1993): 188–202.

of the various ethnic groups within existing or newly formed nation-states and the organizational activities of the migrant communities within these ethnic groups. In the final analysis, the important issues are whether foreigners are being excluded or efforts are being undertaken towards integration with them, whether ethnic minorities are being recognized or not, the levels of support being offered to them by local and national institutions, the organizational relationship between migrants and the homeland, the support of the international community, and the dynamics of the ethnic groups themselves. These, in turn, are determined by the policies practiced by the country of acceptance. If we accept that migrant groups are thereby condemned to existing within an asymmetric relationship with the country of acceptance, we can begin to determine what opportunities are open to them through their collective organizations and associational activities.

Ethnic Enterprises

If we use the concept of "dual labor market," as developed by Piore in his theoretical framework, the reason then becomes clear as to why we see migrants doing the most badly paid, unimportant, unskilled, and undesirable labor in urban environments heavily populated by them throughout Europe. Kreuzberg, Wedding, and Tiergarten in Berlin, Saint Josse in Brussels, and Paris's Strasbourg/St. Denis, all of which are known as Turkish neighborhoods, constitute the most striking examples of these kinds of dense ethnic spatial configurations in which economic activity and housing exist side by side. Paris's haute couture and ready-to-wear clothing sectors rely on the cheap—and often illegal—labor that operates in these areas from homes or overcrowded ateliers. These kinds of economic activities have resulted in the appearance of what may be called "niche" ethnic enterprises that are challenging the norms. Originally established as a result of economic necessity and discrimination, one might expect that these enterprises would at some point adapt to and move towards the constraints of general economic and social life, but instead they have chosen to provide employment opportunities based on kinship and community ties. Here, individuals, in choosing to partially join in the culture in which they were brought up, are also creating a selective assimilation model, which gives migrants the opportunity to speak the language of their original culture and to practice of the traditional ways and customs of the homeland. The only demand that is being made of them is absolute obedience to the formal rules and regulations of the country of acceptance. In other words, these ethnic niche enterprises represent a different adaptation model and cannot be considered as compatible with either the "salad bowl" or the "melting pot" models of integration.

Figure 7.2. Niche Economy

In this way, first-generation migrants, without giving up their culture, identity, or internal solidarity networks, and without going through a process of acculturation, are able to achieve economic success. The climate necessary for the development of successful ethnic enterprise is created when sufficient numbers of migrants exist to constitute an ethnic group and the necessary capital and labor become available. Migrants, whether newly arrived and completely unfamiliar with the country and language, or of the second or third generation but poorly educated, can develop a business in such a climate. In this context, we can add Berlin's Little Istanbul to the sociologist Alejandro Portes's Korea Town in Los Angeles and Chinatown in San Francisco. In Little Istanbul, Turks, either in possession of a work permit or in partnership with a local, have created a segmented market centered on food, green grocers, and the restaurant business—a market that simultaneously functions as a source of temporary employment for illegal migrants.

Ali Gitmez and Czarina Wilpert's research revealed that in the Kreuzberg neighborhood, which houses a quarter of all Turks living in Berlin, 12 percent of the businesses and 40 percent of the service sector were in the hands of Turks.[10] Another study noted that in the 1990s there were 33,000 businesses in Germany owned by Turks that operated in fifty-five different sectors and had created 125,000 jobs. The majority of these enterprises were based on food

[10] Gitmez and Wilpert, "A Micro-Society or an Ethnic Community?" 99.

production and distribution: 37.8 percent sold food products and 17.6 percent were in fast food. However, 83 percent of the businesses were not providing any of the trainee or apprenticeship facilities that in Germany lead to career improvement.[11]

The increase of self-employment is closely related to the major structural changes in the German economy, as industrial jobs have been shifted offshore and employment has moved to high technology production and services. In 2000, the majority of German workers worked in non-manual labor jobs, whereas fewer than 30 percent of foreign residents in the labor market had managed to join the white-collar labor force. This shift did not offer Turkish migrants many opportunities, so self-employment remained the most desirable occupation. According to surveys carried out in 1996[12] and in 2000,[13] the most relevant factor in establishing an enterprise is the independence obtained. To be one's own boss is a highly cherished position. In second place comes the expectation of a higher income; third is the fear of becoming unemployed.

This data indicated that the majority of the self-employed are members of the second generation; the average age is about 29.8 years, and about 37 percent are German citizens. Although there has been a diversification in the distribution of activity areas, retail trade still occupies the largest place. In the field of services, there is a larger spread: from cosmetic shops and taxi companies to doctors, lawyers, architects, and lawyers, and from computer and consulting firms to marketing enterprises.[14]

TABLE 7.1.
Turkish enterprises in Germany according to field of activity, 2005

Area	*Number*	*%*
Commerce	22,400	34.6
Gastronomy	16,600	25.7
Service	14,700	22.8
Construction, handcraft	10,900	16.9
Total	64,600	100.0

Source: *Türkei Studien Zentrum-Essen*, 2005

[11] Ilhan Duymaz, "Selbststaendige Erwerbstaetigkeit von Auslaendern als Integrationsindikator," *Zeitschrift für Auslaenderrecht andauslaenderpolitk* 2 (1988): 27–28; Zentrum für Türkeistudien, *Türkei-Sozialkunde* (Opladen: Leske & Budrich, 1994).

[12] Faruk Şen and Andreas Goldberg, eds. *Türken als Unternehmer* (Opladen, 1996).

[13] Çiğdem Akkaya et al., *Türkische Wirtschaftsleistung in Deutschland und in der EU* (Essen, 2000).

[14] Zentrum für Türkeistudien. *Die ökonomische Dimension der türkischen Selbsstaendigen in Deutschland und der Europaeischen Union* (Essen, 2001).

These ethnic businesses, if ranked by the numbers of employees, can be considered an "ethnic niche." The majority (49.2 percent) of these businesses are owned by males between thirty-five and forty-two years of age, who have a secondary school education, and have lived in Germany over ten years. More than four-fifths of these small entrepreneurs, or 87.7 percent, are focusing on three distinct areas: services, trade, and gastronomy.

TABLE 7.2.
Number of employees in Turkish enterprises

Small family business of up to 3 persons	46.5%
Medium enterprise of 4–9 persons	43.7%
Large enterprise of more than 10 persons	9.8%

Source: Zentrum für Türkeistudien, 2001. Migrationsbericht 2002, p. 357, Graphic 2.

Their dominant motivation is the desire to own one's personal business. They acquired their experiences in working in another enterprise. An additional factor has been the assumption that owning one's business enhances the prestige of the person within his own community.[15]

TABLE 7.3.
Turkish entrepreneurs in Germany (1985–2005)

Variables	***1985***	***1990***	***1995***	***2000***	***2005***
Number of enterprise	22,000	33,000	40,500	59,500	64,600
Average Investment In Euro	88,400	88,400	104,800	116,600	114,000
Total Investment In Billion Euro	1.9	2.9	4.2	6.9	7.4
Total yearly turnover of enterprises in Bil.Euro	8.8	12.8	17.4	28.5	29.5
Average number of Employees	3.5	3.3	4.1	5.5	5.0
Total number of Employees	77,000	100,000	168,000	327,000	323,000

Source: *Türkei Studien Zentrum-Essen,* 2005, www.existenzgruender.de

A similar development has taken place in the Netherlands. Turkish immigrant entrepreneurs have increased over time, from 1,895 in 1986–1987 to 5,385 in 1992, 6,561 in 1998, and 9,047 in 2000.[16]

The importance of ethnic enterprises lies not so much in their employment provision as in the resulting establishment of collective organizations

[15] Hüseyin Boz, *Etnik Girişimcilik* [Ethnic entrepreneurship] (Akdeniz University: European Research Center, 2008), 58–59.

[16] Gamze Avcı, "Comparing Integration Policies and Outcomes: Turks in the Netherlands and Germany," *Turkish Studies* 7, no. 1 (2006): 74–75.

and cultural associations, many of which have homeland-oriented political objectives. Turkish meat trade enterprises in Berlin originated out of the wish to provide Turkish workers with *halal* meat (from animals slaughtered according to Islamic rules). These began by distributing the meat brought to the workers' dormitories and later to the workers' private houses. This trade spread quickly throughout Germany, particularly in Munich, Stuttgart, and Frankfurt. Later, there began the import of conserved food products, and later still cassette recorders and video cassettes produced in Turkey began to be distributed in Germany. The real turning point, however, came with the appearance of large chain stores. Between 1978 and 1984, large wholesale food companies such as Helal Gıda, Elif Gida, and Hicret were established.[17] These businesses were not confined to the sale and distribution of food, but also participated in many other activities, including setting up travel agencies, providing funeral services (including shipping the body to the homeland), establishing Qur'an courses, and managing sports club. Thus, as Ali Gitmez and Czarina Wilpert reported,[18] it became possible for individuals to conduct all of their business and social life within the boundaries of the Islamic community without the need for contact or dealings with non-Muslims.

These enterprises also became an arena in which various Islamic factions conducted their religious and political struggles. Both Elif Gıda and Helal Gıda, which embraced IGMG as a base from which to broaden their market appeal, became an organ of the Turkish National Welfare Party. Hicret, founded later, went even further in its efforts. More radically religious in its outlook, Hicret approached the financial circles in Saudi Arabia to obtain credit. Even though bad management eventually led the enterprise to bankruptcy, this did not signal the end of such economic-ideological efforts. Today in European countries where dense Turkish populations live, e.g., Germany, France, the Netherlands, Belgium, Denmark, and Sweden, one may find various kinds of ethnic enterprises, and it must be said that they are a mark of the success of those who went to these countries as workers or businessmen, and with a little capital, savings, and "know how," gained a respected place in these industrialized economies. Such enterprises may be seen as a model for either high levels of individual motivation or effective mutual interaction. At the same time, ethnic enterprises represent a "niche" and, as such, are convenient for use in the spreading of a particular political program or a politicized worldview. As has been observed in many European countries, political Islam has been strengthened through the economic infrastructure put in place by ethnic enterprises, in that this infrastructure allows for ease in the broadening of social relations to include those holding the same views in neighboring countries.

[17] Gitmez and Wilpert, "A Micro-Society or an Ethnic Community?" 105–106.
[18] Ibid., 104.

An event that occurred in 1994 and led to heated public debate provides a good example: prior to local elections in Turkey on 27 March 1994, the public learned that *Refah* (Welfare) party president Necmettin Erbakan had succeeded in obtaining an additional 5,000 visas for Turks to enter Saudi Arabia to complete their *hajj* (i.e., pilgrimage to Mecca). Saudi Arabia applies a pilgrim visa policy to all Muslim countries by which it allows each country a certain number of pilgrim visas. At that time, Turkey's allowance was set at 60,000. Therefore, such a large addition caused much public debate in Turkey. Erbakan's response to criticism was to say that he had obtained the additional visas to enable workers and their families in Europe to fulfill their religious obligations and that his doing so should simply be regarded as a mark of respect and understanding to these fellow Turkish citizens abroad.[19] In reality, however, the situation was very different. Travel agencies such as Miraç, which operated out of both Germany and Turkey, charged each individual $1,700 (U.S.) for the *hajj* tour, when in fact the cost of such a journey was only $1,300. The $400 difference was divided between the travel agency and the Welfare Party.[20] Those travel agencies forced to operate within the constraints of the actual contingent numbers available solved the problem by first sending their passengers to places such as Baku, Tehran, or Moscow and then flying them to Mecca on charter flights.[21] This situation was subsequently the subject of debate in the Turkish Parliament, after which a special commission was set up to investigate the issue.[22]

Sharing in the profits of companies sympathetic to the Welfare Party was only one of the characteristics of Islamic organizations. The company once known as Royal Holding (later M-Y GmbH) was established by members of the Erbakan family and, operating through Selam GmbH, became a leading distributor of vegetable produce, food, and cosmetics to the more than five hundred mosques and their communities in Germany. Management of this company was in the hands of Ali Yüksel, general secretary of the German Islamic Council, and self-styled "Grand Mufti."[23] The examples mentioned above are all evidence of the close links between ethnic enterprises, political parties, and party leadership. Following closure of the Welfare Party by Turkey's Con-

[19] Necmettin Erbakan, "Kontenjanı hayır için istedim," *Cumhuriyet*, 14 February 1994, 15.
[20] Mustafa Balbay, "RP'nin gerçek yüzü ve Hac ticareti," *Cumhuriyet*, 10 February 1994, 17.
[21] Kemal Yurteri, "Dinci şirketlerden sınır ötesi çalım," *Cumhuriyet*, 10 February 1994.
[22] Saudi Arabian authorities exercise a quota system whereby each country is allowed to have a specific number of its citizens fulfill their pilgrimage duties in any given year. Beşir Darçu, a close associate of Erbakan and owner of the Van der Zee, successfully overcame these restrictions by having Turks living in Europe obtain visas through a third country in order to travel to Mecca. This was seen as a breach of the agreement between Saudi Arabia and Turkey, and in 1994 the company was stripped of the right to be apportioned any of the quota.
[23] Erbakan, "Milli Görüş ticaret hattı," *Cumhuriyet*, 23 March 1994, 19.

stitutional Court, similar efforts at organization were made by those abroad who sympathized with the then newly formed *Saadet* (Happiness) Party, in the hope of drawing in those who had been supporters of the Welfare Party.

Ethnic enterprises will no doubt continue to exist and operate. As Saskia Sassen sees it,[24] in today's metropolises, the service sectors expertly managed by migrant communities are the structures or vehicles that guarantee highest profit margins for individual investment. As a result, we see that the restoration of a number of houses in a neighborhood means greater value for the neighborhood, and the desire to learn a language or taste the food of different cultures serves to create a faithful customer base for the owner of an ethnic enterprise. Employment opportunities continue to exist for migrant workers in the ever increasing numbers of low paying jobs in large cities, despite the high unemployment rates among both the blue and white collar native workforce. However, it must not be forgotten that developing ethnic enterprises still constitute the greatest source of financial support for politically and religiously motivated organizations, and it would be seriously misguided to see the ethnic enterprise industry as a sign of any complete and successful integration into the country of acceptance.

Nevertheless major changes are taking place, which indicate that close ties with the Turkish community are weakening over time while new transnational networks are developing. In 2003, more than 60,000 Turkish businesses in Germany employed approximately 420,000 workers in 100 fields of activity. Only 23 percent of Germany's Turkish businesses are in the traditional strongholds of restaurant and catering industries; 35 percent are involved in retail or trade; and 23 percent are in the service sector.[25]

A study published in 2009 sheds light on the important changes of the last ten years. A survey of 150 young Turkish entrepreneurs in Germany indicate that 72 percent of the successful members of the second generation refer to themselves not as "Turkish entrepreneur" but as "German entrepreneur of Turkish origin." Among them, 40 percent had completed college or the equivalent, and 40 percent had received vocational training. They look with optimism to the economic situation in Germany: 70 percent are expecting higher profits in the coming two years, and 54 percent are determined to create additional jobs. These enterprises are shouldering an important task, offering up to 55 percent in-service training, and enterprises with more than fifty employees are extending this training up to 68 percent. Unlike the first generation of self-employed Turks, 44 percent are not employing any relatives. Their priority,

[24] Saskia Sassen, *The Global City* (Princeton, NJ: Princeton University Press, 1991), 315.

[25] For a detailed analysis of the economic potential of Turkish immigrant entrepreneurs in Germany, see "The Economic Potential of Turks: Migrant Entrepreneurs in Germany," http://www.zfti.de/

Figure 7.3. Tourism: A Lucrative Business

oriented toward governmental policies, is to demand that more money should be spent for educating the next generation.[26]

The "economic transnational nationalism" movement is propelling many of these entrepreneurs out of the niche economy into the bigger league of "transnational operators." For example, in the textile industry, Turkish entrepreneurs in the Netherlands or Germany are establishing production facilities in Turkey with the backing of Dutch or German capital, and selling the products on to a third market. In textiles in particular, however, these developments have been curbed somewhat by the recent fierce competition out of China. It seems that firmly established ethnic businesses will retain their original position and dominate certain sectors of the market, whereas newly created large enterprises by second- and third-generation Euro-Turks will go beyond ethnic-related self-employment and perform a different role in the EU economic sphere.

[26] The study was conducted by PricewaterhouseCoopers LLP. A summary was published by the German weekly *Der Spiegel* on 19 January 2009.

CHAPTER 8
Citizenship and Political Participation

Figure 8.1. Voting for Whom?

In its narrowest definition citizenship describes the legal relationship between the individual and the polity. In Europe one of the key definitions of the polity was originally the city in both ancient and medieval times. Today citizenship and nationality both refer to the nation-state.

Citizenship is comprised of three qualifying dimensions: first, the notion of collective self-determination and democracy; second, the legally guaranteed status of equal political freedom and other rights; and third, membership in a political community.[1] Interest in citizenship has grown because of two trends: political issues and decisions extend beyond national borders, and people are perceived to be crossing state borders on a new scale; and the migration process forces people to think about their citizenship. One of the major goals of the migratory process is to achieve some kind of integration. No doubt the final step is the process of naturalization. This aim is easier realized in countries that recognize dual citizenship. However, for the overwhelming majority of Turks living in Europe, namely in Germany, the demand for naturalization remained for a long period unanswered.

In this chapter I will try to delineate the legal requirements for naturalization and demonstrate how, with the increase of demand for highly skilled labor, unemployment, and to some extent Islamophobia, the legal requirements have been tightened.

Naturalization

Germany

The German constitution, the Basic Law (*Grundgesetz*), does not prescribe how citizenship is recognized or conferred, but the criteria are based first and foremost on ethnic nationality. The Basic Law implicitly prescribes the exclusionary principle of *jus sanguinis* (law of blood or descent), with a very strong emphasis on the holistic notion of culture. The claim for naturalization has always been difficult for non-EU "foreigners" in the Federal Republic of Germany (FRG) and has required repudiation of the country of origin. This repudiation of former citizenship still plays a decisive role among Turkish immigrants who opt against naturalization.

Anxious to integrate those foreigners who continue to lead a lifestyle which separates them from the mainstream society, the former German government, the Red-Green coalition of the Social Democrats and the Greens (1998–2002), facilitated the naturalization process for those who had been living for a longer period in the country, partially changing the principle of *jus sanguinis* into a transitional principle of *jus soli* (law of place of birth). According to an amendment in 1991, "foreigners between the ages of 16 and 23, who lived more than eight years in Germany, attended a school in Germany for at

[1] Thomas Faist, Jürgen Gerdes, and Beate Rieple, "Dual Citizenship as a Path-Dependent Process," in *Rethinking Migration: New Theoretical and Empirical Perspectives*, eds. Alejandro Portes and Josh DeWind (New York: Berghahn Books, 2007), 94.

least six years and had not been convicted for serious offences," received the right of naturalization.[2] Furthermore those "migrants" who have been residents of Germany for at least fifteen years and possess a residence permit were also entitled to naturalization.[3]

But the most important change was realized with the ratification of the new Nationality Law. Since 1 January 2000, a child born on German soil acquires German citizenship as well as the parents' citizenship. However, this dual citizenship is only valid until the age of twenty-three. Such children will have to decide between the years of eighteen and twenty-three whether or not they want to retain their German citizenship. They must opt for one of their two nationalities.[4]

Following the introduction of these new laws, the number of naturalizations rose by around 30 percent in the year 2000, compared with 1999. However, this was not the case for the Turkish population; their rate decreased by around 20 percent, compared to 1999.

Kaya cites a number of reasons for this behavior, such as German-Turks being less keen to possess political rights; they had expected a more democratic citizenship law without any limitation for dual citizenship; and they were discouraged by bureaucratic workload. Probably the most important factor has been the fact that German-Turks prefer to retain their diasporic identity. They would like to live on "both banks of the river."[5]

The Christian Democrat-Social Democrat coalition that came to power in 2005 does not look favorably on the multicultural policies put in place by its predecessors, the Social Democrat-Green Party coalition, and is in pursuit of policies that will serve to accelerate the process of integration. The federal nature of the German constitution allows for individual states to regulate their own educational and cultural activities and policies, which, of course, in turn allows the majority party at state level to play a significant role in policy-making. Thus, for example, since 1 January 2006 in the Christian-Democrat dominated state of Baden-Württemberg, Muslim foreigners applying for citizenship have been subjected to what is called a "conscience test" consisting of thirty questions. Two of the questions included in the test are as follows:

---

[2] Article 85, Basic Law of the Federal Republic of Germany (*Grundgesetz*); can be accessed in English online at http://www.iuscomp.org/gla/statutes/GG.htm.

[3] Article 86, Basic Law of the Federal Republic of Germany (*Grundgesetz*); can be accessed in English online at http://www.iuscomp.org/gla/statutes/GG.htm.

[4] For a detailed account of the contemporary German Nationality Law see the German Interior Ministry, http://www.bmi.bund.de/Internet/Content/Common/Anlagen/Gesetze/Staatsangehoerigkeitsgesetz-englisch,templateId=raw,property=publicationFile.pdf/Staatsangehoerigkeitsgesetz-englisch.pdf.

[5] Ayhan Kaya, *Islam, Migration and Integration: The Age of Securitization* (New York: Palgrave/Macmillan, 2009), 49–50.

TABLE 8.1.
Naturalization of Turkish origin migrants and their Descendants, 1972–2006

Year	*Number of Naturalizations*
1972–1979	2,219
1972–1980	10,361
1990	2,034
1991	3,529
1992	7,377
1993	12,915
1994	19,590
1995	31,578
1996	46,294
1997	42,240
1998	59,664
1999	103,900
2000	82,800
2001	75,600
2002	64,631
2003	56,244
2004	44,465
2005	32,661
2006	33,388
Total	**736,495**

Source: Federal Statistical Office Germany, Wiesbaden, 2007.

"What would your reaction be if your son told you he was homosexual and he wanted to live with another man?" and "Must a woman obey her husband, and if she does not is it acceptable that he beat her?" Should responses be considered incompatible with German values, the application is denied. Practices such as these are evident that what is required of the newcomer is assimilation, as is the practice in some schools that only German be spoken on the school grounds.[6]

[6] The decision in March 2005 by the management at Herbert Hoover School in Wedding in Berlin that only German be spoken throughout the school grounds was the subject of heated debate in the Turkish and German press. With 90 percent of this school's students being of non-German origin, this decision by the headmaster, who gave more productive communication as his reason, was criticized by a number of German politicians and the press in Turkey and Germany. Dr. Lâle Akgün, a Social Democrat Member of Parliament of Turkish origin has said that such a decision was a step on the road to forced assimilation. Güner Mutlu, also of Turkish origin and a Green Party member of the Berlin City Council, said that the mentality that could enforce such a language ban could also enforce bans in other areas in the future. *Die Zeit,* 16 February 2006.

France

Because of the French Revolution, France has historically defined citizenship in political rather than ethnocultural terms. A decree of 1972 granted French citizenship to foreigners who by their writings or acts defended the principles of the Revolution. Alongside the principle of *jus sanguinis* attributing citizenship to those born in France and to French parents, the revolutionaries attributed to the principle of *jus soli* specific conditions that guaranteed attachment and loyalty to France.

The French Civil Code specifies that foreigners can only be naturalized if they are "assimilated to French society" (*assimilation a la communauté française*). French citizenship law contains two provisions embodying the principle of *jus soli:* Article 23 granted citizenship at birth to third-generation immigrants, and Article 44 granted citizenship at age eighteen to second-generation immigrants born in France and resident there since age thirteen, provided they have not opted out of French citizenship and they have not been convicted of certain crimes.[7] However, French citizenship has been criticized by nationalists who say that foreigners are turned into French citizens on paper without making sure that they are "French at heart" (*Français de Coeur)*. Nicolas Sarkozy, then Minister of the Interior, took action in 2003 to reduce the number of immigrants in France by doubling the number of illegal immigrants in France to be expelled.[8] A second law was enacted in 2006. The primary emphasis of the second Sarkozy Law was on "selective immigration" (*immigration choisie*) rather than "imposed immigration" (*immigration subie*). In other words, family reunification and asylum-seekers would be reduced and "selective immigration" would be tailored to France's economic requirements, with the introduction of a renewable three-year residence permit called a "skilled and talents permit" (*carte de competences et talents*) for highly skilled non-EU workers.[9] It is assumed that qualified migrants will assimilate more easily. This assimilationist tone continued after Sarkozy's election as president. At one party meeting Sarkozy stated, "If there are people who are not comfortable in France, they should feel free to leave a country they do not love." This was not very different from National Front leader Jean-Marie Le Pen's slogan in the 1980s: "Love France, or leave it."[10]

However, the French assimilationist policy has changed. It is positioned between assimilation and a timid multiculturalism. In 1970s, the French state

[7] French Civil Code. See http://www.legifrance.gouv.fr/html/codes_traduits/code_civil_textA.htm.

[8] Law 2003-1119 (26 November 2003) on immigration control, residence of alliance in France, and nationality.

[9] Sally Marthaler, "Nicolas Sarkozy and the Politics of French Immigration Policy," *Journal of European Public Policy* 15, no. 3 (April 2008), 390.

[10] Ibid., 391.

actively supported religious pluralism through tolerance of Islamic practices in factories and local public housing, and it promoted cultural pluralism by sponsoring mother-tongue classes for children of immigrant families and developing cultural programs on television.

In 2002, the French Muslim Council (CFCM) was established. It is composed of a board of 17 members, an Administrative Council of 64 members and a General Assembly of 197 members. They are authorized to discuss the issues of mosques construction, organization of religious holidays (e.g., fasting times, pilgrimage trips, ritual slaughter) and the training of religious clergy in France.

Foreigners' access to French nationality is also facilitated by France's traditional indifference to dual nationality. Formally, by signing the convention of the Council of Europe that eliminates cases of dual nationality among member states, France has endorsed the classic conception according to which one must belong to a single nationality. In practice, however, like Great Britain, France has always allowed people taking on French nationality to retain their former nationality as well.[11] The proportion of Turkish-origin immigrants with French citizenship in 2004 was 36 percent.[12]

Belgium

Since 1993, Belgium has been divided into three linguistic and cultural communities—Flemish-speaking, French-speaking, and a small German-speaking one—and into three geographical, political, administrative, and economic regions: Flanders, Wallonia, and Brussels. The Francophone concept is based on the political will to live together.[13] In 1993 the Belgian Constitution officially declared Belgium to be a federal state. Belgium's transition from a unitary state to a federal entity proceeded at the same rate as the EU integration process.[14]

Immigration to Belgium started in the late 1960s; the majority of immigrant workers were of Turkish and Moroccan descent. In 1974 Islam was recognized in law as an official religion. Between 1989 and 1995, underlining the politics of identity and culture, multiculturalism was applied. This policy resulted in the imprisonment of Muslim origin migrants and their children in their own ethnocultural and religious ghettos. From 1995 to 2000, a more judicious approach towards Islam was applied. Muslims were asked to organize

---

[11] Patrick Weil, *How to Be French: Nationality in the Making Since 1789* (Durham: Duke University Press, 2008), 237.

[12] Ayhan Kaya and Ferhat Kentel, *Euro-Turks: A Bridge, or a Breach, Between Turkey and the EU* (Brussels: CEPS Publication, 2005).

[13] Edwige L. Lefebvre, "Belgian Citizenship: Managing Linguistic, Regional, and Economic Demands," *Citizenship Studies* 7, no.1 (2003): 129.

[14] Ibid., 128.

elections for the *Executif des Musulmans de Belgique* (Executive of Muslims of Belgium). At the first election the Moroccans, and at the second the Belgian-Turks, were in the majority. The Belgian immigration law of 1984 had three specific objectives: to limit illegal immigration, to repatriate some immigrants, and to integrate other immigrants by naturalization. The law brought equality for migrant women and men, which also allowed mothers to automatically transmit their Belgian nationality to their children. In 2000 the naturalization process was eased further. Candidates no longer have to prove their allegiance to Belgium.[15]

TABLE 8.2.
Number of naturalized Belgian-Turks, 1990–2006

Year	*Number of naturalized Belgian-Turks*
1990	706
1991	1,020
1992	4,044
1993	3,415
1994	6,263
1995	6,925
1996	7,066
1997	7,835
1998	6,932
1999	4,402
2000	17,282
2001	14,401
2002	7,805
2003	5,186
2004	4,467
2005	3,602
2006	3,204
Total	104,555

Source: National Institute of Statistics, 2007, http://www.npdatabe/

By the 1980s, Belgian immigration had become almost entirely Moroccan and Turkish, with large Turkish communities in Limburg and Gent, and the largest number of Moroccans in Antwerp.

Turkish migrants are more marked by their rural origins, their familial character, and the process of chain migration. Former residents of the district of Emirdağ, a province of Afyon-Karahisar, are flourishing. Turkish migration was initially conceived more as a temporary family project. They are setting up

[15] Kaya, *Islam, Migration and Integration,* 105.

their own solidarity networks ranging from hometown fellowship associations to business associations. Different research projects in Belgium indicate that Turkish immigrants are concentrated according to their ethnic origin, which is particularly visible in Brussels where Kurds, Alevis, Armenians, and Assyrians are leading separate lives. These compartmentalized communities tend to generate their own solidarity networks without communicating with others.[16]

The Netherlands

Dutch society between 1945 and 1965 was characterized by tightly organized subcultures of minorities called *pillars*. Three religious pillars existed, corresponding to Catholicism, Protestantism, and secularism. The Catholics constituted the largest of these groups—approximately 40 percent of the population—and the Protestants made up about 30 percent.

Pillarization structured not only political parties, but also trade unions, hospitals, schools, newspapers, and leisure activities. After the 1967 elections, the religious parties lost a substantial part of their votes. The pillars began to disintegrate. New social movements made their views heard. Since 1985 the rising visibility of immigrants began to preoccupy public opinion. When Muslims came to the Netherlands, it was reasonable that the Dutch would allow them to build their own "Muslim" pillar. The Dutch multicultural ideal presumed that the Muslims would build a Muslim pillar first, and then let it collapse into liberal individualism, like the Protestants and Catholics.[17] However, the Muslims' development indicated a different trend. By 1997 Islam, with more than 1 million Muslims, became the third largest religious group. With around five hundred mosques, forty schools, various associations, and their own media, Islam became a threat for the native Dutch. With international events such as the Iranian revolution of 1979, the Salman Rushdie affair of 1989, and the first Gulf War in 1990, the public began to be uneasy with the rise of Islam. In 1991, Fritz Bolkestein, the leader of the largest opposition party in the Netherlands stated that Islam and Western values were incompatible. This pronouncement led the government to reconsider its ethnic minority policy.[18] The rapid increase in family reunions; immigrants' desire to preserve their cultural identity; constructions of mosques, schools and community organizations; increasing visibility of Islam in the public space; and the murder

---

[16] Ural Manço and Meryem Kanmaz, "From Conflict to Co-operation between Muslims and Local Authorities in a Brussels Borough: Schaerbeck," *Journal of Ethnic and Migration Studies* 31, no.6 (2005): 1105–1123.

[17] Robert Carle, "Demise of Dutch Multiculturalism," *Society* (March/April 2006): 71.

[18] Han Entzinger, "The Rise and Fall of Multiculturalism: the Case of the Netherlands," in *Toward Assimilation and Citizenship: Immigrants in Liberal Nation-States*, eds. Christian Joppke and Eva Morawska (Basingstoke, UK: Palgrave, 2003), 59–86.

of two polemical figures, the conservative politician Pim Fortuyn in 2001, and the filmmaker Theo van Gogh in 2004, created a sharp discontent with "radical" Islam. An increasing number of critical voices in parliament on the position of Muslims in the Netherlands induced the government to tighten its immigration and integration measures. The Integration of Newcomers Act of 1998 was a sharp critique of multiculturalism that aimed at vigorously implementing integration courses for non-Western persons wishing to immigrate to the Netherlands in the context of family reunion or marriage. The existing legal instrument appeared to be not sufficient. In 2003 a new Citizenship Law on Dutch Citizenship was put into effect. The new law includes a formal naturalization test in which the applicant has to demonstrate oral and written knowledge of the Dutch language as well as Dutch society and politics. A third legal instrument was accepted in March 2006, the Civic Integration Abroad Act, which includes a test that is given before the applicant's arrival to the Netherlands. An accompanying orientation package includes the film *Naar Netherlands* (*Coming to the Netherlands*). The film has been violently criticized: it shows a topless woman sunbathing, and two gay men kissing. The film is in the applicant's own languages as well as in Dutch. There is a list of one hundred possible questions that could be asked about the film. During the test at the Dutch consulate, the applicant is connected via telephone to a remote computer that asks the test questions and records the answers given. The language requirement is set at a very high educational level. Both examinations are criticized not only because of their content, but also because of who is to take the test, which is only required for "non-Western" peoples. In actuality the test is oriented particularly towards applicants of Turkish and Moroccan—in other words, Muslim—origin.[19]

As a result of the high number of restrictive legal instruments and the policy of exclusion, an integration industry has developed in the Netherlands. There are people such as researchers, social workers, teachers, doctors, consultants, and officers who are accommodated in the integration sector and who have vested interests in the maintenance of the sector.

Today a large part of public opinion in the Netherlands associates Muslims with essentialism, fundamentalism, violence, terror, and dissidence. Changing from a country of tolerance into a country of bigotry towards Muslims, the Netherlands has adopted new immigration and integration policies similar to those of other countries aimed at attracting qualified immigrants and prevent-

[19] For further detail about the Civic Integration Abroad Act of 2006, see http://english.justitie.nl/themes/immigratin-and-integration/integration/the-act.aspx. Four categories of persons are exempted from the cited examinations: (1) citizens of EU countries, the USA, Sweden, or Switzerland; (2) persons of Surinamese nationality who have completed primary education in Dutch; (3) persons who come for temporary reasons such as au pair work, medical treatment, etc.; (4) persons with a work permit, self-employed persons, or "knowledge" migrants; and (5) family members of a person in possession of an asylum residence permit.

ing unskilled ones from entering the country. It has also become apparent that Muslim origin migrants and their descendants are structurally excluded from the labor market, higher education, and affluent neighborhoods.

As the table below reveals, the largest number of Turks who opted for naturalization are living in Germany, which requires proof of renunciation of former citizenship. The second largest group is living in Belgium, which accepts dual citizenship.

TABLE 8.3.
Turks Changing Citizenship in Europe by Country, 1991–2002

Country	*1991–1993*		*1994–1996*		*1997–1999*		*2000–2002*		*1991–2002*	
	# (x1000)	*%*	*# (x1000)*	*%*	*# (x1000)*	*%*	*# (x1000)*	*%*	*# (x1000)*	*%*
Germany	20.3	27.8	97.0	42.7	129.1	56.8	159.4	63.4	405.8	52.1
Austria	4.7	6.4	6.6	2.9	7.8	3.4	18.3	7.2	37.4	4.8
Belgium	7.2	9.9	13.0	5.7	17.5	7.7	31.7	12.6	69.4	8.9
Denmark	1.1	1.5	2.6	1.1	5.4	2.4	5.9	2.3	15.0	1.9
France	2.8	3.8	8.8	3.9	14.5	6.4	13.8	5.5	39.9	5.1
Netherlands	29.5	40.4	87.6	38.5	39.9	17.6	10.2	4.1	167.2	21.5
The UK	0.2	0.3	0.5	0.2	2.0	0.9	2.5	1.0	5.2	0.7
Sweden	5.8	7.9	7.6	3.3	4.9	2.2	4.2	1.7	22.5	2.9
Switzerland	1.4	1.9	3.6	1.6	6.2	2.7	6.2	2.5	17.4	2.2
Total	73.0	100.0	227.3	100.0	227.3	100.0	251.2	100.0	778.8	100.0

Source: Figures are compiled by İçduygu (2006a) from various sources of OECD and Eurostat.

Dual citizenship is the prevailing norm in the EU in fifteen states. Only Denmark and Austria retain strict renunciation requirements of former citizenship. Germany and the Netherlands are defending this principle but are granting many exceptions. In the new member-states, rejection of dual citizenship is the norm.[20]

Forms of Political Participation in Selected European Countries

Voting Rights at Local Elections

Until the latter half of the twentieth century, each nation-state, operating either on the principle of *jus sanguinis* or *jus soli,* granted to those living within its borders citizenship rights and obligations, which, in turn, determined the

[20] ENACT, Eurasylum interview with Rainer Bauböck, 29 April 2009, http://www. Eurasylum.org/Portal/DesktopDefault.aspx?tabindex=28tabid=19. For a detailed discussion, see Thomas A. Aleinikoff and Douglas Klusmeyer, *Citizenship Policies for an Age of Migration* (Washington, D. C.: Carnegie Endowment, 2002).

exercise by the citizen of his/her economic, social and political rights. Today, some European countries have granted political rights on a local government level to their foreign populations, even though they may not have obtained full citizenship. The following European countries allow foreigners to take part in local elections:

- Ireland (since 1973, local, minimum residency period of six years)
- Sweden (since 1975, local and regional, minimum residency period of three years)
- Denmark (since 1981, local and regional, minimum residency period of three years)
- Norway (since 1983, local, minimum residency period of three years)
- Netherlands (since 1983, local, minimum residency period of three years)

In Switzerland in the cantons of Neuchatel and Jura foreigners are allowed to vote and be candidates in local elections.[21]

Thus, it would appear that legal migrants are close to gaining equal status with the native populations in their countries of acceptance, and these practices have significant consequences: the link between state and territory is being broken, and individuals bearing the citizenship of one country are at the same time able to avail themselves of the rights and privileges offered by another. This fluidity is paving the way to a growing acceptance of the institution of dual citizenship.

Political Associations of Migrants

In countries of the Western world, political organization is a feature of pluralist democracy, and migrant groups engage in this activity in order to pressure the governments of their countries of acceptance. However, attitudes of the country of acceptance towards its migrant populations play a direct role in determining the level of influence these organizational activities may exert. Yasemin Nuhoğlu Soysal has developed a typology on this issue, explored in great detail in her book *Limits of Citizenship.*[22] Soysal examines the activities of migrants within a framework of different approaches. For example, in countries such as Sweden and Holland in which the concept of "ethnic minority" is recognized, there is local and national funding available for the organization of activities. France, although not formally recognizing the existence of minority status, makes available public funding on a local level for the organization

[21] Yasemin Nuhoglu Soysal, *Limits of Citizenship: Migrants and Postnational Membership in Europe* (Chicago: University of Chicago, 1994), 128, table 7.6.
[22] Ibid., 65–83.

of activities. Germany, in which no official recognition exists, displays special treatment to migrant associations. Finally, in Switzerland migrant associations are viewed as representing individual demands.

It is thus clear that the formation of public policies regarding migrant communities and the reinforcement of "islands of isolation" are both heavily dependent on the policies applied by the countries of acceptance. Even the existence of publicly funded organizations in some countries is not enough to untangle the relationship networks based on traditional solidarity among migrant groups—especially those that have resulted from chain migration.

Sweden

Analyses of foreign labor movements in Sweden are based on the notion of the community of minority groups. Migrant associations are viewed as organizations that link the institutions of Swedish society and migrant communities.[23] The associations receive funding from the national government and are involved in the national political process through participating in various advisory and consultative committees. Because each national group must be represented by a national federation, the result is the formation of single umbrella federations.

The Turkish Federation (TF) was founded in 1977. It has close to 9,000 members and is made up of approximately thirty member associations. In 1988, the annual budget of the TF in state funding was 2 million kronor (344,448 U.S. dollars). The state was also involved in the funding of special projects targeting migrant women and children. The same model is applied to migrants' religious organizations: the Swedish Muslim Association (SMA) operates in close cooperation with the TF. Swedish migration institutions also undertake the financing of language courses for newly arrived migrants. These courses consist of 240 hours of language instruction given as part of the working day. Literacy courses are also offered to illiterate Turkish women. Even though the vast majority of Turkish migrants take advantage of these courses, there exists hidden and open discrimination in the labor market, and difficulties in securing accommodation have resulted in high concentrations of Turkish migrants in certain neighborhoods such as Rinkeby in Stockholm. Sema Köksal Erder has analyzed this issue in detail in *Refah Devletinde Getto ve Türkler* [Turks and The Welfare State Ghetto]. On the one hand, the protected lifestyle that is provided by a well-organized society eases adaptation to a new culture, but, on the other hand, it may also create a conflicting situation if it proves an obstacle to integration. Traditional values continue to exist, particularly in low-income migrant centers.

---

[23] Eva Lithman, *Immigration and Immigrant Policies in Sweden* (Stockholm: The Swedish Institute, 1987), 29–31.

The Netherlands

The *Verzuiling* (pillar) system which operates in the Netherlands calls for co-operation among all religious sects and secular groups, based on the idea that all interest groups create vertical structures in all aspects of public life. This tradition in the Netherlands led, in 1980, to the Dutch government formally adopting a multi-ethnic policy with three basic aims: developing and emancipating ethnic groups; increasing equality before the law; and promoting the position of ethnic communities in the social and economic spheres.[24]

The first of these targets the group rather than the individual, and thus the teaching of the groups' mother tongues in both private and public schools was encouraged. The second aim, equality before the law, has been implemented such that members of ethnic minority groups who have been issued residence permits for a period exceeding five years have been granted the political right to participate in local elections. As a result of this, in 1990 thirty-six Turks were elected as members of various city councils.[25] In the 2002 local and national elections there were almost one hundred candidates of Turkish origin elected to local governments, and Turkish-born Nebahat Albayrak, the Dutch Labor Party candidate, was not only elected to the national parliament but was also one of the names put forward for leadership of the party.

The third aim of this multiethnic policy is the successful integration of ethnic minorities into mainstream social and economic life. It would appear, however, that the government has failed in its efforts in the area of unemployment: in the 1990s, 21 percent of Turks and 36 percent of Moroccans were unemployed and being excluded from the labor market. A decrease in employment opportunities for minorities was one result of the national economic restructuring of that time.

An analysis of the first ten years of these policies revealed that their application to ethnic minorities was essentially paternalistic, based more on social assistance rather than any economic participation, and resulted in the exclusion of some migrant groups. Consequently, in 1989 the Dutch Scientific Council adopted a new plan with the main aim of economic and social integration. The plan abandoned the notion of trying to spread minority language and culture through education and left initiatives in this kind of education to migrant groups.[26]

---

[24] Jan Rath, "Political Action of Immigrants in the Netherlands: Class or Ethnicity," *European Journal of Political Research* 16 (1988): 623–644.

[25] Cities in which Turks were elected members of city councils included: Almelo (one), Amesfoot (one), Amsterdam (seventeen), Arnhem (three), Bergen ov Zoom (one), Devenba (one), and Dordrecht (one).

[26] Han Entzinger, "L'immigration aux Pays-Bas du pluri-culturalisme a l'integration," in *Racisme et modernité,* ed. K. A. Wierow (Paris: Deitions la decouverte, 1993), 409–410.

The Turkish Advisory Council is currently made up of ten federations and associations and works in cooperation with the Dutch National Advisory Committee. The current legal framework calls for cooperation among the Turkish Muslim Association, other political organizations, and Turkish associations. Insofar as cooperation occurs between associations dealing with migrant problems and others, this is conducted only on the managerial level; there is only very limited interaction among members of different associations. Nevertheless, all associations are responsible for the presentation of consultative reports regarding various proposed laws. Of fourteen proposals made by migrant organizations between 1986 and 1987, six met with a positive response from the government.[27]

France

Until recent times the political system of France, built as it was on the concept of the unitary nation-state, appeared to have a neutral policy stance and was known as being amicable in its relations with migrants and asylum-seekers. However, the dramatic rise of Jean Marie Le Pen's right-wing anti-migrant National Front Party in 1983, and its attraction of 11 percent of the vote in elections, led the way to important changes in France's citizenship laws. Whereas prior to that time the principle of *jus soli* had entitled second-generation migrants born on French soil French citizenship from birth, today an individual may only attain French citizenship on reaching the age of eighteen. State policy in France on migration has remained unchanged since the start of the twentieth century and is based on the absolute refusal to recognize the existence of any ethnic community. Instead, the system anticipates integration of the migrant into society, through the state fostering the formation of ethnic associations and establishing various local level social service networks. With the arrival on France's shores of ever increasing numbers of Muslim migrants—there are presently approximately 5 million Muslims living in France—Muslim communities began using their religious affiliation as a bargaining tool in negotiations with state authorities. This, in the words of Leveau, led to the "collapse of the French system."[28] In their determination to have their cultural and religious identities recognized, migrants felt the need to mobilize their communities and increase pressure on central government. This strategy con-

[27] Yasemin Nuhoğlu Soysal, "Workers in Europe: Interaction with the Host Society," in *Turkey and the West: Changing Political and Cultural Identities,* eds. Metin Heper, Heinz Kramer, and Ayse Oncu (London: I. B. Tauris, 1993), 250.

[28] Rémy Leveau, "Maghrebi Immigration to Europe: Double Insertion or Double Exclusion," *The Annals of the American Academy of Political and Social Science* 524, no. 1 (November 1992): 176.

flicts directly with the principle of laicism (secularism) as set out in the French Constitution.[29]

This strategy on the part of the migrants clearly proved successful. The first success came in 1973 when migrant workers from Turkey and the Maghreb nations challenged an increase in the rent for their low-cost public housing and entered into direct negotiations with Sunacotra, the company responsible for the running of the housing estates. The company bowed to their demands and, beginning with estates in Bobigny in Paris and later in other areas in which Muslim migrants were concentrated, made alterations to the buildings whereby the rooms set apart for communal television watching and/or games were transformed into *mescit* (prayer rooms). As Keppel pointed out, "the institutions dealing with housing tried to overcome economic deprivation with spiritual concessions!"[30] More action was taken in 1976. The Maoist faction of the French Federation of Unions (CGT), in an attempt to increase membership numbers, led the way in demanding that prayer rooms be set up during Ramadan in the Renault factory in Billancourt. The demands of the Muslims were met in order to maintain peace in the workplace. Finally, in the middle of the 1980s, a group of young Algerians known as Harkis, who possessed citizenship rights as a result of having been born in France, managed to obtain permission from their local authorities to build a mosque. With financial support from the international Muslim missionary organization *Cemaat-el-Tebliğ* and the help of some French church organizations they appeared on the scene as a social partner who would build countless mosques.[31]

There can be little doubt that all these developments were affecting the lives of Turkish migrants. Turkey had signed a labor agreement with France in 1966. Prior to this, in 1962, there were 111 Turkish workers registered in France. Numbers had risen to 50,860 by 1975, and in 2006 the official figure for Turkish citizens in France was 359,887, of which 87,992 had worker status.[32] The rapid spread of Islam throughout France had a noticeable effect on the activities of the Turkish community associations. In Germany, the ideologically oriented political associations benefited from both individual participation and support from private international organizations and carried out their activities with the homeland in mind. The situation was similar in France, where a quasi-state institution called the *Fonds d'Action Sociale* (FAS), in an attempt to halt the rapid growth of Turkish-Islamic associations, began to assist in the funding of leftist, laicist sociocultural associations. As a result, Turkish-Islamic associations began to play a more active role as an opponent

---

[29] Ibid.

[30] Gilles Keppel, *Les Banlieues de l'Islam* (Paris: Le Seuil, 1991), 136.

[31] Gilles Kepel, *The Trail of Political Islam* (London: I.B. Tauris Publishers, 2006).

[32] Employment Ministry, *BÜLTEN*, 2006, 18.

of government policies and thus took a step forward on the path to integration.[33] The opposite occurred with some ethnic and religious organizations styling themselves as "cultural associations" in order to benefit from funding. In 1992, a total of 203 Turkish associations were active all over France,[34] with 76 of these in Paris, 51 in Strasbourg, 17 in Marseilles, and 59 in Lyon. These associations were constantly engaged in processes of establishment, dissolution, and reestablishment. Those with political and religious aims expressed affiliation with the *Refah* (Welfare) Party in the homeland, and following its closure, they transferred their affiliation to the *Saadet* (Happiness) Party and the present government party *Adalet ve Kalkınma* (Justice and Development Party, or AKP). Those associations based on ethnic ties tended to have little if any remaining bonds with the homeland. Meanwhile, the Kurds were claiming to have a distinct ethnic-national identity. Association members wishing to emphasize their "Turkishness" would choose such names as "Association of Turkish Workers" or "Association of Workers from Turkey." Thus, association activities played a part in the formation of redefined political identities abroad.

Germany

Almost fifty years have passed since Turkey signed a labor export agreement with Germany on 10 October 1961.[35] At that time there were only 7,000 Turkish workers in Germany. In 2008 the estimate was 2.1 million.

Despite the constant and steady increase in the numbers of foreigners in Germany—in 1980 they constituted 22.7 percent of the population, and in 1990, 28.2 percent—until 2001 successive German governments had remained adamant that Germany was not a country of migration. This attitude would go some way towards explaining why Germany was so late in granting even local voting rights to its foreigners. The process to become a German citizen was complex and time consuming: in 1992 only 7,377 Turks were granted citizenship, whereas that same year 14,773 of France's Turks became French citizens. However, the situation has changed in recent years. In 1998, 57,374 Turks in Germany were granted German citizenship and currently their numbers exceed 405,000.[36] Despite the fact that federal funding exists to promote the integration of migrants, these monies may not be appropriated by umbrella organizations. Because financial support is provided only on a local level, col-

[33] Kastoryano, *Etre Turc en France*, 76.

[34] Employment Ministry, *1992 Annual Report*, 76, table 2.4.6. There is no further data available on workers' associations in France in later years.

[35] Abadan-Unat, ed., *Turkish Workers in Europe 1960–1975*, 6.

[36] Employment Ministry, *1999 Annual Report*, 11; Ahmet İçduygu and Kemal Kirişçi, eds., *Land of Diverse Migrations: Challenges of Emigration and Immigration in Turkey* (Istanbul: Istanbul Bilgi University, 2009), table 4.

lective enterprises are to a large extent dependent on individual donations and financial aid from other Islamic countries.

Turkish associations follow two distinct paths: those migrants who are long-time residents in Germany have conducted their struggle in the areas of gaining dual citizenship and voting rights and have been supported in this struggle by the "Euro-Turks" in favor of integration. However, a significant number of Turkish associations represent ethnic and cultural groups who display no great interest in German society. Among these are religious, ethnic, extreme right-wing and left-wing groups whose profiles are very different and whose leaders are highly aggressive in their tone. Until recent times, these had refused to enter into any peaceful dialogue with the country of acceptance, a situation which changed following the events of 11 September 2001. The groups in question tend to look more towards Turkey in their activities, and work in cooperation with extreme right-wing, nationalist, or left-wing organizations. Islamic organizations are engaged in trying to effect a power change in Turkey, whereas ethnic groups such as the Kurdish ones are driven by separatist goals, to which end they support terrorist organizations. In their refusal to engage in any efforts towards integration, these kinds of associations played a partial role in the increasing racism and xenophobia that accompanied German reunification and the arrival of increasing numbers of asylum seekers.[37]

The European Federation of Turkish Nationalists (*Avrupa Türk Ülkücüler Federasyonu,* ATÜF) was set up in the 1970s with the support of the National Labor Party in Turkey, and branches were opened in West Germany in 1973. They carried out their activities using the name Grey Wolf (*Bozkurt*), but when these began to take on a violent nature the branches were closed down. Loopholes in the ban on such activities were later used to set up associations such as the *Büyük Ülkü Derneği* (Great Ideals Association), *Türk Cemaat* (Turkish Assembly) and *Türk-Genç* (Turkish Youth). These all had close connections with Alparslan Türkeş's *Milliyetçi Hareket Partisi* (Nationalist Movement Party) in Turkey and joined together as the Federation of European Turkish Nationalists Associations (*Avrupa Türk Ülkücüler Dernekleri Federasyonu,* or ATÜDF). They continue to operate in cooperation with the Nationalist Movement Party. The Federation's ideology is based on taking a stance in opposition to integration into a German society that they believe considers Turks a second-class race.

Two other important ethnic-based associations that were allowed to operate until recently are KOMKAR and BİRKOM. It is estimated that 450,000 Turkish citizens of Kurdish origin reside in Germany. These have organized themselves in various associations, the most powerful of which is the Kurdis-

[37] Nermin Abadan-Unat, "Ethnic Business, Ethnic Communities, and Ethno-Politics among Turks in Europe," in *Immigration into Western Societies: Problems and Policies,* eds. Emek M. Uçarer and Donald J. Puchala (London: Pinter, 1997).

tan Kurdish Workers Association, or KOMKAR. This aims to create a collective consciousness as a base for the establishment of a Kurdish state in southeastern Turkey. The other separatist organization is BİRKOM, founded by supporters of Abdullah Öcalan, who fled Turkey in 1980. This organization's activities were all directed towards the homeland rather than any kind of integration into German society. Violent protest by Kurdistan Workers' Party (PKK) supporters, including the blockading of motorways and arson activities, followed the decision in 1999 by Germany and some other European countries to declare KOMKAR, BİRKOM, and the PKK terrorist organizations. Following the events of 11 September 2001, the PKK made a strategic alteration to its aims and declared that it would henceforth carry out its activities on the political stage only. At its eighth congress on 8 February 2002, the Party Council of the PKK stated that it was bringing to an end its violent activities within the borders of Turkey and the European Union and changing the party name from PKK to KADEK. Just prior to this decision, EU member states, in a consensus vote, had banned all activity by the PKK and the Revolutionary People's Liberation Party/Front (DHKP/C), an association that aims to establish a socialist state in Turkey. It has not yet become clear what the German authorities' assessment is of KADEK.[38]

The way German-Turks form civil society organizations has a strong impact in Turkey. Alevi associations, some other religious organizations like the European Association of National Vision (*Avrupa Millî Görüş Teşklâtı*, or AMGT), and gay-lesbian organizations formed in Germany have generated counterparts in Turkey, and have had a visible impact on social and political life there. Organizations such as *Cojépiennes,* a Turkish youth organization in France, and MUSIAD, a Turkish-origin employer syndicate bringing together small- and medium-sized enterprises strongly imbued with a Calvinist work ethic, provide the present political party in power in Turkey—the Justice and Development Party (AKP)—with strong social and political support from the Turkish diaspora. Agents of these transnational spaces are no more imprisoned in their new home country. Their organizations represent a vibrant bridge between two or more communities.

The many research activities conducted among Turkish communities in Europe have all shown that since the 1980s, they have undergone three stages of development: the spread of ethnic enterprises, the growth in importance of ethnic communities within collective organizations, and the rapid growth of ethnic politics.

During this period, many Turks who had given up on the dream of returning to the homeland began establishing small businesses of their own, which

[38] In *Süddeutsche Zeitung* on 9 February 2002, Christiane Schlötzer commented, "The PKK are late in forming a party." In *Die Tageszeitung,* on the same date, Jürgen Gottschlicht said that "the transformation from terrorist party to democratic party is good news."

led to the growth of successful niche enterprises. There are presently approximately 60,000 such enterprises in Germany, which employ 300,000. There can be no doubt that these businesses, which provide employment for both Turks and Germans, are an indication of adaptation to mainstream economic life. However, the majority of these businesses serve consumers from ethnic communities. For migrants working in these ethnic communities, this type of employment provides a means towards eliminating the effects of social exclusion, and the workplace in this case assists in both resolving personal and financial problems and bettering communication with the migrant community. At the same time, these "niche" enterprises also serve to reinforce the structures of spatial and cognitive "ghetto-ization." By providing potential employment opportunities they often become an obstacle to young migrants progressing with education. They have close ties with religious associations and thus act to promote the interests of groups whose identity is based on religion. In other words, in addition to the establishment of Qur'an courses, boarding schools, and private television and radio channels, ethnic enterprises also play a leading role in the spread of a religiously based political ideology, and are one of the cornerstones in the construction of an ethnic subculture.

All ethnic communities in similar situations live out their lives in spatially dense conditions, and this is particularly true in the case of chain migration, where many individuals who share the same roots and refuse integration with the country of acceptance naturally come together in one space. Migrants' cooperation with local authorities while still attempting to protect their cultural values leads only to the formation of a kind of instrumental multiculturalism, a tendency which, in some cases, may reinforce a de facto apartheid.

When operating through such complex networks, politics based on ethnic or religious identities is fertile ground for the growth of the desire to establish a federal Islamic republic in Turkey or the fulfillment of Kurdish separatist demands. In either case, it is possible for the activities of the associations to result in violence, armed conflict, or illegality. Migrant movements are generally seen as a process that, in situations such as this, allows for new actors to appear on the stage of international relations.

I wonder if the academic community working on migration has paid sufficient attention to the developments I have touched upon above. Heisler said that new forms of international migration, the political measures being taken to deal with these, and fundamental developments in regional/global international relations have all become one and the same issue. In considering these changes Heisler proposes the foundation of a "sociology of institutional politics."[39] The notion of ethnic pluralism, as used to define the inclusion

[39] Martin Heisler, "Now and Then, Here and There: Migration and the Transformation of Identities, Borders and Orders," in *Identities, Borders, Orders,* eds M. Albert et al. (Minneapolis: University of Minnesota Press, 2001), 77–93.

of migrants in the process of integration, contains within it concepts such as multiculturalism, cultural pluralism and pluralist ethnicity, and taking these into consideration leads us to ask the following question: to what extent can unique cultural values be preserved without completely destroying a political community?

One more topic that deserves attention here is the notion, developed by Alain Touraine, of social movements. According to Touraine, social change has its origins in groups organized to support the development of alternative institutions and conflict (1997). The question here is: does the exercising of democratic rights legitimize either legal discrimination as practiced in the country of acceptance by racists and xenophobes, or activities engaged in by migrants as they attempt to make changes to the political system and borders of their home country? With levels of interdependency growing, desires for a more just and equal citizenship increasing, and civil law no longer permitting the denial of basic human rights, questions such as these are critically important. The area of common ground created by globalization is forcing both migrant-accepting and migrant-sending countries to discuss the issue and engage in a search for common solutions.

CHAPTER 9

Political and Economic Asylum Movements and Xenophobia

Figure 9.1. "They Don't Like Us"

It is my present that is foreign, … the past is home, albeit a lost home in a lost city in the mists of lost time. … Thus, we will, in short, create fictions, not actual cities or villages, but invisible ones, imaginary homelands.

—Salman Rushdie, *Imaginary Homelands*

Collective hate eliminates all feelings of loneliness, weakness, powerlessness, exclusion and abandonment. As members of a group, individuals are saved from thoughts of failure or being misunderstood. A strange kind of unconditional brotherhood is created. There is nothing easier than being intolerant in the face of an object that is collectively hated, than sharing in a prejudiced ideology. … It is easy to lay the blame for all wrongs and misery in the world at the feet of Germans, Arabs, Blacks, Vietnamese, Hungarians, Czechs, Gypsies, or Jews. Openly declared hate leads to a hypothesis of legitimacy and creates, at least, a feeling of common sharing.

—Vaclav Havel, "The Anatomy of Hate"

During the last quarter of the twentieth century, international migration revealed itself mainly in asylum movements and illegal labor migration. Wars in Africa, Asia, and Latin America, repressive regimes, and economic poverty impelled almost 20 million individuals to escape in fear of their lives to other countries and continents. With most asylum demands being made to Western countries, those countries adopted the use of four criteria in their response to these demands: What gains are to be made by acceptance or refusal of the demands? What foreign policy gains are to be made by acceptance? What are our labor needs and population levels? And finally, are certain ethnic or religious groups within the country pressuring the state to accept specific asylum-seeking groups?[1] These questions have been answered variously, depending on the political climate of the time.

Two hundred thousand people were forced to leave Hungary following Russia's suppression of the rebellion there in 1956, and almost one hundred thousand were compelled to leave what was then Czechoslovakia following the famous "Prague Spring" of 1968. The asylum demands that followed were not looked at askance but were largely supported, because within the ideological climate of the time they signified a rejection of communism.

This supportive situation began to change in the 1970s. Military takeovers in Chile and Uruguay in 1973 and in Argentina in 1976 forced many to seek asylum in Europe and North America. This time, however, the demands were not responded to quite so tolerantly. The 1980s witnessed a dramatic increase in numbers of asylum-seekers as a result of internecine strife in Africa, Asia, Latin America, and the Middle East, and increases in serious abuses of human rights. Coupled with these political events, the economies of many countries were weakened by the oil crisis of 1973, when oil prices skyrocketed. When labor imports to Europe were halted, asylum became the path chosen by many individuals as the way to better their economic and social condition. Meanwhile, the fall of the Berlin Wall in 1989 and the collapse of the former Soviet state resulted in another unexpected increase in those seeking asylum. In 1976, numbers of asylum-seekers were estimated to be 2.8 million; by 1980, estimates had reached 8.2 million, in 1985, 11.6 million, and in 1990, 18.2 million.[2] Chaotic situations developed in Europe when huge numbers of Albanians attempted to get into Italy in 1991 and 1997, and when individuals from what was then Yugoslavia made attempts to enter Germany and France after 1992. Despite the existence of articles in the Geneva Convention which set out the legal status of asylum-seekers, faced with situations such as these, Europeans began to focus more on their own and their state's interests rather

[1] Robin Cohen, *Frontiers of Identity: The British and the Others* (London: Longman Publishing Group, 1994), 69–70.

[2] United Nations High Commission for Refugees, *The State of the World's Refugees: A Humanitarian Approach* (Oxford: Oxford University Press, 1997).

than humanistic ideals. During the Balkan wars in Bosnia-Herzegovina and Kosovo, Western countries pursued discriminatory policies: doors were more freely opened to those from the east, but were not thrown quite so wide to those coming from the south.

The huge rise in numbers made necessary new legal definitions and descriptions. There were only 13,000 asylum demands made in Europe during the 1970s. By 1980, demands had risen to 158,000, and in 1991, 550,625 asylum cases were heard, 60 percent of which were made to Germany, with 20 percent to France. It was around this time that member countries of the European Union began to take new measures to deal with the situation.[3] The first results of these were the arrangements that led to the Schengen Agreement, which applied to visa requirements for six countries of the EU. In 1988, EU meetings in Dublin resulted in the Dublin Agreement, which established that an application for asylum could be made to a single country only in the EU. Then, in 1995, the visa obligations set out in the Schengen Agreement became applicable to all EU countries, with the exception of England. In 1992, in London, criteria were established to determine which countries were safe havens in the event of an asylum demand being refused and the applicant repatriated. In 1997, the Amsterdam Agreement set out that all asylum applications made in the following five years would be evaluated according to common EU laws. European Council members meeting at Tampere in 1999 reiterated the necessity for asylum applications to be treated with respect, and formally adopted the principle that applicants should not be repatriated to countries whose penal systems accepted death and torture as forms of punishment.[4] At present, the EU has declared all its immediate neighbors to be "safe havens" and has thus, in effect, created a security cordon around itself. In the event of any individual entering the EU from any of these "safe haven" countries and making an asylum application, the individual is automatically sent back to the country where he or she first made the application.[5] During all this time, there have been constant ongoing ethical debates between NGOs defending humanistic values and institutions that are primarily charged with the protection of national interests. Many of the former, firm in their belief that no restrictions should be placed on asylum rights, accused the United Nations High Commission for Refugees (UNHCR), for example, of passively assisting the Serbian state in its policy of "ethnic cleansing" by allowing obstacles to be placed in the way of more than 700,000 Bosnians who tried to enter Germany and other Western countries.

---

[3] Daniele Joly and Clive Nettelton, *Refugees in Europe* (London: Minority Rights Group, 1990).
[4] UNHCR, *The State of the World's Refugees 2000: Fifty Years of Humanitarian Action* (Oxford: Oxford University Press, 2000), 159.
[5] Weiner, *Global Migration Crisis*, 50.

Before we move on to look at the issue from the perspective of Turkish asylum seekers, it is useful first to examine post-1980 Germany as the country that received the most asylum applications and also the country from which most Turks returned to their homeland.

Migration and Asylum in Post-1980 Germany

Despite its insistence that it was not a country of immigration, in 1980 Germany was at the top of the list of European countries accepting migrants. When a halt was brought to the import of labor in 1973, foreigners constituted 7.3 percent of the German population and numbered 4.9 million. By this time, German authorities had come to the realization that these migrants were in Germany to stay. In fact, 59.7 percent of the foreign population had been residents there for more than ten years. In all that time, however, these migrants had been granted no political rights and their level of integration into German society had been limited to its economic life and public institutions. They were known at the time as the "local foreigners." As the 1980s began, public debate in Germany was focused on issues such as how these foreigners could be integrated, multiculturalism, and the idea of bringing more flexibility to the laws governing foreigners. Meanwhile, the 1980s also witnessed the first threats to social peace in the form of growing xenophobia, the origins of which lay, for one, in the tendency among many German politicians in pursuit of votes to consciously blur the lines between foreigner and asylum issues and to present the German public with frightening scenarios of the future.

A second factor was the arrival into what was then West Germany of German citizens from East Germany, thus creating a situation in which there existed dual foreignness: "local foreigners" and "German foreigners." A general xenophobia came into existence with comparisons being made between these two groups and their legal status. A third factor, demographics, also played a role. With the reunification of Germany in 1991, five new states were added to the existing structure and the total population of the new united Germany reached 72.1 million.

Of these three factors, it is the second that is of importance here. Until 1971, German citizenship, as set out in the German constitution, was based solely on the principle of *jus sanguinis,* or blood ties. Today, this principle still holds true but amendments to the law have changed the situation somewhat. Individuals who can prove they have a single German grandparent or who live outside Germany's borders but were resident on German soil prior to World War II have the right to become German citizens. This led to a huge increase in citizenship applications following the collapse of the Communist system, as both East Germans and those of German ancestry living in the old socialist states hoped to exercise this constitutional right. It was after all a very attractive prospect, bringing with it as it did other benefits such as housing, income potential, and financial aid. Those entering Germany were categorized under two titles: *Übersiedler,* or Germans entering from the former East Germany, and *Aussiedler,* or those of German ancestry entering as a result of war, exile, or forced migration. During the most intensive years of this East to West migration movement, a total of 343,854 (1989) and 238,384 (1990) *Übersiedler* entered Germany. In addition, in 1989, 720,909 *Aussiedler* from Poland, Romania, and the former Soviet Union also entered. All the newcomers went by the name of "new citizens," and thus, immediately following German reunification, the population of Germany increased by more than 1 million.[6] The existence of such significant numbers of new Germans had come about as a result of the nationalist policies of the Kohl governments, and within a short time added new dimensions to the conflicts between the "Wessies" of the economically developed former West Germany and the "Ossies" who chose to remain in what had been East Germany. These "new Germans" were, for the most part, people from rural backgrounds who had lived lives far removed from the economically high standards of Western Europe and who had been engaged in different social processes. Among these were German families—some of whom had preserved their native language—settled by Catherine the Great on the banks of the Volga, others who had been forcibly removed to Kazakhstan by the Nazis, and yet others from Transylvania in Romania. Yet more were German families from Poland who had, over time, fully adopted the language and traditions of Poland. It is hardly surprising, therefore, that the average West German should have had difficulty coping with such large numbers of individuals with such different roots. To this mix was later added the asylum-seeking populations from Asia, Latin America, and Africa, numbers of which began to rise after 1980.

Until 1993, the German constitution was considered one of the most liberal in the world with respect to asylum. Taking as its point of departure Article 14 of the 1948 United Nations Declaration on human rights, which stated that individuals had the right to "flee from repression or in fear of life," the second clause of Article 16 of the German constitution generously granted the right to asylum to all who were under political persecution. This rendered the German constitution unique, as no other nation-state has included such a right under its constitution. It was not until the 1980s, when asylum demands reached extraordinary dimensions, that the adoption of such a humanitarian and liberal principle was questioned, following which it became the focus of intense debate. The end result of these debates was compromise between the governing CDU party and the SDP opposition party, and the removal of the

---

[6] Klaus J. Bade, ed., *Deutsche im Ausland* (Munich: Verlag C.H.Beck, 1992), 403.

second clause Article 16. During these debates it was impossible not to hear the extreme, demagogic views being voiced in some of the state-level parliaments, views which declared in no uncertain terms that the raising of the Iron Curtain could only mean the occupation of Germany by Asian peoples. Thus, to ethnic tensions were added nationalist misunderstandings. In 1990, a total of 193,063 applications were made for asylum and this marked the end of the climate of tolerance. At the top of the list of those applying were Romanians, Yugoslavians, Turks, and Lebanese.

Public criticism arose mainly out of the fact that while investigations were conducted into the truth behind these individual's applications, each was given a place to live, a work permit, and had their health needs met by the state. As abuses of this system were brought to light, asylum-seekers came to be regarded by many as little more than parasites feeding off Germany and its good intentions. The most demagogic debates were conducted by politicians during election campaigns. Spokespersons for the conservative CDU (Christian Democrats) called for an acceleration of the investigation process in asylum applications and the speedy deportation of individuals found to be under no immediate threat. In the media were to be found headlines including terms such as the "asylum flood" and the "deluge." Other headlines read, "Germany becomes one large asylum camp," "Fraudsters who wish to take part in the economy," and "Asylum seekers increase alienation," all of which fueled the debate. Finally, in 1993, the asylum right in Article 16 of the German constitution was amended to a much more restrictive code. From then onwards, while court investigations were being conducted into the truth of asylum-seekers' claims, the individuals being investigated would be housed in communal shelter and have no right to work or to benefit from education or state child subsidy payments. Those whose applications were refused would be subject to immediate deportation.[7] These new laws came into effect on 1 July 1993, and asylum-seeker numbers, which had reached 438,000 in 1992, fell to 128,000 by 1995. Other European countries were not long in following Germany's example by bringing in similar restrictions.[8]

Since the early 1980s, Turkish asylum-seekers have been heading for Western Europe, fleeing from the consequences of Turkish military intervention in civilian politics and the increase in the violence surrounding efforts to suppress the PKK, a separatist Kurdish movement in southeastern Turkey. According to UNHCR statistics, between 1981 and 2005 over 664,000 Turkish citizens applied for asylum, mostly in various European countries (see table 9.2). Refugee recognition varied from country to country but overall the numbers have been very low as there were many who tried to make fraudulent use

---

[7] Weiner, *Global Migration Crisis*, 57–58.

[8] Castles and Miller, *The Age of Migration*, 89.

TABLE 9.1.
Numbers of asylum requests made to Germany by Turkish citizens between 1980–1997

Year	*1980*	*1984*	*1985*	*1986*	*1987*	*1988*	*1989*	*1990*	*1991*	*1996*	*1997*
Turkish	57,913	4,180	7,528	8,693	11,426	14,873	20,020	22,082	23,877	23,814	16,840
Total	107,818	35,278	73,832	99,650	57,379	103,076	121,318	193,063	256,112	350,000	320,000

Source: Thomas Faist, *The Volume and Dynamics of International Migration,* 2000, Table 3.6, p.83.

TABLE 9.2.
Turkish Asylum-seekers by Destination, 1981–2005

	1981–85		*1986–1990*		*1991–1995*		*1996–2000*		*2001–2005*		*1981–2005*	
Destination	*#*	*%*	*#*	*%*	*#*	*%*	*#*	*%*	*#*	*%*	*#*	*%*
Europe	45,620185,797		175,557	98.6	141,226	97.9	107,534	97.2	655,734	98.7		
Canada	755	0.4	1,919	1.3	2,451	2.2	5,125	0.8				
Australia	780	0.4	928	0.6	332	0.3	2,040	0.3				
USA	984	0.6	199	0.1	330	0.3	1,513	0.2				
Total	178,076	100	144,272	100	110,647	100	664,412	100				

Source: Figures are compiled by Içduygu (2006) from various sources of OECD and Eurostat

of the asylum channel to emigrate. Because the worst of the conflict between the armed forces and the PKK wound down in the second half of the 1990s, and following the gradual introduction of political reforms, numbers of asylum applications fell. However, an unidentified number of Turkish nationals, often of Kurdish origin, continue to attempt to enter EU countries illegally in search of jobs.[9]

Xenophobia and Enmity towards Foreigners

All these developments and changes led to increasing polarization among the German public on the issues of migration and asylum. This polarization came about as a consequence of debates on the paths Germany must follow in ideology, strategy, and international relations, and as the 1980s progressed, was increasingly expressed as a general fear and anxiety. In 1985, a survey asked members of the public how they felt about the fact that a few million foreigners were living among them, to which 45 percent replied that they were not in favor off this situation, 21 percent approved, and the remaining 34 percent were undecided. In a similar survey in 1989, however, 75 percent of those interviewed felt that there were too many foreigners in Germany. Leggewie (2004) claims that these fears among the German public were to some extent legitimate insofar as German society, which had hitherto been homogenous, was suddenly being surrounded by foreigners, and thus by unknown attitudes and behavior to which individuals within German society were unaccustomed. It seemed that fear of foreigners had become the spirit of the age, as a primary characteristic of post-modern societies is a mobility that threatens the organization of institutions. Urban areas as centers of aggregation increased alienation in the individual, in response to which the individual resorted to believing that those not sharing the same skin color, body language, and speech patterns were strange or odd. In some cases, these feelings even resulted in a reason to be grateful for being German.[10] Nevertheless, this sociopsychological examination does not sufficiently explain the climate of growing xenophobia in Germany throughout the 1990s.

Following German reunification, a 1992 research carried out by *Der Spiegel* magazine revealed that the greater majority of Germans felt no amity towards foreigners. In response to statements such as, "Foreigners are abusing our social security system," 77 percent said they felt this to be true; 74 percent

---

[9] Ahmet İçduygu and Kemal Kirişçi, "Turkey's International Migration in Transition," in *Land of Diverse Migrations: Challenges of Emigration and Immigration in Turkey* (Istanbul: Istanbul Bilgi University, 2009), 5–6.

[10] Claus Leggewie, "Stolz ein Deutscher zu sein—die neue Angst vor dem Fremden," in *Deutsche im Ausland,* ed. Bade, 428–429, footnote 6.

TABLE 9.3.
Reactions to the use of violence against asylum seekers in East and West Germany (%)

	Total	*Primary*	*Middle school*	*Gymnasium*	*Higher education*
West					
I approve/do not approve of the use of violence					
approve	8.0	13.0	10.0	4.0	4.0
do not approve	91.0	86.0	89.0	96.0	96.0
I understand/feel ashamed/unashamed by the use of violence					
ashamed	66.0	54.0	66.0	73.0	72.0
unashamed	25.0	32.0	23.0	24.0	20.0
understand	8.0	13.0	10.0	4.0	5.0
East					
I approve/do not approve of the use of violence					
approve	18.0	24.0	19.0	25.0	8.0
do not approve	82.0	76.0	81.0	74.0	91.0
I understand/feel ashamed/unashamed by the use of violence					
ashamed	58.0	47.0	55.0	54.0	73.0
unashamed	11.0	18.0	11.0	11.0	5.0
understand	18.0	24.0	19.0	25.0	8.0

Source: Einstellungen zu aktuellen Fragen der Innenpolitik 1992 in Deutschland, *Ipos,* Mannheim 1992.

agreed with the statement, "They are adding to Germany's housing problem"; 60 percent agreed that foreigners were "creating unemployment among Germans"; and 50 percent were of the opinion that "foreigners were making the streets unsafe."[11] These feelings were not expressed simply as a social trend, but also in the rise of attacks on asylum-seekers, migrants, and foreigners. In 1991, in the small town of Hoyerswerda in former East Germany, a serious attack, organized by a group of German youths, was made on a shelter housing Asian refugees. The local population was not hesitant about encouraging these youths in the attack, and security forces remained passive throughout the incident. In 1992, Rostock, another town in former East Germany, was the scene of a five-day-long series of attacks, again undertaken with support from the local population, which ended with the refugee shelter having to be evacuated and those it housed removed from the area.

Whether or not fear of foreigners may be considered a natural psychological reaction, when this fear becomes overtly xenophobic there needs to be change brought about in public policy. In the cases outlined above, the public

[11] *International Herald Tribune,* 27 October 1992, 1.

authorities' response was to treat the violence against the refugees as crimes committed by individuals rather than as violent acts rooted in growing xenophobia. In fact, violent acts such as these and others, like public attacks on foreign youths in cafes and the like, and foreign youths being prevented from using the city metro, were being committed by groups of Skinheads, violent youths who supported extreme nationalist political parties, and radical measures were needed to prevent such actions from happening.

The fact that xenophobia was rapidly becoming expressed in acts of open enmity towards foreigners meant that the ugly specter of racism was once more raising its head. Despite clear awareness among public institutions of the dangers entailed in continuing down such a path, the ponderous workings of the political system meant that legal measures were slow in coming.

By the 1990s, this new racism was evident all over Europe, but was most widespread in Germany. In elections in 1998, the German Folk Union (FVU) Party, not satisfied with the usual slogans of "Foreigners out!" and other tactics, garnered 13 percent of the vote in former East Germany by following a campaign in which it posted letters to the electorate outlining its enmity towards foreigners. This party, founded by a Bavarian billionaire industrialist, works in cooperation with other like-minded parties and their leaders throughout Europe, at the top of the list of which is Le Pen and his National Front Party in France, Jirinovski in Russia, and Kjaesgaard in Denmark. The latter is the leader of the DDP (Denmark People's Party) and was part of the coalition that came to power following elections in 2001. Although claiming that she is not racist, Kjaesgaard has said that Arabs and Muslims are not wanted in Christian Denmark. The German Nationalist Democratic Party, another party with a racist program, has brought thousands of its followers onto the streets of Leipzig during May 1 celebrations. Smaller parties on the extreme right of the political spectrum such as these also have an influence on the larger parties. Prior to the 2002 elections, Siegfried Benker from the Green Party in Bavaria stated that Bavaria's CSU (Christian Social Union Party) would be giving much of its campaigning time over to issues such as the deportation, exclusion, and polarization of foreigners.

Meanwhile, the numbers of racist attacks by extreme right-wing parties and neo-Nazis continued to rise. According to reports published by the Organization for the Protection of the German Constitution, 10,791 racially motivated attacks were reported in 1993. This had risen to 11,719 by 1997, an increase of 34 percent. It was clear that Skinhead groups were becoming ever more daring and by now were targeting particularly Turks, blacks, and punks.[12] Germany is home to the greatest number of Skinheads—estimates

[12] A. Shaikh Mohammad, "Germany Leads New Tide of Racism and Xenophobia Sweeping Europe," *Muslimedia*, 16 May 1998.

put the figure at about 5,000—but they are also active in Hungary, Poland, the United States, and England. It was in England that they first became organized in their activities. Groups generally consist of white males aged thirteen to twenty-five. Their beliefs are centered on the principles of deep anti-Semitism, extreme nationalism, and orthodox Nazism. Their appearance is marked by their sh aved heads, tattoos of Nazi symbols, and leather clothing with metal or chains added.

Xenophobic Behavior Directed at Turks

By the 1980s Turks were the most visible and numerous of Germany's ethnic groups, making them a primary target of xenophobia. By the 1990s, attacks had become frighteningly serious: Between 1991 and 1993, a total of eight Turks lost their lives in arson attacks in the cities of Mölln and Solingen. As expected, these were followed by mass protests in the streets by ordinary Germans wishing to make it known that they condemned these attacks. However, it would be wrong to see the attitudes held by those targeting the Turks as simply one more factor of the shockwaves felt in Germany, and indeed all over Europe, following the collapse of the Berlin Wall and the reunification of Germany. The roots of this racism lie further back in German history, in a time that many Germans try to forget.

In an attempt to reach the roots of this thinking, throughout the 1980s Barre Toelken collected from the German media selections of "comic material" based on migrant workers.[13]

One went as follows: "What's the difference between a Turk and a white line? You can't drive your car over a white line." This goes beyond the derision common in such kinds of "jokes" because it contains the element of killing. Everywhere in the world, various groups are the focus of derisive jokes that most often feature individuals from the group in question and are based on a particular trait associated with the group, such as meanness or stupidity. However, the jokes told by some Germans about Turks go beyond the usual ridicule and almost always include an element of death or annihilation: A few more are given here:

> What do you call something black perching in a tree?
> A Turk after a forest fire.
>
> How do you rape a Turkish woman?
> Skirt up and trousers down.

[13] B. Toelken, "Türkenrein and Türken, 'Raus' Images of Fear and Aggression in German Gastarbeiterwitze," in *Turkish Workers in Europe: An Interdisciplinary Study,* eds Ilhan Basgöz and Norman Furniss (Bloomington: Indiana University, 1985), 151–164.

Figure 9.2. After the Arson Attack in Solingen

> Have you heard that Turks can carry a knife all the time?
> Between their shoulder blades and ten centimeters deep.
>
> Have you seen the latest microwave oven?
> There's room in it for a whole family of Turks.
>
> A Turk and a Jew jump out of a plane at the same time. Who hits the ground first?
> Does it matter?
>
> A trainload of Turks leaves Istanbul but arrives in Hamburg empty. How come?
> It came by way of Auschwitz.[14]

According to Richard Albrecht, these jokes represent the potential nostalgia for Fascism and the attitudes of the radical right in Germany. Other writers too have expressed how deeply rooted these ideas and feelings are in some quarters. Consequently, the extraordinary rise in numbers of asylum-seekers and the pressures faced by Germany following reunification are not sufficient in explaining Germany's xenophobia, and particularly its targeting of Turks. Christian Habbe has explained that letters sent to German politicians by members of the public contain evidence of just how deep-seated this rancor and enmity is in the hearts of some. It is also worth noting that it would appear that anti-Jewish sentiment of the Nazi period seems to have been redeployed, this time against Turks. Some letters refer openly to the nostalgia of a superior race:

> Why should German tax charges be spent on this scum? Jews, migrant workers and gypsies are being provided with services. As is done in other countries, the women should have their reproductive organs removed and the men castrated. They breed like rabbits.
>
> What you call xenophobia is a resistance movement to prevent an Islamic take-over of this country.
>
> What do you expect German citizens to say when the first thing asylum-seekers do with money we've given them is hire taxis to have prostitutes brought to them from brothels?
>
> Our mother tongue, our culture, our religion, everything, is slipping through our fingers![15]

Although the above are examples from the more inflammatory end of German media, they nevertheless reveal how deep the roots of xenophobia penetrate, and how great a role is played by thinking that lays blame for all ills on the "other." Racism, thus, is a fine thread that has been woven into much of the fabric of life and features in debates on issues ranging from employment, man-

---

[14] Richard Albrecht, "Was ist der Unterschied zwischen Türken und Juden?" *Zeitschrift für Volkskunde* 78 (1982): 220–229.

[15] Christian Habbe, ed., *Auslaender—die verfemten Gaeste* (Hamburg: Spiegel-Buch, 1983), 157–166.

Figure 9.3. Hidden Threats

ner of dress, and eating habits to language, family size, and marriage patterns, and is a thread which, on issues considered particularly sensitive, is liable to break, thus causing damage to the fabric.

Between 1990 and 1995, German authorities, both federal and state, passed a range of laws attempting to say the ghost of neo-Nazism. In 1993, the German parliament passed a law granting foreigners who were victims of racial attacks the right to compensation on par with German citizens. The following year it was decided to render the display of Nazi symbols in public places a crime. With preventative measures such as these being put into place by Germans not desirous of being labeled racists, it would appear that, ironically, those among them who were the bitterest enemies of foreigners had actually served to improve the lot of their victims. In the end, of course, despite these measures, it is the smaller, marginal political parties who, ever in search of votes, have chosen to continue active campaigning using the racism ticket.

Asylum Seekers from Turkey and Their Organizations

Global changes in the 1990s brought new dimensions to such issues as the search for identity, the exercise of democratic rights, and ethnic group membership. As a consequence of this, on the international stage many societies began to witness the politicization of religious, ethnic, and cultural identities as founding elements of their nations.[16] Reactions to this were different in Europe and Turkey. Europe, influenced by a growing liberalism, chose to adopt a politics of difference and open up new areas for the expression of ethnicity, religion, culture, and gender. In contrast, Turkey adopted an aggressive stance when faced with its national groups making religion or ethnicity-based demands for some form of autonomy or independence. The resulting polarization led to high levels of organization among representatives of these ethnic groups abroad, where they were able to benefit from the wide-ranging democratic rights available to them. Within Turkey's borders, the armed forces, charged above all with the protection of national integrity, went into action against the extensions of these ethnic groups who chose terror and violence as their means of expression. Conflict between the two, concentrated in the south and southeastern parts of the country, resulted in more than 30,000 deaths over a period of fifteen years. Thus, two contrasting policies both served to alter the landscapes of asylum and identity.

With the halt of foreign labor imports by Germany in 1973, economic demands for employment began, more often than not, to conceal themselves behind politically based asylum demands. It was during the period of authoritarian rule following the 1980 military coup in Turkey that the asylum movement became politicized, and the continued politicization was guaranteed in later years by the powerful organizations and networks established by various ethnic groups.

The aim of a military memorandum presented to the government of Turkey on 12 March 1972 was liquidation of the leftist intelligentsia and other elements that had adopted the cause of Kurdish nationalism. Significant numbers of these people fled to Germany at the time, where a small number sought political asylum status. More austere and long-term measures were taken following the coup of 1980, and as a result, even more members of leftist groups or Kurdish organizations sought refuge in Germany, but this time they were accompanied by individuals from the extreme right and fundamentalist Islamists. The new Turkish constitution came into effect in 1983, and significant numbers of those whose asylum demands had been denied by Germany were given temporary, and later permanent, permits to remain in the country. It is estimated that 75 to 80 percent of asylum-seekers at the time made a decision to remain abroad permanently.[17] In the period after the 1990s, it appeared that those leaving Turkey to seek asylum abroad gained citizenship in the countries

---

[16] Ümit Cizre, "Türk Siyaseti: Geçmeyen Geçmiş, Gelemeyen Gelecek," *Görüş* no. 18 (1994–1995): 22.

[17] Jonas Widgren, "Movements of Refugees and Asylum Seekers. Recent Trends in a Comparative Perspective," in *The Changing Course of International Migration* (Paris: OECD, 1993), 87–95.

TABLE 9.4.
Asylum requests to Germany made by Turkish citizens between 1985–1994 and 1996–2001[1]

1985–1994	175.048
1996	23.814
1997	16.840
1998	11.754
1999	9.065
2000	8.968
2001	10.869

[1] Böcker, Refugee and Asylum-Seeking Migration from Turkey to Western Europe, *Bosphorus Journal,* Vol. 10, no. 1–2, p. 57
Kaynak: Eurostat ve Bundesamt für ausl. Flüchtlinge ve www. baft. The numbers given in this table for 1996 onwards have been calculated by the state institution responsible for asylum issues (*Bundesamt für die Anerkennung auslaendischer Flüchtlinge).* The same information presented in graphic form shows that four-fifths of asylum requests come from individauls of Kurdish origin

of destination, regardless of whether or not their legal status merited it. The majority of these are educated and from urban backgrounds and therefore often find employment in local governments and various departments of social services which have dealings with migrants from the same ethnic group.

Kurdish Organizations in Germany

From the very early days of the arrival of migrant labor, Germany supported the establishment of associations, but during the early years, despite the availability of state funds, migrants did not engage in much activity in this area. In later times, however, the associational movement would increasingly come to divide ethnic groups from each other and to radicalize some.

From the 1970s onwards, Turkish and Kurdish migrants began to make changes to the names of their organizations, replacing the traditional "Turkish" with "from/of Turkey." Cultural activities became important. The first large-scale celebration of *Nevruz,* a spring festival most closely associated in Turkey with the Kurdish population, took place in Duisburg in 1978.[18] During the following years, ideological divisions among Kurdish organizations became apparent. Although many migrants of Kurdish origin tended to remain with the Turks, others began to move in directions determined by the agenda of their organizations. In 1979 the Kurdistan Kurdish Workers Association (KOMKAR) was founded, followed three years later by the Federation of Democratic

[18] Gitmez and Wilpert, "A Micro-Society or an Ethnic Community?" 109–110.

Kurdish Migrant Workers' Association (KKDK). In 1984 other urban and regional organizations sprang up and were linked to Feyda-Kurdistan, which had close ties with the PKK.

From 1985 onwards, both KOMKAR and the KKDK were active not only in trying to influence politics in the homeland but also in defending the interests of Kurdish groups in Germany. As part of their activities, they engaged in enormous efforts to have the Kurds recognized as a distinct ethnic group, put pressure on authorities to have Kurdish children in Germany educated in their native tongue, and campaigned for Kurdish language television and radio broadcasts.[19] These campaigns gained support not only from other Kurdish organizations but also Turkish left-wing associations, German churches and unions, and the SPD (Social Democrat Party). Both KOMKAR and the KKDK operated on the principle that the Kurds in Germany were there to stay and therefore directed much of their action towards improving the legal status of migrants, refugees, and asylum-seekers. With this in mind, they worked in close cooperation with other Kurdish associations and organizations throughout Europe. The most significant result of this was the meeting in The Hague in April 1995 of the Kurdish Parliament in Exile, the aim of which was to find a political solution to the Kurdish problem.

Feyda-Kurdistan broke away from both KOMKAR and the KKDK in 1991 and entered into a much closer relationship with the PKK. Its efforts to persuade the German government to withdraw political and military support from Turkey were based on violence and the threat to commit violence, threats which were finally carried out in June 1993, with bomb attacks on Turkish diplomatic offices, banks, and tourist agencies in Berlin, Munich, and twenty-seven other cities throughout Europe. When similar attacks were repeated in November of the same year, the German government responded by clamping down on the PKK, the Kurdish National Salvation Front (ERNK), and thirty-three of their affiliated associations.

Other European states, claiming that if they were to take similar action the organizations would go underground, did not close them, so with their European networks still in place to a large extent, these organizations were weakened only in Germany. According to the Organization for the Protection of the German Constitution, the vast majority of the 400,000–500,000 Kurds resident in Germany have no desire whatsoever to become involved in any manner with PKK. Estimates in 1996 put numbers of "active" PKK members at 7,500 and sympathizer numbers at 40,000–50,000.[20]

---

[19] Sengül Şenol, *Kurden in Deutschland. Fremde unter Fremde* (Frankfurt a.M.: Haag und Heerchen, 1992), 186–202.

[20] Martin Hoch, "Türkische Politische Organisationen in der Bundesrepublic Deutschland," *Zeitschrift für Auslaenderrecht und Auslaenderpolitik* 14 (1994): 17–22.

Migrants, Asylum-Seekers, and Diaspora

Diasporas comprised of ethnic groups who have either voluntarily or forcibly become part of international migration movements constitute one of the most significant elements in modern migration.[21] Two factors are currently strengthening the position of old and new diasporas all over the world: the spread of multiculturalism, and the incapacity or reluctance of states that have active ethnic groups within their borders to take measures that would maintain state control over their activities.[22]

Three factors determine whether a specific ethnic or religious group is viewed as being "a diaspora": identity consciousness, organizational activity, and meaningful contact with the homeland. These three factors also explain conflict and disagreements that arise between the diaspora and the country of settlement or the home country. One more significant characteristic of diasporas is that in contrast to migrants, asylum-seekers, and illegal workers, whose status is determined by law, those who make up a diaspora community are individuals who have consciously chosen to maintain their ties and membership to the home country. States who accept migrants and asylum-seekers are faced with an entirely different situation in dealing with diasporas. These states' initial efforts are usually directed towards dissolving the ethnic group's identity within the dominant culture, restricting their communication channels and, particularly with younger generations, assimilating them into the culture. From examples throughout the world it is clear that in many cases they have failed, and continue to fail in this mission: the Russian diaspora that moved out of the pre-1989 Soviet Union; Armenians and Greeks in both the United States and France; the Kurds in Germany, Belgium, and Holland; the ongoing Tamil conflict in Sri Lanka; and the Palestinians who, on various continents, continue to struggle against the pro-Israeli lobby in the United States.

Globalization is also playing a part in strengthening diasporas, particularly with respect to their gaining new rights and visibility as a minority in public space. In this context, cultural rights have moved to the fore. In their countries of settlement, diasporas engage in campaigns for development of their native languages and the right to use communication channels to broadcast in these languages. A newer strategy they've adopted is the attempt to gain some form of autonomy in countries of settlement through "communal-

---

[21] Until fifty years ago the term "diaspora" was used to describe the scattering of the Jewish peoples following their escape from Egypt. It is now used to describe minority migrant groups who maintain emotional and material ties with the homeland.

[22] There is extensive literature on this subject. See Dimitri Constas and Athanasios Platias, eds., *The Greek Diaspora in a Comparative Perspective* (London: MacMillan, 1992); Mark J. Miller, *Foreign Workers in Europe: An Emerging Political Force* (New York: Praeger, 1981); and Gabriel Sheffer, ed. *Modern Diasporas in International Politics* (New York: St. Martins, 1986).

ism." With the new freedoms being afforded them, diasporas are constructing churches, mosques, synagogues, and other religious institutions, providing social and health services to their communities, and founding private schools and universities. And these efforts are not confined to the larger, financially well supported groups; smaller, less financially well-off groups such as Algerians, Moroccans, Turks, and Kurds, through group solidarity, are also engaged in forming organizations specific to their needs. Thus, it is possible to say that a wide range of resources for communication and possibilities for engaging in solidarity-based activity are being provided for all diaspora communities, whether their resources are limited or not. One important factor being taken into account at this point is the organic nature of the ties diasporas maintain with opposition groups in the homeland. Most conflict is engendered by the security fears of diasporas and the notion of citizenship that is being forced upon them. A striking example of this occurred when, during a state visit to Turkey in August 1999, German Foreign Affairs Minister Joschka Fischer requested that Turkey abolish the death penalty, citing as his greatest concern the violent protest activities Kurdish migrants in Germany would engage in if this request were denied. In reference to Abdullah Öcalan, the PKK leader imprisoned in Turkey, Fischer was not hesitant in saying that Öcalan's execution would affect both security and stability in Europe and constitute an enormous obstacle on the path of negotiations for Turkey's entry into the European Union.[23] Reflecting as they do external dynamics, this power of diaspora communities to sanction or impede governments was visible yet again when it became the cause of a conflict of opinion in the coalition government in Turkey in 2001.

Increasing numbers of Kurdish asylum movements since the 1980s have, in the words of Appadurai, led to the creation of "diasporic public scape."[24] A "long-distance nationalism" or transnational nationalism has emerged, empowered by collective memory, imagination, and symbols broadcast by electronic media rather than national borders, and has begun to question classical nationalism and its parameters. Resolution of identity problems in today's world lies in questioning the hegemony of the nation-state.[25] Global media and migration movements have opened the way to international debate on contemporary political and social values, with the result that we now speak of the "shifting nature of national boundaries." With these terms of Appadurai's, there exist diasporic public spheres in which the nation-state is no longer the single arbiter of important social change,[26] and diasporas gain power in identity negotiations with the nation-state.

[23] *Milliyet,* 23 July 1999.

[24] Arjun Appadurai, *Modernity at Large* (Minneapolis: University of Minnesota Press, 1996), 4.

[25] Ümit Cizre, "Turkey's Kurdish Problem: Borders, Identity, and Hegemony," in *Right-Sizing the State: The Politics of Moving Borders,* eds Brendan O'Leary, Ian Lustick, and Thomas Callaghy (Oxford: Oxford University Press, 2001), 249.

[26] Appadurai, *Modernity at Large,* 4.

Media Consumption Habits among Euro-Turks

Changes in media consumption patterns among Euro-Turks after 1980 were brought about by a twofold process: the end of the state monopoly of television in Turkey and subsequent enterprises in the area of communications technologies, and the differentiation and variety that became part of the life of the media in Turkey. Greater ease in being able to receive television broadcasts from the homeland and in buying Turkish newspapers abroad led to increased numbers following the media in their native tongue. In the 1980s, Turkish migrants in Germany watched more German television broadcasts with only special daily or weekly programs provided in Turkish. From 1990 onwards, however, broadcasts in Turkish became the most watched, a situation which, from the perspective of adaptation and integration, creates a conflict. Turkish language broadcasts have succeeded in filling the gap by providing television programs that deal with issues of less interest to the German media. These broadcasts are of particular significance to the many first-generation migrants who, because of their lack of German language skills, are unable to follow up on such issues as changes to the pension and tax systems in the German media.

On the other hand, this situation also leads to what may be referred to as "media ghettoization," insofar as it facilitates the possibility of creating one-sided views among Turkish migrants who live on a daily diet of Turkish language television and press broadcasts with a more nationalist bias. Until 1990, only TRT, Turkish State Television, and its special channel for Turkish citizens overseas, TRT-Int, were able to broadcast abroad.

Preference for Visual Media

Research completed in 1999 in Germany revealed that the majority of Turkish radio and television audiences there followed Turkish broadcasts with a frequency and intensity that varied depending on age and education level. In the under–thirty-five age group of migrants, 95 percent followed both German

TABLE 9.5.
Media preferences among migrants according to age group (%)

Age group	*Television*	*Radio*	*Daily newspaper*	*Weekly newspaper*
18–25	92.2	47.8	67.2	29.4
26–29	96.8	38.5	51.6	16.7
30–44	95.6	31.8	58.2	18.0
45–59	95.2	26.3	47.2	15.3
60 and older	95.2	22.1	33.7	11.5

Source: *Migrationsbericht 2002,* Zentrum für Türkeistudien, P.72

and Turkish television; 36 percent listened to both German and Turkish radio; and 50 percent read newspapers in both languages.

Media preferences among migrants are closely linked to the issue of identity. There can be little doubt that technological advances of the previous twenty years—the fax, Internet, mobile phone—have paved the way for the growing importance of transnational migrants, who consider their identity as unbound by national borders and who are equally engaged both here and there. With this phenomenon emerging all over the world, with increasing globalization, it has made itself heard in the context of Turkey's forty-year migration history primarily since 2000. It is useful here to outline briefly the development of this process over time.

Foreign Media Maintains a Warm Relationship with Turkey— "Bridge Building" (1960–1980)

In the early years of surplus labor export by Turkey, the Turkish state had two primary concerns: preventing workers' saving from disappearing into the black economy and catering to the need among Turkish workers for information by broadcasting news in Turkish through the Western media. The latter was also an effort to drown out the sound of Bizim Radyo, at that time broadcasting out of Communist East Germany and engaging in pro-Communist propaganda. Following discussions between the Turkish State Planning Organization and the relevant authorities in West Germany, broadcasting of daily news bulletins in Turkish began. The individual responsible for these broadcasts was writer Yüksel Pazarkaya, then editor of German TV station ZDF, broadcasting out of Cologne in West Germany. The broadcasts at that time were more information- than entertainment-based and aimed at keeping workers up-to-date on their social rights and the support services available to them. Meanwhile, the major Turkish daily *Hurriyet* began printing in Europe to cater to the needs of the workers. In the 1970s, the *TV Memleket Haberi* program, prepared by TRT in Ankara and broadcast out of Frankfurt, was added.

Europe Discovers a New Consumer Group: Turkish Advertising in the Media (1985–2000)

In the latter part of the 1970s, and particularly in the wake of the 1973 energy crisis, labor-importing countries in Europe brought a halt to their state-sponsored labor agreements and would accept no more guest workers. The results of this proved unexpected: workers did not return to their homelands and, in fact, began bringing their families to the country of settlement. Thus, with these new consumers, new advertising methods and campaigns began, especially in Germany and other countries with high populations of Turks. In Germany, the press, radio, and television, in order to attract Turkish consumers, began addressing them in their own language. Examples are Etap and

Turkiş broadcasting in German; Merhaba and TD1 in German and Turkish; and Metropol FM in Turkish only. These broadcasts thus created new transnational social spaces.

In 1985 the first private Turkish television channel, Star, made its debut. It was followed in rapid succession by Show TV, ATV, Kanal 6, TGRT, Kanal D, and Kanal 7. TGRT belongs to the Ihlas Group and is nationalist-religious. Kanal 7 has, in turn, been the interpreter of the views of the Refah Party, the Fazilet Party, and, currently, those of AKP.

Three factors were paramount in the appearance of this transnational media: the restructuring of the communications sector in Turkey, the global growth of ethnic media, and the developments in telecommunications in Germany.

Consequent to all these developments, Turks living abroad can receive news from Turkey and be entertained via different channels, and the European economy, by developing marketing strategies of an ethnic nature, has succeeded in directly addressing its Turkish consumers. After all, the yearly income of Turks in Germany alone amounts to 18 billion DM, and in contrast to the early years of migration when savings were sent to the home country, over 97 percent of Turks now choose to utilize and spend their income in the country of settlement.[27] Research completed in 1997 by the Turkish Research Center showed that 56.7 percent of Turks in Germany fulfilled their information needs from Turkish press only, whereas 38 percent followed both German and Turkish press.[28]

It is not only the private sector but also state institutions such as the *Deutsche Bundespost* (the state post administration) and insurance companies that have begun to make their services available through the medium of Turkish. The profits made as a result of these campaigns is reflected, for example, in the fact that TD1, a 24-hour television channel operating in Berlin, secures all of its income from advertising, and TRT-Int, the state-operated Turkish channel, secures more than 98 percent of its advertising from businesses in Germany.

Metropol FM, whose target group is fourteen- to forty-nine-year-old Turks, refuses financial funding from the German authorities, thereby choosing to protect its freedom of expression through economic independence rather than becoming an instrument of a *multikulti* ethnic presentation.[29] The importance of addressing the Turkish population in its own tongue did not go

[27] Matild Jrdanova-Duda, "Von vernachlaessigter deutsch türkischer Zielgruppe ..." *Auslaender in Deutschland* 17, no. 1 (2001): 4–5.

[28] Ayşe Çağlar, "Mediascapes, Advertisement Industries and Cosmopolitan Transformations: German Turks in Germany," *New German Critique* 92 (Spring/Summer, 2004): 43.

[29] *Multikulti* is a public institution in Berlin that allows the voices of its various ethnic groups to be heard via broadcasting in twenty languages. For more detailed information see Steven Vertovec, "Fostering Cosmopolitanism: A Conceptual Survey and a Media Experiment in Berlin," working paper for the Transnational Communities Programme, University of Oxford, 2000.

unnoticed by local German press either, and the Berlin daily *Tageszeitung* now publishes a weekly supplement in Turkish titled *Perşembe* (*Thursday*). These developments are most meaningful in the fact that they allow a broadening of views and interests among Turks living abroad through making it possible for them to get both entertainment and news from at home and abroad, thereby allowing them to create transnational social spaces in which to develop different identities.

They are also significant in that they point to the existence of a new relationship between migration and cosmopolitanism. According to German sociologist Ulrich Beck, cosmopolitanism is not the reverse of localism, and is a process that involves the individual in the formation of nonegalitarian pluralistic loose ties. The individual, rather than being affiliated to one country or nation is affiliated to a city, or even a neighborhood. Metropol FM may be said to have adopted this perspective. One individual, listening to Metropol FM in Berlin's 1001 Café, described his feelings as follows: "We are listening to Istanbul and Izmir here, but we're also connecting with New York via Istanbul. In this café I feel as if I'm in Istanbul, Berlin, Europe, and New York at the same time."[30] This development of ethnic media presents Euro-Turks with the opportunity to express themselves, introduce their lifestyles and pleasures, and take their place in mainstream society. During the Green–Social Democrat coalition government, in attempts to take this even further, a media dialogue took place in 1999 between representatives of Turkish and German media. Out of these meetings came some interesting proposals: creating a consultative committee of both groups; weekly presentations of important news items from the Turkish media to their German counterparts for publication in the German press; and the establishment of a two-language television channel such as ARTE, the currently operating French and German channel. All these proposals were put forward and supported in parliament by Cem Özdemir, then a parliamentary representative for the Greens.

The Islamophobia and antipathy towards Turks that spread throughout the West following 2001 served to strengthen right-wing and conservative political parties in many of the countries with high concentrations of Turkish populations. This sadly resulted in the pushing aside of any efforts to spread the native languages of migrants, of the desire to make them part of school curricula. With unconditional integration now being the aim, native language lessons in school began to be abolished, to the extent that in one Berlin school it was forbidden to speak a language other than German within the school grounds. Positive multicultural policies were abandoned and policies that would bring Turks and the EU closer culturally were discarded. However,

[30] Ayşe Çağlar, "Popular Culture, Marginality and Institutional Incorporation," *Cultural Dynamics* 10, no. 3 (1998): 243–261

global communications systems of today mean that Turkey's state and private channels still operate, and with their nationalist leanings are encouraging the formation of an Islamic identity among Euro-Turks who would otherwise be adopting "transnational" identities. National origin is being put aside, and it is as Muslims that Turks are spoken of more often than as Turks. Prior to the events of 11 September 2001, new identities were about to be born in transnational social spaces. When these efforts failed there developed a mentality among Turks that Reiner Bauböck refers to as "local consumer cosmopolitanism," a mentality encouraged and shaped by business interests and the advertising industry.[31] In light of recent developments it is only possible for ethnic media to play a unifying role if it can overcome the obstacles placed in their path by the majority Christian Democrat Party.

Religion in the Media: The Islamist Multiculturalism Experience, Berlin's AçikTV (1990–2001)

The 1990s witnessed a huge increase in the number and variety of television programs from the homeland available to migrants and the ethnicization of means of mass communication. Both led to the creation of social spaces unique to migrants and heated public debate on the obstacles to integration that all of these created.[32] One product of these debates was the introduction by German public communication organizations of "multicultural" radio and television programs, a decision given impetus by the growing levels of violence against Turks, which culminated in the arson attacks in Mölln and Solingen. Fearful of the competition created by transnational broadcasts, the state began sponsoring what quickly became known as *multikulti* programs. It was hoped that with these broadcasts, migrants would become more involved in the problems of the areas in which they lived, but results proved less positive than expected. Instead, a different kind of communication system, described as the "third social space," gained popularity. This emerged out of the "Open Channels" that were established in many cities and regions in Germany from the middle of the 1980s onwards as a result of cable technology.[33] Through these channels both German citizens and migrants had the opportunity to produce and broadcast in their native languages, an opportunity that Turks,

---

[31] Reiner Bauböck, "Political Community beyond the Sovereign State: Supranational Federalism and Transnational Minorities," paper given at a conference on cosmopolitansim at University of Warwick, 27–29 April 2000, 19

[32] Jörg Becker, "Die Ethnisierung der deutschen Medienlandschaft-Türkischee Medienkultur zwischen Assoziation und Dissoziation," in *Deutschland im Dialog der Kulturen: Medien, Images, Verstaendigung,* eds Siegfried Quandt and Wolfgang Gast (Konstanz: UKW Medien, 1998), 295–302.

[33] Kira Kosnick, "Building Bridges: Media for Migrants and the Public-Service Mission in Germany," *European Journal of Cultural Studies* 3, no. 3 (2000): 321–344.

in particular, utilized extensively: more than a quarter of the programs issuing from Berlin's Open Channel were in Turkish, despite Turks' constituting only 8 percent of the city's population. Views on this new communication system varied across a wide spectrum. Those who spoke in its defense were of the opinion that with the dominant national media in Europe treating foreigners and migrants as a marginal group and showing little interest in their problems, this system allowed their voices to be heard and thus fulfilled a positive role in integration. It was democratic communication, the greatest benefit of which was an opportunity to groups such as women, the unemployed, youth, migrants, the homeless, homosexuals, artists, and even those of school-going age to reflect their wishes and demands. Those who use the Open Channel pay no fee and are given technical help and training. They operate on the principle of first-come, first-served, and their usage is divided into time segments between 2:00 PM and midnight. At the beginning, directors did not meddle in any way with program content, believing that this radio had a significant role to play locally in democratic culture.

However, as fundamentalist Islamic content came to dominate more and more broadcasts, theses uncontrolled programs became the subject of criticism by the Media Council of the state of Brandenberg. The broadcasts became the source of more anxiety following 11 September 2001. In Berlin the Open Channel began to be known as the "Molla Channel." Meanwhile, a number of Turkish followers of the programs also began calling for control mechanisms to be put in place for what they described as anti-democratic militant broadcasts.[34] These developments resulted in the polarization of views among responsible institutions. Until very recent times, the head of the Office for Foreigners in Berlin, Barbara John, was defending the Open Channel as a unique forum for the teaching of tolerance-based discussion of political attitudes in a democratic society.[35] Open Channel Berlin director, Jürgen Linke, believes that it is an extremely influential agent in socialization.

Kira Kosnick has undertaken a detailed analysis of these programs and the results reflect different attitudes. One of the two programs studied in the research, *Halimiz, ahvalimiz,* was prepared and presented by Ramazan Ekici for six years. Ekici came to Germany having completed his primary education in Turkey. During his time in Germany, he worked in several factories and his latest enterprise is a secondhand goods store. The program aired on the Open Channel three times a month from a small studio in which Ekici sat with his papers and a telephone. The program was in three parts: a reading in Turkish of sections of the Qur'an, an interview with a selected guest, and finally a

---

[34] Kira Kosnick, "Extreme by Definition: Open Channel Television and Islamic Migrant Producers in Berlin," *New German Critique* 92 (Spring/Summer 2004), 26.

[35] Ibid., 29.

section whereby the public telephoned in for discussion. The telephone never ceased ringing. Ekici espoused some radical views: according to him, for example, no one may come between the individual and the Qur'an.[36] His views were rejected by many, but because of the program, the Islamic faith became a subject of debate outside mosques and social centers. According to some, this democratic debate based upon Islam is a doorway that may lead to a European Islam.[37]

The second Islamist program studied on Open Channel Berlin had a different character. Saadet began in 1997 and was prepared and presented by Himmet Kabak. It took its inspiration from the teachings of the MIHR Foundation, established by the Mihr sect. Kabak is a disciple of Sheik Iskender Ali Mihr, and the foundation he represents has its headquarters in Ankara with branches in Izmir, the United States, and Germany. The program had a very simple format, with the sheik or his representative would appear from a fixed camera angle. Turkish was the language used, and the program was in the form of a *hadis* lesson; it used as examples events from the life of the Prophet Mohammed. The Kabak family was at the same time using the Internet in their own home to organize video conferencing activities between cities in Germany and Turkey. From 2000, the Mihr sect used the cable system in Berlin to begin live broadcasting on the Internet, a new method with the advantage of bypassing even the rules of Open Channel broadcasting. The aim of Saadet was the spreading of the voice of *ümmet*, the community of the faithful. The program was taken off air after the September 11 attacks. With its closure the MIHR Foundation established a cyber-university to continue its teachings to the faithful on the Internet.

After 2001, debates on public security in Europe brought changes to the usage of the Open Channel. Debate began in the context of freedom of opinion on the views espoused on religious and political issues. Although attitudes remained positive towards the anti-authoritarian and individualistic character of programs like Ekici's, they lost their attractiveness as part of a soft liberalism that allowed the spread of radical global teachings. In most recent times, multiculturalism is being supported only to the degree that it encourages interest and concern in local issues. Open Channel broadcasts are now being controlled, and religious broadcasts are allotted space only on Saturdays and Sundays between 1:00 and 5:00 PM.

---

[36] Ibid., 31. In an interview with Kosnick on 8 May 1998, Ramazan Ekici stated that Muslims must personally read the Qur'an and imams must not come between the individual and the Qur'an.

[37] Gerdien Jonker, "Islamic Television 'Made in Berlin,'" in *Paroles d'Islam,* ed. Felice Dassetto (Strasbourg: Gallimard 2000), 267–280.

CHAPTER 10

Attitudes to the European Union: Euro-Turks and Euroskeptics

Figure 10.1. European Workforce

Turkish immigration has long been important in European-Turkish relations. These relations have a long past. Turkey formally declared in 1959 its intention to foster close cooperation with the European Economic Community (EEC), the European Union of that time. In 1963 the Ankara Agreement was signed declaring the intention of Turkey to become a full member of the European community. This procedure was followed by years of mutual discussions; however, neither side wanted to end the process. In 1995 the Custom Union was finalized. After the Summit Meeting in 1997 in Luxembourg, Turkey halted the political dialogue, indicting its frustration that Turkey's name was not mentioned among the candidate countries. Then in 1999 at the Helsinki Summit the breakthrough took place and Turkey was officially declared a candidate country. A critical turning point was the decision of the European Council's Copenhagen Summit in 2002 to review Turkey's progress in meeting the Copenhagen political criteria. The pitch of objections reached an especially high level in 2004, and in 2005 the decision to finally start negotiations with Turkey was made. Opposition to Turkish membership has been partly based on a fear of a "flood" of Turkish nationals entering EU countries. In addition, many have also pointed to the difficulties faced by Turkish immigrants in integrating themselves into their host society. This "integration" problem has been used as evidence for how Turkey does not and cannot fit culturally into Europe.

The European Commission (EC) regularly monitors public opinion of old and new member states. The surveys concerning public opinion swings are published in printed and digital form by Eurobarometer. The EC also publishes country reports concerning potential members. In order to better understand the reaction and attitudes of Turkish migrants in Europe as well as public opinion within Turkey about the EU, the findings of two major surveys are explored here, both conducted by Dr. Ayhan Kaya and Dr. Ferhat Kentel of the Center for Migration Research at Istanbul's Bilgi University.

The primary importance of the first research survey lies in its revealing the character and nature of the Turkish diaspora, and it is useful here to present its main findings in brief. The aims of the research may be said to have been threefold: bringing to light the heterogeneous structure of the Turkish diaspora in Europe; assisting in breaking down the stereotypical image of this group; and presenting a picture of the main features of the transnational communities these Turks have created.

In this research, 1,065 and 600 surveys were conducted in Germany and France, respectively. In answering the questions posed to them, 20 percent of respondents in France and 36 percent in Germany used the Turkish language. For Turks in Germany, changes brought about with the 1991 Foreigners Law and the 1993 Migrant and Asylum Seeker Law have played a determining role concerning citizenship. Since that time, no further legal amendments have been made, although Kaya and Kentel say that political discourse reveals that more restrictive measures may be possible in the future. In France, Article 23 of the law governing foreigners grants automatic citizenship to third-generation migrant children. For those of the second generation, Article 44 of the same law requires that they must have been born on French soil and resident there since the age of thirteen.

Significant numbers of Euro-Turks have yet to complete the legal formalities that will allow them citizenship status. Kaya and Kentel are of the opinion that this may be explained by the fact that the individuals involved do not feel the necessity to do so and find it more convenient to establish transnational social spaces in which bridges may be built that facilitate both sides, a process which has come to be known as "globalization from below."[1]

As indicated by the research, regional concentrations have occurred in both countries. In Germany, the areas where the greatest numbers of Turks are concentrated are the states of North Rhine-Westphalia, Baden-Württemberg, and Bavaria, and in France, the areas of Ile-de-France, Rhône-Alpes, and Alsace. A quarter of those taking part in the surveys in Germany were born there, and a fifth of those participating in the French surveys were born on French soil. In the sampling used, the numbers of mixed marriages were few: only 6 percent of respondents were married to natives of either France or Germany. The majority of families surveyed had three children; 80 percent were living in rented accommodation; 76 percent owned property in Turkey; 94 percent of German Turks, and 87 percent of French Turks, said they visit the homeland each year. Employment in the sampling was as follows: laborers and paid workers, 40 percent; students, 6 percent; unemployed, 10 percent; and housewives and retired persons, 42 percent. Both qualitative and quantitative data reveal clearly that it is not only unskilled labor that makes up Turkish populations in Europe. Politicians, artists, businesspeople, and journalists are among individuals of Turkish origin whose names are known by the German public. Although a section of the population is upwardly mobile, there remains a significant number of unemployed (22 percent), a high number of whom may be found in Berlin's Kreuzberg, Cologne's Keupstraße, and in Villier Le Bel in Paris. This population, which may be said to be living in ethnic cocoons with low living standards, is subject to a kind of "hyper-exclusion"; they do not place their trust in any state, be it Turkey, France, or Germany. Rather than to either the countries of origin or settlement, their primary loyalties lie with various religious associations (especially the National View Movement), Alevi *Cemevi* (worship places), fellowship organizations, and mosques. It is possible to evaluate these attitudes as a kind of proletarianization that dismisses all

[1] Globalization from below is taking place when individuals, groups, or small communities attempt to build a permanent relationship with equivalent partners living permanently abroad.

value of politics. Among Euro-Turks actively integrated into the labor market, those most satisfied with their socioeconomic situation were Turks in France (36 percent); 44 percent of German Turks and 66 percent of those in France were of the opinion that they had witnessed an improvement in their social conditions in the previous ten years.. Concerning their position in the social structure, 52 percent of German Turks and 41 percent of French Turks described themselves as being lower middle class.

Homeland and the Host Country

The research clearly shows that Turks in Europe no longer plan permanent return to the homeland. Forty-two percent in Germany and 50 percent in France do not follow political events in Turkey. Among those who do, it is the activities of the party presently in power there—AKP (Justice and Development Party)—that are most closely followed. Thirty-two percent of German Turks and 35 percent of French Turks are AKP sympathizers; 7 percent of German Turks and 9 percent of those in France feel closer to the CHP (Republican People's Party); 10 percent of Turks in Germany support the openly Islamic *Saadet* Party, the SP (Happiness Party). The MHP (National Movement Party) finds support among 8 percent of Euro-Turks. Respondents' views on the problems facing Turkey were dependent on their country of settlement: 23 percent of German Turks saw democratization and human rights as the primary issues, whereas 22 percent of those in France were of the opinion that bribery, patronage, and nepotism constituted Turkey's greatest problems. As far as citizenship was concerned, a majority of Euro-Turks (59 percent in Germany; 74 percent in France) was in favor of integration and political participation. More recent statistics reveal that of 2.5 million Turks in Germany, 1.5 million are ready to integrate fully into mainstream society, with that number including many who have already become citizens. On the other hand, 1 million German Turks (41 percent) and 100,000 Turks in France (26 percent) have no desire to change their individual status. This lack of interest may be attributed both to disappointment at the non-acceptance of dual citizenship and an unwillingness to become involved in the bureaucratic formalities that obtaining a new citizenship status entails. Euro-Turks' lack of interest in political events in Turkey is also reflected in a similar apathy towards these events in the country of settlement: 60 percent of Euro-Turks do not follow the internal politics of their country of residence; it may be said that they are apolitical. Among those who follow domestic European politics, the Social Democrats are of primary interest: 7 percent of German Turks and 28 percent of French Turks sympathize with this party. The Social Democrats are followed by the Green parties, with 8.5 percent and 5 percent support among German and

French Turks respectively. German Turkish youth display a greater interest in politics than their French counterparts. Twenty percent of German Turks and 30 percent of French Turks placed their primary trust in the services provided by health and social security institutions. In this context and concerning the mosque, there was an interesting difference between the two groups: although 19 percent of German Turks regarded the institution of the mosque with trust, this figure was only 9 percent among French Turks.

Regarding the primary problems facing them in the country of settlement, there was no consensus of opinion among Euro-Turks. Twenty-six percent of German Turks felt that different moral values constituted a significant problem, whereas in France the greatest problem (expressed by 18 percent) was the lack of language skills. In other words, among German Turks it appears that feelings of group solidarity prevail, whereas French Turks tend to explain their exclusion by pointing to a lack of language skills. The same attitudes were visible in relation to association membership: 45 percent of Turks in Germany were members of a religious association, whereas among their French counterparts, participation tended more towards cultural centers.

One important issue examined in Kaya and Kentel's research is the predisposition among Euro-Turks towards identification with their country of settlement. Twenty-seven percent of German Turks and 36 percent of those in France expressed feelings of affiliation with both homeland and country of settlement. Kaya and Kentel believe that it is this group that could constitute the EU-Turkey bridge to which the researchers refer in the title of their research. The researchers describe this group as having an active, transnational, universal, and cosmopolitan identity, and they say it is a mistake to look upon them as "exiles" any longer because they have become active social actors in their new countries. When the data is examined in light of place of birth, it is clear that second- and third-generation Euro-Turks have ties with both Turkey and the host country, with those to the host country being the stronger. Forty-three percent and 37 percent of those born in France and Germany, respectively, stated that they regarded themselves as having dual identities. In terms of social position, feelings of dual belonging were most prevalent in middle and higher income families (36 and 32 percent) whereas affiliation to the home country was higher among lower income families of German Turks and French Turks (23 and 17 percent). Loyalty toward home country seems to be related to financial status.

Among the values most admired by Euro-Turks who had taken on the citizenship of the host country were the validity of rules, being able to defend one's rights, a democratic mentality, and respect for human rights. According to Kaya and Kentel, these are all held in greater esteem in the liberal multicultural structure of Germany in comparison to the secular and republican structures of both France and Turkey.

Integration/Assimilation

Kaya and Kentel attempted to discover the extent to which Euro-Turks are open to processes of adaptation and assimilation using the criteria developed by Gordon (1964), who theorized seven different types of assimilarion: (1) cultural or behavioral assimilation (acculturation); (2) structural assimilation, which involves entrance into organizations and institutions of the host society at the primary group level; (3) marital assimilation (amalgamation); (4) identity assimilation, or the creation of a sense of "people-hood" at the societal level; (5) attitude receptional assimilation, or the absence of prejudice; (6) behavioral receptional assimilation, or the absence of discrimination; and (7) civic assimilation, or generating a shared identity of citizenship. Gordon considered structural assimilation as the most significant of these.

TABLE 10.1.
Form of Assimilation/Integration in Germany/France

	Germany	*France*
Cultural or behavioral assimilation		X
structural assimilation	X	
marital assimilation		
Identity assimilation	X	X
Attitude receptional assimilation		
behavioral receptional assimilation		X
Civic assimilation	X	X

Source: A. Kaya- F. Kentel, 2005 Euro-Turks, Table.15, p.100

Kaya and Kentel claim that Brubaker's thesis (1992) on French and German migration policies no longer hold true. At the time his book was published, Brubaker held that the universal and inclusive character of French migration policies meant migrants became citizens speedily and easily, whereas the particularistic and exclusionist nature of German policies recognized migrants as settlers only.

Kaya and Kentel, however, point to the fact that while countries such as France, England, the United States, Ireland, and the Netherlands, which at one time embraced democratic and universal values towards migrants, have in more recent times adopted more restrictive policies, since 2000, Germany's migration policies have become more liberal. Because of the Red-Green coalition, which was in power until 2005, debates on multiculturalism and cultural differences continued and resulted in the ever-increasing appearance of Turks in Germany's public space. The visibility of Turks has increased through their activities in fine arts and political institutions, and as entrepreneurs and investors in the private sector. It may therefore be said that Germany is moving towards integration rather than discrimination.

Euro-Turks and the EU

Euro-Turks in both countries expect the following from Turkey's EU membership:

- It will bring more democracy to Turkey (63 percent of German Turks; 67 percent of French Turks)
- It will improve the implementation of human rights in Turkey (70 percent of German Turks; 79 percent of French Turks)
- It will result in migration from Turkey into EU countries (71 percent of German Turks; 69 percent of French Turks)

Concerning their influence on the host country, opinions vary among Euro-Turks. Approximately 32 percent of French Turks and 25 percent of German Turks believe that Turks have had no negative impact on the host society. However, 24 percent of German Turks state that Turks tend to be lazy, and 33 percent of French Turks refer to the Turks as having difficulty in adapting to local values, and as a result, tending to build ethnic enclaves and remain introverted.

Formation of New Identities

Sixty percent and 70 percent of Turks in Germany and France, respectively, describe themselves as having identities based on their various loyalties, a phenomenon now referred to in the social sciences as "hyphenated identity." Sixty percent of Euro-Turks define themselves as "Turkish-European." Eighty percent of this group call themselves "Turkish-European," whereas the remaining 20 percent refer to themselves as "European-Turk." In contrast, 37 percent of German Turks and 24 percent of French Turks refer to themselves as being "Turkish." When pressed for more detail, 27 percent of the German Turk respondents defined themselves as "German citizen," "German Turk," "world citizen," *and* "EU citizen." Percentages of French Turks describing themselves as such were slightly higher.

Euro-Turks and Islam

In the West, Islam is most often perceived as a threat, and fundamentalist Islam as a worldview which embraces racism, xenophobia, and violence. Kaya and

Kentel, however, put forward the notion that Islam plays an important role for individuals who, having to live with unemployment and xenophobia, and having given up their original identities while being subjected to processes of forced assimilation, desire to recover their past. Thus, some European Turks are employing ethnic belonging and religious belief as a basis for individual identity. Religiosity among Euro-Turks appears dependent on birthplace: 9 percent of those born in Turkey describe themselves as "a very religious Muslim," with the percentages being 3 and 5 percent in Germany and France, respectively, for Euro-Turks born in those countries. Meanwhile, 35 percent of Euro-Turks describe themselves as being Muslim, but are not obedient to any of its rules in their daily lives: for this group, religiosity is symbolic.

From the perspective of identity and political leanings, German Turks describe themselves as very religious (33 percent), patriotic (23 percent), nationalist (17 percent), democratic (17 percent), and conservative (17 percent). French Turks describe themselves as nationalist (27 percent), Kemalist (21 percent), religious (21 percent), and secular (19 percent). In light of this data, it may be said that France's Turks are more republican and unitarian, whereas their German counterparts are more communitarian.

A second, and similar, research survey was conducted by the same team of Ayhan Kaya and Ferhat Kentel, under the title of *Turks of Belgium—Are They a Bridge or an Obstacle Between Turkey and the EU?* The findings of this second survey largely confirm the conclusions of the first one. Among the additional findings, the most relevant concerns the attachment of Belgian Turks to their new country. This is proven by large-scale house acquisitions and the firm intention of not returning to their home country. Comparing the results regarding financial status according to regional differences, results showed that Turks living in Brussels and in Flemish regions are faring better than those in Walloon regions. However, another characteristic of Turks in Belgium is the tendency to import brides and bridegrooms. This tendency represents a serious handicap in regards to integration.[2]

In both research surveys, Kaya and Kentel observe that Euro-Turks are constructing their "Europeanness," or more precisely, their French and German identities, through mutual interaction with the majority societies, and state that at the end of a forty-year migration process, there are emerging three major groups of Euro-Turks:

1. **Bridging groups.** These groups, which include more than 40 percent of all Euro-Turks, include those who are equally affiliated to both the host country and the homeland, among whom are the younger generations

[2] Ayhan Kaya and Ferhat Kentel, *Belçika Türkleri. Türkiye ile Avrupa Birliği arasında köprü mü, engel mi?* (Turks of Belgium—Are They a Bridge or an Obstacle Between Turkey and the EU?) (Istanbul: Bilgi University, 2008).

with cosmopolitan and syncretic cultural identities and who construct a dynamic transnational space combining Turkey with Germany and France, such as the Euro-Muslims of the Association of Muslim Entrepreneurs (MÜSIAD) in Germany. Also included are those who indicated hyphenated and multiple identities without essentializing any particular political, religious, ethnic, or racial identity.

2. **Breaching groups.** These groups constitute around 40 percent of Euro-Turks and include those who still have a strong orientation to the homeland, including extreme religious, nationalist, and secular persons/groups.
3. **Assimilated groups.** These groups constitute around 20 percent of Euro-Turks and include those who are assimilated into the majority societies and are usually economically more prosperous.

Kaya and Kentel contend that Euro-Turks do not constitute a threat to any of their host countries, arguing that their orientation towards Islam should be interpreted as a search for fairness and justice. German Turks, it would appear from the research, are organized more along religious and communitarian lines, and a certain section of these would appear to have little interest in integration, and are instead happy to live out their lives within ethnic enclaves and traditional religious and solidarity networks. Another section, however, appears to have adopted cosmopolitan, global, reflexive identities that challenge "Europeannness" itself and seem to exist in a constant state of flux.

As far as Turks in France are concerned, the research suggests that they have chosen to engage in a more modern way of life and orient themselves towards the French language and secular modes of thought. However, they display little interest in such things as French domestic politics, its political parties, or its cultural activities such as the theater or film industry.

There can be little doubt that Kaya and Kentel's research is a significant marker on the way to an understanding of the Turks in Europe, and its greatest contribution may be the final laying to rest of the stereotypical image of the "Turkish migrant worker," because in its detail it revealed their striking diversity.

Kaya and Kentel put forward the view, which I do not share, that a specific understanding of secularism constitutes an obstacle to integration and reinforces the tendency towards exclusion. As the research projects have indicated, the formation of religious-based communities with strong personal ties seems to continue. To break these bonds a gradual transition toward a secular mode of thinking and teaching seems absolutely necessary. A European order based on universal values is irreconcilable with an anti-secular mode of thought. Secularism constitutes the cornerstone of a multicultural, democratic identity. However, the expectation that Euro-Muslims are capable of creating a bridge between cultures has yet to be met. It is also worth discussing the idea put forward by Will Kymlicka (1995) that greater minority rights would provide a more powerful support structure for the construction of an integrated Europe.

Turkish Public Opinion and the EU: The Euroskeptics

Two interesting pieces of research have been carried out on public opinion in Turkey about the EU in recent years. The first was conducted in 2001 by the Turkish Economic and Social Studies Foundation (TESEV) with the collaboration of Dr. Ali Çarkoğlu and Dr. Hakan Yılmaz from Boğaziçi University. The research was conducted among 3,060 adults selected randomly from 176 villages, 25 districts, and 17 provinces throughout Turkey; the findings were announced on 28 June 2002.

The research indicated that at the time, a considerable majority of Turks (64 percent) were in favor of Turkey joining the EU. A study of the finer details of these supporters revealed an interesting distribution across the political spectrum: 86 percent of the Democratic People's Party (HADEP) supporters, 82 percent of the Republican People's Party (CHP) supporters, 80 percent of the Motherland Party (ANAP) supporters, 78 percent of the Democratic Social Party (DSP) supporters, 71 percent of the National Movement Party (MHP) supporters, 70 percent of the Right Path Party (DYP) supporters, and 56 percent of the Justice and Development Party (AKP) supporters favored Turkey entering the EU. Forty-two percent of people in Turkey believed that their lives would improve with entry into the EU because of factors such as economic development (52 percent), freedom of movement throughout Europe (30 percent), and improved democracy (28 percent). It needs to be noted here that Turkish citizens do not plan to migrate in large numbers to Europe once its doors are opened to them: the survey showed that with improved living standards, the vast majority (81 percent) would choose to remain in Turkey.

Forty-two percent of the participants were of the opinion that the EU was not "a Christian club," which was understood as signifying that although there may be a level of doubt and unwillingness on the part of the EU, many Turks do not believe that it practices religious discrimination. Fifty-six percent were not in favor of broadcasts being allowed in mother tongues other than Turkish, and 58 percent felt negatively about the Kurdish language being taught in private language courses. Twenty-one percent were of the opinion that EU membership would prejudice Turkey's independence, whereas the numbers of those who felt it would reinforce separatist and fundamentalist religious movements were low: 17 and 9 percent, respectively.[3]

---

[3] *Radikal*, 29 June 2002, 1, 9.

Euroskepticism

The second important piece of research was also conducted by Dr. Hakan Yılmaz of Boğaziçi University, with the support of the Open Society Institute, in October and November 2003. The survey was conducted among 2,123 adults in Turkey's three largest cities and throughout seventeen provinces. The urban-rural split was 68 versus 32 percent of the adults surveyed.

General Attitudes towards the EU

Respondents were first asked how they would vote were Turkey to hold a referendum on EU membership. Seventy-five percent replied that they would vote in favor of membership, and 17 percent said they would vote against it. In a further analysis of the respondents' political leanings, 79 percent of DYP (center right, moderate, laicist, nationalist) supporters, 84 percent of Democratic People's Party (DEHAP; radical left, Kurdish-Nationalist) supporters, 86 percent of CHP (left of center, Kemalist, secular) supporters, and 71 percent of AKP (center right, Islamist, conservative) supporters were in favor of EU membership. Supporters of the Happiness Party (SP; radical right, Islamist) responded most negatively to EU membership, with 58 percent of supporters replying that they would vote against it.

When answers to the same question were considered under the criterion of the language of the respondent, 78 percent and 73 percent of speakers of Kurdish and Turkish, respectively, were positive about EU membership.

Respondents displayed an interesting variety of expectations about EU membership, with economic development leading at 39 percent. The possibility of freedom of movement among EU states was the leading expectation for 13 percent of respondents. Twelve percent expected that democracy would become more deep-rooted in Turkey as a result of membership, and an equal percentage felt that Turkey's status among nations would be bettered. Nine percent expected that the treatment of the individual by the state would become more equal, and 8 percent foresaw a reduction in bribery and corruption. In short, expectations were not confined purely to economic benefits but reflected political perspectives as well. The survey revealed that Turks were realistic in their views on the time it would take for their expectations to be realized: 18 percent foresaw membership within five years; 25 percent said it would happen in ten years; 22 percent believed that they would not see membership in their lifetimes; and 18 percent expressed the opinion that Turkey would never attain membership. The latter two groups appear to reflect the negative and critical stance of their European counterparts.

Attitudes towards National-Local and European Identities

In reply to the open-ended sentence, "Turkey is a part of Europe because …," 60 percent felt this was true because of geography; 52 percent believed that the two were united by history; 24 percent were of the opinion that economically the two were one; and 24 percent felt that culture was the bond—all answers that reflect an objective evaluation. Fragmented identity revealed itself in answers to the following question: "As a Turkish citizen, with which part of the world do you feel most affiliated?" Replies were divided equally (41 percent each) between East (Asia, Middle East) and West (Europe, Mediterranean, the Balkans).

Fears Concerning the EU and Europe

The research attempted to bring to light the broad spectrum of fears and concerns felt by Turks concerning the EU and Europe. Most hesitancy and concern centers on the issues of exclusion, historical fears, sovereignty fears, religious fears, divisions within the state, and moral concerns.

Exclusion

Exclusion is defined as being excluded or otherwise restricted by Europe. Respondents were asked to comment on the claims that the EU was guilty of applying double standards to Turkey in making demands not made of other potential members. Sixty-one percent were in agreement with this; 20 percent believed that it was not true. When asked to consider Turkey's membership in light of current relations between Turkey and the EU, 50 percent of respondents were of the opinion that even if Turkey were to meet all the criteria set out by the EU, membership would still remain unattainable. Forty percent, however, believed that should the criteria be met in full, Turkey would be accepted as a member. This polarization may be said to show that Turkish public opinion is realistic.

Historical Fears

Historical fears are fears that stretch back to events during the Tanzimat period (a period of reform and Westernization in the Ottoman Empire during the middle of the nineteenth century) and the Treaty of Sevres, which led to the final dissolution of the Turkish Empire. To uncover the extent to which these fears still exist, respondents were asked to comment on the belief that the conditions Turkey must fulfill for membership in the EU are reminiscent of the capitulations during the Ottoman period. Forty-one percent agreed with this belief, 27 percent disagreed, and 32 percent left the question unanswered. In response to a similar question comparing the conditions to those of the Treaty of Sevres, which dissolved the Ottoman Empire, 36 percent said they agreed, whereas 27 percent did not believe this to be true. This question went unanswered by 37 percent of respondents. These figures are a reminder that not insignificant numbers are affected by these deep-seated, historically rooted fears.

Loss of National Independence and Sovereignty

Sovereignty fears are based on the loss of national independence and sovereignty. The extent of these fears were revealed in responses to the statement that fulfillment of EU membership criteria by Turkey would signal the beginning of the end for the Turkish state. Fifty-three percent were of the belief that this was a real possibility; 11 percent had no opinion either way in response to the statement. The importance attributed to the Turkish flag is reflected in the fact that 59 percent stated that they would be discomfited by seeing the EU flag beside the Turkish flag on public buildings and schools. Four percent did not comment on this question. Loyalty to other national symbols was reflected in answers to a similar question regarding the EU anthem and the Turkish national anthem being played together on national holidays. Sixty-six percent said this would cause them unease; 3 percent did not reply to the question. These answers reflect the fact that many Turks are not yet prepared to either bow to a supranational authority or make sacrifices of national sovereignty in the name of desire to join the EU.

Religious Fears

Religious fears are based on the worry that Europe is a "Christian club." Fifty-six percent of respondents agreed that the EU was constructed on Christian values; 13 percent did not reply to the question. A similar statement that the EU was a Christian club that had no place to offer Turkey elicited agreement from 45 percent of respondents. As mentioned previously, these answers are evidence of the sensitivity and polarization that can dominate public opinion.

Divisions within the State

Fears regarding divisions within the state center around the loss of national unity and integrity. When asked for their opinion on the idea that certain EU member states were acting in support of the Kurdish PKK organization and other separatist movements, 66 percent agreed. Forty-five percent also agreed with the statement that Turkey's EU membership would serve to strengthen separatist movements within Turkey. However, 51 percent said that that they did not believe that membership of the EU would bring increased ethnic division within Turkey. In short, it may be said that although Turkish public opinion shows concerns and fear about Turkey's future in the context of the EU, Turks are also of the opinion that, on the issue of national unity, Turkey is sufficiently resilient to resist external pressures.

Moral Concerns

Moral concerns center around the degeneracy of traditional values. As expected, a clear polarization was visible in opinions on this issue. Fifty-five percent of respondents expressed fears concerning possible breakdown in moral values of Turkish youth that they felt would come with EU membership, whereas 54 percent were worried about the possible degeneration and loss of religious values. Concerns about a possible detriment to the Turkish language and family values were not so dominant: 49 percent expressed concern about the effects on the Turkish language, whereas 47 percent had no such worries. Figures were similar concerning family values: 48 percent feared that over time these would be eroded, whereas 49 percent did not share these fears. Thus, it is clear that greatest concern was focused on the erosion of religious values that would come with increasing importance attached to European modernity.

Profile of Euroskeptics

In response to the question concerning the near future and identification, 72 percent of Euroskeptics replied by saying they would identify themselves solely in terms of national unity, whereas 50 percent of those with a positive mindset towards the EU believed that they would retain loyalty to their national identity while embracing a new European identity. As a national average, 54 percent of respondents identified themselves with an unadulterated national unity, whereas 40 percent say they have adopted a pro-European identity.

This empirical research by Hakan Yılmaz in 2003[4] reveals above all that despite the high levels of excitement and enthusiasm expressed in Turkish public opinion regarding Turkey's EU membership, no radical change has occurred in the mindset and attitudes of the Turkish citizen. The high percentages of pro-Europeans may be explained by what we might call a yearning to belong to the West, a yearning that is the expression of a more than one-hundred-year effort on the part of Turkish state officials and intellectuals. This desire was expressed by Atatürk at the founding of the Republic when he stated clearly

[4] Unpublished survey by Hakan Yılmaz, Department of Political Science, Boğaziçi University.

that the aim of the newly born state was the attainment of "modern civilization," with "modern" here equating to western values. Meanwhile, a significant proportion of Turkish public opinion has yet to arrive at a perception of the responsibilities and consequences that will come with participation in a supranational order. The interesting point is the overlap visible between the views of Euro-Turks and the polarized views of Turkish public opinion.

The openly antagonistic discourse of France's President Sarkozy and the position of Germany's Chancellor Angela Merkel, who advocates a "favorized partnership" instead of full membership for Turkey, have disillusioned Turks in the years up to 2009. More and more voices in the Turkish media are expressing the opinion that the EU, in spite of its official denial, desires to remain a Christian club. Another relevant reason has also been repeatedly brought into the foreground: the EU does not want to enlarge the Community with a new member of 72 million inhabitants, which would then possess the second-largest representation in the European parliament.

The findings of these surveys as well as other analyses are indicating that the new international order of the future will be strongly influenced by latent and overt transnational links, ties, and policies.

CHAPTER 11

Globalization, Migration, and the Nation-State

Figure 11.1. Globalization and Migration

The state is becoming ever more "globalized" or "internationalized"; in other words, the politics of the state, instead of orienting itself towards its own territory, is moving beyond its territorial borders. Thus, the state is used as an instru-

> ment for transnational regional and global market forces and operates in favor of multinational corporations, banks and, increasingly, the demands of money merchants.
>
> —Richard Falk, *Predatory Globalization*

> Empire can only isolate, divide and segregate. Imperial capital does indeed attack the movements of the multitude with tireless determination. Within each country it divides and segregates; and in the world of labor it reinforces the cleavages and borderlines of race, gender, language, culture and so forth.
>
> —Michael Hardt and Antonio Negri, *Empire*

Our lives today are shaped to a great extent by two conflicting elements: globalization and the search for identity. The revolution in communications technology and the restructuring of capitalism after the 1990s have brought about new type of society, which Manuel Castells defines as the "network society."[1] The driving force in this new society is economic activity aimed at the implementation of specific strategies. In this new organizational form, in which the traditional notions of time and space have been displaced, most types of employment have become flexible and unstable, and cultures are created by interconnected media and virtual realities. At the same time, this new organizational form is breaking down institutions, subverting cultures, and creating enormous wealth and frightening poverty, along with all that such inequality implies. Richard Falk (2001) has labeled this "predatory globalization." This socioeconomic process, the extent and effect of which the public, to a great extent, is unaware, is causing greats fissures in the structure of the nation-states built on historical processes that claim to be hegemonic and representative. Consequently, we are faced with the emergence of the a triangle, comprised of the "New Economic Order," as determined by multinational companies, "transnational" movements resulting from identity struggles based on social, sexual, religious, national, ethnic differences, and other loyalties, and the nation-states' determination to employ hegemonic powers.

Because of the unprecedented increase in international migration, these three factors are paving the way for the emergence of completely new political and social entities that exist outside the traditional structure of the nation-state. Globalization is creating one-sided and/or mutual dependencies, transnational communities, and regional and/or dual alliances. All of these result in new and unpredictable social and economic formations that affect our understanding of citizenship, the nation-state's power to sanction, and the formation of identities.

The process of economic restructuring brought about by globalization over the last twenty-five years has stimulated the world's highly industrialized

[1] Manuel Castells, *The Power of Identity* (Oxford: Blackwell, 1997), 1–2.

nations to reevaluate the differences in labor and the market economy. The most significant changes wrought during this period are the following:

- Finance capital, led by the United States, has brought about radical changes in international investment patterns, with the least developed countries of the world exporting capital and engaging in the establishment of production industries.
- The electronic revolution has eliminated the need for semiskilled labor. The core states, in attempts to retain their monopoly of the "knowledge society," are working to maintain the "brain drain" from the periphery.
- In highly developed countries traditional occupations based on manual skill are disappearing.
- As a result of the rapid growth of informal sectors in the economies of developing countries, there has been decrease in the protections of labor. In the economies of developing countries the fastest growing sector is the informal one, which is neither taxed nor monitored by the government and is not included in that government's gross national product (GNP). The unwillingness of trade unions to accept workers in this sector leaves them largely unprotected.
- The number of part-time jobs is increasing, whereas opportunities for stable and secure employment are shrinking. During recession, part-time jobs, which in terms of labor rights assure the holder only a limited protection, tend to increase in numbers. Part-time jobs do not carry any kind of tenure and thus can be easily eliminated.
- Mechanisms based on age, ethnic origin, and gender have begun to operate in the labor market. These mechanisms direct female, youth, and members of minority groups towards work in the informal sectors, and force labor with outmoded skills into retirement.[2]

The developments briefly outlined here arise out of our living in a single-centered world. As Gülten Kazgan (2000) has pointed out, among the core countries, it is the United States and the G7 that rule the world.[3] They govern our lives through new inventions and technological development and change; usage of communication channels to formulate and market ideas; control of finance; control of positions of authority in international institutions; and strengthening their monopolies and controlling competition by directing the operations of multinational companies.[4]

---

[2] Castles and Miller, *The Age of Migration,* 78.

[3] The G7 consists of the United States, Japan, Germany, France, England, Canada, and Italy. Russia has joined the the G7 in recent years, and the group is now known as the G8.

[4] Gülten Kazgan, *Küreselleşme ve Ulus-Devlet: Yeni Ekonomik Düzen,* [Globalization and the Nation State: New Economic Order] (İstanbul: İstanbul Bilgi Üniversitesi, 2000), 56–76.

This panorama is sufficient to explain the failure of strategies based on the notion of development. Many third world countries, which at one time were expected to develop, have never succeeded in providing sufficient employment opportunities for their people due to misuse of natural resources, deliberate neglect of agriculture, uncontrolled urbanization, poverty, and low living standards. When we add armed resistance, terrorism movements, and other internecine strife that directly or indirectly fuel the fires of ethnic, religious, or regional conflicts, then it is clear why we have witnessed so many new developments in the area of migration and asylum.

Globalization and the Nation-State

Just as globalization resulted in structural and directional change to international labor markets, it also brought about fundamental alterations in the functions and authority of nation-states. As is often talked about in the media, the nation-state is not about to disappear, but its functions and areas of influence are being transformed. Particularly where migration and asylum are concerned, nation-states are taking fundamental legal steps, even at the expense of democracy, and are not hesitant to pass laws that limit freedoms.

Nation-states are the product of the phasing out of feudalism. They can be defined as "state[s] whose people share a strong linguistic, religious, and symbolic identity."[5] This new type of authority is historically specific and increasingly formalized, embodying territorial jurisdiction and exclusive authority over that territory. Today the nation-state is undergoing radical transformations that will be discussed in further detail below.

The concept of the nation-state is not an old one. The Treaty of Westphalia of 1648, which marked the end of a long series of religious wars known as the Thirty Years War, established the main elements of the concept of the "modern state," which it defined as an institution that has authority over a particular geographic area that has been accepted and is under the protection of international agreements; controls the economic, cultural, and social life of a specific geographic area based on its autonomy; and has the right to exercise absolute control within its borders—control that includes, but is not limited to, the power over goods, capital, and cultural products.

Over time the absolutist state containing these elements evolved into the nation-state in Europe and North America. The notion of nation based on history, culture, and language was developed by middle and working classes as they grew in financial strength and began resisting forms of absolutist authority. The notion of democracy took root wherever a national will found op-

[5] Charles Tilly, *Coercion, Capital, and European States: AD 990–1992* (Oxford: Basil Blackwell, 1990), 127–143.

portunities to express itself through election and representation. Even though many claim that this concept in fact refers to "imagined communities,"[6] in this work "nation" is understood as an independent variable.

The emergence of the nation-state brought with it the struggle for political and social rights, which required the provision of minimum levels of education and welfare. Thus, several elements were added to the modern conception of the nation-state. First, democracy and citizenship were added to the legal state that granted political legitimacy. With revolutions undertaken in the name of democracy, citizens embraced constitutionally guaranteed rights, and due to democratic elections started to participate in the legislative process. As a result, the cultural communities that were the nation and the state, and which represented geographical authority, were united. Next, by bringing about the full participation of the citizen in the political process, social movements and labor activism created the social welfare state. The sovereignty and autonomy vested in the state made it possible to control the labor market and the provision of social services to its citizens.

History shows us that nation-states of today were responsible, either by conquest or colonialism, for the destruction of other states. Indeed, humanity had to wait until 14 December 1960, when the UN granted independence to colonial countries and people, for the final, official liquidation of colonialism. By the end of the twentieth century, the end of colonialism became an international ideal for all countries that desired to be considered a member of the law-abiding global community. For these countries, the creation of a democratic civil state based on the primacy of law had also become an international ideal. Unfortunately the world today is still obliged to deal with so-called rogue states—nations in which the government has totally disintegrated, such as Somalia and the Congo.

The Nation-State and International Migration

Since the end of the twentieth century, the majority of nation-states have been influenced economically, politically, culturally, and socially by the spread of ever more complex international networks and large-scale transnational migration movements,[7] and globalization has begun to transform the very character of the nation-state. Multinational companies and "supranational" institutions are limiting states' autonomy and forestalling them in their economic, political, and social decisions. The democratic system and authority of elected par-

[6] Benedict Anderson, *Imagined Communities: Reflections on the Origin and Spread of Nationalism* (London: Verso, 1983), 13.

[7] David Held, Anthony McGrew, David Goldblatt, and Jonathan Perraton, *Global Transformations: Politics, Economics and Culture*, Cambridge: Polity Press, 1999.

liaments is weakening as power passes into the hands of these supranational institutions.

As a result of the pressure exerted by the flows of goods, ideas, migrants and asylum-seekers, it is becoming increasing difficult for the nation-state to monitor its borders. In addition, in areas where the population is not homogenous, nation-citizen bonds are loosened. Individuals enter into different loyalty and dependency relationships. And as multinational companies and international markets drive states towards privatization and liquidation of monopolies, the social civil state is weakened and in some cases is being forced into liquidation.

Saskia Sassen performs a very useful analysis of these problems. She first cites Charles Tilly's (1990) historical distinction between the national state and the state. According to Tilly, states are "coercion-wielding organizations that are distinct from households and kinship groups and exercise clear priority in some respects over all other organizations within substantial territories," and "national states" are distinguished by "governing multiple continuous regions and their cities by means of centralized, differentiated and autonomous structures."[8] Sassen adds a new dimension to this definition. She speaks about the "denationalized state."[9] This distinction is very important because it is this third type of state that in recent years has been subject to analysis. As Sassen points out, the global economy is increasingly dominated by deregulation, privatization, and the growing authority of non-state actors. As a result, these external processes become embedded into the nation-state. While yesterday the authority of nation-states was exclusively exercised over its territory, today globalization is invading existing state structures and transforming them. Thus since the late 1980s, the rights of non-national firms, the deregulation of cross-border transactions, and the growing influence or power of some supranational organizations become a part of what can no longer be called only a "nation-state ". This partial "denationalization" can also take place in domains such as human rights, in which national courts can be used to sue foreign firms and dictators or to grant undocumented immigrants certain rights.[10]

These important structural changes arise out of the fundamental changes in the demographic structure of societies. Although the concept of national unity on which states have been built remains valid, it is gaining new dimensions as the social sciences begin to examine and explore new entities. As individuals move out of their countries of birth for economic or political reasons, high levels of human mobility are creating new conjunctions in the societies

---

[8] Tilly, *Coercion, Capital, and European States,* 1–2.

[9] Saskia Sassen, *A Sociology of Globalization* (New York: W. W. Norton & Co., 2007), 49–50.

[10] Saskia Sassen, *Territory, Authority, Rights: From Medieval to Global Assemblage* (Princeton: Princeton University Press, 2008), 310–311.

of both countries of departure and destination. Although some of these are still in an embryonic stage, the majority is based on social realities. Scientific literature defines these new conjunctions as transnational communities, and we will be returning to them later in the chapter.

Control of Differences

Although ethnic groups settling within nation-states as a result of international migration constitute a problem for states, in more recent times the global networks woven by modern communication systems and transportation networks have begun to allow these groups to live more independent lives, which, in turn, have intensified debates in the arena of public policy. As can be seen in the *Gastarbeiter* policy that Germany pursued in the early years of labor importation, the problem was considered a temporary one, because the process itself was designed to be temporary. Therefore, it was felt that control was not an issue. Later, however, when it became clear that the new arrivals were to become more or less a permanent fixture in their societies, nation-states began to express a desire to implement the sovereign rights that had been eroded.

States accepting migrants employed various policies in attempting to control the ethic differences that subsequently emerged in their societies. The policies may be examined under three specific headings: assimilation, differential exclusion, and multiculturalism.[11]

The policy of assimilation preached that the way forward for newcomers involved learning the language of the country of acceptance, its social and cultural practices and, in some cases, even changing one's citizenship. According to Jacqueline Costa-Lascoux, the assimilation project was designed to "eliminate foreignness."[12] Its primary aim was to render the migrant the same as a citizen of the majority society, and at its core the goal was to fully equip the migrant with the language of the receiving country. Thus linguistic education by itself would act as a decisive facilitator in a migrant's entrance into the mainstream society of the country of acceptance. As a policy, its leading example is the so-called "melting pot" of the United States. By the middle of the twentieth century it was recognized that this approach was not bringing the expected results, and it was unsuccessful in most European migrant-accepting countries of the postcolonial period as well. These states had to switch to a more flexible policy described as "integration," the aim of which became the adaptation of the newcomers, with the hope that, in the long term, their integration

[11] Castles and Miller, *The Age of Migration*, 244.

[12] Jacqueline Costa-Lascoux, *De l'immigré au citoyen* (Paris: La Documentation Francaise, 1989), 10.

would follow. Costa-Lascoux sees the process of integration as an exchange dynamic that links the ideas of reciprocity and respect of differences.[13] In fact, integration is a watered-down version of a strict assimilation policy, and it encompasses all the exclusionist elements of assimilation. In other words, these policies can be considered as policies of differential exclusion.

Since the 1980s, in migrant-accepting European countries it became clear that, with increasing migrant family reunifications, many migrant families with younger generations brought up in those countries had, regardless of their citizenship status, decided to remain permanently. Because each host country adopted different policies to deal with this situation, different ethnic communities and affiliated institutions emerged among Europe's foreign populations, which by the 1990s exceeded 17 million.

Yasemin Nuhoğlu Soysal identifies four different types of policies within the European Union with respect to relations among the individual, the community, and the state.[14] The most important characteristic of these models is their attempt to integrate the migrant (to some extent) into the structure of the nation-state. Soysal prefers to use the term "incorporation," as used in scientific and political debates in the United States. These four types of "incorporation" are defined by Soysal as corporatist, liberal, statist, and fragmentary.

Corporatist Inclusion (Centrist)

The term "corporatist," as it is used here, refers to organizations that are established jointly by the state, society, and the individual. Thus, corporatist groups, based on vocation, ethnicity, religion, or gender, are sources of authority and action. Although they may claim certain natural rights in opposition to the state, they are bound by the public administration of the state in which they function. It is also claimed that this model functions for the welfare and benefit of the public and thus influences the decision-making mechanisms of migrants.

Sweden and the Netherlands are two primary examples of countries that have adopted this model. In response to the wishes of migrants, state and local governments provide financial support for the establishment of associations and the provision of schools for education in the mother tongue(s) of the migrant group(s). In the political discourse of each country, migrants are referred to as "ethnic minorities." The migration policy adopted by Sweden in 1975 stated that its three main aims were: (1) equality between Swedes and migrants; (2) the provision of cultural freedoms to migrants; and (3) solidarity and cooperation between the native and migrant populations. In practice, this

[13] Ibid., 10–11.

[14] Soysal, *Limits of Citizenship*, 37.

was supported by education in the mother tongue for minorities with different languages and the provision of television and radio broadcasts in minority languages. Migrant policy in the Netherlands also works on the basis of four collective categories: Surinamese, migrant workers and their families, the Rom (Gypsies), and asylum-seekers. In both countries, minorities are provided with specific budgets by state and local governments, from which religious organizations may also benefit.

The centrist approach indicates two major characteristics. Immigration policies are implemented as highly organized and centrally formulated policies that are carried out by governmental administrative agencies together with a network of umbrella organizations and consultative commissions that act as intermediaries between the state and the migrant groups.[15]

Society-Centered Inclusion (Noncentrist)

What we may define as the liberal model operates in direct contrast to the corporatist model, in that it holds the individual to be the source of all power and action. Its policies are generally applied through loosely organized public administration, with the decision-making process organized autonomously. The partner in enterprise is usually a local government. This model is used principally by England and Switzerland.

In Switzerland, with respect to decisions concerning migrants, the state is involved only in deciding annual migrant acceptance quotas, in which migrant deaths and repatriation figures play a determining role. However, because the decision to apply for asylum is an individual one, asylum figures cannot be estimated, and use of this option seems to have increased greatly in recent years.[16] The needs and wants of foreigners are determined on the federal level by a mixed commission. Such commissions are solely created on the local level with representatives of local administration and migrants association. The accepted principle is that migrants benefit from the social services provided by local government. In more recent years, consultation committees have been established at the commune and canton levels, and citizenship applications are also decided at this level.

In England, since 1976 the responsibility for migrants mixing and integrating with general society has been in the hands of the Commission for Racial Equality. The Commission operates under the auspices of the Home Affairs Ministry and is responsible for the protection and care of individuals who have been victims of racial discrimination. Apart from this, the system operates in a

---

[15] Ibid., 66.

[16] H.-J. Hoffmann-Nowotny and M. Killias, *Das Fremde in der Schweiz* (Zürich: Seismo, 2001), 16.

manner similar to Switzerland, and social care of migrants is provided by local authorities. With the aim of providing more coordinated public services, both countries have recently begun to establish more administrative units. Society-centered inclusion is looked upon as noncentrist because at no level is there an administrative or executive interference of federal power. Decision-making remains at the local level.

State-Centered Inclusion (Centrist)

This statist model directly contrasts with the corporatist model in which all policies are directed from the center. Statist policies refer to the individual as the point of contact, and decisions emerging out of migrant policies are communicated from the top downwards. France adopted this model and has left the application of migrant policy in the hands of its Social Work and Integration Ministry. To assist migrants in the integration process there is a nine-member Supreme Integration Council. The Fund for Social Action operates under the Ministry and is responsible for the funding of all migrant associations and institutions down to local level. In the statist model the unit of incorporation is the individual. Individuals benefit from an equal standing vis-à-vis the state, and incorporation is achieved through existing institutions. The incorporation process is centralized and bureaucratic. Individuals can participate in consultation at both national and local levels. Thus, in accordance with its republican tradition, France does not legally recognize the concept of "community" or any efforts linked to this that may be attempts to gain autonomy of any kind.[17] This approach defies any kind of communitarian approach that would grant certain groups rights. The inclusionary process is uniquely based on the individual.

Statist-Corporatist Inclusion

In Germany, efforts to integrate migrants into society are conducted by centralized semi-state bodies. Alongside the official *Bundeslandbeauftrage für Auslaenderfragen,* the government department responsible for migrant issues, the state bureaucracy operates in cooperation with the Catholic and Protestant churches, and organizations such as *Türk-Danış,* the consulting organization set up by the Social Democrat Party's *Arbeiterwohlfahrt,* the office that monitors the rights of migrant workers. On the regional level, depending on budgetary allocations and the numerative concentration of foreigners, German states have established administrative units to deal with foreigners' issues, and the city of Berlin also has an administrative representative specifically designated to deal with issues concerning foreigners. Germany encour-

[17] Kastoryano, *Kimlik Pazarlığı,* 95–96.

ages the formation of identity based on culture, and thus ethnic colonies and religious communities exist there. These ethnic and religious communities do not enjoy any formal recognition; however, districts such as Kreuzberg and Wedding in Berlin and Mülheim in Köln are sociologically looked upon as ethnic colonies. Similar observation applies to Köln, where ultra-conservative Islamic organizations are based, being considered "Europe's Mecca." None of these groups enjoy any political recognition; they count as part of civil society within the realm of Germany's states, namely the city of Berlin and the state of Nordrhein-Westfalen.

In the fragmentary model, although the state keeps its sovereign role, it is organizationally weak and circumscribed in its interaction with society. The state only exists as a framework. Instead, primary groups such as the family, clan, or church are dominant in social and public life. In such a situation, migrant groups remain only partially integrated in society. They are integrated fully into the labor market but remain outside the social arena. This model is particularly common in the Asian oil-exporting countries.

With the exception of the fragmentary model, we can see that within their policy frameworks, these European states grant migrants a legal status equivalent to the native population with respect to permanent residence rights, education, health and social services, and employment. They are also legally allowed to form associations and join unions and political parties. Therefore, the primary factor distinguishing foreigners from the native population is their lack of voting rights in national elections.

It would appear that individuals who are long-term residents of a foreign country and whose legal status, in an abstract sense, is different from that of citizens have been brought close to being on a parallel level with the native population. This situation has brought with it a number of changes.

First, the tie between state and geography, as part of the notion of citizenship, is being broken. In today's world an individual, although carrying citizenship of one country, may benefit from the rights and privileges available in another. This fluidity is becoming ever greater with the increasing practice of dual citizenship: Sweden, the Netherlands, and Belgium, for example, recognize this status. In Germany, all babies that are born to foreigners after 2000 are considered German citizens until the age of twenty-three, at which time they must choose which citizenship they will adopt permanently.

The second important change is that differences in status are linked to citizenship. In Europe today there are individuals in many different positions legally: those who have the right to permanent residence and employment, those who do not possess these rights, those with asylum status, those with dual citizenship, and those with the citizenship of a European Union member country. These legal complexities are propelling individuals into seeking identities based on culture.

Also undergoing a process of change is the base and legitimacy of citizenship. Under the traditional model, individual rights within a nation-state were gained by living within and remaining loyal to the borders of that state. New models, however, mean that an individual's citizenship status does not remain bound by nationality status. Instead, one may benefit from and take advantage of the rights and privileges set out in the universal ideology of human rights. As Soysal rightly reminds us in regard to immigration, the global system rests upon the recognition of two major principles: national sovereignty and universal human rights. These two precepts constrain and enhance the nation-state's scope of action. On one hand, nation-states are enlarging their responsibilities by agreeing to implement human rights. On the other hand, as the logical consequence of national sovereignty, nation-states are exercising border control. Thus receiving countries grant the protection of human rights to their foreign residents during their stay, while reinforcing their borders through restrictive measures.[18] International treaties and agreements, in overriding the decisions of nation-states, bring individuals to a position that transcends citizenship, to what Soysal defines as a "postnational" position. The duality embedded in the principles of the global system is further reflected in the incongruence between identity and rights, the two elements of modern citizenship. As an identity, national citizenship—as it is promoted, reinvented, and reified by states and other societal actors—still prevails. But in terms of its translation into rights and privileges, it is no longer a significant construction. Thus, the universal status of personhood and postnational membership coexists with assertive national identities and intense ethnic struggles.[19]

Multiculturalism

Multiculturalism signifies an abandonment of the homogenous single-culture myth of the nation-state. However, it also implies that the nation-state will exercise control over differences within its borders—the notion of multiculturalism does not abandon the principle of territorial attachment. The concept is utilized on two levels, the philosophical and the political. In accordance with Charles Taylor's (1992) definition of the concept as the "recognition of cultural identities," multiculturalism may emerge in its philosophical form. In that form, the notion of identity is the point of departure, and the desire being expressed is for subgroups in society to be equally respected. Taylor insists on the need for recognition, which leads to politics of difference.[20] Another approach calls for the state authorities to provide space for different cultures

[18] Soysal, *Limits of Citizenship,* 156–157.

[19] Ibid., 159.

[20] Charles Taylor, "Multiculturalism and the Politics of Recognition," in *Multiculturalism: Examining the Politics of Recognition,* ed. Amy Gutman (Princeton: Princeton University Press, 1992).

in order to create a counterweight to the hegemonic culture. These kinds of services, although being provided in the name of equality, may on occasion give rise to greater polarization. For example, in Berlin, the decision of the Supreme Administrative Court to recognize the IGMG association as the legitimate representative of Muslim migrants and, beginning in autumn 2002, grant it the authority to provide lessons on Islam in German in all schools in the city, while granting the same rights to the Alevite Federation, was an exercise in indirect control of migration policy. For as long as multiculturalism remains a means of control in the hands of the state, it would appear that the possibility of its creating a democratic climate of tolerance is less likely than its leading to a situation in which identities are bargained for and the result is ever greater polarizations.

As Kaya (2009) has pointed out, institutions that hold multiculturalism as their aim, although having an important function, are simply assisting in the process of "culturalization," which, masquerading as multiculturalism, entails the existence of ethnic minorities being only recognized on the basis of representing a different group with folk dances, music, and cuisine of their own. This actually results in their exclusion from the process of allocation and distribution of material resources. In other words, multiculturalist ideology may also stress social inequality as the result of cultural differences.

Transnational Communities

Research on these communities is a new area in the social sciences and, as a concept, is most closely linked to migration, ethnicity, culture, and nationalism. As we enter the twenty-first century, one of the most prominent elements in the nation-state, namely the national territory on which it is founded, is to a certain degree becoming less important. High levels of geographic mobility; cyclical, transient migration; cheap and easy travel; and the constant communication allowed by technology all serve to weaken the notion that an individual belongs to one nation or country. Individuals in these transnational communities are not bound by a specific geography when forming their identities. Thus, the notion of globalization has begun to be used in the concept of "glocalization." Globalization theorist Ronald Robertson tells us that globalization must be redefined in the context of conflict among local cultures.[21]

Transnational communities are groups whose identities are unlinked to any particular geography. Among other definitions of these communities, Portes, Guarnizo, and Landolt define transnational activities as follows:

---

[21] Ronald Robertson, "Globalization: Time-Space and Homogeneity-Heterogeneity," in *Global Modernities*, eds. Mike Featherstone, Scott Lash, and Ronald Robertson (London: Sage, 1995), 25–44.

> These are activities which transcend borders and regularly and meaningfully absorb the time of those who participate in them. In as much as these kinds of activities may be conducted by national governments and representatives of multinational companies, they may also be conducted on a more modest scale by individuals such as migrants and their families and friends. These activities are not limited to the field of economy but may also encompass political, cultural and religious undertakings.[22]

In reference to transnational nationalism, Portes, Guarnizo, and Landolt also make a useful distinction between "transnational nationalism from above" (i.e., that practiced by multinational companies and governments in their activities) and "transnational nationalism from below," in which migrants and their second and third generations, as groups who have been deprived of rights and subjected to discrimination, play a significant role.[23]

Transnational communities are generally institutionalized reactions to the oppressive policies of governments, powerful companies, and intergovernmental organizations. These movements have previously been referred to in the scholarly literature with the term "diaspora," but the world of social science today prefers to use the more neutral term "transnational communities." It is possible for these communities to develop traditional organizational structures, but in general, activities are conducted through informal networks, the very nature of which render governments less powerful in their efforts to control them.

There is an important issue worth mentioning at this point: Not all migrants are transnational migrants. For this term to be used, the individual involved must have crossed two or more different national borders and take part in developed social, familial, political, economic, or religious organizations. The essential element is that the transnational activities in which the individual is engaged constitute the most important part of his or her life.[24]

Castles and Miller suggest the following typology with respect to transnational communities:[25]

1. **Partnerships and enterprises that emerge out of the international activities of multinational companies or other small- and medium-sized companies.** Small enterprises that bring goods from the home country and sell them in the local ethnic market and send ready goods

[22] Alejandro Portes, Luis E. Guarnizo, and Patricia Landolt, "The Study of Transnationalism: Pitfalls and Promise of an Emergent Research Field," *Ethnic and Racial Studies* 22, no. 2 (1999): 217–237.
[23] Ibid.
[24] Nina Glick Schiller, "Citizens in Transnational Nation-States: The Asian Experience," in K. Olds, P. Dicken, P. Kelly, L. Kong, and H. Yeung, eds., *Globalization and Asia Pacific: Contested Territories* (London and New York: Routledge, 199) 203.
[25] Castles and Miller, *The Age of Migration*, 45.

and money to the home country may be considered a "transnational enterprise from below." In contrast to this, a multinational company that has abandoned the culture of its country of origin and adopts an international corporate ethic may be defined as "a transnational enterprise from above."

2. **Transnational political communities.** These are activities engaged in by ethnic groups that live in two or more countries as part of an effort to create political or other desired changes in the lives of the members of the group. A good example would be the activities of Armenian, Jewish, Greek, and Kurdish communities in securing international sanctions by strengthening the ties they had already developed through their institutionalized diasporas. Two of the most recent examples of such activities are the hindering of official state relations between Turkey and Armenia, and the draft bill passed through the French parliament, both of which were the result of pressure from the Armenian diaspora. Another example is the attempt by European Kurdish migrants to politicize the Kurdish Workers Party (PKK) in the hope that a peace process would begin under the auspices of the European Union.
3. **Transnational cultural communities engaged in a struggle to protect cultural heritage and languages.** These communities, which place great importance on and wish to maintain their emotional ties with their homeland, demand cultural services from their home country and the right to vote while living abroad. From Turkey's perspective, it is in contact with its Eurasian neighbors that these communities play their most significant role. One such type of transnational cultural community may also be seen in Berlin, where bands such as Cartel and singers like Azize-A give voice to protest through their music.[26] Azize-A speaks of her music as follows:

   > I want to show the different talents and characteristics of Turkish women. My aim is to clear our minds of the constant question of whether we're Turks or Germans, and shout out that we're multicultural and cosmopolitan. I want people to know that we're not falling into the gap between two chairs, we're sitting on a third one in the middle![27]

4. **Transnational social communities.** These may also be called the "labor diasporas." Their function is to deal with the problems of international migrants, locate support organizations in cases of asylum, and generally act as a guide. In some cases these communities, in choosing to develop their own unique lifestyle, create a citizenship-like status for members. Arjun Appadurai defines these situations as the creation

---

[26] Ayhan Kaya, "Sicher in Kreuzberg," *Constructing Diasporas: Turkish Hip-Hop Youth in Berlin,* (Bielefeld: Transcript, 2001), 13.

[27] Quoted in Kaya, "Sicher in Kreuzberg," 13.

> of "new diasporic scapes." Examples are Sikhs in England creating a virtual Khalistan; the realized dreams of native South Africans of an apartheid-free home; and Sri Lankan asylum-seekers who envision a free Tamil homeland.

Meanwhile, besides thinking about political change, these transnational communities are working towards realizing their ideas through the creation of unique and new cultural spaces, in which they concentrate on issues concerning the environment, human rights, and women—issues in which the intellectuals and students in those communities play a determining role.

In his analysis of modernity, Appadurai (1996) claims that these communities, through a reinterpretation of the global order, give local cultures the opportunity to redefine their authentic cultural characteristics. He explains that these spaces have created cultural globalization, and he defines their characteristics as follows:

- Ethnoscapes: the spaces created by people who make up the shifting world we live in (e.g., tourists, migrants, refugees, and others on the move)
- Technoscapes: the spaces created by the flow of technology, both high and low, both mechanical and informational, which is so powerful and rapid that it can cross boundaries previously considered impenetrable
- Finanscapes: the spaces in which international markets operate
- Mediascapes: the spaces in which information is produced and disseminated by electronic media, e.g., newspapers, magazines, television stations, and film studios
- Ideoscapes: the spaces in which ideologies and opinions, especially related to such concepts as freedom, welfare, rights, sovereignty, representation, and democracy, are disseminated

The interaction of these spaces, by bringing with it the notion of deterritorialization, creates an environment in which different actions may take place and different ideas may be expressed and even legitimized. One step beyond this point is global virtualization, where different communities interact in cyberspace.[28]

Changes Brought by Transnational Communities

One important consequence of these communities has been the end of the "homogenous nation-state" dream. Today, Berlin is as much a Turkish city as it

[28] Appadurai, *Modernity at Large*, 33.

is a German one, just as London is as much Indian and Caribbean as English.[29] The world is made up now of cities that shelter ever increasing cosmopolitan subidentities carried by individuals bearing transnational identities. As more and more countries come face to face with the reality of migration, the notion that the ethnically homogenous nation-state can remain alive grows ever more unlikely. Thus, we must review yet again the concepts of national identity and national culture. When we attempt to integrate communities made up of multicultural and transnational identities, we must consider the issue of emotional belonging and how this is to be achieved.

Another consequence of these developments is the issue of how migrants are to be integrated into the various countries of acceptance. Given that it is now accepted that the assimilation model is unworkable, is it possible for "transnational communities from below" to assist in the integration process? Is it possible for transnational sociocultural activities to provide the support necessary to second- and third-generation migrants if they are to resist external pressures? Kaya (2001) is optimistic about this, and his research on the Turkish hip-pop youth in Berlin has shown that, through their diasporic consciousness, they have become a sociological subject that has succeeded in creating a "home away from home" and a completely new cultural identity. As a diasporic space, Kreuzberg in Berlin has become a symbolic wall that shields Turkish migrants from racism, xenophobia, unemployment, discrimination, exclusion, and prejudice. Thus, through belonging to a nation with a different history and traditions, or by being the "other," the diasporic subject becomes different and distinctive.[30]

In other words, ethnic resources, solidarity, and symbols may assist migrants in overcoming the exclusion to which they are subjected. According to Portes (1997) this type of "transnational nationalism from below" may play a role in preventing these newly arrived second-class citizens from identifying themselves with the lowest stratum of society in the country of acceptance.

Another outcome of transnational nationalism is the spread of the notion of the "landless state," a process that also brings with it extreme nationalism. Intolerant attitudes and behavior, which are incompatible with universal standards of human rights, towards certain national or religious groups, in both Europe and the United States following the atrocities of 11 September 2001, may be considered manifestations of this process.

One aim of transnational communities is a reevaluation of the notion of citizenship, and one method of institutionalizing multi-identities is through acceptance of dual or multiple citizenships. The existence of perpetually excluded minorities, forced to live as second-class citizens with regard to civic

---

[29] Saskia Sassen, *Globalization and Its Discontents* (New York: The New Press, 1998), 179–80.

[30] Kaya, "Sicher in Kreuzberg," 199–200.

rights, results in constant tension in the society in which they live. This two-speed lifestyle common throughout European societies is the most visible manifestation of exclusion on the continent.

Recognition of transnational nationalism, ease in changing citizenship status, and dual citizenship remain dreams in many countries, while social realities continue to alter social structures. However, as Jellineck (1928) has told us, at some point, *de facto* situations will begin to impel lawmakers to make normative adjustments.

Globalization, Migration, and Paradoxes

> The institution of multicultural citizenship requires specific policies and regulations. The identity of each citizen is intertwined with a common identity which rests upon relations of mutual respect. Therefore, for a multicultural society, it is essential that a politics of respect be applied. … In a situation in which political culture fails to achieve this society splits into sub-cultures whose aim is to destroy each other.
>
> —Jürgen Habermas, *Die Postnationale Konstellation*

In today's world, the globalization process is the most important force behind social change. This process, in which millions of individuals seek new homes, is creating extraordinary tensions in the social fabric of both sending and receiving countries. Although the most immediate effects of migration may be observed in the economic sphere, in time, its effects on other areas of life such as culture, social relations, national politics, and international relations become apparent.

Migration exerts its most powerful influence on the structure of the nation-state. The liberal market economy of globalization, in limiting the state's room for maneuver, has rendered it less capable, or even incapable, of providing public services. Demographic mobility is creating more complex ethnocultural differentiation within the borders of the nation-state, and thus is blurring the lines between identities and traditions. Stephen Castles (1997) has written about seven major paradoxes that he sees embedded in these large-scale migration processes.[31]

The Insertion-Exclusion Paradox

In the new economic order, self-sufficient families and communities are foundering as they enter national and international markets. Global markets em-

[31] Stephen Castles, "Globalization and Migration: Some Pressing Contradictions," *International Social Science Journal* 50, no. 165 (June 1998): 179–186.

brace citizens with qualities that enable them to keep in step with international competition levels, and it is to these citizens that civic, political, and social rights are being granted. In contrast to this, citizens and communities who fail to meet the standards demanded by the global market are being cast aside and deprived of even the most basic rights of food and employment.

International migration movements are being most closely affected by these processes of insertion and exclusion. Individuals attempting to travel great distances, be they workers, experts or asylum-seekers, are reunited with their families and loved ones through transnational relationship networks. Whatever the initial intentions, migration movements result in family reunifications and the emergence of new ethnicities in the new countries. Today, more than 120 million people are residing outside their country of birth.

Migrant-exporting countries undergo deep and constant transformations. A significant number of people leaving these countries' shores are of the opinion that they have been excluded and thus are seeking their destiny elsewhere.

Countries of acceptance are also caught up in the process of change: the structure of urban space is changing its character, and traditional value systems are being questioned by the newcomers. Many migrants also feel deprived of certain rights and excluded in these countries too. Thus, be it in the homeland or the country of settlement, migration policies constantly conflict with migrants' identity claims and social relations.

The Market-State Paradox

It is now the anonymous market powers that decide who will be included in or excluded from the labor market. Millions of people the world over have been abandoned to poverty with this development, for which no individual, institution, or state is prepared to take responsibility. Indeed, the inequality that has come with this victory of national and international markets, represented by the multinational corporations, is fast becoming invisible. This situation may be explained by the productivity of the economic system. The unease created by uncontrolled markets was felt as far back as the nineteenth century. In the twentieth century, class struggles and two world wars led to the development of the welfare state. By the late 1980s, the collapse of the Communist system brought to the fore the thesis that the interests of global capital were one and the same with the interests of all humankind.

Although the world economy today is not managed from one particular center, powerful supranational institutions (e.g., the World Bank and the International Monetary Fund) force more than eighty countries worldwide to comply with the requirements of the market economy. The new international division of labor maintains the trade dominance of OECD countries and opens up new channels of integration of newly industrializing economies, but this integration is extremely uneven and highly selective.[32]

Meanwhile, the conflict between states and world markets reveals itself most clearly in the issue of migration. Some states speak of a "brain drain": the loss through emigration of a skilled workforce in which the state has made a significant investment. In countries of acceptance, of course, employers welcome this skilled workforce with open arms. With respect to unskilled labor, the situation is reversed: governments in labor-exporting countries encourage emigration in the hope that returns will be secured in terms of hard currency and an easing of the pressures created by unemployment, whereas the labor-accepting countries do not want unskilled laborers and, at best, are prepared to turn a blind eye while they work illegally for a certain period of time.

Governments' attempts to halt these flows of people have resulted in the global migration market. The social relationship networks that have arisen out of migration profit through their organization of migration, both legal and illegal. Meanwhile, governments, which allow the flow of capital, goods, and ideas, fail in their attempts to halt human mobility, and the way is paved for even more conflict by the human trafficking that, under the most brutal of conditions, continues.

The Wealth-Poverty Paradox

A growing social polarization can be observed in both developed and developing countries. The combination of free market mechanisms and nonintervention of state structures is leading to ever more inequalities, the greatest of which is to be seen in some Asian and African countries that have missed out on development. There, educational opportunities, health standards, and life expectancy are all on a downward trend: 815 million persons are undernourished, 1.1 billion lack access to safe water, 2.4 billion lack access to basic sanitation, and 854 million adults are illiterate.[33] The flash points of the conflicts resulting from these inequalities have changed. Traditionally, conflict took place between workers and capitalists, between the liberal-democratic and Communist models. Today, the situation is more complex. A schism between those who participate in and those who are excluded from mainstream economic and social life has begun to appear in every society. Social scientists now prefer to use the term "two-speed society" rather than the older "class society." By this they refer to the fact that although the great majority is integrated and has been able to enter the world of employment, there exists an

[32] Manuel Castells, "Global Informational Capitalism," in *The Global Transformation Reader*, eds. David Held and Anthony McGrew (Cambridge: Polity, 2003), 312.

[33] United Nations Development Programme (UNDP) Annual Report (2002), http://www.undp.org/annualreports/2002/english.

ever-growing excluded minority. Among these minorities are women and other ethnic or racial minorities, and migration plays a primary role in their formation. The last fifty years have witnessed the appearance of new minorities in all migrant-accepting countries—minorities that even if they have gained new citizenship, remain excluded because of race, ethnicity, or religion, and form marginalized, impoverished aggregations that carry within them potential sources of conflict.

The Network-Ego Paradox

One of the most confounding problems modernity has brought to light is the tension that exists between the never-ending demands of rational economic and social organizations, and those of individual and groups. According to Castells (1996), societies are becoming increasingly polarized because of the restructuring that is constantly occurring between the "network" and "I."[34] Castells speaks of global networks of wealth, power, and image that are being created by new communications technologies. These networks operate unhindered and are capable of rendering individuals, groups, regions, and even countries visible or invisible. Under the new dominant logic of the space of flows (Castells 1996), areas that are non-valuable from the perspective of informational capitalism and that do not have significant political interest for the powers that be are bypassed by flows of wealth and information. This process induces an extremely uneven geography of social and territorial exclusion and inclusion.[35] This system, although being productive economically, cannot provide people with a meaning for their lives, and one method individuals have developed in order to escape from such abstract universality is the use of identities based on ethnicity, religion, regionalism, or nationalism. This situation explains why most conflicts do not originate in rational economic and social interests. In some cases, resistance against globalizing powers is conducted using cultural symbols related to honor and dignity. With respect to migration, the "network-I" contradiction is most striking on two levels. The first is in racial anti-migration movements, which appear more in homogenous societies, where those who feel discomfited by the structural change that is happening fail to perceive that it is being brought about by globalization and instead see the problem as emanating from the most immediately visible aspect of this change, namely migrants.

The second reaction emerges directly from the migrant communities themselves. In wishing to change this situation, marginal groups are either engaging in discrimination or acquiring radical views that are politically or religiously

[34] Manuel Castells, *The Rise of the Network Society* (Oxford: Wiley, 1996), 3.

[35] Manuel Castells, "The Rise of the Fourth World," in *The Global Transformations Reader*, eds. David Held and Anthony McGrew (New York: Polity, 2004), 430.

motivated, or, as a cultural group with a clear identity, are conducting a democratic struggle to gain rights and recognition.

The Global-Local Paradox

This is probably the greatest of the contradictions. If global integration and economic development is to benefit all of humankind, local units must share in the decision-making process. At the moment, market mechanisms do not allow for this, and states place greater importance on national interests.

The greatest impact of international migration is felt at the local level. Significant numbers of the workforce migrating may lead to the collapse of agricultural production and handcraft industries. Local problems created by migration play a central role in political action and research. One factor to emerge from the 1974–1975 Boğazlıyan research project, outlined in detail in a previous chapter, was the fact that more than four-fifths of all the savings and investment money entering the district's forty villages as a result of migration ended up being directed outside again. The flow of migrant remittances has neither brought any substantial increase in production in the district nor created many jobs. Investments in farm machinery have made many farmers redundant. And non-migrants in the lowest income group have had to look about for alternate sources of living; their search has taken increasing numbers away from the district.[36]

The Economy-Environment Paradox

Constant economic growth involves the equally constant use of natural resources and the ecosystem. Market powers ignore the degeneration of the environment because active players in the market do not add long-term effects to their balance sheets. The depredation of forests, air pollution, and the drying up of natural resources have little to do with borders and thus cannot be halted by national laws. Supranational regulations are almost invariably put into place too late to be of any real use.

In some regions, environmental degradation is directly responsible for migration flows. Desertification, deforestation, soil erosion, drought, and flood all play a role in forcing people to move, and as a result, in addition to the more traditional political refugee, we now have the environmental refugee.

Rapid uncontrolled urban growth and unplanned tourism are further additions to pressures on the environment, and it is now clear that it is only through close international cooperation in understanding and managing human mobility that these problems may be dealt with.

---

[36] Penninx and Van Velzen, "Evaluation of Migrants' Investments and their Effects on Development in Boğazlıyan District," in *Migration and Development*, 324–325.

The Modernism-Postmodernism Paradox

Some contemporary theorists tell us that the problems we have in today's world are part of the painful transition from modernism to postmodernism. If the history of modernism is to be examined in light of Enlightenment philosophy, then progress is all about creating a good society. In contrast, postmodernism casts aside this meta-narrative and includes instead the breakdown of policies, cultures, and identities. In the latter of the two approaches, relativism and pessimism are dominant.

Stephen Castles does not share this view (2003). According to him, the meta-narrative of modernism is stronger today than ever. The globalization of markets is a one-sided realization of the Enlightenment project. Production, control, and communications technologies are universal. Whether it is viewed from an economic or a cultural perspective, globalization is the natural child of modernism.

What is missing here, however, is the political and social project, which would involve strong democratic states engaged in the struggle to obtain equal rights and material comfort for all. Indeed, it is precisely at this point that fragmentation begins, and at its roots are free markets. Thus, globalization constitutes an arena of modernist integrated economy but postmodernist fragmented politics. This paradox is particularly striking in the area of migration.

Neoclassical economists claim that free movement of labor paves the way to wage equality among countries. At the same time, however, the lack of a political framework prevents migrants from being protected by basic human rights, and from their social needs being fulfilled. Thus, we may say that rather than speaking of wage equality, it is clear that migration instead brings with it new inequalities between and among countries.

However rational and productive the markets, they fail to create equality and social balance just as nation-states fail to resolve supranational issues. Even as supranational measures are put in place, new integration and exclusions result. The EU has engaged in great efforts to equalize the rights of the five million individuals within its borders who move between and among its member states, but has done little for the more than ten million migrants from countries outside the EU who are resident in EU member states.

The National Citizen-Global Citizen Relationship

The greatest success story of the nation-state model has been the creation of the democratic citizen, who is not only in possession of rights but is also an active participant in law and decision-making processes. At the same time, it must be said that although there are very few places in the world where this democratic citizenship is practiced at its optimum level, this nevertheless remains an ideal for much of the world's peoples. Democratic citizenship also carries within itself a certain ambiguity: the individual citizen of the nation-state is at one and the same time a member of a political community and, from a cultural perspective, a national community. The political community views all citizens as equal and disregards such characteristics as social, gender, ethnic, or religious identities. Yet, the nation-building process will have generally meant the fusion of different ethnic groups to form national unity. This process then will have entailed these groups becoming assimilated into the whole at the cost of giving up their identity, or at least choosing to forget their differences over long periods of time.

Cultural homogeneity has also created problems because minority cultures have been more resistant than expected, and in today's age of migration, this resistance is beginning to weigh more heavily. Flexible, shifting borders and growing ethnocultural differences mean cultural homogeneity is no longer possible. Today, many individuals constantly move between and among countries and maintain familial, economic, and social ties across borders. These are people who carry within themselves more than one identity, and even if governments try to stop this process, many individuals bear two or more citizenship statuses. Cultural exchange and intercultural marriages are another part of the blend of this new consciousness.

All these experiences, for the moment, reflect the situations of limited numbers of individuals, but there can be little doubt that globalization will put these trends on an upward course, and it would appear that the principle whereby each individual belongs to one nation-state culturally and politically is becoming more and more difficult to actually put into practice. The ultimate goal today is to have a "global" citizenship based not on the rights one has as a result of belonging to a particular place, but on the concept of human rights.

Outlook

Turkish citizens are continuing to establish roots in Europe at a steady rate In 2007, out of 625,000 Turkish homes, 125,000 were of Turkish ownership. The growth of entrepreneurship is also continuing. Bursting out of the ethnic niche, there are 70,000 self-employed Turks who have created 330,000 jobs alone in Germany in 2009. New investment forms created by Turks are taking hold in former socialist states such as Poland, the Czech Republic, and Hungary. Within the borders of the EU, Turkish businesspeople have created up to 640,000 new jobs in 2009. A large number of these enterprises are in the food and restaurant sector, and have created, particularly in northern Italy, a sharp cricism against *döner kebab.*[1] Several cities are trying to push these shops outside the town center, and others are claiming their merchandise is unhygienic. The relevant point is the fact that commercial competition begins to carry the color of ethnic discrimination.

The Turks—the largest immigrant community in Europe—are an easy target for anti-immigrant feelings and xenophobia. Against this background, there are many in Europe who fear that if Turkey were to become a member of the EU, more migration from Turkey would occur. This fear is aggravated by the social and cultural difficulties that Turkish immigrants encounter in integrating into host societies. Actually this difficulty results to a large degree in the intention to retain two-side allegiances, which in turn forges strong transnational links. Although a significant proportion of second- and third-generation immigrants do poorly, especially in respect to education and employment, there is a growing Turkish immigrant civil society in Europe that is making its voice heard. Their annual turnover in Europe is about 50 billion euros. In Germany, this figure exceeds 32.7 billion euros.[2]

Globalism has transformed the modern welfare state into a *prudential* state, where more and more responsibility for the well-being of the citizen is put on the shoulders of the individual. For many second- and third-generation migrants, such as Turks living in Europe, who face unemployment, exclusion, institutional racism, and Islamophobia, integration does not seem to offer a solution to their problems. Instead they tend to find a refuge in the comfort of religious, ethnic, cultural, and fellowship communities. For example, the ban

[1] Grilled meat rotating on a skewer and served with pita and salad.

[2] See Turkish Republic Ministry of Foreign Affairs, available at http://www.mfa.gov.tr/yurtdisinda-yasayan-turkler_.tr.mfa

on building minarets in Switzerland following the 29 November 2009 referendum will create a boomerang effect by strenghtening the bonds of Islamic communities.

Globalization has also changed the perception of Islam for many migrants.[3] The global circuity of modern communications has created the *individualization of Islam* through which youngsters attempt to liberate religion from the conservative parental culture. However, these young migrants represent the minority; the majority prefers to rally around official institutions. This represents the *institutionalization of Islam.* Official efforts to institutionalize Islam through the establishment of some Islamic organizations and councils—such as in France, Germany, Austria, and Belgium—may not facilitate integration but discourage those who are unwilling to assimilate.

The twenty-first century carries the label of *transnationalism*. Host societies should do better to recognize the value of the social capital migrants have brought with them and accrued during their prolonged stays. Through their presence, the countries where they have settled have changed in structure and culture. To achieve a harmonious coexistence in a state of law, a thorough reevaluation of the principles of liberalism, secularism, and democracy seems unavoidable.

---

[3] Ayhan Kaya, *Islam, Migration and Integration: The Age of Securitization* (New York: Palgrave/Macmillan, 2009).

Appendix

TABLE 1.
Turkish labor migration, by destination (1961–2005)

Host Countries	*1961–1974*		*1975–1980*		*1981–1990*		*1991–1995*		*1996–2000*		*2001–2005*		*Total*	
	#	%	#	%	#	%	#	%	#	%	#	%	#	%
Europe	790,017	97.5	13,426	12.8	2,612	0.6	9,647	2.8	10,465	9.3	16,561	9.1	842,728	42.4
Arab Countries	2,441	0.3	74,181	70.6	423,208	97.7	208,274	60.4	32,195	28.5	57,974	31.9	798,273	40.2
Australia	5,806	0.7	2,647	2.5	2,478	0.6	1324	0.4	515	0.5	176	0.1	12,946	0.7
CIS Countries		—		—		—	115	0.0	65,521	58.0	89,623	49.3	155,259	7.8
Others	12,235	1.5	14,792	14.1	4,875	1.1	125,238	36.3	4256	3.8	17,533	9.6	178,929	9.0
Total	810,499	100	105,046	100	433,173	100	344,598	100	112,952	100	181,867	100	1,988,135	100

Source: Compiled by İçduygu (2006a), based on various official sources in Turkey.

TABLE 2.
Turkish migrant stock abroad in the mid-1980s, mid-1990s, and mid-2000s

	Mid-1980s		*Mid-1990s*		*Mid-2000s*	
	# (x1000)	*%*	*# (x1000)*	*%*	*# (x1000)*	*%*
Austria	75.0	3.1	147.0	4.4	127.0	3.8
Belgium	72.5	3.1	79.5	2.4	45.9	1.4
France	146.1	6.2	198.9	6.0	208.0	6.3
Germany	1,400.1	59.3	2,049.9	62.0	1,912.0	57.9
Netherlands	156.4	6.6	127.0	3.8	160.3	4.9
Scandinavian Countries	41.2	1.7	73.0	2.2	51.6	1.6
Switzerland	51.0	2.2	79.0	2.4	79.5	2.4
Other European Countries	42.0	1.8	87.0	2.6	130.0	3.9
Total Europe	1,984.6	84.0	2,841.3	85.9	2,714.3	82.1
Arab Countries	200.0	8.5	127.0	3.8	105.0	3.2
Australia	35.0	1.5	45.0	1.4	60.0	1.8
CIS Countries	0.0	0.0	50.0	1.4	75.0	2.3
Other Countries	140.0	5.9	245.0	7.4	350.0	10.6
Total	2,359.6	100.0	3,308.3	100.0	3,304.3	100.0

Source: Figures are compiled by İçduygu (2006a) from various sources of OECD and Eurostat.

TABLE 3.
Estimates of Turkish migrant stock worldwide

Country	*Turkish Citizens*
Germany	1,738,831
France	423,471
Netherlands	364,333
US	250,000
UK	52,893
Northern Cyprus	31,977
Austria	113,635
Saudi Arabia	120,000
Switzerland	73,861
Australia	64,500
Denmark	54,859
Greece	48,880
Canada	41,000
Belgium	39,664
Sweden	63,580
Israel	30,000
Russian Federation	22,808
Norway	15,356
Azarbaijan	16,000
Italy	14,124
Romania	12,000
Kazakistan	9,593
Lebanon	7,748
Finland	7,000
Turkmenistan	7,000
Japan	6,309
United Arab Emirates	5,484
Afghanistan	4,500
Kyrgizistan	3,380
Kuwait	3,260
Dubai	3,000
Poland	2,500
Jordan	2,500
Syria	2,350
Lybia	1,350
Others	35,375
Total	**3,693,121**

Source: Turkish Ministry of Labour and Social Security as of 31 December 2006

TABLE 4.
Germany's non-German population and Turkish minority

Year	*Non-German population*	%	*Turkish minority*	%
1961	686,200	1.2	6,700	1.2
1970	2,600,600	4.3	249,400	16.5
1973	3,966,200	6.4	605,000	15.2
1977	3,948,300	6.4	508,000	12.9
1987	4,240,500	6.9	1,453,700	34.3
1989	4,845,900	7.7	1,612,600	33.3
1990a	5,342,500	8.4	1,675,900	32.0
1991b	5,882,300	7.3	1,779,600	30.3
1992	6,495,800	8.0	1,854,900	28.6
1993	6,878,100	8.5	1.918,400	27.9
1994	6,990,510	8.6	1.965,577	28.1
1995	7,173,900	8.7	2,014,311	28.1
1996	7,314,000	8.9	2,049,060	28.0
1997	7,365,800	9.0	2,107,400	28.6
1998	7,319,600	9.0	2,110,223	28.8
1999	7,343,600	8.9	2,053,600	27.9
2000	7,296,800	8.8	1,998,500	27.3
2001	7,318.600	8.7	1,947,900	26.6
2002	7,335,592	8.9	1,912,169	26.2
2003	7,334,765	8.7	1,877,661	25.6
2004	6,717,115	8.1	1,877,661	27.9
2005	6,755,881	8.2	1,764,041	26.1
2006	6,751,000	8.2	1,738,000	25.7

Notes: a. Data from 1961-1990 for the 'old' Laender.
b. Data from 1991 for the 'old' and 'new' Laender.

Sources: Statistisches Jahrbuch für die Bundesrepublik Deutschland, 2007.

TABLE 5.
Turkish asylum seekers, by destination (1981–2005)

Destination	*1981–1985*		*1986–1990*		*1991–1995*		*1996–2000*		*2001–2005*		*1981–2005*	
	#	%	#	%	#	%	#	%	#	%	#	%
Europe	45,620		185,797		175,557	98.6	141,226	97.9	107,534	97.2	655,734	98.7
Canada					755	0.4	1,919	1.3	2,451	2.2	5125	0.8
Australia					780	0.4	928	0.6	332	0.3	2040	0.3
USA					984	0.6	199	0.1	330	0.3	1513	0.2
Total					178,076	100.0	144,272	100.0	110,647	100.0	664,412	100.0

Source: Figures are compiled by İçduygu (2006a) from various sources of OECD and Eurostat.

TABLE 6.
Naturalization of Turkish origin migrants and their descendants in Germany (1980–2006)

Year	*Turks*
1980	399
1981	534
1982	580
1983	853
1984	1,053
1985	1,310
1986	1,492
1987	1,184
1988	1,243
1989	1,713
1990	2,034
1991	3,529
1992	7,377
1993	12,915
1994	19,590
1995	31,578
1996	46,294
1997	42,240
1998	59,664
1999	103,900
2000	82,800
2001	75,600
2002	64,631
2003	56,244
2004	44,465
2005	32,661
2006	33,388
Total	**683,391**

Source: Statistisches Bundesamt 2007.

TABLE 7.
Number of naturalized Belgian-Turks (1990–2006)

Year	*Number of naturalized Belgian-Turks*
1990	706
1991	1,020
1992	4,044
1993	3,415
1994	6,263
1995	6,925
1996	7,066
1997	7,835
1998	6,932
1999	4,402
2000	17,282
2001	14,401
2002	7,805
2003	5,186
2004	4,467
2005	3,602
2006	3,204
Total	**104,555**

Source: National Institute of Statistics, 2007, http://www.npdata.be

TABLE 8.
Number of people who migrated to Turkey, by region (1923–1997)

Country	*1923–1939*	*1940–1945*	*1946–1997*	*TOTAL*
Bulgaria	198,688	15,744	603,726	818,158
Greece	384,000	—	25,889	84,431
Romania	117,095	4,201	1,266	122,562
Yugoslavia	115,427	1,671	188,600	428,260
Turkistan	—	—	2,878	2,878
Others	7,998	1,005	8,631	17,634
TOTAL	823,208	22,621	830,99	1,676,819

Figures compiled by Ahmet İçduygu – Mirkoç 2007

TABLE 9.
Number of Turks sent abroad for specific tasks as of 2009 (approximate)

Number of Turkish teachers residing abroad, employed by Turkish government	1,264
Number of Turkish teachers residing in Germany, employed by Turkish government	480
Number of Turkish university students abroad	130,000
Number of Turkish university students in Germany	25,000
Number of Turkish students at primary and secondary schools level abroad	838,000
Number of Turkish religious personnel sent by Turkish government	1,074
Number of Turkish religigious personnel sent by Turkish government in Germany	544
Number of Turkish Associations abroad	3,900
Number of Turkish Associations in Germany	2,500
Number of Turkish mosques in Germany	1,500

Source: T.C. Dışişleri Bakanlığı, 2010

Selected Bibliography

In Turkish

Abadan-Unat, Nermin. 1964. *Batı Almanya'daki Türk İşçileri ve Sorunları*. Ankara: Başbakanlık DPT.

———. 1971. "Federal Almanya'nın 1966/7'de gecirdigi ekonomik buhran acisindan yabanci isgucu ve Turk iscilerin durumu." *A.Ü.S.B.F. Dergisi* 26, no. 4:159–180.

———. 1972a. "Yurt Dışına Göçen Türk İşgücü ve Dönüş Eğilimleri." *A.Ü.S.B.F. Dergisi*. 27, no. 2:183–206.

———. 1972b. "Türkiye'nin Dış Göç Akımı ve Sosyal Hareketlilik." *A.Ü.S.B.F. Dergisi* 27, no. 4:17–52.

———. 1973. "Teşvik Edilen Beyin Göçü." *Türkiye Mühendislik Haberleri* 19, no. 216: 92–93.

———. 1977. "Dış Göç Akımının Türk Kadının Özgürleşme ve Sözde Özgürleşme Sürecine Etkisi." *Âmme İdaresi Dergisi* 10, no. 1:107–132.

———. 1979. "Göçmen İşçi Çocuklarının Sosyo-Psikolojik ve Eğitimsel Sorunları." In *Yurt Dışındaki Türk Çocuklarının Eğitim Sorunları*. Ankara: A.Ü.E.F.

———. 1983. "Batı Avrupa ve Ortadoğu'ya Göç Eden Türk İşgücünün Sosyal yasalar ve toplum Yapısı Üzerindeki Etkisi." In *Prof. Dr. İbrahim Yasa'ya Armağan*. Ankara: A.Ü.S.B.F.

———. 1984. "Uluslararası Göç Akımının Kadınların Toplumsal Rolleri Üzerindeki Etkisi: Türkiye Örnek Olay." *Prof. Aziz Köklü'nün Anısına Armağan*. Ankara: A.Ü.S.B.F.

———. 1986. "Türk Dış Göçünün 24 Yıllık Bilimsel Bilançosu,1960–84." In *Türk Dış Göçü, 1960–1984. Yorumlu Bibliyografya*, eds. Nermin Abadan-Unat and N. Kemiksiz. Ankara: A.Ü.S.B.F.

———. 2000. "Küreselleşme, Göç ve Toplumsal Değişme." In *Mübeccel Kıray için Yazılar*, ed. F. Atacan. İstanbul: Bağlam.

———. 2002, 2006. *Bitmeyen Göç. Konuk İşçilikten Ulus-Ötesi Yurttaşlığa*. İstanbul: İstanbul Bilgi Üniversitesi.

———. 2005. "Her iki Ülke de Göçe Hazırlıksızdı." *Evrensel*, no. 168: 65–69.

Abadan-Unat, Nermin, and Neşe Kemiksiz. 1986. *Türk Dış Göçü, 1960–1984. Yorumlu Bibliyografya*. Ankara: A.Ü.S.B.F.

Abadan-Unat, Nermin, and Ruşen Keleş, et al. 1976. *Göç ve Gelişme. Uluslarası İşgücü Göçünün Boğazlıyan İlçesindeki Etkilerine İlişkin bir Araştırma*. Ankara: A.Ü.S.B.F.

Akçapar, Şebnem. 2007. "Batı Avrupa'da Yaşayan Türk 'ithal' Gelinleri ve Entegrasyon Sorunları: Belçika Örneği." In *Kökler ve Yollar*, eds. Ayhan Kaya and Bahar Şahin. İstanbul: İstanbul Bilgi Üniversitesi.

Aker, Ahmet. 1972. *İşçi Göçü.Nisan 1970 ile Nisan 1971 Arasında Almanya'ya Giden Türk İşçileri Üzerinde Sosyo-Ekonomik bir Örnekleme Araştırması*. İstanbul: Sander.

Aksel, L. 1968. *Dış Ülkelerde Çalışan Türk İşçilerinin Sosyal Güvenlik Hakları*. Ankara: Anka.

Anderson, Benedict. 1995. *Hayalî Cemaatler, Milliyetçiliğin Kökenleri ve Yayılması*. Istanbul: Metis.

Andrews, Peter. A. 1992. *Türkiye'de Etnik Gruplar*. İstanbul: Ant.

Ansay, Tuğrul. 1972a. "Almanya'da Boşanan Türklerin Hukukî Sorunları." *A.Ü.S.B.F. Dergisi* 27, no. 3:353–369.

———. 1972b. "Evlilik Dışında Doğan Çocukların Tanınması Alanında Kanunlar Çatışması (Türk-Alman Olayları)." *A.Ü. Hukuk Fak. Dergisi* 29, nos. 3–4:159–183.

Araslı, Oya, and Doğan. Araslı.1973. *Almanya'daki İşçiler Hak ve Menfaatleri*. Ankara: Ayyıldız.

Ayata, Ayşe. 1988. "Türkiye'de Kimlik Politikalarının Doğuşu." In *75 Yılda Tebaa'dan Yurttaş'a Doğru*, ed. A. Ünsal. Istanbul: Tarih Vakfı /İş B.

Bauman, Zgymunt. 1977. *Küreselleşme: Toplumsal Sonuçlari*. İstanbul: Ayrıntı.

Canatan, Kadir. 1990. *Göçmenlerin Kimlik Arayışı: Konuk İşçilikten Yerleşik Göçmenliğe*. İstanbul: Endülüs.

Çalışma ve Sosyal Güvenlik Bakanlığı. 1999. *Avrupa Birliğinde Yaşayan Türk İşçilere ve Ailelerine Mevzuatiyle Tanınan Haklar ve Avrupa Toplulukları Adalet Divanı Kararları*. Ankara: Çalışma Bakanlığı Y.İ.G.M.

Çetinkaya, Hikmet. 31 December 2001. "Avrupa'da radikal Islamcı örgütlenme" [The Organization of Radical Islam in Europe] *Cumhuriyet*.

Çetinkaya, Hikmet. 2002. *İrticanın Kara Yüzü*. İstanbul: Günizi.

Cizre, Ümit. 1994–1995. "Türk Siyaseti: Geçmeyen Geçmiş, Gelemeyen Gelecek." *Görüş*, no. 18.

Connolly, William E. 1995. *Kimlik ve Farklılık. Siyasetin Açmazlarına Dair Demokratik Çözüm*. Istanbul: Ayrıntı.

Ecevit, Bülent. 1964. *Yurt Dışındaki Türk İşçileri*. Ankara: Çalışma Bakanlığı.

Ekin, N. 1970–1971. "Yurt Dışı İşgücü İstihdamının Ekonomik ve Sosyal Analizi." *İ.Ü.İktisat Fak. Mecm* 30, nos. 1–4:73–96.

———. 1980. "Türkiye'den Dış Göç ve Ekonomik Gelişme." *İ.Ü.İşletme Fak. Dergisi* 9, no. 2:1–15.

Erder, Sema. 2006. *Refah Toplumunda Getto*. İstanbul: Istanbul Bilgi Üniversitesi.

Erdentuğ, Nermin. 1968. *Hal Köyünün Etnolojik Tetkiki*. Ankara: Ankara Üniversitesi Dil ve Tarih Coğrafya Fakültesi Yayınları.

Ergil, Doğu. 1982. "Avrupa'da Yaygınlaşan Yabancı Düşmanlığı Üzerine Düşünceler." *A.Ü.S.B.F. Dergisi* 37, nos. 3–4:153–157.

Ergun, T. 1978. *İşgücü Göçünün Türkiye Ekonomisi Üzerindeki Etkileri*. İzmir: Ege Üniversitesi, İ.F.

Esposito, John Lee et al. 2003. *Avrupa ve Amerika Müslümanlar*. İstanbul: Gelenek.

Evrenosoğlu, İskender. 1973. *Federal Almanya Türkye İşgücü İlişkileri*. Eskişehir: Sanayi Odası.

Faist, Thomas. 2003. *Uluslararası Göç ve Ulusaşırı Toplumsal Alanların Dinamikleri*. İstanbul: Bağlam.

Gezgin, M. F. 1994. *İşgücü Göçü ve Avusturya'daki Türk İşçileri*. İstanbul: I.Ü.İ.F.

Gitmez, Ali. 1979. *Dış Göş Öykusü*. Ankara: Maya.

———.1983. *Yurtdışına İşçi Göçü ve Geri Dönüşler*. İstanbul: Alan.

Gökdere, Ahmet. 1974. "Batı Avrupa Ülkelerine İşgücü Göçünün Türk Sanayi Üzerindeki Muhtemel Etkileri." In *T. C. 50 ci yılında Türkiye'de Sanayileşme Ve Sorunları Semineri*. Ankara: A.Ü.S.B.F.

———.1978. *Yabancı Ülkelere İşgücü Akımı ve Türk Ekonomisi Üzerine Etkileri.* Ankara: T.İş B.

———. 1983. "Batı Göçünün Türk Demografik Yapısına Etkileri," *Fadıl H.Sur Armağanı.* Ankara: A.Ü.S.B.F.

Gökmen, Oğuz. 1972. *Federal Almanya ve Türk İşçileri.* Ankara: Ayyıldız.

Güler, Müzeyyen. 2004. *Okyanus Ötesine: ABD'de Türk Göçmenler.* İstanbul: Kendi.

Gülsün, İlhan. 1974. *Sayılarla Yurtdışındaki Işcilerimiz ve sorunlarına ait istatistikler.* Ankara: IIBK.

Günay, Ünver. 2003. "Göç, Din ve Değişme: Batı Avrupadaki Türk İşçileri Örneği." *Bilimname,* no. 3:35–64.

Gürel, Seval, and Ayşe Kudat. 1978. "Türk kadınının Avrupa'ya Göçünün Kişilik, Aile ve Topluma Yansıyan Sonuçları." *A.Ü.S.B.F. Dergisi* 33, nos. 3–4:109–134.

Güven, H. S. 1977. *Dış Göç ve' İşçi Yatırım Ortaklıkları'.* Ankara: TODAİE.

———. 1996. *Uluslararası İşçi Göçünün Sosyal Politika Sorunları.* Bursa: U.Ü.G.V.

Güzel, Ü. 1981. *Avrupa'da Göçmen İşçiler ve Türk İşçi Tasarruflarının Değerlendirilmesi.* Ankara: DPT.

Hamuroğlu, Alman. 2001. *Alman İslamı.* İstanbul: Kaynak.

Işıklı, Alpaslan. 1963. "Milletlerarası İşgücü Hareketleri." *A.Ü.S.B.F. Dergisi* 18, no. 1: 75–101.

Kaçkar, Mahmut, and Nilüfer Kuryazıcı. 2001. *Gurbeti Vatan Edenler: Almanca Yazan Almanlaşan Türkler.* Ankara: Kültür Bakanlığı.

Kandiyoti, Deniz, and Ayşe Saktanber. 2003. *Kültür Fragmanları.* İstanbul: Metis.

Karahan, Tonguç. 2005. "Gurbet Vatan Olunca." *Evrensel,* no. 168:78–80.

Karakaşoğlu, Aydın. 1999. "Almanya'da Okullarda ve Üniversitelerde Başörtüsü Olayı." *Toplum ve Bilim,* no. 83:58–77.

Karamustafaoğlu, Tunçer. 1967. "Yurt Dışındaki İşçilerimizin Seçme Hakları." *A.Ü. Hukuk Fak. Dergisi* 24, nos. 1 and 4:97–104.

Karlsson, Ingmar. 1996. *İslam ve Avrupa-İnanç Ayrılığı-Yaşam Birliği,* Istanbul: Cem.

———. 2006. *Avrupa'nın Üvey Evlatları.* İstanbul: Homer.

Karul, Orhan. 1990. *Değişen Avrupa ve Göçmen Türkler.* İstanbul: Yapı Kredi Yayını.

Kastoryanu, Riva. 2000. *Kimlik Pazarlığı—Fransa ve Almanya'da Devlet ve Göçmen İlişkileri.* İstanbul: İletişim.

Kaya, Ayhan. 2001. "Sicher in Kreuzberg." *Constructing Diasporas: Turkish Hip-Hop Youth in Berlin* (Bielefeld: Transcript).

———. 2005a. "Euro-Islam ve Korkunun Siyaseti." *Karizma,* no. 24:25–36.

Kaya, Ayhan, and Ferhat Kentel. 2005. *Euro-Türkler. Türkiye ile Avrupa Birliği Arasında Köprü Mü, Engel Mi?* İstanbul: İstanbul Bilgi Üniversitesi.

Kaya, Ayhan, and Turgut Tarhanlı. 2005. *Türkiye'de Çoğunluk ve Azınlık Politikaları. AB Sürecinde Yurttaşlık Tartışmaları.* İstanbul: TESEV.

Kaya, Ayhan, and Bahar Şahin. 2007. *Kökler ve Yollar-Türkiye'de Göç Süreçleri.* İstanbul: İstanbul Bilgi Üniversitesi.

Kazgan, Gülten. 2000. *Küreselleşme ve Ulus-Devlet: Yeni Ekonomik Düzen.* İstanbul: İstanbul Bilgi Üniversitesi.

Keyman, Fuat, and Ahmet İçduygu. 1998. "Türk Modernleşmesi ve Ulusal Kimlik Sorunu: Anayasal Vatandaşlık ve Demokratik Açılım Olasılığı." In *75 Yılda Tebaa'dan Yurttaşa Doğru,* ed. A. Ünsal. İstanbul: Tarih Vakfı ve İş Bankası.

Kıray, Yusuf. 1964. *Cukurova Bolgesi Pamuklar. ve di. er Kultur bitkilerinde Zarar yapan* Earias insulana *(Boisd.) boce.inin biyolojisi ve mucadelesi uzerinde ara.t.rmlar.* Doctoral thesis. Kemal Motbaas, Adana.

Kirişçi, Kemal, and Gareth Winrow. 2000. *Kürt Sorunu, Kökeni ve Gelişimi.* İstanbul: Tarih Vakfı.

Köksal, Sema. 1986. *Refah toplumunda "Getto" ve Türkler.* İstanbul: Köksal.

Odman, Mesut Tevfik. 1995. *Mülteci Hukuku.* Ankara: A.Ü.S.B.F.

———. 1996. *Kadın Mülteciler.* Ankara: A.Ü.S.B.F.

Oğuzkan, Turhan. 1971. *Yurtdışında Çalışan Doktoralı Türkler: Türkiye'den Başka Ülkelere Yüksek Seviyede Eleman Göçü Üzerinde Bir Araştırma.* Ankara: ODTÜ.

Ohmae, Kenichi. 1996. *Ulus-Devletin Sonu; Bölgesel Ekonomilerin Yükselişi.* Istanbul: Türk-Henkel Dergisi Yayınları.

Ören, Aras. 1980. *Niyazi'nin Naunyn Sokağı'nda İşi Ne?* Istanbul: Remzi Kitabevi.

Özdemir, Cem. 1999. *Ben Almanyalıyım-Alman Parlamentosundaki İlk Türk Asıllı Milletvekili.* İstanbul: İletişim Yayınları.

Özdemir, Y. 2005. "Avrupa'da Türk Basını: Dördüncü Kuvetten Birinci Kuvvete Terfii." *Evrensel,* no. 168:70–75.

Pazarkaya, Yüksel, ed. 1995. *Mölln ve Sollingenden sonra Almanya Üzerine.* İstanbul: Sis Çanı.

———. 1977. *Oturma İzni.* Istanbul: Derinlik.

Petras, James, and Morris Morley. 1996. *İmparatorluk mu? Cumhuriyet mi? Amerika'nın Küresel gücü ve İç Çürümesi.* İstanbul: Sarmal.

———. 2005. "Eski ve Yeni Göç Modelleri ile Türkiye'nin Ulusal Kimliği." In *Türkiye Kültürleri,* eds. G. Pultar and T. Erman. İstanbul: Tatragon.

Pur, Necla. 1974. *Uluslararası İşgücü Hareketleri ve Türkiye.* İstanbul: İstanbul Matbaa.

Reisoğlu, Safa. 1973a. *Ortak Pazar Hukuku Özellikle İşçi Dolaşım, Yerleşme ve Hizmet Edimi Serbestisini Düzenliyen Kurallar.* Ankara: A.Ü.H.F.

———. 1973b. *Yabancı İşçiler Yönünden Alman İş ve Sosyal Güvenlik Hukuku.* Ankara: A.Ü.H.F.

Richter, Michael. 2005. *Geldiler ve Kaldılar … Almanya Türklerinin Yaşam Öyküleri.* İstanbul: İstanbul Bilgi Üniversitesi.

Roy, Olivier. 2003. *Küreselleşen Islam.* İstanbul: Metis.

Schnapper, Dominique. 2005. *Sosyoloji Düşüncesinin Özünde. Öteki ile İlişki.* İstanbul: İstanbul Bilgi Üniversitesi.

Semprun, Jorge, and Dominique de Villepin. 2005. *Avrupa İnsanı.* İstanbul: Agora.

Şenel, Şengün. 1977. *Yurtdışında Çalışan İşçilerin Kurdukları Şirketler ve İşçi Halk Şirketleri.* Ankara: İş ve İşçi Bulma.

Seven, Y. B. 2005. "Almanya'daki Türk Sinemasına 'kısa ve acısız' bir bakış," *Evrensel,* no. 168:76–77.

Somersan, Semra. 2004. *Sosyal Bilimlerde Etnisite ve Irk.* İstanbul: İstanbul Bilgi Üniversitesi.

Subaşı, Necdet. 2005. "Gecikmiş bir Kimlik Tartışması: Euro-İslam." *Karizma,* no. 24:85–95.

Şimşek, Çağlar Ayşe. 2002. "İki Elde bir Sehpa." In *Kültür Fragmanları, Türkiye'de Gündelik Hayat,* eds. Deniz Kandiyoti and A. Saktanber. İstanbul: Metis.

Talas, Cahit. 1980. "Avrupa'da Göçmen İşçiler ve İnsan Hakları," *İnsan Hakları Yıllığı,* no. 2:95–110.

———. 1986. "Federal Almanya'daki Türk İşçileri ve Durumları." *Fadıl H.Sur'a Armağan.* Ankara: A.Ü.S.B.F.

Taylor, Charles. 1996. *Çokkültürcülük: Tanınma Politikası.* İstanbul: Yapı Kredi.

Teber, Serol. 1980. *İşçi Göçü ve Davranış Bozuklukları*. İstanbul: Konuk.

Tekarslan, E. 1982. "Avusturya'da Yabancı İşçiler ve Linz Kentinde Türk İşçileri Arasında Yapılan Bir Araştırmanın Bulguları." *İ.Ü.İşletme F. Dergisi* 11, no. 1:261–275.

Timur, Serim. 1972. "Türkiye'de Aile Yapısı." Ankara: Hacettepe University Publications.

Toprak, Zafer. 1981. "Almanya'ya İlk İşçi ve Öğrenci, Göçü: 1916–1918." *Bilim ve Sanat*, no. 3:26–27.

Tuna, Orhan, and Nusret Ekin. 1966. *Türkiye'den F.Almanya'ya İşgücü Akımı ve Meseleleri*, vol. 1. İstanbul: I.Ü.İ.F.

———. 1966. *F. Almanya'ya İşgücü Akımı ile İlgili Organlar ve Meseleleri*, vol. 2. İstanbul: I.Ü.İ.F.

———. 1966. *F. Almanya'da Çalışan Türk İşçilerinin İşledikleri Suçların Tahlili*, vol. 3. İstanbul: I.Ü.İ.F.

Tuncer, Bulutay. 1970. "İşgücü Hareketlerinin Gönderen ve Kabul Eden Ülke Ekonomileri Üzerindeki Etkileri." In *Ortak Pazar İşgücü Hareketleri*. Ankara: Türk-İş.

Uludağ Üniversitesi, 1980. *Federal Almanya'da Çalışan Türk İşçilerinin Toplu Dönüşleri ve Türkiye ile F. Almanya'da Uyum sağlamaları Semineri*. Bursa: U.Ü.Y.

Ünver, Can. 2006. "Almanya'da Türk Kimliğinin Algılanma ve Tanımlama Sorunları." *Türk Yurdu* 224, no. 26:22–27.

Üstel, Füsun. 1999. *Yurttaşlık ve Demokrasi*. Ankara: Dost Yayınları.

Vassaf, Gündüz. 2002. *Daha Sesimizi Duyuramadık: Avrupa'da Türk İşçi Çocukları*. İstanbul: İstanbul Bilgi Üniversitesi.

Walzer, Michael. 1997. *Hoşgörü Üzerine*, İstanbul: Ayrıntı.

Yalçın-Heckman, Lale. 2002. "Kimlikler Üzerinde Pazarlık: Almanya'daki Farklı Türk Göçmen Kuşaklarının Medyadaki, Yansımaları." In *Kültür Fragmanları: Türkiye'de Gündelik Hayat*, eds. Deniz Kandiyoti and Ayşe Saktanber. İstanbul: Metis.

Yalçın-Heckmann, Lale, and Horst Unbehaun. 1999. "Fransa ve Almanya'daki Göçmen Toplulukları: İki Orta Büyüklükteki Şehirde Dernekleşme ve Cemaatleşme Süreçleri." *Toplum ve Bilim*, no. 82:78–89.

Yasa, İbrahim. 1955. Hasanoglan Koyu. Ankara.

———. 1979. *Yurda Dönen İşçiler ve Toplumsal Değişme*. Ankara: TODAİE.

Yasa, İbrahim, and Ömer Bozkurt. 1974. "Orta Anadolu'dan Batı Avrupa'ya: Göç ve Toplumsal Değişme." *Âmme İdaresi Dergisi* 7, no. 3:45–72.

Yasa, İbrahim, and Hasan Sami Güven. 1975. "Yurtdışında Çalışan İşçilerimizin Yaygın Tabanlı Halk Girişimciliğine Katkıları: Şerefli Koçhisar Örneği." *Âmme İdaresi Dergisi* 8, no. 3:85–115.

Yeğenoğlu, Meyda. 1995. "Sömürge Sonrası Dünyada Göçmen Kimliği." *Mürekkep*, nos. 3-4:78–82.

Yılmaz, Hakan, ed. 2005. *Avrupa Haritasında Türkiye*. İstanbul: Boğaziçi Üniversitesi.

In Other Languages

Abadan-Unat, Nermin. 1966. "Studie über die Lage und die Probleme der Türkischen Gastarbeiter in der Bundesrepublik Deutschland." In *Arbeitsplatz Europa*, ed. W.R. Schloesser et al. Köln: Europa Union.

———. 1971. "La Récession de 1966/67 en Allemagne Fédérale et ses répercussions sur les ouvriers turcs." In *Turkish Yearbook of International Relations*, no. 11:39–62.

———. 1972. "Le non-retour a l'industrie, trait dominant de la Chaine migratoire turque." *Sociologie du Travail* 3:278–293.

———. 1973. "La migration turque et la mobilité sociale." *Studi Emigrazione* 30, no. 10: 222–235.

———. 1974. "Turkish External Migration and Social Mobility." In *Turkey: Geographic and Social Perspectives,* eds. Peter Benedict, Erol Tümertekin and Fatma Mansur. Leiden, Belgium: E. J. Brill.

———. 1975. "Educational Problems of Turkish Migrants'Children." *International Review of Education* 21, no. 3:311–322.

———, ed. 1976a. *Turkish Workers in Europe 1960–1975: A Socio-Economic Reappraisal.* Leiden, Belgium: E. J. Brill.

———. 1976b. "Turkish Migration to Europe (1960–1975): A Balance Sheet of Achievements and Failures." In *Turkish Workers in Europe 1960–1975,* ed. Nermin Abadan-Unat. Leiden: E. J. Brill.

———. 1976c. "Migration as an Obstacle to Re-integration in Industry: The Turkish Case." *Turkish Public Administration Annual* 3:191–208.

———. 1977. "Implications of Migration on Emancipation and Pseudo-emancipation of Turkish Women." *International Migration Review* 11 (Spring): 31–57.

———. 1979. "Die politischen Auswirkungen der türkischen Migration im In und Ausland." *Orient,* no. 1:17–33.

———. 1982. "The Effect of International Labour Migration in Women's Roles: The Turkish case." In *Sex Roles, Family and Community,* ed. Çiğdem Kâğitçibaşi. Bloomington: Indiana University.

———. 1984. "International Labour Migration and Its Effect upon Women's Occupational and Family Roles: A Turkish View." In *Women on the Move: Contemporary Changes in Family and Society,* ed. UNESCO. Paris: UNESCO.

———. 1985a. "Identity Crisis of Turkish Migrants. First and Second Generation." In *Turkish Workers in Europe: An Interdisciplinary Study,* eds. Ilhan Başgöz and Norman Furniss. Bloomington: Indiana University.

———. 1985b. *Die Frau in der türkischen Gesellschaft.* Frankfurt a.M.: Dağyeli.

———. 1985c. "Die Auswirkungen der internationalen Arbeitsmigration auf die Rolle der Frau am Beispiel der Türkei." In *Die Frau in der türkischen Gesellschaft.* Frankfurt a.M.: Dağyeli.

———. 1986a. "Turkish Migration to Europe and the Middle East: Its Impact on Social Legislation and Social Structure." In *Social Legislation in the Contemporrary Middle East,* eds. L. O. Michalak and J. W. Salacuse. Berkeley: University of California Press.

———. 1986b. "Türken in der Bundesrepublik." In *Deutschland Portraet einer Nation* 10. Gütersloh: Bertelsmann Lexikotek.

———. 1987. "Summary of Main results." In *The Future of Migration.* Paris: OECD.

———. 1988. "The Socio-Economic Aspects of Return Migration in Turkey." *A European Journal of International Migration and Ethnic Relations,* no. 3:29–59.

———. 1989. "Die Migrationspolitik der Türkei." In *Die Türkei im Umbruch,* eds. I. Halil Özak, and Y. Dağyeli. Frankfurt a.M.: Dağyeli.

———. 1993a. "Impact of External Migration on Rural Turkey." In *Culture and Economy: Changes in Turkish Villages,* ed. Paul Stirling. Huntingdon: The Eothen Press.

———. 1993b. "Turkey: Late Entrant into Europe's Work Force." In *The Politics of Migration Policies,* 2nd ed., ed. Daniel Kubat. New York: Center for Migration Studies.

———. 1994. "Vom Gastarbeiter zum Pendler: 30 Jahre Auswanderung aus der Türkei." In *Jahrbuch für Vergleichende Sozialforschung 1991.* Berlin: Parabolis.

———. 1995. "Turkish Migration to Europe." In *The Cambridge Survey of World Migration,* ed. Robert Cohen. Cambridge: Cambridge University Press.

———. 1997. "Ethnic Business, Ethnic Communities, and Ethno-Politics among Turks in Europe." In *Immigration into Western Societies: Problems and Policies,* eds. Emek M. Uçarer and Donald J. Puchala. London: Pinter.

———. 2003. "Moving Towards European Transnationalism: A Turkish View." In *Migration and Labour in Europe: Views from Turkey and Sweden,* eds. Emrehan Zeybekoğlu and Bo Johansson. Istanbul: Şefik.

Abadan-Unat, Nermin, and Ruşen Keleş et.al. 1976. *A Study on the Effects of International Labor Migration on Boğazlıyan District.* Ankara: A.Ü.S.B.F.

Abadan-Unat, Nermin, Ruşen Keleş, Rinus Pennix, *Herman van Renselaar, Leo Van Velzen,* and Leyla Yenisey, eds. 1975. *Migration and Development: A Study of the Impact of International Labor Migration on the District of Boğazlıyan.* Ankara University–NUFFIC.

Adler, Stephen. 1981. "A Turkish Conundrum: Emigration, Politics and Development: 1961–1980." World Employment Programme working paper. Geneva: ILO.

Akpınar, Aylin. 1988. *Challenged Family and Kinship Ideals: Family Crisis and Social Networks Among Turkish immigrants.* Stockholm: Institutet för Social Forskning.

Akkaya, Çiğdem. et al. 2000. *Türkische Wirtschaftsleistung in Deutschland und in der EU.* Essen.

Aleinikoff, Thomas Alexander and Douglas Klusmeyer. 2002. *Citizenship Policies for an Age of Migration.* Washington, D. C.: Carnegie Endowment.

Allen, Chris. 2005. *Islamophobia: Its Meaning and Manifestations in UK and Europe.* Switzerland: University of Friburg.

Allen, Chris, and Jorgen Nielsen, eds. 2002. *Summary Report on Islamophobia.* (Vienna: EU Monitoring Centre on Racism & Xenophobia).

Alba, Richard, and Victor Nee. 1997. "Rethinking Assimilation Theory for a New Era of Immigration." *International Migration Review* 31, no. 4:826–874.

Albrecht, Richard. 1982. "Was ist der Unterschied Zwischen Türken und Juden?" *Zeitschrift für Volkskunde* 78:220–229.

Alpay, Şahlin, and Halil Sarıarslan. 1984. *Effects of Emigration: The Effects on the Town Kulu in Central Turkey of Emigration to Sweden.* Stockholm: EIFO.

Alund, Alexandra., and Schierup, Carl-Ulrick. 1991. *Paradoxes of Multiculturalism: Essays on Swedish Society.* Aldershot: Avebury.

Anderson, Benedict. 1983. *Imagined Communities: Reflections on the Origin and Spread of Nationalism.* London: Verso.

Appadurai, Arjun. 1996. *Modernity at Large.* Minneapolis: University of Minnesota Press.

Appleyard, Reginald, ed. 1988. *International Migration Today: Trends and Prospects,* vol. 1. Paris: Unesco/University of Western Australia.

Archibugi, Daniele, David Held, and Martin Kohler, eds. 1998. *Re-Imagining Political Community.* Stanford: Stanford University Press.

Aydınoglu, İsmail. 1976. "Manpower and Employment Policies under the Five Year Plans and Emigration." In *Turkish Workers in Europe 1960–1975,* ed. Nermin Abadan-Unat. Leiden, Belgium: E. J. Brill.

Avcı, Gamze. 1999. "Immigrant Categories: The Many Sides of One Coin?" *European Journal of Migration and Law* 1, no. 2:199–213.

———. 2005. "Religion, Transnationalism and Turks in Europe." *Turkish Studies* 6, no. 2 (June): 201–213.

———. 2006. "Comparing Integration Policies and Outcomes: Turks in the Netherlands and Germany," *Turkish Studies* 7, no. 1:67–84.

Aydın, Hayrettin. 2003. "Heiratsmigration bei Türkinnen und Türken." In *Migrationsbericht der Stiftung Zentrum für Türkeistudien*, vol. 5, eds. Andreas Goldberg, Dirk Halm, and Martina Sauer. Hamburg, Germany: LIT Verlag.

Azmaz, Adviye. 1984. *Migration and Reintegration in Rural Turkey: The Role of Women Behind.* Göttingen: Herodot.

Bach, Monika. 1984. *Mediennutzung und türkische Jugendliche.* Berlin: Hitit.

Bade, Klaus J. 1993. *Deutsche im Ausland. Fremde in Deutschland. Migration in Geschichte und Gegenwart.* Munich: C. H. Beck.

Bakanlığı, T. C. Çalışma. *2004 Report* (Turkish Ministry of Labour).

Barth, Fredrik. 1969. *Ethnic Groups and Boundaries. The Social Organization of Cultural Differences.* Oslo: University Press.

———. 1989. "The Analyses of Culture in Complex Societies." *Ethnos* VOL?, no. 54: 120–142.

Basch, Linda, Nina Glick Schiller, and Christina Szanton Blanc. 1994. *Nations Unbound: Transnational Projects, Postcolonial Predicaments and Deterritorialized Nation-States.* New York: Gordon and Breach.

Basch, Linda, Christina Blanc-Szanton, and Nina Glick Schiller, eds. 1992. *Towards a Transnational Perspective on Migration: Race, Class, Ethnicity and Nationalism Reconsidered.* New York: New York Academy of Sciences.

Başgöz, Ilhan, and Norman Furniss, eds. 1985. *Turkish Workers in Europe: An Interdisciplinary Study.* Bloomington: Indiana University Press.

Baubérot, Jean, ed. 1994. *Religion et Laicité dans l'Europe des Douzes.* Paris: Syros.

Bauböck, Rainer. 1994. *Transnational Citizenship: Membership and Rights in International Migration.* Aldershot: Edward Elgar.

———. "Political Community beyond the Sovereign State: Supranational Federalism and Transnational Minorities." Talk at conference on cosmopolitansim, University of Warwick, 27–29 April 2000.

Bauböck, Rainer, Agnes Heller, and Aristide R. Zolberg, eds. 1996. *The Challenge of Diversity: Integration and Pluralism in Societies of Immigration.* Aldershot: Avebury.

Bauböck, Rainer, and Hannes Wimmer. 1988. "Social Partnership and 'Foreigners Policy': On Special Features of Austria's Guest-Worker System." *European Journal of Political Research* 16:659–682.

Baumgartner-Karabak, Andrea, and Gisela Landesberger. 1978. *Die verkauften Braeute: Türkische Frauen zwischen Kreuzberg und Anatolien.* Hamburg: Rowohlt.

Beaugé, Gilbert, and Friedmann Buttner. 1991. *Les Migrations dans le Monde Arabe.* Paris: Centre National de la Recherche Scientifique.

Becker, Jörg. 1998. "Die Ethnisierung der deutschen Medienlandschaft-Türkische Medienkultur zwischen Assoziation und Dissoziation." In *Deutschland im Dialog der Kulturen: Medien, Images, Verstaendigung,* eds. Siegfried Quandt and Wolfgang Gast. Konstanz: UKW Medien.

Beck-Gernsheim, Elizabeth. 2007. *Wir und die Anderen.* Frankfurt: Suhrkamp.

Benedict, Peter, Erol Tümertekin, and Fatma Mansur, eds. 1974. *Turkey: Geographic and Social Perspectives.* Leiden: E. J. Brill.

Benhert, H., L. Rorn, and H. Fraistein. 1974. "Psychische Störungen bei auslaendischen Arbeitnehmer." *Nervenarzt,* no. 45:76–87.

Berliner Institut für Vergleichende Sozialforschung, 1990. *Bibliographie zur Türkischen Migration.* Berlin: Edition Parabolis.

Bhabha, K. Homi. 1994. *The Location of Culture.* London: Routledge.

Bielefeld, Uli. 1988. *Inlaendische Auslaender.Zum gesellschaftlichen Bewusstsein türkischer Jugendlicher in der BDR.* Opladen: Campus.

Bingemer, Karl, Edeltrud Meistermann-Seeger, and Eberhard Neubert. 1970. *Leben als Gastarbeiter.* Köln: Westdeutscher.

Birks, J. S., and C. A. Sinclair. 1980. *Arab Manpower: The Crisis of Development.* London: Croom Helm.

Blaschke, Jochen. 1984. "Islam und Politik unter Türkischen Arbeitsmigranten." In *Jahrbuch zur Geschichte und Gesellschaft des Vorderen und Mittleren Orient,* eds. Jochen Blaschke and M. van Bruinessen. Berlin: Parabolis.

Bodenbender, Wolfgang. 1977. "Zwischenbilanz der Auslaenderpolitik." In *Türkische Kinder in Deutschland,* ed. Franz Ronneberger. Nuremberg: Nuernberger Forschungsvereinigung.

Boos-Nünning, Ursula, M. Hohmann, H. H. Reich, and F. Wittek. 1983. *Aufnahmeunterricht, Muttersprachlicher Unterricht, Interkultureller Unterricht.* München: Oldenburg.

Boos-Nünning, Ursula, R. Grube, and H. H. Reich, eds. 1990. *Die türkische Migration in deutschsprachigen Büchern 1961–1984.* Opladen: Leske and Budrich.

Boos-Nünning, Ursula, and Yasemin Karakasoğlu. 2004. *Viele Welten.Lebenslagen von jungen Frauen mit griechischem, italienischem, jugoslawischen, türkischem und Aussiedlerhintergrund.* Berlin: Bundesministerium für Familien, Senioren, Frauen u. Jugendlichen.

Bourdieu, Pierre. 1977. *Outline of a Theory of Practice.* Cambridge: Cambridge University Press.

Boyd, Monica. 1989. "Family and Personal Networks in International Migration: Recent Developments and New Agendas," *International Migration Review* 23, no. 3:638–670.

Bozkaya, Volkan, 1997. *Life Situation, Identity, and Integration of Turks in the Federal Republic of Germany.* Essen: Zentrum für Türkeistudien.

Brouwer, L., and M. Priester. 1983. "Living in Between. Turkish Women in Their Homeland and in the Netherlands." In *One Way Ticket: Migration and Female Labour,* ed. Annie Phizaklea. London: Routledge and Kegan.

Brubaker, William Rogers, ed. 1989. *Immigration and Politics in Europe and North America.* Lanham, MD: University Press of America.

———. 1992. *Citizenship and Nationhood in France and Germany.* Cambridge: Harvard University Press.

Bundeszentrale für politische Bildung. 1987. *Auslaender und Massenmedien.* Bonn: Bundeszentrale für politische Bildung.

Butterwegge, Christoph, and Siegfried Jaeger, eds. 1993. *Rassismus in Europa.* Köln: Bund.

Çağlar, Ayşe. 1990. "The Prison House of Culture in the Studies of Turks in Germany." *Sozialanthropologische Arbeitspapiere* 31. Berlin: Freie Universitaet.

———. 1994. *German Turks in Berlin: Migration and Their Quest for Social Mobility.* Montreal: McGill University.

———. 1998. "Popular Culture, Marginality and Institutional Incorporation." *Cultural Dynamics* 10, no. 3.

———. 2004. "Mediascapes, Advertisement Industries and Cosmopolitan Transformations: German Turks in Germany." *New German Critique* 92 (Spring/Summer): 39–61.

Çağlar, Nakleden Ayşe. 1998. "Popular Culture, Marginality and Institutional Incorporation." *Cultural Dynamics* 10, no. 3:243–261.

Carle, Robert. 2006. "Demise of Dutch Multiculturalism." *Society* 43, no. 3:68–74.

Castells, Manuel. 1996. *The Rise of the Network Society.* Oxford: Wiley.

———. 1997. *The Power of Identity.* Oxford: Blackwell.

———. 2003. "Global Informational Capitalism." In *The Global Transformations Reader,* eds. David Held and Anthony McGrew. Cambridge: Polity.

———. 2003. "The Rise of the Fourth World." In *The Global Transformations Reader,* eds. David Held and Anthony McGrew. Cambridge: Polity.

Castles, Stephen. "Globalization and Migration: Some Pressing Contradictions." *International Social Science Journal* 50, no. 165 (June 1998): 179–186.

———. 2000. *Ethnicity and Globalization: From Migrant Worker to Transnational Citizen.* London: Sage.

Castles, Stephen, and Godula Kosack. 1973. *Immigrant Workers and Class Structure in Western Europe.* London: Oxford University Press.

Castles, Stephen, Mary Kalantzis, Bill Cope, and Michael Morrisey. 1990. *Mistaken Identity: Multiculturalism and the Demise of Nationalism.* Sydney: Pluto Press.

Castles, Stephen, and Mark J. Miller. 2003. *The Age of Migration: International Population Movements in the Modern World.* 4th ed. New York: Guilford Press.

C.E.M.O.T.I. 1992. *L'Immigration Turque en France et en Allemagne.* Paris: C.E.M.O.T.I.

Cesarani, David, and Mary Fulbrook. 1996. *Citizenship, Nationality and Migration in Europe.* London: Routledge.

Christlich Demokratischen Union Deutschlands. 1989. *Bundesparteitag der Christlich Demokratischen Union Deutschlands: Niederschrift.* Bonn, Germany: Union.

Çiçekli, Bülent. 1998. *The Legal Position of Turkish Immigrants in the European Union.* Ankara: Karmap.

Cizre, Ümit. 2001. "Turkey's Kurdish Problem: Borders, Identity, and Hegemony." In *Right-Sizing the State: The Politics of Moving Borders,* eds. Brendan O'Leary, Ian Lustick, and Thomas Callaghy. Oxford: Oxford University Press.

Cohen, Robin. 1987. *The New Helots: Migrants in the International Division of Labour.* Aldershot: Avebury.

———. 1994. *Frontiers of Identity: The British and the Other.* London: Longman.

———, ed. 1995. *The Cambridge Survey of World Migration.* Cambridge: Cambrige University Press.

———. 1997. *Global Diasporas: An Introduction.* London: UCL Press.

Constas, Dimitri, and Athanasios Platias, eds. 1992. *The Greek Diaspora in a Comparative Perspective.* London: MacMillan.

Cornelius, Wayne A., Philip L. Martin, and Hollifield, James Frank, eds. 1994. *Controlling Immigration: A Global Perspective.* Stanford: Stanford University Press.

Costa-Lascoux, Jacqueline. 1989. *De l'immigré au citoyen.* Paris: La Documentation Francaise.

Council of Europe. 1995. *Immigrant Women and Integration.* Strasbourg: Council of Europe.

Crul, Maurice, and Hans Vermeulen. 2003. "The Future of the Second Generation."*International Migration Review* 37, no. 4:965–986.

Davis, F. J., and B. Sherman. 1986. "Turkish Women and Guestworker Migration to West Germany." In *International Migration: The Female Experience,* eds. R. J. C. Simon and H. Brettl. Totowa, NJ: Roman and Allanheld.

Deutsche Bundesregierung. 1980. "Weiterentwicklung der Auslaenderpolitik." *Beschlüsse der Regierung vom* 19, no. 3.

Dewitte, Philippe, ed. 1999. *Immigration et intégration, l'état des savoirs.* Paris: La Découverte.

Dörr, Silvia, and Thomas Faist. 1997. "Institutional conditions for the integration of immigrants in welfare states: A Comparison of the literature on Germany, France, Great Britain and the Netherlands." *European Journal of Political Research,* no. 31: 401–426.

Dösen, Kristine, and Irene Molina, eds. 2000. *Divided Cities: Best Practices for the Social Inclusion of Ethnic Minorities in Local Communities.* Norköping: PfMI.

Dostal, Walter, H Helmuth W. Niederle, and Karl R. Wernhart, eds. 1999. *Wir und die Anderen, Islam, Literatur Und Migration.* Wien: Universitaetsverlag.

Ebert, F. Stiftung. 1998. *Deutschland und die Türkei im Spiegel der* Medien. Istanbul: FES.

Eck, Clementine van. 2003. *Purified by Blood: Honour Killings amongst Turks in the Netherlands.* Amsterdam: Amsterdam University Press.

Eller, J. D., and R. M. Coughlan. 1993. "The Poverty of Primordialism: The Demystification of Ethnic Attachments." *Ethnic and Racial Studies* 16, no. 2:183–202.

Elsner, Lothar. 1970. *Fremdarbeiterpolitik in Westdeutschland.* Berlin: Verlag Tribüne.

Elwert, Georg. 1982. *Probleme der Auslaenderintegration. Gesellschaftliche Integration Durch Binnenintegration.* Biefeld: Fakultaet für Soziologie.

Endruweit, Günther. 1981. "Integration oder Interkulturation?" *Zeitschrift für Kulturaustausch* 31:261–267.

Engelbrektsson, Ulla-Britt. 1978. *The Force of Tradition: Turkish Migrants at Home and Abroad.* Göteborg: Acta Universitatis.

Entzinger, Han. 1993. "L'immigration aux Pays-Bas du pluri-culturalisme a l'integration." In *Racisme et Modernité,* ed. K. A. Wierow. Paris: Deitions la decouverte.

———. 2003. "The Rise and Fall of Multiculturalism: The Case of the Netherlands." In *Toward Assimilation and Citizenship: Immigrants in Liberal Nation-States,* eds. Christian Joppke and Eva Morawska. Basingstoke, UK: Palgrave.

Erder, Sema, and Selmin Kaşka. 2003. *Irregular Migration and Trafficking in Women: The Case Of Turkey.* Geneva: IOM.

Erman, Tahire, and Emrah Göker. 2000. "Alevi Politics in Contemporary Turkey." *Middle Eastern Studies* 36, no. 4:99–118.

Esman, Milton. 1994. *Ethnic Politics.* Ithaca: Cornell University Press.

Esser, Elke. 1982. *Auslaenderinnen in der Bundesrepublik Deutschland. Eine soziologische Analyse des Eingliederungsverhaltens auslaendischer Frauen.* Frankfurt a.M.: R. G. Fischer.

Esser, Hartmut. 1980. *Aspekte der Wanderungssoziologie. Assimilation und Integration von Wanderern, ethnischen Gruppen und Minderheiten.* Darmstadt: Luchterhand.

Esser, Hartmut, and Jürgen Friedrich, eds. 1990. *Generation und Identitaet: Theoretische und empirische Beitraege zur Migrationssoziologie.* Opladen: Westdeutscher.

Essinger, Helmut, and Achim Hellmich, eds. 1981. *Auslaenderkinder im Konflikt* [Migrant Children amidst Conflict]. Königstein, Germany: Athenaeum.

Even, Herbert, Kadir Yeşilyaprak, Georg Elwert, and Georg Stauth, eds. 1984. *Sozio-ökonomische Differenzierung und Arbeitsmigration in der laendlichen Türkei.* Saarbrücken: Breitenbach.

Faist, Thomas. 1993. "From School to Work: Public Policy and Underclass Formation among Young Turks in Germany During the 1980s." *International Migration Review* 27, no. 2:306–331.

———. 2000a. *The Volume and Dynamics of International Migration and Transnational Social Spaces.* Oxford: Clarendon Press.

———. 2000b. "Transnationalization in international migration: implications for the study of citizenship and culture. *Ethnic and Racial Studies* 23, no. 2:189–222.

———. 2003. "Amalgamating Newcomers, National Minority and Diaspora: Integration(s) of Immigrants from Poland in Germany." In *Identity and Integration: Migrants in Western Europe,* eds. R. Sackman, B. Peters, and Thomas Faist. Aldershot/Burlington, UK: Ashgate.

———, ed. 2006. *Dual Citizenship in Europe: From Nationhood to Social Integration.* Aldershot, UK: Ashgate.

Faist, Thomas, Jürgen Gerdes, and Beate Rieple. 2007. "Dual Citizenship as a Path-Dependent Process." In *Rethinking Migration: New Theoretical and Empirical Perspectives,* eds. Alejandro Portes and Josh DeWind. New York: Berghahn Books.

Faist, Thomas, and Eyüp Özveren, eds. 2004. *Transnational Social Space: Agents, Networks and Institutions.* Avebury, UK: Ashgate.

Falk, Richard. 1995. *On Human Governance:Toward a New Global Politics.* Cambridge: Polity Press.

———. 2001. *Predatory Globalization: A Critique.* Cambridge: Polity Press.

Falk, Svenja. 1998. *Dimensionen kurdischer Ethnizitaet und Politisierung: Eine Fallstudie ethnischer Gruppenbildung in der BDR.* Baden-Baden: Nomos.

Fassman, Heinz, and Rainer Münz. 1994. *European Migration in the Late Twentieth Century.* Aldershot: Edward Elgar.

Feindt-Riggers, Nils, and Udo Steinbach. 1997. *Islamische Organisationen in Deutschland.* Hamburg: Deutsches Orient Institut.

Fijalkowski, Jürgen, Hans Mertens, and Folker Schmidt. 1990. *Dominant National Cultures and Ethnic Identities.* Berlin: Free University.

Galtung, Johan. 1971. "A Structural Theory of Imperialism." *Journal of Peace Research* 8:81–117.

Gans, Herbert J. 1997. "Toward a Reconciliation of 'Assimilation' and 'Pluralism': The Interplay of Acculturation and Ethnic Retention." *International Migration Review* 31, no. 4:875–892.

Gaspard, François, and Farhad Khosrokhavar. 1995. *Le foulard et la république.* Paris: La Découverte.

Geertz, Clifford. 1973. *The Interpretation of Cultures.* New York: Basic Books.

Geiger, Andreas, and Franz Hamburger. 1984. *Krankheit in der Fremde.* Fulda: Express Edition.

Geiselberger, Siegmar, ed. 1972. *Schwarzbuch: Auslaendische Arbeiter.* Frankfurt a.M.: Fischer.

Gellner, Ernest. 1992. *Postmodernism, Reason and Religion.* London: Routledge.

———. 1994. *Conditions of Liberty: Civil Society and Its Rivals.* London: Hamish Hamilton.

Gerholm, Tomas, and Yngve Georg Lithman, eds. 1988. *The New Islamic Presence in Western Europe.* London: Mansell.

Gewerkschaft, Erziehung und Wissenschaft (GEW) [Teachers' Trade Union]. 1979. *Blickpunkt; Auslaendische Schüler—keine Chance für Auslaender.* Frankfurt: GEW.

Gietl, Stefan, Hans-Dieter Schwind, and Gabriele Zwenger. 1991. "Der 'non-helping bystander' Effekt. Wie kommıt es zu unterlassener Hilfeleistung," [The 'Non-Helping

Bystander' Effect: How did it Come to Denial of Help?] *Kriminalistik* 45, no. 4 (April): 233–238.

Giordan, Henri. 1982. *Démocratie Culturelle et Droit a la Différence.* Paris: Documentation Française.

Gitmez, Ali, and Czarina Wilpert. 1987. "A Micro-Society or an Ethnic Community? Social Organizations and Ethnicity amongst Turkish Migrants in Berlin." In *Immigrant Associations in Europe,* John Rex, Danièle Joly, Czarina Wilpert eds. Aldershot, UK: Gower.

Glazer, Nathan. 1993. "Is Assimilation Dead?" *The Annals of the American Academy of Social and Political Sciences* 530, no. 1:122–136.

———. 1997. *We Are All Multiculturalist Now.* Cambridge: Harvard University Press.

Gökdere, Ahmet. 1994. "An Evaluation of Turkey's Recent Migration: Flows and Stocks," *Turkish Journal of Population Studies,* no. 16:29–56.

Goldberg, Andreas, and Martina Sauer. 2004. "Die Lebenssituation von Frauen und Maenner türkischer Herkunft in Nordrhein-Westfalen." Ergebnisse der sechsten Mehrthemenbefragung. Im Auftrag des Ministeriums für Gesundheit, Soziales, Frauen und Familie des Landes Nordrhein-Westfalen. Universität Duisberg-Essen.

Goldberg, David Theo. 1994. *Multiculturalism: A Critical Reader.* Oxford: Blackwell.

Göle, Nilüfer. 1996. *The Forbidden Modern: Civilization and Veiling.* Ann Arbor: University of Michigan Press.

Göle, Nilüfer, and Ludwig Ammann, eds. 2004. *Islam in Sicht. Der Auftritt von Muslimmen im öffentlichen Raum.* Bielefeld: Transcript.

Gordon, Milton Myron. 1964. *Assimilation in American Life.* New York: Oxford University Press.

Greve, Martin, and Tülay Çınar. 1997. *Das Türkische Berlin.* Berlin: Die Aulaenderbeauftragte des Senats.

Greve, Martin, and Ayhan Kaya. 2003. *Islamic Force, Takım 34 und andere Identitaetsmixturen türkischer Rapper in Berlin und Istanbul.* In Eva Kimminich, ed., *Rap: More than Words.* Frankfurt a.M.: F. Lang.

Guibernau, Montserrat. 1999. *Nations without States: Political Communities in a Global Age.* Cambridge: Polity Press.

Gür, Metin, and Alaverdi Turhan. 1996. *Die Solingen—Akte* [The Records of Solingen Trial]. Düsseldorf: Patmos Verlag.

Gutman, Amy, ed. 1994. *Multiculturalism: Examining the Politics of Recognition.* Princeton: Princeton University Press.

Habbe, Christian. 1983. *Auslaender—die verfemten Gaeste.* Hamburg: Spiegel-Buch.

Habermas, Jürgen. 1998. *Die Postnationale Konstellation: Politische Essays.* Frankfurt: Suhrkamp.

Hammar, Tomas. 1985. *European Immigration Policy.* Cambridge: Cambridge University Press.

Hammar, Tomas, Grete Brochmann, Krisof Tamas, and Thomas Faist, eds. 1997. *International Migration, Immobility and Development.* Oxford: Berghahn Books.

Hannoun, Michel. 1987. *L'Homme est l'ésperance de l'Homme.* Paris: La Documentation Française.

Hardt, Michael, and Antonio Negri. 2001. *Empire,* 7th ed. Cambridge: Harvard University Press.

Hartz, Louis, ed. 1964. *The Founding of New Societies: Studies in the history of the United States, Latin America, South Africa, Canada, and Australia.* New York: Harcourt, Brace & World.

Havel, Vaclav. "The Oslo Conference on 'The Anatomy of Hate.'" Speech. Oslo, 28 August 1990.

Hebenstreit, Sabine. 1986. *Frauenraeume und weibliche Identitaet.* Berlin: Express Edition.

Heckmann, Friedrich. 1981. *Die Bundesrepublik: ein Einwanderungsland? Zur Soziologie der Gastarbeiterbevölkerung als Einwanderungsminoritaet.* Stuttgart: Klett-Cotta.

———. 1992. *Ethnische Minderheitn, Volk und Nation.* Stuttgart: F. Enke.

Hegland, Mary Elaine. 2001. Review of "Crimes of Honour" and "Our Honour and his Glory." *Middle East Women's Studies Review* 15, nos. 1–2.

Heitmeyer, Wilhelm, Joachim Müller, and Helmut Schröder. 1997. *Verlockender Fundamentalismus. Türkische Jugendliche in Deutschland.* Frankfurt: Suhrkamp.

Held, David. 1995. *Democracy and the Global Order: From the Modern State to Cosmopolitan Governance.* Cambridge: Polity Press.

Held, David, Anthony McGrew, David Goldblatt, and Jonathan Perraton. 1999. *Global Transformations: Politics, Economics and Culture.* Cambridge: Polity.

Hirschman, Charles, Josh DeWind, and Philip Kasinitz, eds. 1999. *The Handbook of International Migration: The American Experience.* New York: Russell Sage Foundation.

Hirst, Paul, and Grahame. Thompson. 1996. *Globalization in Question.* Cambridge: Polity Press.

Hoch, Martin. 1994. "Türkische Politische Organisationen in der Bundesrepublic Deutschland." *Zeitschrift für Auslaenderrecht und Auslaenderpolitik* 14:17–22.

Hoeber, Rudolph Susanne, and James Piscatory, eds. 1997. *Transnational Religion.* Boulder, CO: Westview.

Hoffmann, Barbara, Michael Opperskalski, and Erden Solmaz. 1981. *Graue Wölfe, Koranschulen Idealistenvereine: Türkische Fschisten in der BDR.* Köln: Pahl-Rugenstein.

Hoffmann-Nowotny, Hans-Joachim. 1973. *Soziologie des Fremdarbeiterproblems.* Stuttgart: Enke.

———. 1981. "A Sociological Approach towards a General Theory of Migration." In *Global Trends in Migration: Theory and Research on International Population Movements,* eds. Mary Kritz, Charles Keely, Silvano Tomasi. New York: Center for Migration Studies.

Hoffmann-Nowotny, Hans-Joachim, and Martin Killias. 1979. "Switzerland." In *International Labor Migration in Europe,* ed. Ronald E. Krane. London: Praeger.

———, eds. 2001. *Das Fremde in der Schweiz.* Zürich: Seismo.

Hoffmeyer-Zlotnik, J. H. P., ed. 1986. *Segregation und Integration.* Berlin: Quorum.

Hollifield, James Frank. 1992. *Immigrants, Markets and States: The Political Economy of Immigration in Postwar Europe.* Cambridge, MA: Harvard University Press.

Holtbrügge, Heiner. 1975. *Türkische Familien in der Bundesrepublik.* Duisburg: Verlag der Sozialwissenschaftlichen Kooperative.

Horowitz, Donald L., and Gérard Noiriel, eds. 1992. *Immigrants in Two Democracies: French and American Experience.* New York: New York University Press.

Horrocks, David, and Eva Kolinsky. 1996. *Turkish Culture in German Society Today.* Oxford: Berghahn Books.

Hutchinson, John, and Anthony D. Smith. 1996. *Ethnicity.* Oxford: Oxford University Press.

İçduygu, Ahmet. 1996. "Transit Migrants and Turkey." *Boğaziçi Journal-Review of Social, Economic and Administrative Studies* 10, nos. 1–2:127–142.

———. 2008. *International Migration and Turkey, 2007: The Country Report for Turkey for SOPEMI/OECD.* Paris: OECD, 2008.

———. 2000. "The Politics of International Regimes: Transit Migration Flows in Turkey." *International Social Science Journal* 52, no. l65:357–367.

İçduygu, Ahmet, and Ayşem Biriz Karaçay. "The International Migration System between Turkey and Russia: The Case of Project-Tied Migrant Workers in Moscow." Paper, Migration Research Program, Koç University, Istanbul, 18–21 June 2009.

İçduygu, Ahmet, and Kemal Kirişci, eds. 2009. *Land of Diverse Migrations: Challenges of Emigration and Immigration in Turkey.* Istanbul: Istanbul Bilgi University.

İçduygu, Ahmet, and Kemal Kirişçi. 2009. "Turkey's International Migration in Transition." In *Land of Diverse Migrations: Challenges of Emigration and Immigration in Turkey,* eds. Ahmet İçduygu and Kemal Kirişçi. Istanbul: Istanbul Bilgi University.

Ilkkaracan, Pınar, ed. 2000. *Women and Sexuality in Muslim Societies.* Istanbul: Kadının Insan Hakları Projesi Yayını.

International Labour Organization. 1984. *The Rights of Migrant Workers,* Geneva: ILO.

International Social Science Journal. 2000. *International Migration 2000.* Paris: UNESCO.

Isajiv, W. W., ed. 1997. *Multiculturalism in North America and Europe: Comparative Perspectives on Interethnic Relations and Social Incorporation.* Toronto: Canadian Scholar's Press.

ISOPLAN. 1973. *Türkische Arbeitnehmergesellschaften in der B.D.R.* [Turkish Workers Investment Companies in West Germany]. Bonn: Saarbrücken.

Jelen, Christian. 1993. *La famille, secret de l'intégration.* Paris: Robert Lafont.

Jellineck, Walter. 1928. *Verwaltungsrecht.* Berlin.

Jenkins, Shirley, ed. 1988. *Ethnic Associations and the Welfare State: Services to Immigrants in Five Countries.* New York: Columbia University Press.

Joly, Daniele, ed. 1998. *Scapegoats and Social Actors: The Exclusion and Integration of Minorities in Western and Eastern Europe.* New York: St. Martin's Press.

Joly, Daniele, and Clive Nettelton. 1990. *Refugees in Europe.* London: Minority Rights Group.

Jonker, Gerdien. 2000. "Islamic Television 'Made in Berlin.'" In *Paroles d'Islam,* ed. Felice Dassetto. Strasbourg: Gallimard.

Joppke, Christian, ed. 1998. *Challenge to the Nation State: Immigration in Western Europe and the United States.* Oxford: Oxford University Press.

Jordanova-Duda, Matilda. 2001. "Von vernachlaessigter deutsch türkischer Zielgruppe … ," *Auslaender in Deutschland* 17, no. 3:4–5.

Kandiyoti, Deniz, ed.1991. *Women, Islam and the State.* Philadelphia: Temple University Press.

Karacabey, Makfi. 1996. *Türkische Tageszeitungen in der BDR: Rolle-Einfluss-Funktionen.* Dissertation, J. W. Goethe Üniversitesi, Frankfurt.

Karakaşoğlu, Yasemin, and Gerd Nonneman. 1997. "Muslims in Germany with Special Reference to the Turkish-Islamic Community." In *Muslim Communities in the New Europe,* eds. Gerd Nonneman, Tim Niblock, and Bogdan Szajkowski. Berkshire: Ithaca Press.

Karasan-Dirks, Sabine. 1980. *Die türkische Familie zwischen gestern und morgen.* Hamburg: Selbstverlag.

———. 1983. *Die Geschichte der Fatma Hanım in Köln.* Göttingen: Edition Herodot.

Kastoryano, Riva. 1987. *Etre Turc en France.* Paris: L'Harmattan.

———. 1994. "La présence Turque en France." *Hommes et migrations* 1172/1173: 71–78.

———. 1996. *La France, l'Allemagne et leurs immigrés: négocier l'identité.* Paris: Armand Colin.

———. 1998. *Quelle Identité pour l'Europe ? Le multiculturalisme a l'épreuve.* Paris: Presses de la Fondation Nationales des Sciences Politiques.

Kaya, Ayhan. 1998. "Multicultural Clientelism and Alevi Resurgence in the Turkish Diaspora: Berlin Alevis." *New Perspectives on Turkey* 18:23–49.

———. 2002. "Aesthetics of Diaspora: Contemporary Minstrels in Turkish Berlin," *Journal of Ethnic and Migration Studies* 28, no. 1:43–62.

———. 2009. *Islam, Migration and Integration: The Age of Securitization.* New York: Palgrave/Macmillan.

Kaya, Ayhan, and Ferhat Kentel. 2005. *Euro-Turks: A Bridge, or a Breach, Between Turkey and the EU.* Brussels: CEPS Publication.

Kazal, Russell. 1995. "Revisiting Assimilation: The Rise, Fall, and Reappraisal of a Concept in American Ethnic History." *American Historical Review* 100, no. 2:437–471.

Kazancıgil, Ali. 1991. "Democracy in Muslim Lands: Turkey in Comparative Perspective." *International Social Science Journal,* no. 128:343–360.

Kelek, Necla. 2005. *Die Fremde Braut—Ein Bericht aus dem Inneren des türkischen Lebens in Deutschland,* 4th ed. Cologne, Germany: Kiepenheuer und Witsch.

Kelson, Gregory A., and Debra L. Delaet. 1999. *Gender and Immigration.* New York: New York University Press.

Keppel, Gilles. 1991. *Les Banlieues de l'Islam.* Paris: Le Seuil.

Keskin, Hakki, ed. 1984. *Menschen ohne Rechten?* Berlin: Express Edition.

Keyder, Çağlar, and Ayhan Aysu-Koç. 1988. *External Labour Migration from Turkey and Its Impact: An Evaluation of the Literature.* Ottawa: International Development Research Center.

Keyman, Fuat, and Ahmet İçduygu. 2005. *Citizenship in a Global World: European Questions and Turkish Experiences.* London: Routledge.

Kıray, Mübeccel. 1976. "The Family of the Immigrant Worker." In *Turkish Workers in Europe 1960–1975,* eds. Nermin Abadan-Unat et al. Leiden: E. J. Brill.

Kirişçi, Kemal. 1991a. "Refugee Movements and Turkey," *International Migration* 29, no. 4:545–560.

———. 1991b. "The Legal Status of Asylum Seekers in Turkey: Problems and Prospects." *International Journal of Refugee Law* 3, no. 3:510–528.

———. 2002. *Justice and Home Affairs-Issues in Turkish-EU Relations.* Istanbul: TESEV.

Kirişçi, Kemal, and Gareth Winrow. 1997. *The Kurdish Question and Turkey.* London: Cass.

Kleff, Hans-Günter. 1984. *Vom Bauern zum Industriearbeiter: Zur kollektiven Lebens-Geschichte der Arbeitsmiganten aus der Türkei.* Ingelheim: Manthano.

Kleff, Sanem. 2005. *Islam im Klassenzimmer: Impulse für die Bildungsarbeit.* Hamburg: Körber Foundation.

Klein, Jürgen. 1977. *Unsere auslaendische Arbeiter sind Fremdarbeiter.* Bamberg: Stiftung Europa.

König, Karin. 1989. *Tschador, Ehre und Kulturkonflikt. Veraenderungsprozesse türkischer Frauen und Maedchen durch die Emigration und ihre soziokulturellen Folgen.* Frankfurt a.M.: Verlag für Interkulturelle Kommunikation.

Körner, Heiko, and Ursula Mehrlaender, eds. 1986. *Die "neue" Auslaenderpolitik in Europa.* Bonn: Neue Gesellschaft.

Kosnick, Kira. 2000. "Building Bridges: Media for Migrants and the Public-Service Mission in Germany." *European Journal of Cultural Studies* 3, no. 3:321–344.

———. 2003. "Extreme by Definition: Open Channel Television and Islamic Migrant Producers in Berlin." *New German Critique* 92 (Spring/Summer 2004): 21–38.

Kritz, Mary Monaca, Lim, Lin Lean, and Hania Zlotnik. 1992. *International Migration Systems: A Global Approach.* Oxford: Clarendon Press.

Kubat, Daniel, and Hans-Joachim Hoffmann-Nowotny. 1981. "Migration: Towards a New Paradigm." *International Social Science Journal* 33, no. 2:307–329.

Kudat, Ayse. 1975. *Stabilitaet und Veraenderung der türkischen Familie* [Stability and Change in the Turkish Family at Home and Abroad: Comparative Perspectives]. Berlin: Wissenschaftszentrum. Pre-print series nos. 75–76, 87.

Kymlicka, Will. 1995. *Multicultural Citizenship.* Oxford: Oxford University Press.

Labor Ministry, Foreign Relations Directorate. 2002. BÜLTEN no. 1 (January/March).

Labor and Social Security Ministry. 1981. *Report about Migration to Oil-Producing Countries.* Ankara.

Landau, Jacob M. 1995. "Ethno-nationalism and Pan-nationalism in Turkey and the Ex-Soviet Republics," *Migration: A European Journal of International Migration and Ethnic Relations* 28:67–84.

Layton-Henry, Zig. 1990. *The Political Rights of Migrant Workers in Western Europe.* London: Sage.

Lefebvre, Edwige Liliane. 2003. "Belgian Citizenship: Managing Linguistic, Regional, and Economic Demands." *Citizenship Studies* 7, no.1:111–134.

Leggewie, Claus. 1993. "Stolz ein Deutscher zu sein—die neue Angst vor dem Fremden." In *Deutsche im Ausland. Fremde in Deutschland. Migration in Geschichte und Gegenwart,* ed. Klaus J. Bade. Munich: C. H. Beck.

———, ed. 2004. *Die Türkei und Europa: Die Positionen.* Frankfurt a.M.: Suhrkamp.

Lerner, Daniel. 1958. *The Passing of Traditional Society: Modernizing the Middle East.* Glencoe: Free Press.

Leveau, Rémy. 1992. "Maghrebi Immigration to Europe: Double Insertion or Double Exclusion." *The Annals of the American Academy of Political and Social Science* 524, no. 1 (November 1992): 170–180.

Lewis, Bernard, and Dominique Schnapper, eds. 1994. *Muslims in Europe.* London: Pinter.

Lindo, Flip. 2000. "Does Culture Explain? Understanding Differences in School Attainment between Iberian and Turkish Youth in the Netherlands." In *Immigrants, Schooling and Social Mobility,* eds. Hans Vermeulen and Joel Perlman. London: MacMillan.

Lissot, René, Nadir Boumaza, and Ghislaine Clement. 1994. *Ces migrants qui font le proletariat.* Paris: Meridian.

Lithman, Eva Lundberg. 1987. *Immigration and Immigrant Policies in Sweden.* Stockholm: The Swedish Institute.

Lohrmann, Reinhard, and Klaus Manfrass. 1974. *Auslaenderbeschaeftigung und internationale Politik: Zur Analyse transnationaler Prozesse.* München: Oldenburg.

Lundberg, Ingrid, and Ingvar Svanberg. 1991. "Turkish Voluntary Associations in Metropolitan Stockholm." *Migration: A European Journal of International Migration and Ethnic Relations* 19, no. 2:35–76.

MacManus-Czubinska, Clare, William L. Miller, Radosław Markowski, and Jacek Wasilewski. 2003. "Understanding Dual Identities in Poland." *Political Studies* 51:121–143.

Magnarella, Paul J. 1979. *The Peasant Venture. Tradition, Migration and Change Among Georgian Peasants in Turkey.* Cambridge, MA: Schenkman Publications.

Mandel, Ruth. 1989. "'Turkish Headscarves' and the 'Foreigner Problem': Constructing Differences through Emblems of Identity." *New German Critique,* no. 46 (Winter): 27–46.

———. 1990. "Shifting Centres and Emergent Identities: Turkey and Germany in the Lives of Turkish Gastarbeiter." In *Muslim Travellers: Migration and the Religious Imagination,* eds. Dale Eickelman and James Piscatori. London: Routledge.

———. 2008. "Veiling Modernities." In *Cosmopolitan Anxieties: Turkish Challenges to Citizenship and Belonging to Germany,* ed. Ruth Ellen Mandel. Durham, NC: Duke University.

Manço, Ural, and Meryem Kanmaz. 2005. "From Conflict to Co-operation between Muslims and Local Authorities in a Brussels Borough: Schaerbeck." *Journal of Ethnic and Migration Studies* 31, no.6:1105–1123.

Marshall, Thomas Humphrey. 1950. *Citizenship and Social Class.* Cambridge: Cambridge University Press.

Marthaler, Sally. 2008. "Nicolas Sarkozy and the Politics of French Immigration Policy." *Journal of European Public Policy* 15, no. 3:382–397.

Martin, Philip. L. 1991. *The Unfinished Story: Turkish Labour Migration to Western Europe.* Geneva: ILO.

Martin, Philip. L., and Jonas. Widgren. 1996. *International Migration: A Global Challenge.* Washington, D.C.: Population Reference Bureau.

Massey, Douglas. 1994. "An Evaluation of International Migration Theory: The North American Case." *Population and Development Review* 20, no. 4:699–751.

———. 1999. "International Migration at the Dawn of the Twenty-First Century: The Role of the State." *Population and Development Review* 25, no. 2:303–322.

Maturi, Giacomo. 1964. *Arbeitsplatz: Deutschland.* Mainz: Krauskopf.

Mehrlaender, Ursula. 1974. *Soziale Aspekte der Auslaenderbeschaeftigung.* Bonn: Verlag Neue Gesellschaft.

———. 1983. *Türkische Jugendliche-Keine beruflichen Chacen in Deutschland?* Bonn: Neue Gesellschaft.

———. 1987. *Auslaenderforschung 1965 bis 1980: Fragestellungen, theoretische Ansaetze, empirische Ergebnisse.* Bonn: Neue Gesellschaft.

Meier-Braun, Karl-Heinz. 1979. *"Freiwillige Rotation": Auslaenderpolitik am Beispiel der baden-würtembergischen Landesregierung.* München: Minerva.

Meier-Braun, Karl-Heinz., and Martin A. Kilgus, eds. 1995. *40 Jahre "Gastarbeiter" in Deutschland.* Baden-Baden: Nomos.

Melikoff, Irene. 2004. *Hacı Bektaş: Efsaneden Gerçeğe* (*Hacı Bektaş: From Mythos to Reality*). Istanbul: Cumhuriyet kitapları.

Mertens, Gabriele, and Ünal Akpınar, 1977. *Türkische Migrantenfamilien.* Bonn: AGG.

Meske, Sigrid. 1983. *Situationsanalyse türkischer Frauen in der BDR.* Berlin: Express Edition.

Mıhçıyazgan, Ursula. 1990. *Moscheen türkischer Muslime in Hamburg.* Hamburg: Behörde für Arbeit, Gesundheit und Soziales [Department of Labor, Health and Social Services].

Miller, Mark J. 1981. *Foreign Workers in Europe: An Emerging Political Force.* New York: Praeger.

———. 1999. "Prevention of Unauthorized Migration." In *Migration and Refugee Policies: An Overview,* eds. A. Bernstein and M. Weiner. London: Pinter.

———. 2002. "Continuity and Change in Postwar French Legalization Policy." In *West European Immigration and Immigrant Policy in the New Century,* ed. Anthony Messina. Westport, CT: Praeger.

Mirdal, Gretty M. 1985. "The Condition of 'Tightness': The Somatic Complaints of Turkish Migrant Women." *Acta Psychiatrica Scandinavia* 71, no. 3:287–296.

Murck, Manfred, Hans Peter Schmalzl, and Hans-Martin Zimmermann, eds. 1993. *Immer dazwischen-Fremdenfeindliche Gewalt und die Rolle der Polizei.* Hilden/Rhineland: Deutsche Polizeiliteratur.

Narmann, Halil. 1978. *Türkische Arbeiter in Münster.* Münster: Coppenrath.

Neumann, Ursula. 1980. *Erziehung auslaendischer Kinder. Erziehungsziele und Bildungsvorstellungen in türkischen Arbeiterfamilien.* Düsseldorf: Schwann.

Nikolinakos, Marios. 1973. "Die Dritte Welt unter uns: Zur politischen Organisierung der Gastarbeiter." *Die Dritte Welt* 2, no. 1:73–86.

———. 1975a. *The Concept of the "European South" and the North–South Problem in Europe.* Berlin: Wissenschaftszentrum.

———. 1975b. *Politische Ökonomie der "Gastarbeiter."* Hamburg, Germany: Rowohlt.

Noelle-Neumann, Elizabeth, and Renate Köcher, eds. 1997. *Allensbacher Jahrbuch der Demoskopie, 1993–1997,* vol. 10. Allensbach am Bodensee, Germany: K. G. Saur.

Nonnemann, Gerd, Tim Nibblock, and Bogdan Szajkowski, eds. 1997. *Muslim Communities in the New Europe.* Berkshire: Ithaca Press.

O'Brien, Peter. 1996. *Beyond the Swastika.* New York: Routledge.

———. 2009. *European Perceptions of Islam and America.* New York: Palgrave.

OECD. 1998. "Trends in International Migration." *SOPEMI Annual Report.* Paris: OECD.

———. 2004. *Learning for Tomorrow's World.* Paris: OECD.

Olsson, Tord, Elisabeth Özdalga, and Catharina Raudvere, eds. 1989. *Alevi Identity: Cultural, Religious, and Social Perspectives.* Istanbul: Swedish Research Institute.

Osmay, Sevim. 1975. *Türkische Dorfentwicklungsgenossenschaften* [Turkish Village Development Cooperatives]. Bonn, Germany: Bundesministerium für Wirtschaftliche Zusammenarbeit.

Öztekin, Z. et al. 1977. "Health Problems of Turkish Migrant Workers' Children Living in West-Berlin." Paper presented at International Conference on Migrant Children, Ankara.

Özyürek, Esra. 2009. "'The Light of the Alevi Fire was Lit in Germany and Then Spread to Turkey': A Transnational Debate on the Boundaries of Islam." *Turkish Studies* 10, no. 2:233–253.

Paine, Susanne. 1974. *Exporting Workers: The Turkish Case.* Cambridge: Cambridge University Press.

Papademetriou, Demetrios G. 1996. *Coming Together or Pulling Apart: The European Union's Struggle with Immigration and Asylum.* Washington, D.C.: Carnegie Endowment for International Peace.

Penninx, Rinnus, and Herman van Renselaar. 1978. *A Fortune in Small Change.* The Hague, the Netherlands: Nuffic/Imwood Remplod Project.

Penninx, Rinnus, and Leo Van Velzen. 1975. "Evaluation of Migrants' Investments and their Effects on Development in Boğazlıyan District." In *Migration and Development,* eds. Nermin Abadan-Unat et al. Ankara University–NUFFIC.

———. 1975. "Alternate Routes Abroad." In *Migration and Development,* eds. Nermin Abadan-Unat et al. Ankara University–NUFFIC.

———. 1976. "The Economic Impact of External Migration on the District of Boğazlıyan." In *Migration and Development*, eds. Nermin Abadan-Unat et al. Ankara: SBF Yayınları.

Phizacklea, Annie, ed. 1983. *One Way Ticket: Migration and Female Labour.* Boston: Routledge.

Piore, Michael. 1979. *Birds of Passage: Migrant Labor in Industrial Societies.* Cambridge: Cambridge University Press.

Portes, Alejandro, ed. 1995. *The Economic Sociology of Immigration: Essays on Networks, Ethnicity and Entrepreneurship.* New York: Russell Sage Foundation.

Portes, Alejandro, Luis E. Guarnizo, and Patricia Landolt. 1999. "The Study of Transnationalism: Pitfalls and Promise of an Emergent Research Field." *Ethnic and Racial Studies* 22, no. 2:217–37.

Radtke, F. O. 1994. "The Formation of Ethnic Minorities and the Transformation of Social and Ethnic Conflicts in a So-Called Multicultural Society: The Case of Germany." In *Ethnic Mobilisation in a Multi-Cultural Europe*, eds. J. Rex and B. Drury. Hampshire, UK: Avebury.

Raetsel, Nora. 1991. "Germany: One Race, One Nation?" *Race and Class* 32, no. 3:31–48.

Ramadan, Tarıq. 1999. *Être Musulman Européen.* Lyon: Tawhid.

Rasuly-Palecsek, Gabriele, ed. 1996. *Turkish Families in Transition.* Frankfurt: Peter Lang.

———. 1999. "Kollektive Identitaeten und ihre Transformationen am Beispiel Afghanistan." *Mitteilungen der Anthropologischen Gesellschaft in Wien (MAGW)* 129:175–187.

Rath, Jan. 1988. "Political Action of Immigrants in the Netherlands: Class or Ethnicity." *European Journal of Political Research* 16:623–644.

Renner, Erich. 1975. *Erziehung und Sozialisationsbedingungen türkischer Kinder.* Heidelberg: Schindele.

Renselaar, Herman van, and Leo Van Velzen. 1975. "Public and Private Initiatives Aimed at Using External Labour *Migration* for *Development*." In *Migration and Development*, eds. Nermin Abadan-Unat et al. Ankara University–NUFFIC.

Rex, John, Danièle Joly, and Czarina Wilpert, eds. 1987. *Immigrant Associations in Europe.* Aldershot, UK: Gower.

Rist, Ray C. 1978. *Guestworkers in Germany: The Prospect for Pluralism.* New York: Praeger.

Robertson, Ronald. 1995. "Globalization: Time-Space and Homogeneity-Heterogeneity." In *Global Modernities*, eds. Mike Featherstone, Scott Lash, and Ronald Robertson. London: Sage.

Ronneberger, Franz, ed. 1976. *Türkische Kinder in Deutschland.* Nuremberg: Nuernberger Forschungsvereinigung.

Rogers, Rosemary, ed. 1985. *Guests Who Come to Stay: The Effects of Labor Migration on Sending and Receiving Countries.* Boulder, CO: Westview Press.

Rogers, Rosemary, and Emily Copeland. 1993. *Forced Migration: Policy Issues in the Post-Cold War World.* Medford: Tufts University.

Roy, Olivier. 2003. "Euro-Islam: The Jihad Within?" *National Interest* (Spring).

Roy, Olivier. 2004. *Globalized Islam: The Search for a New Ummah.* New York: Columbia University Press.

Rushdie, Salman. 1992. *Imaginary Homelands: Essays and Criticism.* New York: Penguin.

Sachs, Lisbeth. 1983. *Evil Eye or Bacteria? Turkish Migrant Women and Swedish Health Care.* Stockholm: Studies in Social Anthropology.

Sakonoto, Yoshikazu, ed. 1994. *Global Transformation: Challenges to State System.* Tokyo: UN University Press.

Saktanber, Ayşe. 2007. "Cultural Dilemmas of Muslim Youth: Negotiating Muslim Identities and Being Young in Turkey." *Turkish Studies* 8, no. 3 (September): 417–434.

Salt, John. 1985. "West German Dilemma: Little Turks or Young Germans?" *Geography* 70:162–168.

Sander, Åke. 1990. "Islam and Muslims in Sweden." *Migration: A European Journal of International Migration and Ethnic Relations* 8:83–134.

Sanguin, André-Louis. 1993. *Les Minorités Ethniques en Europe.* Paris: Edition l'Harmattan.

Sassen, Saskia. 1981. "Towards a Conceptualization of Immigrant Labor." *Social Problems* 29, no. 1:65–84.

———. 1989. *The Mobility of Labor and Capital: A Study in International Investment and Labor Flow.* Cambridge: Cambridge University Press.

———. 1991. *The Global City.* Princeton: Princeton University Press.

———. 1998. *Globalization and Its Discontents.* New York: The New Press.

———. 1999. *Guests and Aliens.* New York: The New Press.

———. 2007. *A Sociology of Globalization.* New York: W. W. Norton & Co.

———. 2008. *Territory, Authority, Rights: From Medieval to Global Assemblage.* Princeton: Princeton University Press.

Schiffauer, Werner. 1983. *Die Gewalt der Ehre. Erklaerungen zu einem türkisch-deutschen Sexualkonflikt.* Frankfurt a.M.: Suhrkamp.

———. 1984. "Religion und Identitaet." *Schweizerische Zeitchrift für Soziologie* 10, no. 2:485–516.

———. 1997. *Fremde in der Stadt.* Frankkfurt a.M.: Suhrkamp.

———. 2000. *Die Gottesmaenner, Türkische Islamisten in Deutschland* [The Men of God, Turkish Islamists in Germany]. Frankfurt: Suhrkamp.

———. 2001. *Die Boten von Allah.* Frankfurt a.M.: Suhrkamp.

Schiller, Nina Glick. 1999. "Citizens in Transnational Nation-States: The Asian Experience." In *Globalization and Asia Pacific: Contested Territories,* eds. Kris Olds, Peter Dicken, Philip Kelly, Lilly Kong, and Henry Wai-Chung Yeung. London and New York: Routledge.

Schulz, M. 1985. *Meine Name ist Keskin.* Darmstadt: Selbstverlag.

Schwartz, Thomas. 1987. "Ethnische Koloniebildung und die Organisation des Sports türkischer Zuwanderer in Berlin." *Migration: A European Journal of International Migration and Ethnic Relations* 1: 169–172.

———. 1992a. "The Turkish Community Berlin: Youth Cultures in the System of the German Welfare System." In *Ethnicity in Youth Culture,* eds. C. Pamfren, K. Löfgren and G. Bolin. Stockholm: University of Stockholm Press.

———. 1992b. *Zuwanderer im Netz des Wohlfahrtsstaat—Türkische Jugendliche und die Berliner Kommunalpolitik.* Berlin: Parabolis.

Schwarzer, Alice, ed. 2004. *Die Gotteskrieger und die falsche Toleranz.* Köln: Kiepenheuer & Witsch.

Scott, Franklin D. 1968. *World Migration in Modern Times.* New York: Prentice Hall.

Scott, Joan Wallach. 2007. *The Politics of the Veil.* Princeton: Princeton University Press.

Sellach, Brigitte. 1985. *Das Vertraute im Spiegel des Fremden: Forschungsbericht Aus einem Projekt mit Frauen in der Türkei.* Frankfurt a.M.: Institut für Sozialarbeit.

Şen, Faruk, and Regine Erichsen. 1987. *Hinwendung zur Selbststaendigkeit bei "Gastarbeitern" mit besondere Berücksichtigung von Türken* [Tendency toward Self-Employment of Guestworkers with Particular Regard to Turks]. Geneva: ILO.

Şen, Faruk, and Andreas Goldberg, eds. 1996. *Türken als Unternehmer.* Opladen.

Şen, Faruk, and Gerhard Jahn. 1985. *Wahlrecht für Auslaender.* Frankfurt: Dağyeli.
Şenol, Sengül. 1992. *Kurden in Deutschland. Fremde unter Fremde.* Frankfurt a.M.: Haag und Heerchen.
Sertel, Yıldız. 1987. *Nord-Sud: crise et immigration – le cas Turc.* Paris: Ed. Publisud.
Seyran, Ateş. 2003. *Grosse Reise ins Feuer. Die Geschichte einer deutschen Türkin.* Berlin: Rowohlt.
Sheffer, Gabriel, ed. 1986. *Modern Diasporas in International Politics.* New York: St. Martin's.
Sirman, Nükhet. 2004. "Kinship, Politics and Love: Honour in Post-Colonial Contexts—The Case of Turkey." In *Violence in the Name of Honour,* eds. Shahrzad Mojab and Nahla Abda. Istanbul: Istanbul Bilgi Üniversitesi.
Smith, J., C. Chatfield, and R. Pagnucco, eds. 1997. *Transnational Social Movements and Global Politics: Solidarity Beyond the State.* Syracuse, NY: Syracuse University Press.
Söhn, Janina, and Veysel Özcan. 2008. "The Educational Attainment of Turkish Migrants in Germany." In *Turkish Immigrants in The European Union,* eds. Refik Erzan and Kemal Kirişçi. London: Routledge.
SOPEMI. 1985. Continuous Reporting System on Migration. Paris: OECD.
Soysal, Nuhoğlu Yasemin. 1993. "Workers in Europe: Interaction with the Host Society," in *Turkey and the West: Changing Political and Cultural Identities,* eds. Metin Heper, Heinz Kramer, and Ayse Oncu. London: I. B. Tauris.
———. 1994. *Limits of Citizenship: Migrants and Postnational Membership in Europe.* Chicago: University of Chicago.
Spiess, C. Katharina, Felix Büchel, and Gert G. Wagner. "Children's School Placement in Germany: Does *Kindergarten* Attendance Matter?" *Early Childhood Research Quarterly* 18, no. 2:255–270.
Spijkerboer, T. 1994. *Women and Refugee Status: Beyond the Public/Private Distinction.* The Hague: Emancipation Council.
Spuler-Stegemann, Ursula. 1998. *Muslime in Deutschland. Nebeneinander oder Miteinander?* Wien: Herder Spektrum.
Stalker, Peter. 2000. *Workers without Frontiers: The Impact of Globalization on International Migration.* Boulder, CO: Lynne Rienner.
Strasser, S. 1995. *Die Unreiheit ist fruchtbar! Grenzüberschreitungen in einem türkischen Dorf am Schwarzen Meer.* Wien: Wiener Frauenverlag.
Statistisches Bundesamt. 1995. *Statistisches Jahrbuch.* Bonn, Germany: Metzler & Poeschel.
Stastistisches Bundesamt, Bildung und Kultur. 1999–2000 statistics.
State Planning Organization. 1962. *Turkish Five-Year Development Plan.* Ankara.
———. 1966. "Dış Ülkelere İşgücü Göndermede Kooperatif Kuran Köylülere Öncelik Tanınması Projesinin Uygulanması Üzerine Bir Inceleme" [Study of the Realization of Recognizing Priority In Sending Farmers who founded cooperatives to foreign countries]. Ankara.
Stirling, Paul. 1965. *Turkish Village.* Oxford: John Wiley & Sons.
Stüwe, Gerd. 1982. *Türkische Jugendliche.* Bensheim: Paedextra.
Taib, E.1998. *Immigrés: l'effet générations. Rejet, assimilation ,intégration d'hier et d'aujourdhui.* Paris: Edition de l'Atelier.
Tapper, Richard, ed. 1991. *Islam in Modern Turkey: Religion, Politics and Literature in a Secular State.* London: I. B. Tauris.
Taylor, Charles. 1992. "Multiculturalism and the Politics of Recognition." In *Multiculturalism: Examining the Politics of Recognition,* ed. Amy Gutman. Princeton: Princeton University Press.

Tertilt, Hermann. 1996. *Turkish Power: Ethnographie einer Jugendbande.* Frankfurt a.M.: Suhrkamp TBV.

Thoma-Venske, Hanns. 1981. *Islam und Integration: Zur Bedeutung des Islams im Prozess der Integration türkischer Arbeiterfamilien İn die Gesellschaft der BDR.* Hamburg: E. B. Rissen.

Tilly, Charles. 1990. *Coercion, Capital, and European States: AD 990–1992.* Oxford: Basil Blackwell.

Timmerman, Christiane. 2008. "Gender Dynamics in the Context of Turkish Marriage Migration: The Case of Belgium." In *Turkish Immigrants in the European Union,* eds. Refik Erzan and Kemal Kirişçi. London: Routledge.

Todd, Emmanuel. 1994. *Le Destin des Immigrés: Assimilation et ségrégation dans les Démocraties occidentales.* Paris: Seuil.

Toelken, B. 1985. "Türkenrein and Türken, 'Raus' Images of Fear and Aggression in German Gastarbeiterwitze." In *Turkish Workers in Europe: An Interdisciplinary Study,* eds. Ilhan Basgöz and Norman Furniss. Bloomington: Indiana University.

Toksöz, Gülay. 1990. *"Ja, sie kaempfenn-und sogar mehr als die Maenner": Immigrantinnen-Fabrikarbeit und gewerkschaftliche Interessenvertretung.* Berlin: Verlag für Wissenschaft und Bildung.

Touraine, Alain. 1997. *Pourrons-nous vivre ensemble? Egaux et différents.* Paris: Fayard.

Trebous, Madeleine. 1969. *Migration and Development: The Case of Algeria.* Paris: OECD.

Trokhymchuk, Stepan, and Solomiya Zinko. 2004. "Muslim Migrants in Europe: A Challenge to a Social Policy of a State." In *Proceedings of 4th International Immigration Conference,* Warsaw, Poland: Independent University of Business.

Turner, B. S. 1993. *Citizenship and Social Theory.* London: Sage Publications.

Üçüncü, Sadi. 1984. *Integrationshemmender Faktor: Auslaenderfeindlichkeit in der BDR.* Pfaffenweiler: Centaurus.

UNESCO, 1984. *Women on the Move: Contemporary Changes in Family and Society.* Paris: UNESCO.

United Nations High Commission for Refugees. 1997. *The State of the World's Refugees: A Humanitarian Approach.* Oxford: Oxford University Press.

———. 2000. *The State of the World's Refugees 2000: Fifty Years of Humanitarian Action.* Oxford: Oxford University Press.

Veblen, Thorstein. 1979. *The Theory of the Leisure Class: An Economic Study of the Institutions.* New York: Penguin.

Vernart, J. 1988. "Turkish Coffeehouses in Holland," *Migration: A European Journal of International Migration and Ethnic Relations* 3:97–113.

Vertovec, Steven. 1996. "Berlin Multikulti. Germany, 'Foreigners' and 'World-openness.'" *New Community* 22, no. 3:381–389.

Vertovec, Steven, and Robin Cohen, eds. 1999. *Migration, Diaspora and Transnationalism.* Cheltenham: Edward Elgar.

Wallerstein, Immanuel. 1998. "Culture as the Ideological Battleground of the Modern World System." In *Global Culture, Nationalism, Globalization and Modernity,* ed. M. Featherstone. London: Newbury Park; Delhi: Sage.

Weidacher, Alois. 1983. "Policy with Respect to Aliens and Migration Research in the Federal Republic of Germany: 1973–1983." *International Migration* 11, no. 4:463–486.

Weil, Patrick. 2008. *How to Be French: Nationality in the Making Since 1789.* Durham, NC: Duke University Press.

Weiner, Myron, ed. 1993. *International Migration and Security.* Boulder, CO: Westview.

———. 1995. *The Global Migration Crisis: Challenge to States and to Human Rights.* New York: HarperCollins.

———. 1997. *Japan's Minorities: The Illusion of Homogeneity.* London: Routledge.

Westerlund, David, and Ingvar Svanberg, eds. 1999. *Islam Outside the Arab World.* New York: St. Martin's Press.

Widgren, J. 1993. "Movements of Refugees and Asylum Seekers. Recent Trends in a Comparative Perspective." In *The Changing Course of International Migration.* Paris: OECD.

Wieworcka, M., ed. 1996. *Une sociétée fragmentée? Le multiculturalisme en débat.* Paris: La Découverte.

Wilpert, Czarina. 1980. *Die Zukunft der Zweiten Generation: Erwartungen and Verhaltensmöglichkeiten auslaendischer Kinder.* Königstein: Anton Hain.

———. 1981. "Bedeutung von sozialer und kultureller Identitaet für auslaendische Frauen und Maedchen." In *Situation der Auslaenderin,* ed. U. Welzel. München: Minerva.

———. 1988. *Entering the Working World.* Aldershot, UK: Gower.

Wilpert, Czarina, and Mirjana Morokvasic. 1983. *Bedingungen und Folgen Internationaler Migration.* Berlin: Institut für Soziologie, TUB.

Wolbert, Barbara. 1995. *Der getötete Pass. Rückkehr in die Türkei: Eine ethnologische Migrationsstudie.* Berlin: Akademie.

Wülfing, S. 1977. *Türkische Vorschulkinder in Köln.* Köln: Selbstverlag.

Yalçın-Heckmann, Lale. 1997. "Anthropological Studies on Turks in Turkey and in European Migration: Recent Works in German Language." *New Perspectives on Turkey* 16:105–114.

Yeşilada, Karin. 2000. *Topographien im 'tropischen Deutschland': Türkisch-Deutsche Literatur nach der Wiedervereiniung.* Frankfurt a.M./New York: Peter Lang.

Yurdakul, Gökçe, and Ahmet Yükleyen. 2009. "Islam, Conflict, and Integration: Turkish Religious Associations in Germany." *Turkish Studies* 10, no. 2 (June): 217–231.

Gottschlich, Jürgen, Dilek Zaptçioglu, and Metin Yilmaz. 2005. *Das Kreuz mit den Werten. Über deutsche und türkische Leitkulturen.* Hamburg: Körber Stiftung.

Zarka, Yves Charles, Sylvie Taussig, and Cynthia Fleury. 2004. *L'Islam en France.* Paris: Presses Universitaires de France.

Zentrum für Türkeistudien. 1991a. *Zum Integrationspotential der türkischen Tagespresse in der BDR.* Opladen: Leske and Budrich.

———. 1991b. *Gesundheitsbewusstsein der Migranten aus der Türkei in NRW.* Bonn: Ministerium für Arbeit, Gesundheit und Soziales NRW.

———. 1995. *Türkische Muslime in Nordrhein-Westfalen.* Pulheim: Ministerium für Arbeit, Gesundheit und Soziales des Landes Nordrhein-Westfalen.

———. 1999. *Türkische Unternehmer und das duale Ausbildungssystem.* Münster: Lit Verlag.

———. 2001. *Die ökonomische Dimension der türkischen Selbsstaendigen in Deutschland und der Europaeischen Union.* Essen.

———, ed. 1995a. *Migration und Emanzipation-Türkische Frauen in Nordrhein-Westfalen.* Opladen: Leske and Budrich.

———, ed. 1995b. *Das Bild der Auslaender in der Öffentlichkeit.* Opladen: Leske+Budrich.

Zolberg, Aristide R. 1989. "The Next Waves: Migration Theory for a Changing World." *International Migration Review* 23, no. 3:403–430.

Zolberg, Aristide R., Astri Suhrke, and Sergio Aguayo. 1989. *Escape from Violence.* New York: Oxford University Press.

Name Index

Subject Index